AMERICA AND THE JUST WAR TRADITION

AMERICA AND THE JUST WAR TRADITION

A HISTORY OF U.S. CONFLICTS

Edited by
MARK DAVID HALL
AND J. DARYL CHARLES

University of Notre Dame Press
Notre Dame, Indiana

University of Notre Dame Press
Notre Dame, Indiana 46556
undpress.nd.edu

Copyright © 2019 by the University of Notre Dame

All Rights Reserved

Published in the United States of America

Library of Congress Cataloging-in-Publication Data

Names: Hall, Mark David, 1966- editor. | Charles, J. Daryl, 1950- editor.
Title: America and the just war tradition : a history of U.S. conflicts /
edited by Mark David Hall and J. Daryl Charles.
Description: Notre Dame, Indiana : University of Notre Dame Press, 2019. |
Includes bibliographical references and index. |
Identifiers: LCCN 2018055518 (print) | LCCN 2018056151 (ebook) |
ISBN 9780268105273 (pdf) | ISBN 9780268105280 (epub) |
ISBN 9780268105259 (hardback : alk. paper) | ISBN 0268105251
(hardback : alk. paper) | ISBN 9780268105266 (pbk. : alk. paper) |
ISBN 026810526X (pbk. : alk. paper)
Subjects: LCSH: United States—History, Military. | United States—History,
Military—Moral and ethical aspects. | United States—History,
Military—Social aspects. | United States—History,
Military—Religious aspects. | Just war doctrine.
Classification: LCC E181 (ebook) | LCC E181.A36   2019 (print) |
DDC 355.00973—dc23
LC record available at https://lccn.loc.gov/2018055518

∞ *This book is printed on acid-free paper.*

We dedicate this book to the men and women who serve, or have served, in America's armed forces, and to professors who keep the just war tradition alive in our nation's colleges and universities.

CONTENTS

Foreword   ix
James Turner Johnson

Acknowledgments   xv

ONE
The Just War Tradition and America's Wars   1
J. Daryl Charles and Mark David Hall

TWO
"Fear, Honor, and Interest": The Unjust Motivations and Outcomes of the American Revolutionary War   50
John D. Roche

THREE
The War of 1812   74
Jonathan Den Hartog

FOUR
James K. Polk and the War with Mexico   97
Daniel Walker Howe

FIVE
The Fractured Union and the Justification for War   114
Gregory R. Jones

SIX
Just War and the Spanish-American War   136
Timothy J. Demy

SEVEN
The Great War, the United States, and Just War Thought   155
Jonathan H. Ebel

EIGHT
The United States and Japan in the Second World War: 175
A Just War Perspective
Kerry E. Irish

NINE
America's Ambiguous "Police Action":   203
The Korean Conflict
Laura Jane Gifford

TEN
Vietnam and the Just War Tradition   226
Mackubin Thomas Owens

ELEVEN
The First and Second Gulf Wars   251
Darrell Cole

TWELVE
The War on Terror and Afghanistan   271
Rouven Steeves

Contributors   300
Index   305

FOREWORD

James Turner Johnson

As I considered what I might contribute as a foreword to this book on bringing a just war perspective to reflection on America's wars, among the thoughts that came to mind were various examples of books and shorter pieces whose authors have employed their own understandings of the just war idea to argue against the justice of American uses of armed force in particular cases, against the use of particular weapons or ways of fighting by American military forces, or against war itself as inherently unjust today, measured by just war standards. This book is different from these in conception and execution; yet since it appears in a landscape populated by such examples, they need to be acknowledged in order for readers to appreciate the contribution this book makes.

Among the examples that came to my mind were three books that used somewhat different understandings of just war to criticize the 2003 use of armed force to invade Iraq and overthrow the Saddam Hussein regime. One of these extended the author's political opposition to the government officials who favored this use of force and argued for it during the period of deliberation that ended with the decision to use force: here the introduction of just war reasoning came in second, not first, place, and the interpretation of just war was shaped by the author's political commitments. Two other books also came to mind, works that defined the idea of just war in terms of lengthy lists of criteria and then used as a checklist by which to weigh, and find wanting, various aspects of the decision process and the use of armed force itself. This way of describing and using the idea of just war not only manifested a simplistic kind of moral reasoning divorced from the complexity of actual moral reflection and decision making, but it eviscerated the idea of just war itself, which, understood in its fullness, is the composite product of centuries of interactions among various formative forces—religion, philosophy, law, government, and military experience—all intertwined in the wisdom of a moral tradition.

I also thought of various books and articles, as well as statements produced by various groups, using elements from just war thinking to oppose war itself, to oppose the use of particular kinds of weaponry, or to oppose any and every use of force by states—often especially the U.S.—as inherently immoral. Sometimes the thought in these works turned just war reasoning back on itself, arguing that just war thinking justifies immoral uses of armed force and so ought to be discarded completely.

Happily, the present book is of a very different sort from any of the kinds of examples I have mentioned. First and fundamentally, in the first chapter of the book the editors rightly insist that just war should be thought of as a *tradition*, not a *theory*. This properly acknowledges two core truths about just war thought: that it is the product of a long and rich history of experience and efforts to think morally about that experience in connection with the place of the use of armed force in the service of the goods of order, justice, and peace within and among political communities; and further, that the moral content of just war tradition is not simply intellectual in nature but also empirically engaged in recognizing and meeting the responsibilities of life in an ever-challenging world. Augustine, often cited as the first Christian just war thinker, formulated his own thoughts on just war in fashioning responses to the teachings and actions of Christian heretics like the Manichees and the Donatists, and at the end of his life his thinking about just war reflected the grave military and religious threats posed by Arian Vandal armies that laid siege to his home city of Hippo Regius. In the face of all these challenges he argued for restoring and maintaining justice in the face of injustice. This, for him, was what the idea of just war was about: it was an element in Christian responsibility to take part in holding together a world menaced by injustice and chaos, so that God's purpose for that world might be completed. His was an engaged understanding of just war, not simply a theoretical conception.

The same goes for the thinkers who contributed to the definition of the first systematic understanding of just war, the canonists of the twelfth and thirteenth centuries. Their focus was on just war as a responsibility of temporal government, a tool for securing the common good of all in every political community. Justice and peace for them were not ideal goods for a perfect world but real forms of human interrelations which those responsible for political order should continuously seek to achieve. The same applies to the theological thinkers who followed, importantly illustrated by Thomas Aquinas, who seconded the canonists in emphasizing use of just war as an aspect of the responsibility of sovereign rule and understood the decision for or against just war as a form of moral discernment of the natural law. The same too for those thinkers of the early modern period who rethought just war in the context of new forms of warfare and new experiences of cultural diversity, and so also those thinkers who transformed just war into a way of ordering and regulating the world of nation-states that followed the Peace of Westphalia. Such was the nature of the thinking of those who in earlier times gave shape to just war tradition, and stepping into that tradition today means taking up the same lines of reflection.

One who engages in just war reasoning, on this conception, is one who enters the ever-developing stream of tradition on moral responsibility and the use of armed force, joining in dialogue not only with contemporaries in their own context in the world but also with those who have dealt with similar and other challenges in earlier historical contexts. The result of thinking of just war in this way is to conceive it as significantly more diverse than can be captured in any checklist of moral criteria that might be offered. Nor is it simply a set of ideal norms; it is also a way of thinking that recognizes the contingency of human moral reflection and activity. The standard here is not moral perfection, which can only be reached in some ideal realm but only approximated as best possible in history.

If one surveys recent and present-day writing on the topic of just war, one encounters a wide variety of representations of just war. Rather than argue for one or another of the theoretical conceptions of just war found in these, chapter 1 of this book, written by the two editors to define the purpose and scope of the book, develops a synthetic overview of the essential elements of just war thinking as they have been defined in this tradition of responsible moral engagement with life in the world. At the same time, the references cited in this chapter draw broadly from examples of the different understandings of just war in recent and present-day debate. As a result, the reader is provided with a comprehensive understanding of what just war is, understood as a tradition, while also receiving a detailed bibliographic resource on contemporary debates over just war. Chapter 1 alone is worth the price of the book, both as an anchor for how to think about just war and as a point of entry into the varied religious, philosophical, political, historical, and legal thinking that has treated the idea of just war in recent decades.

While I have argued in my own work that just war reasoning first and foremost seeks to guide moral decision making about the use of armed force looking forward in particular urgent contexts, at the same time I believe one cannot think seriously about moral choice in each new case without taking into account the moral choices made by others in similar contexts in the past. To assist in this is the purpose of this book. On the model of just war reasoning described above, entering a stream of tradition within which one engages in dialogue with others from earlier times as well as with one's own contemporaries, this book does not seek to offer single, once-for-all determinations on the rightness or wrongness of particular decisions or actions taken in the context of any of America's wars examined here. To be sure, the authors of the chapters below take their own stands on these matters. But the overall purpose is to stimulate and aid the readers' reflections, so as to extend the dialogue inherent in just war reasoning. Any individual reader may disagree with the analysis, arguments, and judgments offered in particular chapters while agreeing with those offered in others. This is as it should be: the aim is not to provide final answers, but rather to provoke new thought.

Professional moralists who read this book, bringing to it a desire for theoretical discourses on one or another aspect of just war thinking, may well be disappointed by the extended historical discussion found in every chapter. But a sincere effort at historical reconstruction of each context is essential for serious moral analysis of the decisions made and actions taken in it, and thus it is a necessary basis for just war judgments relating to each of the wars discussed. History has real moral importance, and these chapters should be read with this in mind. Moral actions always take place in historical context, and moral analysis accordingly must always take account of such context.

Early in chapter 10 this same point is put in the words of British Field Marshal Viscount Slim, reflecting on a decision he had made in a particular context early in his career. The chapter's author writes, "It is necessary to apply prudence to the evaluation of actions in wartime. Different times and conditions may make one condition more important than another. Moreover, a reasonable judgment that a condition was met in a particular situation can be changed as a result of additional experience, information, or insight." Then, quoting Slim, he continues: "The soldier always knows that everything he does on such an occasion [of combat] will be scrutinized by two classes of critics—by the Government which employs him and by the enemies of that government. As far as the Government is concerned, he is a little Admiral Jellicoe and this his tiny Battle of Jutland. . . . Lucky the soldier if, as in Jellicoe's case, the tactical experts decide after twenty years' profound consideration that what he did in three minutes was right." This is the challenge for any and all moral decision making, whether by the individual soldier or by a head of state or anyone in between in the chain of responsibility, and it is a challenge that just war tradition aims to help the moral agent to meet while also standing as a resource for judging that action in its aftermath. There is no place in either for moral hubris. Nor should the present book be read as a source of such hubris.

Just war tradition has taken different forms in different historical periods and as expressed by different authors. The synthetic overview of just war provided in chapter 1, which provides a reference point for readers as well as the authors of the following chapters, provides a view of just war as it is today. Working from such a standard is needed for a book of this sort. But at the same time readers should keep in mind that in the cases of all except the most recent of the wars covered, the standards for just war were different.

There was in fact no concerted religious or philosophical moral reflection on just war from the early seventeenth century until the end of World War II. During this period just war tradition was carried and developed not through moral theology or philosophy but by theory on the law of nations, customary and, in time, positive international law, and military customs and practice. We can see the effects of this in the case of the American Revolution. In this historical context the status of revolutions was in debate. While the main line of just war thinking earlier on had strongly questioned whether revolutions were examples of immoral sedition, Grotius's argument on behalf of the Dutch rebellion against Spanish rule challenged the earlier consensus and, through the next century and a half, was working its way into the thought of others and into the nascent conception of a politics based on human rights, importantly exemplified by the work of Locke. Thus the meaning of the needed authority and justification of war were in debate and, in the practical world, in flux. As far as the conduct of war was concerned, the standard was the kind of chivalric bravery well described in chapter 2, but the reverse side of this was a kind of cruelty: soldiers who broke and fled under volley fire from muskets could be summarily put to death. Similar things can be said about the standards of the times when later American wars were fought. How this all relates to just war thinking and moral judgments based on it is too big a topic for this book (I have spent much of my career trying to take it into account), but what to make of it is a matter for readers of this volume to keep in mind as they reflect on each chapter of this book.

Another historical fact to keep in mind, especially for those readers interested in the specifically Christian element in thinking about war, is that during the nineteenth century major Christian influences pushed in two opposite directions. On the one hand, Evangelical Protestantism in England and the U.S. promoted wars for the purpose of establishing Christian morality, including the Indian Mutiny, the war against the Mahdi in Sudan, and the American Civil War, while encouraging the idea of "manifest destiny" in America's wars of that era. Simultaneously, though, other forces within Protestantism, as well as important thinking within the Catholic Church, promoted pacifism and the end of all war. How to factor these opposite developments into just war judgments on the wars of this period should also be kept in mind by readers of this volume.

All in all, this book is a valuable resource for reflection on morality, warfare, and political decision making during American history. But it will succeed best when it stimulates its readers to engage with it in dialogue and to cast their thinking more broadly to encompass the changes in the idea of just war over the period of America's wars.

ACKNOWLEDGMENTS

Mark and Daryl have been collectively fascinated by the just war tradition for more than half a century. We see in this venerable two-thousand-year-long conversation on qualifying coercive force much-needed wisdom of the ages—wisdom that is needed in the present age. We thank our teachers—ancient and modern—who introduced us to the tradition, and we thank innumerable students over the years with whom we have discussed issues of war and peace, especially in the American context. Teachers and colleagues who have been particularly influential in our day include James Turner Johnson, Mark R. Amstutz, David Corey, Nigel Biggar, Timothy Demy, Marc Livecche, and Eric Patterson, not to mention the recently deceased Jean Bethke Elshtain, who is greatly missed.

Daryl is particularly grateful to the Institute on Religion and Democracy, whose leadership under Mark Tooley has been responsible for creating the only journal of its kind, *Providence: A Journal of Christianity and American Foreign Policy*, edited by Marc Livecche. *Providence* offers serious and sustained reflections on Christian faith and foreign policy, and although it is not intended to be a journal *solely* dedicated to the ethics of war and peace, much of its content is devoted to this realm of ethical reflection and policy analysis, which, quite frankly, is absent from public discourse.

Mark is thankful for a Fellowship Research Grant from the now defunct Earhart Foundation which permitted him to spend the summer of 2014 doing preliminary work on this project. The Foundation will be sorely missed. As well, George Fox University has provided important and ongoing support for his research and writing. He is particularly grateful to his pacifist colleagues who have sharpened his thinking on these issues.

Mark and Daryl have both benefited from working with the fine editors at the University of Notre Dame Press. We are especially thankful for the insights of Stephen Little, and manuscript editor Bob Banning of Turning Leaves Editorial. Of course, any errors that remain in the volume are our responsibility.

Finally, we are grateful for our long-suffering wives, who have had to hear far more than they would have liked about *ius ad bellum*, *ius in bello*, and *ius post bellum*. Their love and support has been indispensable.

ONE

The Just War Tradition and America's Wars

J. Daryl Charles and Mark David Hall

How Americans think about war cannot be properly understood apart from reflecting on the American experience in our relatively brief history. That experience, it goes without saying, has evolved in ways that previous generations would have thought unfathomable. Any attempt to reflect on war, of course, is biased by numerous factors, not least of which is historical vantage point. One of the great obstacles confronting anyone who approaches the study of war, as one historian of just war has well noted, is that contemporary expectations, values, and social context color one's understanding of the nature of war and its purposes.[1] To consider the relative justness or unjustness of, say, the Spanish-American War or World War II is one thing. To measure the justness of American involvement in Afghanistan or of fighting global or regional terrorism is quite another.

And yet the matter of war—past or present, conventional or nonconventional—does not occupy some nebulous realm that is detached from the human experience and transcending moral norms and human obligations. Much to the contrary. Armed conflict may be properly conceived as "an extraordinary extension of ordinary acts of judgment."[2] Indeed, much can be learned by studying these "acts of judgment." Which is why the present volume has come into being. Historians and students of international affairs, of course, have spilled a great deal of ink describing and analyzing America's wars. Political philosophers and ethicists have written boundlessly on the ethics of war and peace and, more recently, on just war theory; significantly, in the last fifteen years the literature on just war ethics has proliferated.[3] Intriguingly, however, there has been relatively little serious analysis of the extent to which America's wars have been justified. Two general tendencies characterize the literature, both past and present. The first is to offer a moral judgment with respect to a particular war without engaging in careful theoretical analysis, and the second is to offer a moral judgment about a war without carefully studying the historical context. This collection of essays seeks to provide a careful analysis of America's wars, from the nation's inception to the present ongoing "war on terror," and it does so from the perspective of just war doctrine that has been nurtured and refined in the West chiefly, when not solely, within the Christian moral tradition.[4] In other words, this volume subjects American involvement in war to rigorous moral scrutiny while being attentive to historical context.

Of the writing of books on war and peace there is no end, or so it would seem. And even of the writing of books on individual American wars, one might argue, there is almost no end. Of the writing of books on *American wars cumulatively*, however, there is no evidence of anyone having undertaken the task. To our knowledge, no one has assessed from an ethical standpoint in a coherent work American military conflicts from the nation's founding to the present day.[5] And who would be sufficient to the task? Such an endeavor exceeds the expertise and purview of any one scholar or analyst. To this end, then, the editors of this volume have enlisted the wisdom and insights of historians, ethicists, political philosophers, and military strategists whose expertise extends to those particular wars—and periods of American history—contained in this volume.

We reiterate the aim of this work: to subject the relative justness of major American military campaigns to moral scrutiny and to do so being attentive to historical context. Clearly, a great deal has been written about the justness of particular wars immediately before, during, and after the conflict. Not all of this commentary demonstrates a moral seriousness, even when offered by professional scholars. Of course, it is difficult to do serious historical analysis in the heat of the moment. To "subject the relative justness of American military involvement to moral scrutiny" assumes and requires that a nonfluid moral standard avails itself to ultramodernism in the twenty-first century, permitting us to do moral evaluation and make moral judgments.

Those who have contributed to this volume represent a considerable range of vocational callings. Some are historians, others are political philosophers, others teach ethics or religion, and yet others wrestle with military strategy. All, however, share in common several qualities necessary for a work such as this to take shape—in particular, (1) a commitment to the just war tradition as articulated in this introduction, (2) a willingness and capacity to do the hard-historical analysis necessary for evaluating particular conflicts, and (3) the ability to offer a fair and balanced appraisal of America's wars. In the essays that follow, each author discusses the causes of a particular war, the degree to which the justice of the conflict was a subject of debate at the time, and the extent to which that particular conflict measured up to traditional *ad bellum* and *in bello* criteria. As well, where appropriate, they offer *post bellum* considerations, insofar as justice is concerned with helping to foster a better peace and end result than what had existed in the prior state of affairs.[6] And where appropriate, contributors reflect on lessons that may be learned from the wars they cover that are relevant to present and future debates. Our modest proposal, then, is to join a centuries-long conversation in which enduring resources—resources that imbue our own cultural tradition—are reaffirmed.

THE TRADITION OF JUST WAR

The just war tradition may be viewed as the chief moral grammar in the Western cultural tradition by which moral judgments concerning war and interventionary force have been shaped. In the words of one political ethicist, "just war" is "a way of thinking that refuses to separate politics from ethics."[7] As described by another, it is a particular "understanding of political responsibility that is rooted in neighbor-regarding love."[8] We intentionally refer to the *tradition* of just war and not to "just war *theory*," since this way of thinking about war and peace is embedded prominently within the wider Western cultural heritage. A "tradition" (from the Latin *traditio*: a "handing down") implies that a cumulative wisdom, in its development and refinement, accrues over time. Tradition is important both in a cultural-political and moral sense, given the cumulative differentiating work of multiple generations and the resultant insights. As a tradition, "just war" has been supremely eclectic in character, spanning the domains of theology, philosophy, politics, international law, and military strategy. The great value of this tradition is that it supplies a map, as it were, of the complexities of armed conflict as well as a history of paradigmatic attempts to think through these complexities. The result is a firmer grasp of the ethical terrain surrounding questions of justice and war, allowing an informed citizenry to participate more effectively in indirectly shaping policy and allowing those in authority to be effectively informed in their policy-making capacity. To the extent that American citizens are aware of this tradition, they are all too prone to view it in narrow terms as a theory, as an outmoded vestige of our Christian past, or as something rendered obsolete by international law.[9]

The just war idea presupposes not that war or coercive force can ever be perfectly "just"; such a state of affairs is not part of temporal realities. Rather, it assumes *relative* justice as an ideal in the affairs of human beings and nations and consequently seeks moral wisdom and discernment in arriving at judgments about war and peace. Hence, by "just war" we are indicating war that is *justified* or *morally defensible*—not war that is perfectly or purely just. Paul Ramsey, in our view, was correct to admonish that we speak not of "just war" but of "justified war," since virtue and justice are matters of moral discernment, proper intention, and responding to human need.[10]

Embodying a moral realism that is ideologically distinct from both militarism/holy war on the one hand and pacifism on the other, the just war tradition represents "a discipline of deliberation" that provides us with moral principles, moral wisdom, and categories of moral measurement that are indispensable in making sense of the ethics of war and peace and coercive intervention. Properly viewed, the just war idea is a morally guided approach to statecraft that both qualifies the administration of coercive force and views peace as the result of justly ordered relationships. As a framework, just war thinking takes its bearings not from positive law but from moral law, whether that form is natural or revealed in character. Because not all applications of force create conditions for bringing about peace and justice, the use of coercive force must be highly qualified. Peace is not to be understood as the absence of conflict; rather, it is the fruit or by-product of a justly ordered community.

Pacifists such as John Howard Yoder and Stanley Hauerwas have argued that just war reasoning, as well as the natural law thinking that supports it, is used merely to justify war, violence, and military conflict.[11] Particularly in light of the destructiveness of modern weaponry, some would argue that "justice" in conducting war is a moral absurdity. But calls to "abolish war," whether in the name of religious ethics or any other name, are viewed by just war thinkers as an abdication of human moral reasoning, since they give little thought to responsible public policy and fail to wrestle with the common good.[12] The moral wisdom of the just war tradition—a tradition with pre-Christian traces and extending from Ambrose, Augustine, and Aquinas to the Protestant Reformers, and beyond, from early-modern theorists such as Vitoria, Suárez, Grotius, Vattel, and Locke to twentieth-century and contemporary exponents such as Paul Ramsey, William V. O'Brien, Michael Walzer, James Turner Johnson, and Jean Bethke Elshtain—shows itself capable of ever adapting to changing social-political and geopolitical challenges. Representative voices within the tradition, whether past or present, affirm that a "will to peace" *can and should* guide the use of force.[13]

At the most basic level, just war thinking presupposes certain moral realities that not infrequently are ignored or forgotten, if not denied, by contemporary theorists, strategists, and commentators. These fundamental moral assumptions include the idea that good and evil are a part of human nature—a reality that informs responsible policy considerations—and that human nature is such that not only do persons do evil things to fellow human beings but also states and regimes can do intolerable things to humans—things that must not be tolerated. Moreover, certain features of humanity are constant, having both a universal and a culturally specific character. Hence, we should not be surprised that all cultures have moral codes with norms that inform what is morally regulative and restrict the taking of human life.[14]

The tradition assumes as well that justice without force is a myth—because there will always exist evil humans—and that evil individuals must be hindered, in order that the very goods of *human flourishing* be protected. This leads, it seems to us, (1) to a distinction between a presumption against *war* or coercive force and a presumption against *injustice* and (2) to an insistence that to claim that the just war idea begins with a general presumption against *war* is a mutation and distortion of the classic just war tradition, inasmuch as it confuses force—not injustice—with evil. This distinction is not mere academic or moral-philosophical gnat-straining. It is critical as a starting point for thinking about war and, *inter alia*, exposes the difference between pacifism and the just war tradition, even when the former may masquerade under the cloak of "just peacemaking," as several writers have attempted to do in recent decades.[15]

Moral realism about human nature should cause us to think soberly about the use—and abuse—of power while at the same time preventing us from opting out of political reality altogether in favor of utopian ideals. This sobriety requires of us participation, action, and moral discernment in a world of limits, estrangements, and partial justice wherein we recognize the provisional nature of all political arrangements.[16] Similarly, a moral distinction between criminal behavior and victimhood, between relative guilt and relative innocence, can be discerned, even when this distinction might seem blurred by unbridled nationalism, political complexities, and nonstate actors. "War" and "peace" are *not* "two discontinuous and incommensurable worlds of existence and universes of discourse," each with its own set of rules, whereby "peace" is the equivalent of morality and "war" is the equivalent of evil.[17]

Another important assumption is that "peace" can be unjust and therefore illicit in character; hence, it must be justly ordered. It follows, then, that "it is not possible to disavow war absolutely without disavowing the task of establishing justice."[18] Peace and stability themselves are the fruit of justice. For this reason, peace is incompatible with a tolerance of evil. Peace and justice are both human goods, but neither is an absolute good. Peace must be the goal of justice, while justice must properly order peace if human beings are to flourish.[19]

The just war tradition insists that qualitative moral difference can be seen to exist between "violence" and "force." According to John Courtney Murray, force is "the measure of power necessary and sufficient to uphold the valid purposes both of law and politics. What exceeds this measure is violence, which destroys the order both of law and politics."[20] Force, then, is morally neutral and can be used for either good or ill. Coercive force is *both* permissible and limitable,[21] thereby avoiding two extreme positions—on the one hand, that coercive force can never serve just purposes (pacifism), and on the other hand, that coercive force need not be severely qualified (militarism and holy war/jihad).[22]

A final set of assumptions concerns means. First, a correlation must be discerned between the injustice being thwarted and its response, whereby consequences and fallout caused by the response must be evaluated in moral terms; and, consequently, a hierarchy of moral values must guide military and humanitarian intervention—not a mere utilitarian estimate of material damage but the realization of human death and suffering caused by war. Second, a moral symmetry exists between military ends and means, between *ius ad bellum* and *ius in bello*, based on the justice of a cause for intervention and the right intention that governs both ends and means.[23] Practically speaking, the means *are* the end in the making; a just end cannot be advanced by unjust means.[24] Technology or strategy per se does not remove the possibility of morally guided coercive force, even when such can be used for unjust purposes.[25] Third, even when moral judgment can be clouded—or violated—in war, this potential itself does not render war or coercive force unjustifiable. And fourth, the same moral criteria yield different moral judgments in different wars.[26]

In anticipating the modern objection that warfare cannot be "just"— that is, that moral principle cannot guide us in approaching war and that conduct in war cannot be morally guided and "humanized"—just war thinking presumes that to deny human intellectual and moral judgment in the midst of *applying* coercive force (in any military context) is to deny who we are as human beings. Such is to succumb to a radically deterministic pessimism in human affairs that must be resisted at every turn. For if discerning and implementing various levels of coercive force is not possible, then we shall have to concede that neither is criminal justice attainable at the level of domestic policy, nor are just norms in *any* human context plausible. Just principles do not exist hermetically sealed in some universe removed from daily living; rather, they embody justice everywhere and at all times—in civilian and domestic life as well.

Insofar as policy, properly viewed, is the convergence of moral principle and governing, the pertinent issue is *not* whether a war is perfectly just; it is whether war can be justified on moral and prudential grounds (*ius ad bellum*) and whether it can be limited and guided by moral intent and design (*ius in bello*). In the words of Michael Walzer, "There never was a golden age of warfare when just war categories were easy to apply."[27] *Relative* justice is therefore needed to order human relationships and provide what Augustine calls the *tranquillitas ordinis*, the tranquility of order.[28] This justly ordered peace, motivated and contextualized by the leavening agent of *caritas* (neighbor love),[29] which treats others with equal human dignity, serves the function of preserving human society, which otherwise would self-destruct. Augustine describes this expression of *caritas* as "benevolent harshness" (*asperitas benigna*), insofar as it does the unjust aggressor the important service of restraining him from doing evil, confronting him with the need to repent, and forcing him to regard peace.[30] Alas, one discovers through an examination of wars ancient and modern that it *is* possible to limit war and not succumb to the temptation of "all-out war." It is *not* inevitable that means dishonor ends. In truth, because war is not an end in itself but rather "an instrument of policy"[31] to bring about a better peace, all war must be limited, whereby ends and means are organically connected in the service of a morally justifiable aim.[32]

Just war thinkers maintain that the tradition of which they are a part does not merely consist of a checklist of immutable rules so much as it (a) qualifies and clarifies scenarios that justify a state going to war (*ius ad bellum*) and (b) qualifies what measure of force is or is not permissible in the conduct of war (*ius in bello*). This full-throated chastening of Realpolitik adds up to a "vision of civic virtue"[33] that requires a willingness to make difficult moral discriminations. Just war thinking emphatically rejects the obtuseness of militarism, which eschews moral reasoning in general. Therefore, a morally formed citizenry is a precondition for just war thinking. Neither relativism nor withdrawal is an option in the just war scheme, regardless of the cultural Zeitgeist.

The structure of the just war tradition mirrors two chief concerns for moral qualification, as has already been suggested. The same moral reasoning that leads to (a) determinations about going to war informs decisions about (b) the means by which war is to be executed. Undergirding the just war tradition are the baseline moral assumptions that coercive force must be severely qualified and that unjust means may not be employed to obtain a "just" end; in this tradition, ends and means are inextricably related. Historically, two groups of moral categories or criteria serve as guidelines that help determine the relative "justness" or "rightness" of military action according to the tradition: these moral criteria assist us in determining whether to go to war (*ius ad bellum*) and how to conduct war (*ius in bello*).[34] Although typical discussions of just war contain longer lists of the former that are familiar to most people, all conditions derive from three principle criteria that constitute the heart of just war moral reasoning—just cause, proper authority, and right intention—which are interlocking. That is, war can be justified only by a conjunction of all three conditions. While identified by a host of just war thinkers both ancient and modern, these core criteria are specified by Thomas Aquinas, whose account has served as a basis for subsequent just war thinking to the present.[35]

Ius ad Bellum

1. *Just Cause.* To establish the justness of a cause is to make fundamental moral distinctions—for example, between innocence and guilt, between the criminal and punitive act, between retribution and revenge, and between egregious human rights violations ("crimes against humanity") and the need for humanitarian intervention. Augustine observes that "the wise man will wage only just wars.... It is the iniquity on the part of the adversary that forces a just war upon the wise man."[36]

In principle, just cause is motivated by one of two chief concerns: to rectify injustice or to prevent further injustice. Hence, Aquinas can argue that "those who are attacked are attacked because they deserve it on account of some wrong they have done."[37] The sixteenth-century Spanish theologian Francisco de Vitoria agrees, observing that there is only one just cause for resort to war, and that is *iniuria accepta*, a "wrong done."[38] Citing Augustine, Aquinas identifies a just war as "one that avenges wrongs, that is, when a nation or state has to be punished either for refusing to make amends for outrages done by its subjects, or to restore what it had seized injuriously."[39] Sufficient justification for war, according to Hugo Grotius, includes reclaiming stolen or occupied territory, oppressive injury or harm (even in another nation) that requires punishment or prevention of humanitarian abuses, threat to or rescue of nationals, terrorism, and preventive attack.[40] War, for Grotius, is justifiable only "to continue the work of peace."[41]

For a response to be considered just, it must be in proportion to the injustice committed. But this response may not be narrowly punitive—which is to say, vindictive—in nature; it must also aim at some greater good. Not every injustice, it goes without saying, necessitates coercive intervention or war. Military intervention is just to the extent that it restores inalienable rights that have been violated. Just cause wrestles with an appropriate response where and when gross injustice and moral culpability are established; in this way, it seeks to defend the basic order of justice that has been violated.[42]

Two challenges in our day serve as a potential impediment to establishing "just cause" in a manner consistent with traditional just war thinking. One is to view justice in absolutist and triumphalistic terms, which is characteristic of both "realism" and "holy war." Therein belligerents operate apart from a conviction of moral restraint and limitations and a commitment to achieve a better peace. The other obstacle presents itself in the form of a deep-seated moral skepticism that refuses to acknowledge that we can arrive at moral judgments about relative justice.[43] At the most fundamental level, however, just war thinking proceeds on the assumption that human beings *are* equipped to discern basic justice and injustice. We must therefore reject the implication or thinking, found in many circles, that because we can never know whether a cause is *absolutely* just, we cannot discern basic justice. For to assume that a cause cannot be identified as just or unjust in the end paralyzes the moral agent in a state of nonaction.

Given human beings' imperfect attempts at realizing justice, we recognize the necessity of a degree of moral skepticism in the process of establishing just cause. While just war theorists have disagreed on whether a war could be just on both sides, Augustine and Aquinas (and those in their debt) considered this an impossibility, even when one might grant that *legitimate grievances* on both sides are to be found. The notions of "innocence" and "guilt," after all, disappear if a war is "just" on both sides. It is, therefore, preferable to speak of a *preponderance* of justice and injustice in the anatomy of a conflict.[44] Just cause is best understood "in terms of a *balance* (or perhaps more accurately an imbalance) of justice and injustice.... That it is a question of the balance of justice is a recognition of the complexities and ambiguities of international relations and of the likelihood that neither justice nor injustice will be the monopoly of one side or the other."[45] For this reason, Vitoria found it necessary to distinguish between objective wrongs and apparent wrongs resulting from "ignorance either of fact or of law."[46] And where just cause was "certain" on both sides, Vitoria considered it "unlawful" to go to war. In this regard, the wisdom of one just war thinker bears repeating: "Where we ignore the complexities of just cause, we stand in danger of licensing fanaticism and unleashing powerful emotional forces that may overwhelm moral restraint"[47]—forces that would seem to fuel "holy war" in its varied forms. Hence, the capacity for moral action, in the words of one theorist, is necessarily tempered by "the exercise of a certain humility and ... a restraint of the moral imagination."[48]

It is surely of necessity that the criterion of just cause be reassessed in our own day, and this for multiple reasons. Among these, three need identification: the problem of moral inadequacy of the very notion of "just cause" in the sphere of positive international law (whereby little agreement on what constitutes "aggression" can be found); the lack of responsible teaching and interpretation of the just war tradition in religious circles; and the matter of contemporary adaptation, based on the shift from convention to nonconventional forms of warfare (inclusive of nonstate actors capable of attacking states).[49] Given their increase, also belonging to the category of nonconventional interventionary force today there are numerous catastrophic scenarios that require some military assistance and, hence, just cause deliberation. These include—but are not limited to—genocide, mass starvation, widespread human rights abuses, refugee crises, interstate conflict and civil war, and failed states. As one just war theorist has noted, "When a people are being massacred, we don't require that they pass the test of self-help before coming to their aid."[50] At the same time, regardless of the specific character of the injustice being redressed, a state contemplating intervention will weigh—both for moral and prudential reasons—the dangers and risks being imposed both on the people being directly aided and people of the surrounding region.

In the end, just cause is a necessary condition for recourse to war, but it is not a sufficient condition when standing alone. Moral and prudential considerations in the just war tradition, even where just cause has been reasonably established, may point in the direction of *not* intervening. Part of the reason for this is that the moral efficacy of just cause depends upon the existence of *right intention*, which is discussed below. At bottom, right intention concerns itself with the proper motives for intervention, requiring that intervention be based wholly on a commitment to help facilitate a better peace than heretofore existed. The great challenge for a nation—its political leaders, its military, and its citizenry—lies in "identifying the moment when ultimate human values are genuinely at stake, and not just some . . . disproportionate cause, to which a spurious moral value is being attached."[51]

2. *Proper Authority*. To address matters of sovereignty, to declare a war and wage it, there must exist a public authority that has responsibility for the people. Aquinas writes that "it is not the business of a private person to declare war. . . . Moreover it is not the business of a private person to summon together the people, which has to be done in wartime. And as the care of the common weal is committed to those who are in authority, it is their business to watch over the common weal of the city, kingdom or province subject to them."[52] War, then, is necessarily an act by "the authority of a sovereign by whose command the war is to be waged."[53] Private acts of justice—*duellum* over against *bellum*—are rooted in vengeance and thus are illegitimate, as are rioting, insurrection, and other quasi-public acts of injustice which lack representative as well as juridical-legal authority. Only public acts of justice are legitimate. Hence, only governments may make war, "for the same reason that only police and magistrates may arrest and only judges [may] sentence, namely, that they require representative persons, acting for the community, to perform them."[54] As an instrument of justice, coercive force is not "random, uncontrolled violence" or "violence as an instrument of terror for terror's sake"; rather, it is "the use of force at the behest of *right*

authority."⁵⁵ Indeed, such is the nature of the polis, the political community; justice requires representative consensus, even when it does not require perfection.

Justice in war is a moral and legal judgment. Although beyond the mere confines of domestic criminal justice, and thus extraordinary rather than ordinary in character, war requires—like criminal justice—representative authority for its enactment. Its legitimacy is anchored in the legitimacy of sovereignty and political authority, which are moral and legal in nature.⁵⁶ In the words of one theorist: "'Reasons of state' are valid only so long as the state itself has reason."⁵⁷ Perhaps the best way to illustrate the nature of public authority that must stand behind war-enacting is to note three distinct ways in which a belligerent party may lack authority. It is lacking when (1) the cause of belligerence lies *outside* the party's sphere of authority from the very beginning; (2) authority has collapsed from *within*, for whatever reason; and (3) a claim to authority is not authorized as being representative of a people and government. These conditions illustrate why terrorism, along with piracy and other forms of nonstate criminal action, is a moral abomination irrespective of time and culture. It simply cannot lay claim to authority. Terrorism forces us, as few things do, to recognize the indispensability of government.⁵⁸

As it applies to political authority, just war thinking performs two moderating functions. On the one hand, it holds in check excessive claims to state sovereignty by conceiving of justice and rights in universal—and thus international—terms. This has the effect of curbing nationalist tendencies and imperialist pretensions.⁵⁹ On the other hand, it affirms the right of government qua government to adjudicate over justice and rights in a way that private individuals and special-interest groups are not permitted to do. This very attempt to balance the claims of justice and power is itself one of the great moral safeguards that just war thinking furnishes against totalitarian schemes, be they secular or religious in character. The proper-authority condition focuses our attention not on who controls power but rather on representative authority and who has the right to govern.

3. *Right Intention.* Establishing just cause alone is insufficient to justify going to war. Morally guided force will seek to advance a greater

good and secure a greater peace than previously existed. Aquinas insists that belligerents should have a right intention "so that they intend the advancement of good, or the avoidance of evil," although it may happen that "the war is declared by the legitimate authority, and for a just cause, and yet be rendered unlawful through a wicked intention."[60] Unjust war is perhaps best illustrated by what does *not* constitute right intention. Such scenarios include a sovereign's pride or reputation, vengeance, national aggrandizement, bloodthirst or lust for power, and territorial expansion.[61]

In just war thinking, ends and means must be interlocking. Right conduct of war requires that moral limitations be placed upon the mode employed; in this way, morally calibrated means have the effect of "verifying" the justness of an interventionary cause.[62] A particular point of emphasis for Grotius is that, in the pursuit of any object, the means must derive the complexion of its moral character from the nature of the end toward which it is directed.[63] Human beings may never do evil that good might be achieved; thus, we may not hold to a moral calculus that permits a "lesser evil" in order to resist a greater evil. Without right intention, there can be no continuity between ends and means and, hence, no moral justification. Anthony Coates states the matter well: "The dynamic way in which just war criteria are related is nowhere more evident than in the case of right intention.... Principles are important but they remain ineffective without the will and disposition to apply them. This is why right intention, understood in its traditional and dispositional sense, may be (strategically) the most important of all the criteria of *ius ad bellum*. Without an appropriate and moral disposition, the other criteria of a just war become distorted or inoperable."[64] For a war to be just, then, its aim must be a greater good, and that greater good is a justly ordered peace. To intend to create or foster peace for others, according to Aquinas, is a property of the virtue of charity.[65] Where the political sovereign is acutely aware of his or her responsibility to protect the commonweal, chances are greater that just criteria have been met for going to war. Where a just peace is established as the aim of intervention, the chances for the possibility of territorial domination, revenge, or other wrong motives are severely minimized, if not ruled out.[66] Within just war thinking, the goal of war is to stop the strongman, to incapacitate and defeat the opponent, not necessarily to kill; the goal is liberation and not merely brute conquest. Oliver O'Donovan has framed the matter in the following way: "It is not essential to war-making that you kill, merely that you should intend to remove by all sound means the forces that oppose you. The scale of loss of life, important as it is in any concrete moral decision, does not define the distinctive nature of war as such."[67] At bottom, to defeat the opponent is to overcome the enemy's will, which is a humane goal.

As one might expect, a not infrequent criticism of the criterion of right intention concerns its sheer vagueness; it is impossible, so the argument goes, to know whether a state has done its due diligence and probed deeply enough to establish the justness of a cause with good and proper aims. While this concern in and of itself is legitimate, it can easily be exaggerated, as one just war theorist cautions:

> Intentions can be, and ought to be, discerned through *a reasoned examination of publicly accessible evidence*, relying on behaviour, consideration of incentives and explicit avowals of intent. Intentions are neither infinitely redescribable nor irreducibly private—they are connected to *patterns of evidence*, as well as constrained by norms of logical coherence—and so right intention is not a vacuous criterion for moral judgment during war. Though difficult, it *is* possible to tell whether a state is prosecuting a war out of ethnic hatred, for example, as opposed to vindicating its right of self-defence. That kind of dark motivation produces distinctive and noticeable results, such as torture, massacres, mass rapes and large-scale displacements.[68]

Because it looks to the inner ethical quality of the agent's action rather than to the mere external act, right intention distinguishes between moral retribution and revenge. At its base, the moral outrage that expresses itself through retributive justice is first and foremost rooted in moral principle and not hatred or passion. For this reason, Augustine can speak of retribution in terms of "benevolent harshness."[69] Thus, for example, in his letter to Publicola, Augustine renders legitimate (based on the wedding of justice and charity) an exception to the prohibition of killing. It is legitimate precisely when and where it involves the public good—for example, in the case of a soldier or public official carrying out his public trust by establishing a justly ordered peace.[70] For this reason, Augustine can write elsewhere to Boniface, a governor of a northern African province, "Do not think that it is impossible for anyone serving in the military to please God."[71] Of the soldiers who came to John the Baptist with questions, based on the Lukan gospel narrative, Augustine observes that John "surely did not prohibit them from serving in the military when he commanded them to be content with their pay."[72]

Conceptually, revenge (i.e., vengeance or retaliation) and retribution are worlds apart. Whereas revenge strikes out at real *or* perceived injury, retribution speaks to an objective wrong. Because of its retaliatory mode, revenge will target both the offending party and those perceived to be akin. Retribution, by contrast, is targeted yet impersonal and impartial, thereby distinguishing itself from "vigilante justice." (It is for this reason that "Lady Justice" is depicted as blindfolded.) Moreover, whereas revenge is wild, insatiable, and not subject to limitations, retribution acknowledges both upper and lower limits.[73] By its very nature, vengeance has a thirst for injury, delighting in bringing further evil upon the offending party. The avenger will not only kill but rape, torture, plunder, and burn what is left, deriving satisfaction from the victim's direct or indirect suffering. Augustine condemns this "lust for revenge,"[74] a propensity prompting C. S. Lewis, who experienced war's brutality, to observe: "We may kill [in wartime] if necessary, but we must never hate and enjoy hating. We may punish if necessary, but we must not enjoy it. In other words, something inside us, the feeling of resentment, the feeling that wants to get one's own back, must be simply killed. . . . It is hard work, but the attempt is not impossible."[75] Despite the assumptions of modernity, it needs to be emphasized that the impulse toward retribution is not some primitive instinct. Rather, it issues out of the awareness that human beings have an intrinsic dignity as moral agents. It is precisely *because* of this dignity (not *in spite of* it) that we hold fellow humans accountable for their actions. Civilized human beings will not tolerate murder and mayhem; the uncivilized, however, will. As it is expressed in just war thinking, the retributive response is both discriminating and proportionate to the offense committed. Both of these properties are anchored in an awareness of human dignity and a commitment to treat fellow human beings as responsible moral agents.

While the three aforementioned core criteria of just cause, proper authority, and right intention constitute the heart of *ad bellum* thinking, together they give rise to other related prudential conditions. To distinguish between primary and secondary conditions is not to suggest that the latter are insignificant. It is only to recognize that they are derivative, issuing out of primary considerations. As such, they mirror the obligations of justice, express political prudence, and call for discernment in terms of concrete application. We include among these "secondary" conditions reasonable chance of success, last resort, peace as the ultimate aim, and formal declaration of war.

Because the secondary criteria are frequently the primary focus of contemporary discussions of just war, we offer a brief word of commentary on last resort, which more often than not is the starting point for contemporary debates.[76] Going to war can be justified only in exceptional conditions. That is, only when the core conditions of just war moral reasoning have been met without any solution is war to be considered. The prudential wisdom of just war thinking, which is rooted in moral principle and restraint, is captured by one contemporary theorist:

> Recognition of the potential moral instrumentality of war is not to be confused with moral enthusiasm for war. There are those for whom war, far from being a regrettable necessity, is in fact the preferred option.... For those who regard it in this way war is more a matter of *first* than of last resort. Such ready acceptance of war is foreign to the just war approach. Given the horrors of war, moral as well as physical, a just recourse to war should be marked by extreme reluctance and a sense of moral tragedy and foreboding.[77]

To grapple with last resort is to reckon with the gravity of acts of force; at the same time it is a factor only when the other principle conditions have been considered. Have all reasonable efforts to utilize nonmilitary (i.e., diplomatic, economic, political, and cultural) alternatives been exhausted? The operative word here is *reasonable*, since those who oppose war in principle will *never* see diplomatic possibilities as having been exhausted. Unhappily, "last resort" not infrequently serves as "a useful device of concealment" by those who are ideologically committed to the logic of deploring all war.[78] Taken literally and not reasonably, as Michael

Walzer points out, last resort would render all war morally impossible, for we can "never reach lastness, or we can never know that we have reached it."[79]

A common misunderstanding of the principle of last resort is to view the qualifier "last" as indicating the final move in a chronological series of actions. Such *might* be the case, as, for example, in a police action involving a crime suspect who is fleeing. The law enforcement agent goes through particular steps in apprehending the suspect—first, a verbal warning; second, a verbal warning that she will shoot; third, firing a warning short in the air, and finally, if all else fails, firing a shot at the fleeing suspect. And in some scenarios—for example, hostage-taking by terrorists who then announce that the hostages will be killed within a certain time frame—coercive force would be justified as a *first* (and perhaps only) option.[80]

And then there is the question of *who* is qualified to judge "last resort." Some readers will perhaps recall the very heated (and in some ways comical) debate in 1990 and 1991 between two prominent Oxford University theologians—Richard Harries and soon-to-become Archbishop of Canterbury Rowan Williams. The former argued that in the case of Iraq #1 "last resort" had been reached, while the latter rejected this contention. The point needing emphasis is that "last resort" is a political-diplomatic-military judgment that is removed from the purview of even brilliant theologians. Churchman are not rulers; neither are they usually privy to military intelligence. For better or worse, rulers must exercise moral judgments in enacting policy.

In light of the priority given to last resort in contemporary debates, and attendant confusion surrounding the concept, James Turner Johnson makes an important clarification: "The criterion does not mean always postponing use of military force until every possible means short of force has been tried. If one comes into a situation late in the day, as is almost by definition the case when a conflict has created urgent humanitarian needs, working the gradualist way might simply postpone what is necessary until still later, perhaps making the situation worse and requiring a more robust, costly, and dangerous intervention when force is finally brought in."[81] To claim, as some do, that *ius ad bellum* requirements begin with a presumption against *war* (over against a presumption against *injustice*) is false, as we have already noted, revealing a fundamental misunderstanding of the just war tradition. Properly understood, last resort leads us to deliberate not over forestalled timing per se but over what sort of morally appropriate action should be taken. All possibilities are considered, including the military option. Last resort, then, is properly construed as a subordinate to just cause.

Ius in Bello

The moral reasoning that leads to determinations about going to war contributes to conduct in war. Ends and means are organically related; thus Hugo Grotius: "Least of all should that be admitted which some people imagine, that in war all laws are in abeyance. On the contrary war ought not to be undertaken except in pursuit of what is right and, when once undertaken, it should be conducted only within the bounds of law and good faith. . . . But in order that wars may be justified, they must be carried on with no less scrupulousness than judicial processes are wont to be."[82] If particular policies or strategies violate the normative *ius in bello* conditions from the outset, then this may well indicate that it is wrong to begin war at all.[83]

1. *Discrimination.* The linkage between ends and means, of course, is all but lost on the militarist and crusader or jihadist, who can justify war but fail to apply any restraint in prosecuting war. The most basic moral prohibition, even in war, is the taking of innocent life. This proscription is part of the natural moral law and confirmed in legal codes both ancient and modern. Guilt is predicated on intention, and a justified war, in Thomistic terms, is one that is waged against those who deserve it.[84] The noncombatant—including civilian populations, wounded soldiers, prisoners, noncombatant women, children, and noncombatant males— may not be held "guilty" as may a government or military representatives of that regime.

A justified war is one that, as Aquinas puts it, is waged against those who deserve it. The distinction between "guilty" and "innocent"— categories that are moral and legal in nature and rooted in the natural law—is a distinction that is qualified by *intention* and established by "direct material cooperation in the doing of wrong."[85] In prosecuting war we oppose a state, as represented by its military apparatus, and not a society. Hence, one is a "combatant" to the extent that he or she *stands in relative proximity* to participation in that wrong—that is, as one "involved in the chain of agency directing the perceived aggression or wrongdoing."[86] In other words, by reason of *material cooperation* one becomes a legitimate object of attack.[87] As a result of *function*, then, one stands within "a proximate nexus to 'war-fighting.'"[88] Immunity, therefore, relates to the function of not bearing arms,[89] and one loses immunity from attack, even as a civilian, by virtue of direct or material contribution to hostility. That is to say, by virtue of one's *choosing* (a) to be a combatant or (b) to contribute (in any number of ways) to the combatant's cause, one forfeits immunity from direct attack. The just war tradition distinguishes between persons qua persons and persons qua combatants. Those who do not *abet* war are not guilty.[90]

While the precise meaning of noncombatant status might vary according to time period and military technology, the nature of "immunity" is not fluid, given the fact of military strategy and what is *intended* or *deliberated*. Combatant and noncombatant status, then, are grounded in the same moral principle of establishing culpability—that of agency in prosecuting war, material cooperation with that effort, and subsequent threat. Deliberately inflicting any suffering or injury that is not directly related to morally legitimate and strategic purposes is strictly prohibited. A fundamental flaw of both militarism and totalitarianism is their indiscriminate attitude toward human life. Accordingly, all and any may be sacrificed for the greater political end.

But what if a war must be waged in locations where the belligerents and civilians are closely intermixed, as contemporary conflicts often are and as terrorists intend? Here the moral imperative approximates that of law enforcement in the domestic context, even when the stakes are incalculably greater.[91] When and where violent crime has occurred or is about to occur, law enforcement authorities must plan, calculate, and collude in order to avoid needless casualties. However, when the threat has reached critical mass and where the murder of innocents is likely, there comes a point at which action must be taken against the belligerent, even if it means the possibility of innocent bystanders being hurt or killed. Military activity is based on deliberation and intent. For this reason, just war thinking makes a distinction between deliberate and unintended liability. In the military context, the fact that there are (or well may be) civilian casualties does not in and of itself render a war or military campaign unjust. Intention is not deduced from the consequences; that is, the physical nature of human acts is not to be confused with their moral nature. In just war thinking, this means that the intention of the agent is oriented toward the good and not toward evil.

What's more, it has never been presupposed in just war thinking that, in war, noncombatants would be immune from being injured or killed; only from being directly or intentionally targeted. Even police work proceeds on the same basis. Noncombatants thus have never been (nor can they be) "roped off" and somehow "hermetically sealed."[92] We need not—indeed, we cannot—know the certainty of who and where noncombatants are. Human beings cannot require both justice and perfection; if both could be required, even in a moral tragedy such as a wartime scenario, we would need to give up on all forms of justice, including criminal justice in domestic policy.[93]

We might illustrate through events of the Second World War. For tactical purposes, a city's communications network, railroad system, ammunitions plans, and factories are bombed. In these operations, civilians are killed. These deaths are simultaneously grave and yet unavoidable; what needs emphasis is that these individuals were not targeted. This sort of strategic bombing is permissible, but the indiscriminate firebombing of Dresden and Tokyo and the use of nuclear weapons against Hiroshima and Nagasaki are difficult to justify—if they can be justified at all.

Just war advocates do not intend or wish deaths. At the same time, they do not, with pacifists, require on putatively moral grounds the nonuse of lethal force. In the task of resisting social-political evil, we cannot have it both ways; it needs reiteration that we cannot require both justice *and* perfection, since working for justice is always an *approximate* endeavor. The ambiguities that attend our imperfection demonstrate why just war moral reasoning must be applied with political prudence, insofar as military intervention always entails imprecise calculation and different situations call for different solutions within the wider sphere of moral parameters.[94]

Can evils be inflicted upon the innocent neighbor in our attempts to defend the innocent? Unquestionably. Such is the nature of living in the temporal order—an order that exhibits the effects of human "fallenness."

Sometimes defending or protecting the innocent cannot be done without inflicting further unintended evil and suffering. But what renders this imposition of force "just" is that its primary intention was to *protect* and not harm. Not only does discrimination express the heart of *in bello* conditions; it is implicit in *ius ad bellum*, insofar as only by means of moral discrimination can judgments about going to war be made.

2. *Proportionality*. The principle of proportionality has to do with the shape of the act of retributive judgment being administered. It concerns economy in the use of force and, specifically, in "the proportioning of means of violence to the effective protection of endangered interests or values."[95] But that economy of force must be morally guided. Resting on several basic assumptions, it begins with the baseline recognition that a moral loss through injustice has occurred (just cause) prior to the consideration of whether force is justified to restore what was lost and, if so, how. As a moral property, it seeks to balance the good that an application of force will create over against the evil that will result from not forcibly intervening. Force is an entity that can be *regulated*, and the degree of force applied is not to be greater than what is needed to render the enemy compliant. If the aim of war is to correct injustice, then creating a new, greater injustice is immoral. In principle, all-out war would be counter to the reason-for-being of the armed forces in nontotalitarian nations. It is for this very reason that we speak of "military force" and not "military violence."

Just war thinking distinguishes itself from crusading or militarism by its commitment to *limit* war. This is a moral stricture that is all but ignored by the militarist, who is willing to enter into total war and whose motivation might be nationalist or religious (or both). Any necessary means is thought justifiable in order to obliterate the enemy. By contrast, for the just war proponent, to wrestle with proportionality of response is to discern not only what is reasonable in terms of economy of force in a given situation but also what is a truthful approximation of the wrong done. After all, punishment is measured strictly by desert. Although justice does not require that the retributive act must "match" the offending act with precision, justice (as intuited by moral common sense and natural law) is "unjust" where responses are not in moral proportion to the acts committed. For this reason, in regular parlance we use the language of "travesty of justice" and "miscarriage of justice" to depict such outrages.

In war, as in criminal justice, this principle remains constant. Responses that are proportionate to the crimes committed are a reflection and requirement of justice. The retributive response in warfare, according to Grotius, must be commensurate with the evil being redressed. Thus, for example, a draconian response to lesser abuses is illegitimate. Wisdom must cause kings and those with representative authority to assess the cost of war as it affects not only the enemy but also other nations and people groups.[96]

At the same time, to hope that we can judge proportionality in mere terms of mathematical calculation and quantitative assessment, thereby reaching precise and certain conclusions, is pure fantasy. Cost-benefit analysis, in the words of one theorist, cannot settle the moral issue.[97] Purely utilitarian thinking "ignores the obvious fact that the many goods and evils involved—on the one hand, the vindication of the innocent, the maintenance of international order, and freedom from serious oppression; on the other hand, the deaths of individuals, social breakdown, economic destruction, and long-standing resentments—are incommensurable. There is no common currency in terms of which they can all be measured and weighed against each other to produce a reliable answer."[98] This is not to suggest that we cannot or should not make responsible and principled estimations of military operation; indeed, we must. It is only to underscore the fact that any attempts at estimation will be inexact and uncertain. What's more, no judgments of proportionality can be made "until they have been ordered according to a particular hierarchy of goods, and until conflicts between equal goods have been resolved by appeal to particular moral rules."[99]

We might illustrate the sheer difficulty of measuring proportionality as one just war theorist has done by depicting the nature of German Nazism several generations removed and the need—an incalculable need—to fight against it. Nazism was "an ultimate threat to everything decent in our lives." It was "an ideology and a practice of political domination so murderous, so degrading even to those who might survive, that the consequences of its final victory in World War II were literally beyond calculation"; the sum total of its influence in the world was "immeasurably awful." Nazism was "evil objectified in the world," and "in a form so potent and apparent that there never could have been anything to do but fight against it."[100]

And yet those who resist tyranny are not doomed to imitate or perpetuate it. Proportionality is governed by a just moral, social, and political aim toward which war must be directed.[101] That the limitation of war and its execution is a *moral mandate* lies at the heart of just war thinking. This limitation prevents "military necessity" from being removed from the exercise of moral reason and morally responsible decision-making. In its ethical orientation, proportionality is both retrospective and prospective, assessing the past in order to consider future possibilities. Just war will seek to secure the *peace*, whereas political realism, militarism, and crusading will merely strive for *conquest*.

The moral logic of *in bello* reasoning, which expresses itself in the two complementary and integrated directions of discrimination and proportionality, is rooted in the inner dispositions that give rise to right intention. To the extent that charity—which desires the best, the highest, for others—and human dignity combine with the demands of justice, right intention has the effect of humanizing justice. Discrimination and proportion together belong to the very nature of moral judgment. Hence, to lose the will both to discriminate between relative guilt and innocence and to render in proportion what is due based on the nature of the offense is, in the end, to disregard human dignity and moral agency. One is, therefore, justified in contending that the emergence of rules of conduct—even when they surface in antiquity in sources that predate Christianity—is a characteristically Christian feature.[102]

Ius post Bellum[103]

In his important work *Just and Unjust Wars*, Michael Walzer writes that there can be no justice in war if, in the end, there are not just men and women.[104] This basic truism bears repeating, even when both the militaristic cynic and the ideological pacifist would deny such. Nowhere is the truth of this statement demonstrated more forcefully than in the aftermath of war. Traditional accounts of just war theory focus on two categories of moral analysis—*ius ad bellum* and *ius in bello*. Until more recently, little attention has been given to yet a third and related category—*ius post bellum* (justice after war).

Events of the last decade and a half, however, have changed this. And if, as we have argued, the moral efficacy of just war thinking is guided by right intention and a concern for proper ends, then *ius post bellum* considerations are integral to—and requisite for—coercive intervention. What is the overall aim in order for a conflict to be declared just? While the militarist thinks chiefly in terms of victory or conquest and destruction of the enemy, just war proponents seek to bring about— and help establish—a state or condition that is qualitatively better than what existed previously. In positive terms, the bare minimum that might be cited as necessary in the aftermath of war is threefold: (1) the restoration or imposition of basic human and political rights that either did not exist previously or were eradicated from social life, (2) compensation for victims who suffered egregiously as a result of the prior regime, and (3) affirmation of political sovereignty as well as territorial integrity. Negatively expressed, justice requires that the initiators of the aforementioned suffering and oppression be held accountable for the crimes that they perpetrated, which violated basic—that is, universally acknowledged—canons of justice.

In thinking through the nature of the *post bellum* task, Brian Orend utilizes the metaphor of radical surgery to describe an extreme yet necessary measure undertaken in the interest of a future greater good. He posits that if a war is justly prosecuted, "then the justified conclusion to such a war can only be akin to the rehabilitation and therapy required after surgery, in order to ensure that the original intent is effectively secured—defeating the threat, protecting the rights—and that the 'patient' in this case can only be the entire society of states."[105] James Turner Johnson similarly argues that the just war criteria of right intention and goal of peace presuppose a readiness to engage in postwar nation-building: "In some cases, nation-building may be a necessary adjunct to the provision of humanitarian relief or protection of relief efforts or the endangered population. In such cases, the idea of military intervention should include the possibility of not only fighters but engineers, communications teams, military police, and civil affairs units, or of civilian teams that would fulfill these functions and others necessary to the rebuilding of a stable civil order."[106] A useful reminder of this lesson stands in the not-too-distant past. Post–World War II Germany required Allied support and reconstruction, to the extent that it was not Germany qua Germany but Nazi Germany that was intolerable. Walzer frames the Allies' responsibility in this way: "Pending the establishment of a post-Nazi and an anti-Nazi regime, the Germans were to be placed in political tutelage." Why? Because of their failure to overthrow Hitler themselves. This forfeiture of independence, however, "entails no further loss of rights . . . [since] the punishment was limited and temporary; it assumed, as Churchill said, the continued existence of a German nation."[107] In the words of another just war theorist, "The threat of Nazism and German militarism was something with deep roots in German institutions, and the Allies could hardly just walk away. At a bare minimum, Germany needed to be reshaped."[108]

From the standpoint of just war moral reasoning, to walk away from any nation in a postwar scenario is to invite anarchy and thus to contradict the very essence of foundational just war principles. In the aftermath of conflict, a broad array of efforts is necessary in reconstructing any semblance of "civil society" in war-torn and politically decimated regions. Such efforts include (but are not limited to) the "extended hands" of the military, diplomatic activity, the private sector, nongovernment organizations, educational services, even the work of the church. Despite the great challenges to concerned nations that reconstruction poses, post–World War II Germany is a reminder—a glorious reminder—that there is nonetheless hope.

It needs emphasis that education is particularly vital in rebuilding war-torn and decimated countries. Education has a peculiarly humanizing effect for people who have known only (or chiefly) totalitarian, repressive rule. Hence, an exposure to ideas, history, law, literature, science and technology, and other cultures is critical. On a practical level, citizens need to learn job skills to make productive use of their gifts and creativity. Learning to be self-motivated, to serve others, to make basic wise economic decisions—these capacities require a fundamental change in the way that a people might think, inasmuch as the previous government siphoned off from the people whatever resources they had in order to consolidate and maintain power. What's more, a future generation of leaders will need to be raised up as part of the recovery process.

Thus, to emphasize the importance of *post bellum* considerations is nothing less than to take seriously the aims of justice and peace that have been declared before conflict is entered. Nothing less than justice is due a formerly oppressed people, in order that they might flourish as human beings. From a purely "humanitarian" standpoint, the failure of a "victorious" or intervening nation (or coalition of nations) to provide assistance in postconflict reconstructive efforts in another nation calls into question the very claim to have waged a "just" war in the first place.

REFLECTING ON THE MEANING OF AMERICA'S WARS

The present volume, it needs emphasizing, is neither a textbook, nor a manual, nor a military history. Thus, it will not read as such but rather as a series of narratives—independent (though not unrelated) narratives that are constitutive parts of America's history. At the same time, the volume has been crafted under the operating assumption that, in the just war tradition as classically developed and refined, there exists a common frame of reference, a moral compass, if you will. Undergirding this frame of reference is the conjoining in the tradition of the universal dispositions of justice and charity, which are expressions of the natural moral law.[109] In the ethics of war, the implications of this union are particularly crucial.[110] Indeed, wisdom, prudence, and our common humanity demand that we work toward such a union and that we approach and evaluate war with the awareness that we are moral agents.[111] We do not have the luxury of not making moral judgments in this world, even when we might evade or be dismissive of this responsibility.

We noted that *America and the Just War Tradition* is not intended to be an exercise in military history, and properly so. At the same time, this volume was birthed in the conviction that serious study of social upheaval and military conflict has much to teach us. In the words of one commentator, "The praxis of mortal combat is not destructive to human sociality as such; it is simply a moment at which human sociality regroups and renews itself."[112] In "regrouping" and "renewing" (whether in each new generation or in times of social upheaval), we might well ask ourselves, what values or ideals animate the civic polity, and what qualities constitute a virtuous citizenry? Why are the varieties of pacifism—whether secular and religious—so attractive in any age? What leads to an unthinking militaristic mind-set? Do relatively "free" people have a moral obligation to relieve the plight of the masses in other regimes who suffer egregiously? Why or why not, and when? Why must "freedom" be morally qualified? What is the appeal behind utilitarian approaches to ethics? Once relatively "democratic" freedoms have been mortgaged or lost, can they be recovered? And what forces within a culture are necessary to preserve "civil society" and the "common good"?

The "common good," of course, presupposes (a) public argument about (b) a consensus regarding "the good." Thus John Courtney Murray: "The whole premise of the public argument, if it is to be civilized and civilizing, is that the consensus is real, that among the people everything is not in doubt, but that there is a core of agreement, accord, concurrence, acquiescence. We hold certain truths; therefore we argue about them."[113] Where, however, a consensus does *not* exist and where public argument itself is difficult or impossible, the question is whether that society is still "civilized." Again, Murray: "As a heritage and as a public philosophy, the American consensus needs to be constantly argued. If the public argument dies from disinterest, or subsides into the angry mutterings of polemic, or rises to the shrillness of hysteria, or trails off into positivistic triviality, or gets lost in a morass of semantics, you may be sure that the barbarian is at the gates of the City."[114] It has been said that barbarism is the lack of reasonable conversation according to reasonable laws. By this definition, a society becomes uncivilized when people cease having dialogue together, when they fail—or are unable—to have open and rational conversations about human affairs. We confess that this volume, in a very real way, is intended to *stimulate* conversations—lively and provocative conversations—about human affairs.

Victor Davis Hanson, codirector of the Group on Military History and Contemporary Conflict at the Hoover Institution, observes that a public that is illiterate and not conversant about past conflicts will easily find itself confused during wartime developments.[115] That is, without standards by which to judge, people show themselves to be ill equipped at making informed judgments when faced with catastrophic scenarios. While the study of past wars does not promise cookie-cutter comparisons and while just war thinking by no means furnishes us with a shortcut around moral complexity, study of the past *does* provide parameters within which we may think, and ultimately act. At the very least, studying past wars has moral and pedagogical value in that we are confronted with the phenomenon of human sacrifice, by which the universal virtues of justice and neighbor-love express themselves, often in remarkable ways. Some sacrifice, of course, is needless, unjust, and tragic; some, however, is justified and honorable, when directed—based on the symbiosis of justice and charity—toward an innocent party—what has been called a "preferential ethics of protection."[116] By reflecting thereupon we learn much about human nature, about human moral obligation, and about "civil society" as we presently know it.

The questions of whether America's wars can be said to have been "just" or "unjust," and if so, to what extent, will invoke sharp disagreement, depending on how policy and principle are gauged, and depending on our historical and cultural vantage point. Even among those who acknowledge the authority of just war moral reasoning, we will not find uniform thinking. Such latitude of conviction, however, need not prevent us from probing. We are grateful that each contributor to this volume has engaged in this exercise with both a historical and moral seriousness. This is not to say that we agree with the conclusions of each author—indeed, we have disagreements with several of them. But we are pleased to include their chapters anyway as we are confident that they advance the conversation about how Americans have thought and should think about war.

OVERVIEW

By the historian Harry S. Stout's count, the United States of America has been involved with at least three hundred wars or military interventions.[117] Selecting which of these conflicts to cover in this volume was no easy task. One of our first decisions was to include only wars that occurred after America became a nation on July 4, 1776.[118] We had initially wanted to include chapters on the Pequot War, King Philip's War, and the French and Indian War, all conflicts that deserve serious consideration, but we simply did not have the space to do so. It is only a partial consolation that we have begun discussing the possibility of a sequel to this volume that will remedy these and other omissions.

Limiting the scope of our volume to wars fought after the U.S. came into being did not eliminate our hard choices. America has engaged in an almost continuous series of military conflicts, both overt and covert.

For instance, the nation fought numerous small wars against different Native American tribes.[119] As well, the country has engaged in drawn-out conflicts with foreign powers, such as the so-called war against the Barbary pirates and the Cold War. And there have been plenty of small military interventions, which between 1950 and 2000 include at least "Iran (1953), Guatemala (1954), Lebanon (1958), Panama (1958), Cuba (1961), Iraq (1963), Indonesia (1965), Oman (1970), Angola (1976–92), Libya (1986), Somalia (1992–94), and Haiti (1994)."[120] Space constraints permit us to cover only America's major, most notable wars—and even so one may reasonably contend that we should have made room for a chapter on, say, America's wars against Native Americans, even if it required us to cut one of the other chapters in this volume.

This book explores America's wars in light of a just war tradition nurtured and developed in the Christian West. It does not explore America's wars from a Christian perspective per se, but because Christianity has been so influential in informing the tradition and, more generally, has been a source of guidance and comfort for many Americans, a brief word should be said about its role in this nation. Scholars debate whether America was founded as a Christian nation; answers often depend upon how terms are defined.[121] But this much is clear—in 1776 virtually every white American would have identified himself or herself as a Christian, and 98 percent of these would have been reasonably classified as Protestants. In the nineteenth century, waves of immigrants significantly increased the number of Roman Catholics in America, but well into the mid-twentieth century most Americans were accurately classified as Christians. Only in the late twentieth and early twenty-first centuries did significant numbers of Americans identify themselves as members of other religions or as nonbelievers, yet as late as 2017 approximately 70 percent of Americans continued to call themselves Christians.[122]

Identification with the Christian faith does not mean that all Americans acted in accord with Christian moral standards, or even that they agreed on what these standards require. But there has been a general consensus that Christian ethics should matter with respect to society and politics, and religious language and arguments have played important roles in supporting and opposing wars and in debating how they should be fought and for what ends. As one might expect, clergy and denominations utilize such arguments, but so do political and military leaders and regular citizens. Some of our chapters address the use of religious arguments, but again it bears emphasizing that the task of this volume is to explore America's wars from a just war perspective, not in light of Christianity more generally.

The first war covered in the volume, the American Revolution, arguably violates the chronological rule mentioned above, as hostilities began well before July 4, 1776. But it was, at least eventually, fought and concluded by the U.S., and the conflict is so central to the history of this nation that we simply could not exclude it. John Roche considers the interesting question of whether patriots violated Romans 13's admonition for Christians to obey their rulers, but he focuses on whether the war is justifiable in light of the just war tradition. He concludes that the Revolutionaries should not have gone to war, that the war was unjustly concluded, but that the Continental Army's conduct throughout the conflict was largely just.

Critics of the just war tradition sometimes contend that it is merely used to justify conflicts. Jonathan Den Hartog's chapter on the War of 1812, like several other chapters in this collection, demonstrates that the tradition has also been used by American civic and religious leaders to oppose wars. In this case, the opposition was significant indeed. Moreover, Den Hartog contends that the critics were correct; President James Madison led the nation into an unjust war. Notably, the conflict violated *ius ad bellum* principles as Americans abandoned a policy of calculated neutrality and launched a war of aggression focused on vindicating "rights" rather than defending territory.

In the mid-nineteenth century, advocates for the westward expansion of the U.S. used Christian ideas and language to support what they called America's "Manifest Destiny." Daniel Walker Howe shows how President James K. Polk of the Jacksonian Democratic Party invoked such ideas to legitimate a war of aggression against Mexico. A philosophical tradition defining when warfare was just did exist, and it disapproved of waging war to acquire territory. To be sure, few Americans in the age of Manifest Destiny were aware of this tradition. Nevertheless, a strong opposition to the war with Mexico did develop, especially among the rival political party of the time, the Whigs. When we today evaluate the moral case for and against the Mexican War, we revisit the arguments contemporaries themselves voiced. Howe makes his own position clear: the war was unjust.

Perhaps the most tragic war fought by Americans was the Civil War, also known as the War Between the States. Gregory Jones deftly shows that the North and the South were each convinced they were justified in going to war and that God favored their cause. Abraham Lincoln noted in his Second Inaugural Address: "Both [parties] read the same Bible, and pray to the same God; and each invokes His aid against the other."[123] This infusion of religious fervor into the conflict may have led both sides to ignore the requirements of *ius in bello* far too often. Today, most Americans agree that preserving the union and eliminating slavery were just outcomes of the war, but Jones reminds us that even these results were controversial at the time.

Timothy Demy's chapter on the Spanish-American War begins by suggesting that much of what Americans "know" about the war is wrong. He shows that the conflict coincided with an expansionist foreign policy and the great Protestant missionary efforts of the late nineteenth and early twentieth centuries. In the U.S., religious identification of the kingdom of God with the American Republic enhanced support for the war. In the American press, images were presented of a democratic Protestant "Christian America" that was fighting an imperial Roman Catholic Spain. Additionally, political and religious rhetoric of "humanitarian intervention" helped gain support for the war. Demy concludes that the U.S. justly entered and fought the war but that it attempted to impose an unjust peace on the Filipino people, resulting in the Philippine-American War of 1899–1902.

The cultural, political, and civil religious attention afforded the First World War, specifically the American experience of that war, is undeniably small. There are many reasons for the shrinking of the Great War, most of them understandable. The U.S.'s involvement was brief, casualties were comparatively few, and it wasn't long before the noble aims that gave so many Americans a sense of purpose in and around the war proved to be unrealizable in the short term. Within two decades of the armistice, the world was again spinning toward global conflagration. However, Jonathan Ebel shows that students of the just war tradition cannot afford to overlook this conflict.

After December 7, 1941, few Americans thought that war against the Empire of Japan was immoral or avoidable. Adolf Hitler's decision to declare war on the U.S. just four days after the shocking Japanese assault on Pearl Harbor seemed to leave the American people with little choice but to defend themselves against two of the most aggressive and ruthless adversaries the world had ever known. But the ferocity and brutality of the war, along with its atomic ending, eventually brought intense scrutiny not only to the conduct of the conflict but to its origins as well. It is tempting to conclude that this war is the most obviously just of the wars covered in the volume, but Kerry E. Irish shows that America's decision to go to war is not as simple as most Americans suppose, and elements of how America prosecuted the war should certainly be condemned. Nevertheless, the American people fought a necessary war for the laudable goal of building a lasting and equitable peace on the ashes of much of the old imperial world.

The Korean War of 1950–53 inaugurated an era in which the only unambiguous characteristic of American involvement in armed conflict was its very ambiguity. Korea was a war fought over divisions in the geographic and political landscape of a country noted for its cultural homogeneity and geographic integrity—until the day in 1945 when American planners first partitioned the peninsula. American involvement began with a defensive response to North Korean aggression—until North Korean troops were first pushed back beyond the 38th Parallel, forcing the question of whether to hold to a post–World War II status quo or pursue Korean reunification on Allied terms. Korea was fought under the auspices of the U.N., but it involved a dominant—though not exclusive—role for American troops, leadership, and equipment. It was a war which the U.S. entered without a congressional declaration, using the notion of "crime control" to justify this departure from traditional practice. Korea was a Cold War conflict whose origins and execution were deeply influenced by questions about the U.S.'s commitment to democracy in Asia, given its preoccupation with Stalin's intentions in Europe. Laura Jane Gifford's essay sifts through the ambiguities of the Korean conflict to discern the degree—itself ambiguous—to which the U.S. was justified in intervening, fought justly, and attempted to bring about a just peace.

The Vietnam War remains controversial on many levels, not the least of which is the justness of the conflict. The standard narrative is that the war was uniquely unjust in terms of both *ius ad bellum*, the American decision to fight the war in the first place, and *ius in bello*, the actual conduct of the war. Mackubin Thomas Owens offers a provocative challenge to this narrative, contending that America was justified in entering the conflict and that while there were violations of *ius in bello*, these were aberrations, not policy. Indeed, he points out that the U.S.'s conduct in this conflict was, in fact, more just than its conduct in the Second World War or Korea.

The Greek historian Thucydides once argued that all war is caused by some combination of fear, honor, and interest. Not surprisingly, these are the rubrics referred to in all but name by the presidents who initiated the Gulf wars. Darrell Cole contends that the U.S. fought the First Gulf War for reasons of honor and interest—honor in living up to the treaty with Kuwait and interest in preserving stability in the Gulf region. The Second Gulf War was fought for reasons of fear, honor, and interest— fear of Iraq providing terrorist groups with the means to attack the U.S. or its allies with weapons of mass destruction, honor in striking at any political regime that would support elements that lent their power to the terrorist attacks on 9/11, and interests in ridding the Gulf region of a destabilizing force and, again, protecting the U.S. and its allies from terrorist groups gaining possession of weapons of mass destruction. Cole argues that the U.S. had good reasons to enter the first Gulf war, that entry into the second war was far more questionable, but that the military made every effort to fight both wars in a just manner.

Terrorism is not a new phenomenon, although the scale of a modern terrorist attack can bring with it a level of unprecedented destruction. The 9/11 terrorist attack marked an instance of what modern terrorism could accomplish, though by no means its most horrific extent. Hence, the question of how—if at all—just war theory can apply to terrorism is not new but has taken on heightened importance. Although there has traditionally been a measure of critical doubt regarding the value and viability of applying just war theory or particular criteria to preventing terrorism or engaging in operations against terrorists, Rouven Steeves argues that the just war tradition is sufficiently elastic to address the exigencies of terrorism. Indeed, there is no viable alternative to ensure an effective and just response to what is intrinsically unjust and most often outside the historic pale of normal military operations.

As JAMES TURNER JOHNSON argues in this volume's foreword, how Americans have thought about war is inextricably linked to how this country has fought the wars in which it has been engaged. For better or worse, arguments about war have often been made in light of the just war tradition. Given the number of America's conflicts, only a portion of which have been covered in this book, it is easy to despair either that the tradition is used to justify wars or that it is ignored when it is inconvenient.

Yet in some ways this volume may be misleading. A major success of the just war tradition, particularly *ius ad bellum*, is not found in justifying wars but in preventing unjust and unnecessary ones. For instance, in the mid-nineteenth century the U.S. and Great Britain engaged in a long series of disputes that began with the burning of the American ship *Caroline* by Canadian soldiers in 1837, included the so-called Aroostook War of 1838 and the negotiation of the Maine-New Brunswick border in 1842, and ended with the Oregon Treaty of 1846 (which set the Oregon-Canada border at the Forty-ninth parallel despite American hotheads who insisted "Fifty-four forty or fight!"). Without minimizing the role of practical interests and other realities, one reason all-out war was avoided may have been that American and British statesmen shared a commitment to the basic principles of just war tradition. We are not saying this was necessarily the case, but it is a possibility that is worth exploring. The U.S. has engaged in literally thousands of serious conflicts with other nations that have not resulted in the use of military force. At least some of the credit for these results may be attributable to the just war tradition.

Many of this volume's chapters suggest that America's political and military leaders have made good faith efforts to follow the principles of *ius in bello*. Doing so became progressively harder in the era of total war—arguably inaugurated in the Civil War and certainly a reality by the Second World War—but, ironically, advances in military technology since the Vietnam War permit military leaders to target combatants with a great deal of specificity. In any event, it is certainly praiseworthy that so many Americans attempted to abide by the doctrines of discrimination and proportionality.

Finally, we are heartened to see the recent interest in *ius post bellum*. It is not enough to enter into only just conflicts and to fight them in a just manner. Policy makers must consider what a just peace looks like. The contrast between the end of the First and the Second World Wars suggests that how wars are ended may well be more important than considerations of entering them in the first place.

The just war tradition, as it has developed in the West, leaves plenty of ambiguity with respect to when nations should go to war, how wars should be fought, and how they should be ended. This ambiguity has been cynically abused by those who would enter wars for unjust causes. Yet it has also served as an important check on the use of military force and has reduced the death and destruction that has occurred in wars. It remains an important guide for policy makers and citizens who wish to think seriously about when, how, and why America should and should not go to war.

NOTES

1. James Turner Johnson, *Just War Tradition and the Restraint of War* (Princeton: Princeton University Press, 1981), xxxi–ii.

2. Oliver O'Donovan, *The Just War Revisited* (Cambridge: Cambridge University Press, 2003), 14.

3. Consider, for example, this representative sampling of works published within the last fifteen years: Tamar Meisels, *Contemporary Just War Theory and Practice* (2018); Marcus Schulzke, *Just War Theory and Civilian Casualties: Protecting the Victims of War* (2017); Daniel R. Brunstetter and Cian O'Driscoll, eds., *Just War Thinkers: From Cicero to the 21st Century* (2017); Todd Burkhardt, *Just War and Human Rights: Fight with Right Intention* (2017); A. J. Coates, *The Ethics of War*, 2nd. ed. (2016); James M. Dubik, *Just War Reconsidered: Strategy, Ethics, and Theory* (2016); Fritz Allhoff, Nicholas G. Evans, and Adam Henschke, eds., *Routledge Handbook of Ethics and War: Just War Theory in the 21st Century* (2015); Joseph E. Capizzi, *Politics, Justice, and War: Christian Governance and the Ethics of Warfare* (2015); James G. Murphy, *War's Ends: Human Rights, International Order, and the Ethics of Peace* (2014); Nigel Biggar, *In Defence of War* (2013); Nicholas Rengger, *Just War and International Order* (2013); Anthony Lang, Cian O'Driscoll, and John Williams, eds., *Just War: Authority, Tradition, and Practice* (2013); Richard J. Regan, *Just War: Principles and Cases* (rev. ed. 2013); David Fisher, *Morality and War: Can War Be Just in

the Twenty-First Century? (2012); Eric D. Patterson, *Ending Wars Well: Just War Theory in Post-Conflict* (2012); Patterson, *Ethics beyond War's End* (2012); David D. Corey and J. Daryl Charles, *The Just War Tradition: An Introduction* (2012); Steven P. Lee, *Ethics and War: An Introduction* (2012); Larry May and Andrew T. Forcehimes, eds., *Morality, Jus Post Bellum, and International Law* (2012); Larry May, *After War Ends* (2012); Sohail H. Hashmi, *Just Wars, Holy Wars, and Jihads: Christian, Jewish, and Muslim Encounters and Exchanges* (2012); James Turner Johnson, *Ethics and the Use of Force: Just War in Historical Perspective* (2011); Helen Frowe, *The Ethics of War and Peace: An Introduction* (2011); J. Daryl Charles and Timothy J. Demy, *War, Peace, and Christianity: Questions and Answers from a Just War Perspective* (2010); Paola Pugliatti, *Shakespeare and the Just War Tradition* (2010); J. Mark Mattox, *Saint Augustine and the Theory of Just War* (2009); Eric D. Patterson, *Just War Thinking: Morality and Pragmatism in the Struggle against Contemporary Threats* (2009); Eric A. Heinze and Brent J. Steele, eds., *Ethics, Authority, and War: Non-State Actors and the Just War Tradition* (2009); Daniel M. Bell Jr., *Just War as Christian Discipleship* (2009); David Rodin and Henry Shue, eds., *Just and Unjust Warriors: The Moral and Legal Status of Soldiers* (2008); Cian O'Driscoll, *The Renegotiation of the Just War Tradition and the Right to War in the Twenty-First Century* (2008); Carsten Stahn and Jann K. Kleffner, eds., *Jus Post Bellum: Towards a Law of Transition from Conflict to Peace* (2008); Larry May, *War Crimes and Just War* (2007); Charles Reed and David Ryall, eds., *The Price of Peace: Just War in the Twenty-First Century* (2007); Nicholas Fotion, *War and Ethics: A New Just War Theory* (2007); C. A. J. Coady, *Morality and Political Violence* (2007); Charles Guthrie and Michael Quinlan, *Just War: The Just War Tradition; Ethics in Modern Warfare* (2007); Igor Primoratz, ed., *Civilian Immunity in War* (2007); Michael W. Brough et al., eds., *Rethinking the Just War Tradition* (2007); Steven P. Lee, *Intervention, Terrorism, and Torture: Contemporary Challenges to Just War Theory* (2007); Michael Walzer, *Just and Unjust Wars: A Moral Argument with Historical Illustrations* (4th ed., 2006); Alex J. Bellamy, *Just Wars: From Cicero to Iraq* (2006); Brian Orend, *The Morality of War* (2006); Gregory M. Reichberg, Henrik Syse, and Endre Begby, eds., *The Ethics of War: Classic and Contemporary Readings* (2006); J. Daryl Charles, *Between Pacifism and Jihad: Just War and Christian Tradition* (2005); Michael Evans, ed., *Just War Theory: A Reappraisal* (2005); A. F. C. Webster and Darrell Cole, *The Virtue of War: Reclaiming Classic Christian Traditions East and West* (2004); Michael Walzer, *Arguing about War* (2004); Peter Temes, *The Just War: An American Reflection on the Morality of War in Our Time* (2003); Oliver O'Donovan, *The Just War Revisited* (2003); and Jean Bethke Elshtain, *Just War against Terror: The Burden of American Power in a Violent World* (2003).

4. In the words of ethicist Paul Ramsey, just war doctrine is "as Lutheran and Calvinistic as it is Roman Catholic." *The Just War: Force and Political Responsibility* (repr.; Lanham, MD: Rowman & Littlefield, 2002), 261.

5. The closest approximation is Ronald Wells's *The Wars of America: Christian Views* (Grand Rapids: Eerdmans, 1981). Wells brought together eight historians to write essays that analyzed America's major wars from an explicitly Christian standpoint. While Wells's book has virtues, it has flaws as well. Several of the contributors either misconstrue or reject the validity of the just war tradition, and the chapters are not tightly focused on evaluating the justice of particular wars. In addition, the Korean and Vietnam Wars are treated in one chapter, and, understandably, there is no coverage of wars or conflicts since Vietnam. Occasionally in recent literature one finds single chapters devoted to particular recent wars—for example, Michael Walzer's *Arguing about War* (New Haven and London: Yale University Press, 2004), chapter 11, and Nigel Biggar's *In Defence of War* (New York: Oxford University Press, 2013), chapter 7. As one might expect, any number of volumes have been devoted to the war in Iraq—among them, James Turner Johnson, *The War to Oust Saddam Hussein: Just War and the New Face of Conflict* (Lanham, MD: Rowman & Littlefield, 2005); Craig M. White, *Iraq: The Moral Reckoning* (Lanham, MD: Lexington Books, 2010); Albert L. Weeks, *The Choice of War: The Iraq War and the Just War Tradition* (Santa Barbara, CA: ABC-CLIO, 2010); and Craig J. N. de Paulo, Patrick A. Messina, and Daniel P. Tompkins, eds., *Augustinian Just War Theory and the Wars in Afghanistan and Iraq* (New York: Peter Lang, 2011).

6. After all, at the end of a military campaign, we cannot simply walk away. To disavow the task of "nation building" is simply to renounce the conditions of doing justice, as Oliver O'Donovan has maintained (*Just War Revisited*, 31). Just war thinkers have become increasingly concerned with *post bellum* considerations in recent years. See, for instance, Eric Patterson, *Ending Wars Well: Just War Theory in Post-Conflict* (New Haven: Yale University Press, 2012); Patterson, *Ethics beyond War's End* (Washington, DC: Georgetown University Press, 2012); Larry May and Andrew T. Forcehimes, eds., *Morality, Jus Post Bellum, and International Law* (Cambridge: Cambridge University Press, 2012); Larry May, *After War Ends: A Philosophical Perspective* (Cambridge: Cambridge University Press, 2012); and Carsten Stahn and Jann K. Kleffner, eds., *Jus Post Bellum: Towards a Law of Transition from Conflict to Peace* (The Hague: T.M.C. Asser, 2008).

7. Jean Bethke Elshtain, "Just War and Humanitarian Intervention," *Ideas* 8, no. 3 (2000): 4.

8. Ramsey, *The Just War*, 151.

9. This is not merely the tendency of most lay persons; it also characterizes many analytical philosophers and international lawyers, who too often fail to understand "just war" as a wider *tradition* and hence do not recognize the moral assumptions and principles that are refined over the better part of two millennia. See David D. Corey and J. Daryl Charles, *The Just War Tradition: An Introduction* (Wilmington, DE: ISI Books, 2012), 1–21, for a discussion of why the tradition matters today.

10. Paul Ramsey, *War and the Christian Conscience: How Shall Modern War Be Conducted Justly?* (Durham, NC: Duke University Press, 1961), 16. See as well Johnson, *Just War Tradition and the Restraint of War*, xxxi–xxxv.

11. For example, Hauerwas reasons that "if just war is based on natural law, a law written in the conscience of all men and women by God, then it seems that war must be understood as the outgrowth of legitimate moral commitments." Hence, "just" use of force and going to war for justified purposes are necessarily—and therefore *always*—"the compromise we make with sin" and "cooperating with sin," which renders them *always unjust* (Stanley Hauerwas, "Should War Be Eliminated? A Thought Experiment," in *The Hauerwas Reader*, ed. John Berman and Michael Cartwright [Durham, NC: Duke University Press, 2001], 404). See also John Howard Yoder, *The Original Revolution: Essays on Christian Pacifism* (Scottdale, PA: Herald, 1971); Yoder, *What Would You Do?* (Scottdale, PA: Herald, 1983); Yoder, *Nevertheless: The Varieties and Shortcomings of Religious Pacifism*, 2nd ed. (Scottdale, PA: Herald, 1992); Yoder, *The Politics of Jesus*, 2nd ed. (Grand Rapids: Eerdmans, 1994); and Yoder, *When War Is Unjust: Being Honest in Just-War Thinking*, 2nd ed. (Maryknoll, NY: Orbis, 1996).

Perhaps it is more than a curiosity that one of this volume's coeditors, Daryl, was raised within a religious pacifist context, Anabaptism, which since its inception in the sixteenth century as part of the "radical reformation" has been attentive to the abuse of "the sword"—an abuse that emanated from both Catholic *and* Protestant sides—and to this day remains committed ideologically to nonviolence. The second coeditor, Mark, teaches in a school founded by Quakers. Both editors have the utmost respect for pacifists, and like them we long for the day when "nation shall not lift up sword against nation, neither shall they learn war any more" (Isa. 2:4).

12. Theological ethicist Oliver O'Donovan (*Just War Revisited*, 8) has observed that the pacifist position, which *politically* denies the significance of participating in making moral judgments, in consequence cannot treat international affairs wholly seriously as *politics*—a sphere which, from the standpoint of Christianity, is a God-given realm of earthly responsibility. O'Donovan's

observation finds support in the assumption, adopted by religious pacifists, that "just war theory" was incubated in a "Constantinian" religio-cultural climate in which religious believers, "coopted" now by the state, were (reluctantly) led to justify coercive force against the backdrop of earlier patristic pacifist nonviolence. But this view of the development of just war reasoning within a Christian context needs modification. On the one hand, it fails to acknowledge, as more recent patristic scholarship has shown, that the early Christian fathers represented diverse views regarding soldiering and the military; they were neither only pacifists nor only patriots. On the other hand, it is unable to discern (or acknowledge) that charity can undergird the implementation of force for the good of others. The mainstream Christian position through the ages is that both military service and political service can express an obligation of neighbor love. While traditions of pacifism or nonviolent activism as well as crusading can be found in Christian history, they do not represent the church's consensual or mainstream thinking and teaching on matters of war and peace and the use of coercive force.

13. For a comprehensive and authoritative "state-of-the-art" review of just war thinking as it affects military ethics, see James Turner Johnson and Eric D. Patterson, eds., *The Ashgate Research Companion to Military Ethics* (Surrey and Burlington: Ashgate, 2015).

14. In the West, this is often referred to in terms of the natural law tradition. The essence of natural law, observes Aquinas (*Summa Theologiae* [hereafter *S.T.*] I-II, q. 94, a. 2), is that good is to be sought and done and evil is to be avoided; all other natural-law precepts, he notes, are based on this first principle. For a lucid historical overview of how natural law ethics has informed the just war tradition, see Johnson, *Just War Tradition and the Restraint of War*, 85–118.

15. On the necessity of making this critical distinction, see especially Paul Ramsey, *Speak Up for Just War or Pacifism* (University Park: Pennsylvania State University Press, 1988); James Turner Johnson, "The Broken Tradition," *National Interest*, Fall 1996, 27–36; and J. Daryl Charles, "Presumption against War or Presumption against Injustice? The Just War Tradition Reconsidered," *Journal of Church and State* 47, no. 2 (Spring 2005): 335–69.

16. These assumptions about political reality, rooted in Augustinian thinking about the "two cities"—the city of God and the city of man—and calling us to live "between the times" in a way that takes both citizenships seriously, are set forth variously in chapters 4 and 7 and the epilogue of Jean Bethke Elshtain, *Women and War*, rev. ed. (Chicago: University of Chicago Press, 1995), and in chapter 3 of Elshtain, *Just War against Terror: The Burden of American Power in a Violent World* (New York: Basic Books, 2003). In her

writings, Elshtain is attentive to the obligations that issue out of the "two cities" metaphor in Augustinian thought and *Civitate Dei* in particular. See, for example, her important work *Augustine and the Limits of Politics* (Notre Dame, IN: University of Notre Dame Press, 1995).

17. John Courtney Murray, *Morality and Modern War* (New York: Council on Religion and International Affairs, 1959), 12–13; Grotius (*The Law of War and Peace* 2.1.9–11) believes the laws governing war and peace to be binding and anchored in the same principles of justice that hold together all domains of civil society. Thus, to argue that engaging in a justified war is per se a necessary or lesser *evil* (so, e.g., Michael Ignatieff, *The Lesser Evil: Political Ethics in an Age of Terror* [Edinburgh: Edinburgh University Press, 2004], and Alex J. Bellamy, *Just Wars: From Cicero to Iraq* [Cambridge, UK, and Malden, MA: Polity Press, 2006], 3, who are merely representative) is misguided. By analogy, law-enforcement officers and agencies are trained to use lethal force if and when it is necessary. This public duty, however, is not a necessary or lesser "evil"; guided by moral constraints, it is a public service and a genuine "good."

18. Reinhold Niebuhr, *An Interpretation of Christian Ethics* (New York: Harper, 1935), 103.

19. Michael Walzer, *Just and Unjust Wars: A Moral Argument with Historical Illustrations*, 4th ed. (New York: Basic Books, 2006), 329–35.

20. John Courtney Murray, *We Hold These Truths* (New York: Sheed and Ward, 1960), 288.

21. Restraint, which is alien to the very nature of war, is the animating assumption that undergirds just war thinking. The reconciliation of permission and limitation was the great burden of Grotius as he agonized over the devastation of the Thirty Years War. In this light, he writes: "For both extremes [militarism and pacifism] a remedy must be found, that men may not believe either that nothing [ever] is allowable, or that everything [always] is" (*Law of War and Peace* 1.1; here we are relying on the translation of Grotius by R. L. Loomis [Roslyn, NY: Walter J. Black, 1949]). For two perspectives on how moral theory informs the limitation of war, see Walzer, *Just and Unjust Wars*, and Johnson, *Just War Tradition and the Restraint of War*. The former is secular in orientation, while the latter blends secular and religious perspectives.

22. The wisdom of this mediating position is expressed by Grotius in his introduction to *The Law of War and Peace*. Murray describes the just war position as "a way between the false extremes of pacifism and bellicism." Murray, *We Hold These Truths*, 258.

23. Not only is this linkage lost on the militarist/crusader/jihadist, but it is also denied even by some who claim to represent the "just war" perspective. Thus, for example, Paul Christopher, who contends that "questions of *jus ad*

bellum are not relevant to *jus in bello* proscriptions," and "soldiers can never be held responsible for the crime of war, qua soldiers" (*The Ethics of War and Peace: A Introduction to Legal and Moral Studies*, 2nd ed. [Upper Saddle River, NJ: Prentice Hall, 1999], 91, 96), and James Murphy, who asserts that "*jus ad bellum* is independent of *jus in bello*" (*War's Ends: Human Rights, International Order, and the Ethics of Peace* [Washington, DC: Georgetown University Press, 2014], 2). But this sentiment does not represent classic just war thinking, in which moral continuity exists between ends and means.

24. Hence, Aquinas (*S.T.* II-II, q. 40, a. 1) writes, "It is necessary that those waging war should have a rightful intention, so that they intend the advancement of good, or the avoidance of evil. . . . For it may happen that the war is declared by the legitimate authority, and for a just cause, and yet be rendered illicit through a vile intention." Here we are utilizing the translation supplied by Gregory M. Reichberg, Henrik Syse, and Endre Begby, eds., *The Ethics of War: Classic and Contemporary Readings* (Malden, MA: Blackwell, 2006), 177. None has demonstrated with greater clarity in our day the moral continuity between ends and means than Anthony Coates in "Is the Independent Application of *ius in bello* the Way to Limit War?," in *Just and Unjust Warriors: The Moral and Legal Status of Soldiers*, ed. David Rodin and Henry Shue (Oxford and New York: Oxford University Press, 2008), 176–92.

25. Just war thinking has no intrinsic bias against weapons of mass destruction—only against indiscriminate and disproportionate usage. Hereon see William V. O'Brien, *The Conduct of Just and Limited War* (New York: Praeger, 1981); Ramsey, *The Just War*; and Nigel Biggar, "Christianity and Weapons of Mass Destruction," in *Ethics and Weapons of Mass Destruction: Religious and Secular Perspectives*, ed. Sohail H. Hashmi and Steven P. Lee (Cambridge: Cambridge University Press, 2004), 168–98.

26. The analogy employed by Walzer (*Arguing about War*, xii) is helpful: a doctor who diagnoses one patient with cancer is not obliged to supply a similar diagnosis for the next patient, or for all patients. Moreover, the fact that disagreements exist itself does not invalidate just war thinking, just as medical professionals can disagree over a patient's diagnosis.

27. Walzer, *Just and Unjust Wars*, 86.

28. Augustine, *City of God* 19.13.

29. It is significant that Aquinas's discussion of just war in the *Summa Theologiae* (II-II, q. 40) is contextualized in the section on charity (*de vitiis oppositis caritati*) and not justice. The implication is that princes and policy makers, soldiers and civilians, are to be motivated by neighbor love and do everything within their power (humanly speaking) to resist social-political evil. On the seeming contradiction between charity and resort to force, see J. Daryl

Charles and Timothy J. Demy, *War, Peace, and Christianity: Questions and Answers from a Just-War Perspective* (Wheaton: Crossway, 2010), 356–61, wherein the authors trace the condition of charity in the just war thinking of Augustine, Aquinas, Luther, Suárez, and Grotius, as well as contemporary theorists.

30. *Epistle* 138, "To Marcellinus."

31. O'Brien, *Conduct of Just and Limited War*, 223.

32. This, of course, is what distinguishes totalitarian regimes from relatively free societies.

33. Elshtain, *Women and War*, 152.

34. *Ius post bellum*—justice after war—has been a notable accent in just war discourse over the last ten to fifteen years. Insofar as postconflict justice is part of the overall just war idea (standing in relationship to right intention and securing a better peace), we understand *ius post bellum* to inhere in—and derive from—*ius ad bellum*.

35. Aquinas, *S.T.* II-II, q. 40.

36. *City of God* 19.17; we are relying on the translation of M. W. Tkacz and D. Kries in *Augustine: Political Writings*, ed. Ernest L. Fortin and Douglas Kries (Indianapolis and Cambridge: Hackett, 1994), 149.

37. Aquinas, *S.T.* II-II, q. 40.

38. Francisco de Vitoria, *On the Law of War* 1.3.

39. Aquinas, *S.T.* II-II, q. 40.

40. Grotius, *Law of War and Peace* 2.1–3.1.

41. Grotius, *Law of War and Peace* 1.1, trans. Loomis.

42. O'Donovan helpfully summarizes the three objectives of righting a wrong which have been at the heart of the just war tradition: they are penal, defensive, and reparatory (*Just War Revisited*, 53, 134). To these O'Donovan adds a fourth: vindicating international authority (*Just War Revisited*, 134), but this element must be severely qualified.

43. Recourse to war is predicated on our discernment of *relative* justice; absolute justice does not exist in the context of temporal realities.

44. A. J. Coates, *The Ethics of War*, 2nd ed. (Manchester and New York: Manchester University Press, 2016), 167.

45. Coates, *Ethics of War*, 167.

46. Vitoria, *On the Law of War* 2.4.

47. C. A. J. Coady, "The Status of Combatants," in Rodin and Shue, *Just and Unjust Warriors*, 165.

48. Coates, *Ethics of War*, 172.

49. While a discussion of these factors is beyond the scope of the present chapter, addressing all three of these elements in an abbreviated but insightful and helpful fashion is James Turner Johnson, "Just Cause Revisited," in *Close*

Calls: Intervention, Terrorism, Missile Defense, and Just War' Today, ed. Elliott Abrams and James Turner Johnson (Washington, DC: Ethics and Public Policy Center, 1998), 3–38.

50. Walzer, *Just and Unjust Wars*, 106.
51. Coates, *Ethics of War*, 177.
52. *S.T.* II-II, q. 40.
53. *S.T.* II-II, q. 40.
54. O'Donovan, *Just War Revisited*, 21–22.
55. Elshtain, *Just War against Terror*, 54, emphasis original.
56. Hence, the U.N. lacks the "legitimacy" to declare or wage war, not least of all because it is not a juridical body, i.e., a "government," with legal authority. It has not replaced—nor can it replace—nation-states. Moreover, its verdicts are just as likely to sanction injustice as justice. And there is little reason to think that it will be any more effective in mediating international conflict than its defunct predecessor, the League of Nations.
57. Ramsey, *The Just War*, 419.
58. This reality has been eloquently described by Elshtain, *Just War against Terror*, and O'Donovan, *Just War Revisited*, 18–32.
59. Thus, in just war thinking, defense of the homeland or the spread of democratic principles cannot be erected as "a self-contained, moral absolute."
60. *S.T.* II-II, q. 40.
61. So Augustine, *Contra Faustum* 22.74, and Aquinas, *S.T.* II-II, q. 40.
62. Ramsey, *War and the Christian Conscience*, 8.
63. This accent is pronounced in book 3 of *The Law of War and Peace*, wherein rules for the conduct of war are discussed.
64. Coates, "Independent Application of *jus in bello*," 191.
65. Aquinas, *S.T.* II-II, q. 29, a. 4.
66. Moral realism causes us to affirm this truism, even as it acknowledges that *wholly pure* intentions and motivations on the part of both individuals and nations are illusory.
67. O'Donovan, *Just War Revisited*, 21.
68. Brian Orend, "Michael Walzer on Resorting to Force," *Canadian Journal of Political Science* 33, no. 3 (2000): 532, emphasis added.
69. Augustine, *Epistle* 138, "To Marcellinus."
70. Augustine, *Epistle* 47, "To Publicola." In *City of God* 1.21 Augustine argues similarly.
71. Augustine, *Epistle* 189, "To Boniface," trans. Tkacz and Kries, in Fortin and Kries, *Augustine: Political Writings*, 219.
72. Augustine, *Epistle* 189, trans. Tkacz and Kries, in Fortin and Kries, *Augustine: Political Writings*, 219; Augustine cites Luke 3:14.

73. The concept of the *lex talionis* presupposes these upper and lower limits (cf. Exod. 21:24, Lev. 24:20, and Deut. 19:21), even when in the first century its application was distorted by pharisaical religion (Matt. 5:38).

74. Augustine, *City of God* 4.6 and 14.28.

75. C. S. Lewis, *Mere Christianity* (repr.; New York: Simon & Schuster, 1996), 109.

76. Not only does the supplanting of primary conditions by secondary or prudential concerns in contemporary debates invert the logic of classic just war moral reasoning, but it also fundamentally distorts the purpose and rationale of the just war idea, which is "to determine when the use of armed force is just (and not unjust), rather than to avoid the use of armed force as itself always an evil to be avoided." James Turner Johnson, *Ethics and the Use of Force: Just War in Historical Perspective* (Surrey and Burlington: Ashgate, 2011), 3.

77. Coates, *Ethics of War*, 189, emphasis original.

78. O'Donovan, *Just War Revisited*, 132.

79. Walzer, *Just and Unjust Wars*, xiv.

80. For a very useful discussion of last resort and representative scenarios, see Robert L. Phillips, *Justice and War* (Norman: University of Oklahoma Press, 1984), 14–16.

81. James Turner Johnson, "The Just-War Idea and the Ethics of Intervention," in *The Leader's Imperative: Ethics, Integrity, and Responsibility*, ed. J. Carl Ficarotta (West Lafayette, IN: Purdue University Press, 2001), 123.

82. Grotius, prolegomena to *The Law of War and Peace*, no. 25. We are here relying on the translation of Grotius found in Reichberg, Syse, and Begby, *Ethics of War*, 390.

83. On the organic nature of ends (*ius ad bellum*) and means (*ius in bello*), see Coady, "Status of Combatants," 153–75, and Coates, "Independent Application of *jus in bello*," 176–92.

84. As Ramsey has noted, following G. E. M. Anscombe ("War and Murder," in *War and Morality*, ed. Richard A. Wasserstrom [Belmont, CA: Wadsworth, 1970], 42–53), pacifism teaches people to make no distinction between the shedding of *innocent* blood and the shedding of *any* blood. That is, "pacifism teaches people to believe that there is no *significant moral* difference . . . between murder and killing in war," between "soldiers and licensed murderers," between "the murderous and non-murderous *intentions* of men." Ramsey, *The Just War*, 146, 297, emphasis original.

85. O'Donovan, *Just War Revisited*, 36.

86. Coady, "Status of Combatants," 162.

87. Ramsey, *The Just War*, 153–56, distinguishes between "close" and "remote" cooperation. The principle of discrimination (or distinction) exists not

only between combatants and civilians but also between military objectives and civilian objects. Thus, article 48 of the First Additional Protocol to the Geneva Conventions states that parties in conflict "shall at all times distinguish between the civilian population and combatants and between civilian objects and military objectives and accordingly shall direct their operations only against military objectives."

88. Yoram Dinstein, *The Conduct of Hostilities under the Law of International Armed Conflict*, 2nd ed. (Cambridge: Cambridge University Press, 2010), 96.

89. James Turner Johnson, "The Meaning of Non-Combatant Immunity in the Just War/Limited War Tradition," *Journal of the American Academy of Religion* 39, no. 1 (1971): 157–65.

90. Thus John Locke, *Two Treatises of Government*, ed. Peter Laslett (New York: Mentor, 1960), 435.

91. As Jean Bethke Elshtain observes, "Just war argument insists one must not open an unbridgeable gulf between 'domestic' and 'international' politics" ("Just War and Humanitarian Intervention," 4).

92. Ramsey, *The Just War*, 156.

93. Because, morally speaking, death can be caused in different ways, the intention of the one causing death is critical and thus central to just war thinking, which distinguishes between effects of lethal force that are intended and those that are not, between direct and indirect or "primary" and "secondary" effects. This distinction is well illustrated by the moral difference between self-sacrifice (which is others-regarding) and suicide (which is purely self-regarding). This principle of "double effect," explained most famously by Thomas Aquinas—"Moral acts take their species according to what is intended and not according to what is beside the intention, since this is accidental" (*S.T.* II-II, q. 64, a. 7)—remains, as one might expect, the source of intense controversy and disagreement among ethicists and philosophers. Nevertheless, as Ramsey insists, the "heart and soul" of the principle is charity, which seeks "to save human life when not all killing could responsibly be avoided" (*The Just War*, 316). What opponents of double effect ignore is how many lives are *saved* as a result of intervention. How many deaths are thereby prevented?

94. Here a bit of moral insight from Aristotle (*Nicomachean Ethics* 1.3, 7) bears repeating. Wisdom does not demand the same degree of exactness or certitude as, say, mathematics and the sciences. Moral intentions and moral actions are inherently imprecise; hence, greater experience (resulting in virtue and wisdom) is needed in making moral evaluations and applying moral principle. As it affects conduct in war, Michael Gross's *Moral Dilemmas of Modern War: Torture, Assassination, and Blackmail in an Age of Asymmetric Conflict*

(Cambridge: Cambridge University Press, 2010) probes some of the challenges that emerge when the traditional distinction between combatants and noncombatants collapses.

95. Ramsey, *The Just War*, 403.

96. Grotius, *Law of War and Peace* 2.20, 24.

97. John Finnis, Joseph M. Boyle Jr., and Germain Grisez, *Nuclear Deterrence, Morality and Realism* (Oxford: Clarendon, 1987), 252.

98. Biggar, *In Defence of War*, 146. We wholly acknowledge that there is a "trade-off" in terms of minimizing civilian casualties and achieving military objectives and that our justification of the latter in moral terms is supremely cloudy; there is quite simply no pat formula for decision making that seeks to reconcile the two.

99. Biggar, *In Defence of War*, 146.

100. Michael Walzer, "World War II: Why Was This War Different?," in *War and Moral Responsibility*, ed. Marshall Cohen, Thomas Nagel, and Thomas Scanlon (Princeton: Princeton University Press, 1974), 86.

101. Grotius, *Law of War and Peace* 2.20, 24.

102. In the language of the Christian scriptures, charity fulfills the law (thus Jesus, James, and Paul). This moral intuition is sensed by Christian thinkers through the ages who have helped shape the contours of the just war idea.

103. In addition to those sources listed in note 6, see Eric D. Patterson, "Security and Political Order: The Ethics of Who Is in Charge and Enforcing the Peace at War's End," in Johnson and Patterson, *Ashgate Research Companion to Military Ethics*, 335–47; Timothy J. Demy, "How Should This Conflict End?," in Johnson and Patterson, *Ashgate Research Companion to Military Ethics*, 349–57.

104. Walzer, *Just and Unjust Wars*, 288.

105. Brian Orend, *Michael Walzer on War and Justice* (Cardiff: University of Wales Press, 2000), 139.

106. Johnson, "Just War Idea," 124.

107. Walzer, *Just and Unjust Wars*, 115.

108. Gary Bass, "Jus Post Bellum," *Philosophy and Public Affairs* 32, no. 4 (2004): 397.

109. For Aquinas (*S.T.* I-II, q. 94, a. 2), "The order in which commands of the law of nature are ranged corresponds to that of our natural tendencies"; chief among our "natural tendencies" is "an appetite for the good."

110. On the importance of this union, Suárez is insistent: "I hold that whoever initiates a war without just cause . . . sins not only against charity, but also against justice" (*De triplici virtute theologica*, disputation 13 ["On War"],

sec. 4, no. 8). Here we are utilizing the translation found in Reichberg, Syse, and Begby, *Ethics of War*, 351.

111. On the ethical imperative of reconciling justice and charity as a *unity*, especially as it affects policy prescriptions, see J. Daryl Charles, "Toward Restoring a Good Marriage: Reflections on the Contemporary Divorce of Love and Justice and Its Cultural Implications," *Journal of Church and State* 55, no. 2 (2013): 367–83.

112. O'Donovan, *Just War Revisited*, 4–5.

113. Murray, *We Hold These Truths*, 10.

114. Murray, *We Hold These Truths*, 11–12.

115. Victor Davis Hanson, *The Father of Us All: War and History, Ancient and Modern* (New York: Bloomsbury, 2010), 12.

116. Paul Ramsey, *Basic Christian Ethics* (New York: Scribner's, 1954), 165. The animating spirit of just war thinking, according to Ramsey, is that "social charity comes to the aid of the oppressed" (*Speak Up for Just War or Pacifism*, 109). In this vein, Ramsey provocatively writes: "While Jesus taught that a disciple in his own case should turn the other cheek, he did not enjoin that his disciples should lift up the face of another oppressed man for him to be struck again on his other cheek. It is no part of the work of charity to allow this to continue to happen" (*The Just War*, 143). Charity, then, requires that we honor and respect, and if necessary, protect, defend and resist.

117. Harry S. Stout, "Review Essay: Religion, War, and the Meaning of America," *Religion and American Culture: A Journal of Interpretation* 19 (2009): 275–89.

118. Students of American political thought debate the exact date the United States of America came into being. Other common dates include July 2, 1776 (when Congress voted for independence), and June 21, 1788 (when New Hampshire became the ninth state to ratify the U.S. Constitution). Although it does not resolve the debate definitively, it is worth noting that the U.S. Supreme Court has long considered the nation's birthday to be July 4, 1776. On this debate see Mark David Hall, "Did America Have a Christian Founding?" First Principles Series, The Heritage Foundation, June 7, 2011, http://www.heritage.org/research/lecture/2011/06/did-america-have-a-christian-founding; Hall, "The Declaration of Independence in the Supreme Court," in *The Declaration of Independence: Origins and Impact*, ed. Scott Douglas Gerber (Washington, DC: Congressional Quarterly Press, 2002), 142–60.

119. Stout, "Review Essay," 278.

120. Stout, "Review Essay," 275. This list does not include covert activity, blockades, isolated bombings, etc.

121. On this debate see Hall, "Did America Have a Christian Founding?"; John Fea, *Was America Founded as a Christian Nation?* (Louisville: Westminster John Knox Press, 2011).

122. Pew's *Religious Landscape Study* (2015), http://www.pewforum.org/religious-landscape-study/; Frank Newport, "2017 Update on Americans and Religion," Gallup, December 22, 2017, https://news.gallup.com/poll/224642/2017-update-americans-religion.aspx.

123. Abraham Lincoln, *Lincoln: Selected Speeches and Writings*, ed. Don E. Fehrenbacher (New York: Vintage Books, 1992), 450.

TWO

"Fear, Honor, and Interest"

The Unjust Motivations and Outcomes of the American Revolutionary War

John D. Roche

> Fear of an uncertain danger [is] no just cause of war.[1]
> —*Dutch Jurist Hugo Grotius, 1655*

The United States of America was born in the crucible of war. Following twelve turbulent years of political struggles against Great Britain, hostilities exploded into open warfare on Lexington Green during the morning of April 19, 1775. As the nation's founding events, the American Revolution and the War of Independence it spawned are critically examined by few Americans, who instead take the justice of both events for granted.[2] However, the Whigs of the era went to extraordinary lengths to legitimize their actions both domestically and to a wider European audience. While the patriots masterfully exploited Enlightenment thinking to make a compelling case to their contemporaries, the probity of their rebellion and subsequent civil war did not satisfy traditional just war requirements. Using *ius ad bellum*, *ius in bello*, and *ius post bellum* criteria as its lens, this paper argues that the Continental Army's conduct throughout the war was largely just, but the causes and consequences of the war were not. This contradictory situation resulted from the disparate motives of the American colonists. As the fifth-century Athenian general and historian Thucydides noted, "fear, honor, and interest" are three of the most powerful causes of war.[3] His triumvirate was clearly at work during the American Revolution and War of Independence because fear undergirded American rationale for the war, honor dictated the conduct of the Continental officers, and interest drove the terms of the peace settlement.

The American Revolution raises interesting questions from the perspective of just war theory as, unlike virtually all of the other wars discussed in this book, it was a rebellion. Historically, Christian thinkers have held that biblical passages such as Romans 13 clearly prohibit rebellion. Although a few Catholic writers such as John of Salisbury argued that tyrannicide may be justified in extreme circumstances, prior to the Protestant Reformation the vast majority of Christian thinkers rejected its legitimacy. Early Protestant leaders, including Martin Luther and John Calvin, initially accepted this view, but by most accounts they eventually embraced the position that inferior magistrates may actively resist tyrants. Within a generation, Calvinist thinkers such as John Ponet, Christopher Goodman, George Buchannan, and Samuel Rutherford had embraced this position.[4] That Calvinists developed such a robust resistance ideology is particularly important in the American context as this tradition was, according to Sydney Ahlstrom, "the religious heritage of three-fourths of the American people in 1776."[5]

But it was not only Calvinists who argued that tyrants may be resisted. Particularly important in the American context is John Locke's *Second Treatise on Civil Government* (1689). Locke was likely influenced by earlier Calvinist thinkers, but he secularized and helped popularize the idea that the people themselves could justly overthrow tyrannical governments.[6] As well, patriot colonists were influenced by the Whig political ideology which developed between the turn of the seventeenth and the early eighteenth century.[7] Whigs, also known as the Commonwealth Men or Country opposition, believed, like many of their counterparts, that Britain's Constitution had made it the freest nation on earth.

What frightened the Whigs was their suspicion that corruption was undermining the British Constitution.

Unlike later constitutions, Britain's was a collection of documents and practices which ensured freedom and political stability. Some of the key documents were the Magna Carta (1215), which made the king subject to the laws of the land; the Petition of Right (1628), which restricted the king from making arbitrary arrests, levying taxes without Parliament's consent, billeting troops in private homes, or implementing martial law; and the Bill of Rights (1689), which confirmed Parliament's power of the purse and made standing armies in peacetime illegal without Parliament's consent. The British government's structure was another key element of the constitution. The king represented the monarchy, while the House of Lords represented the aristocracy, and the House of Commons represented everyone else. These three bodies balanced the interests of the social groups within British society to maintain freedom and order. However, Whigs believed that the king and his courtiers were unduly influencing other branches of the government. Historians Stanley Elkins and Eric McKitrick pithily explain:

> A power-grasping ministry was already at work to paralyze the independence of Parliament through the arts of bribery, the sale of honors and offices in government and Church, and the control of pocket boroughs, thus giving rise to luxury, extravagance, profligacy, dependence and servility. The time might not be far off when the ministry, with its legion of parasites, pensioners, and placemen, a subservient Church, a rising and compliant money power, costly wars, ever-heavier taxes and excises, public debts, and eventually an overgrown standing army, would enfold the entire people in its coils of oppression and enslavement.[8]

Using this framework as the interpretive lens to the imperial crises of the 1760s, the patriots firmly believed there was a conspiracy afoot to deprive them of all their rights.[9]

Well before the Stamp Act Crisis, American clergy reminded their congregations of the importance of opposing tyranny. For instance, Boston Congregationalist minister Jonathan Mayhew penned a sermon entitled "Discourse Concerning Unlimited Submission and

Non-Resistance to the Higher Powers" in 1750 that argues that Christian conscience is a valid reason for opposing a government that is not promoting the public good. The sermon asserts that "Common tyrants, and public oppressors, are not entitled to obedience from their subjects, by virtue of anything here laid down by the inspired apostle."[10] Whigs on both sides of the Atlantic enthusiastically read the sermon, and even John Adams testified to its importance, writing, "If the Orators on the 4th. of July really wish to investigate the principles and Feelings which produced the Revolution, they ought to Study this Pamphlet and Dr. Mayhew's Sermon on Passive Obedience and Non Resistance."[11] Another noteworthy Whig minister was the Presbyterian Abraham Keteltas. Keteltas preached a sermon entitled "God Arising and Pleading His People's Cause" in 1777 during which he expounded upon the religious dynamics of the American struggle, arguing that "the cause of this American continent, against the measure of cruel, bloody, and vindictive ministry," was "the cause of God" and that, since the colonies were God's chosen people, Britain's war against the colonies was "unjust and unwarrantable."[12]

American colonists thus had multiple resources upon which to draw as conflicts arose with Parliament and the Crown. But important questions remain. If the people themselves are justified in resisting tyrannical governments, who speaks for them? If resistance must be led by inferior magistrates, who are these magistrates? Colonial legislatures? National bodies with no clear constitutional standing such as the Stamp Act Congress or the Continental Congress? And, perhaps most importantly, were Parliament's and the Crown's actions legitimately characterized as being tyrannical?

The issue of taxation was by far the most critical one for Britain and America's imperial relationship because it questioned Parliament's sovereignty. As a result of the French and Indian War (1754–63), which began when George Washington ambushed a French diplomatic party in western Pennsylvania and ended nine years later in the removal of the colonists' Catholic foes from New France and Spanish Florida, Britain's national debt nearly doubled to £146 million sterling.[13] King George III's decision to keep ten thousand regular British troops in North America to consolidate the territorial acquisitions after the war further exacerbated Britain's financial hardship. As a result, imperial administrators implemented a number of reforms in an effort to improve the efficiency and profitability of the empire. These measures immediately came under colonial scrutiny.

The question of Parliament's authority to tax the American colonists first reared its ugly head following the passage of the American Duties Act in 1764. The measure, which became known as the Sugar Act to Americans, sought to increase revenue from American trade in three ways: by enhancing customs enforcement, by creating new duties, and by altering existing ones to make them more profitable.[14] Notably, the new act cut the 1733 Molasses Act duty of six pence per gallon in half. These measures angered merchants who had grown accustomed to smuggling and bribing customs officials. In response, Boston lawyer James Otis penned *The Rights of the British Colonies Asserted and Proved* (1764) as the opening salvo against Parliament's right to tax the colonies. His key assertion was, "I cannot but observe here, that if the parliament have an equitable right to tax our trade, it is indisputable that they have as good an one to tax the lands, and every thing else."[15] However, he disputed this notion by insisting on Parliamentary representation as a prerequisite for levying taxes under the British Constitution and asked, "Can it be said with any colour of truth or justice, that we are represented in parliament?"[16] After replying in the negative, Otis suggested that Parliament ought to seat Members of Parliament (MPs) for the colonies.

The next major event in the colonial dispute over taxation was the passage of the Stamp Act on March 22, 1765. The Stamp Act required stamps for printed material such as legal documents, newspapers, and pamphlets in addition to playing cards and dice. Prime Minister George Grenville expected the act would generate 60,000 pounds annually to help offset the approximately 350,000 pounds required to keep ten thousand regulars in the colonies.[17] The Maryland attorney Daniel Dulany issued one of the first challenges to the Stamp Act when he wrote *Considerations on the Propriety of Imposing Taxes in the British Colonies* (1765). Dulany attacked British officials' claims that Americans possessed "virtual representation" in Parliament: "If it appears that the Colonies are not actually represented by the Common; of Great-Britain, and that the Notion of a double or virtual Representation, doth not with any Propriety apply to the People of America; then the Principle of the Stamp Act must be given up as indefensible on the Point of Representation."[18] Like Dulany, House of Burgesses delegate Patrick Henry also challenged the legality of the Stamp Act. In the *Virginia Resolves* (1765) Henry echoed the now familiar sentiments regarding the right of the colonists to tax themselves under British law, and he referred to the colonists' rights as Englishmen under Virginia's charters granted by King James I. However, Henry took the argument further by directly challenging Parliament's sovereignty on the taxation question. The fifth article stated, "Resolved, Therefore that the general Assembly of this Colony have the *only and sole exclusive* Right and Power to lay Taxes and Impositions upon the inhabitants of this Colony."[19]

Unfortunately for the future of the imperial relationship, Colonial Agent Benjamin Franklin's testimony before Parliament provided an inaccurate account of the colonists' feelings regarding Parliamentary taxation prior to 1763. Franklin responded, "I have never heard any objection to the right of laying duties to regulate commerce; but a right to lay internal taxes was never supposed to be in Parliament, as we are not represented there."[20] Patriot allies in London, most notably William Pitt, used this reasoning in their efforts to repeal the Stamp Act. When Grenville discounted the difference between internal and external taxes, Pitt responded, "If the gentleman does not understand the difference between internal and external taxes, I cannot help it; but there is a plain distinction between taxes levied for the purpose of raising a revenue, and duties imposed for the regulation of trade."[21] The colonists' rejection of all Parliamentary taxes, whether internal or external, was based on their belief that they were not and could not be represented in Parliament.[22] This misunderstanding about the legitimacy of external versus internal taxes not only survived the Stamp Act difficulties but directly led to the next confrontation over taxation.

Realizing that concerted effort would produce better outcomes, nine colonies sent twenty-seven delegates to a Stamp Act Congress in New York City from October 7 to 25, 1765. Attorney John Dickinson drafted, and the Congress adopted, fourteen resolutions which became known as the *Declaration of Rights and Grievances* (1765). After declaring loyalty to George III, the document uses the next five resolutions to explain the delegates' legal and historical understandings of representation and why the Stamp Act is in violation. The colonists also complain about the new duties and suggest that they will be unable to purchase British goods under these new taxes and regulations.[23] British mercantile pressure persuaded Parliament to rescind the Stamp Acts in 1766, but jealous of its authority, Parliament passed "The Declaratory Act," which stated that Parliament had "full power and authority to make laws and statutes of sufficient force and validity to bind the colonies and people of America, subjects of the crown of Great Britain, in all cases whatsoever."[24] In the immediate wake of their victory over the Stamp Act, the colonists largely ignored the Declaratory Act, but it was later pointed to as evidence that Parliament was claiming tyrannical powers for itself.

The patriots only enjoyed a short reprieve, for by June 26, 1767, Britain passed the Townshend Revenue Act. Charles Townshend, chancellor of the exchequer, punctiliously observed the supposed distinction between internal and external taxes and therefore only levied taxes on trade items. This act imposed duties on paper, lead, glass, paint, and tea in an effort to generate £42,000 to pay the salaries of royal officials in the colonies and thus make them less beholden to the colonial legislatures.[25] Dickinson responded again, this time authoring twelve *Letters from a Farmer in Pennsylvania* (1767–68). He further refined the concept of internal versus external taxes by insisting that revenue generated through trade regulations had to be incidental rather than the intended purpose of the act. Since the Townshend Duties specifically sought to generate revenue, Dickinson declared them unconstitutional. He wrote, "It is true, that impositions for raising a revenue, may be hereafter called regulations of trade, but names will not change the nature of things."[26] The Massachusetts Assembly echoed these sentiments when its members approved the *Massachusetts Circular Letter* (1768) which not only invited the other colonies to "harmonize with each other," but maintained, "Imposing duties on the people of this province, with the sole and express purpose of raising a revenue, are infringements of their natural and constitutional rights; because, as they are not represented in the British Parliament, his Majesty's commons in Britain, by those acts, grant their property without their consent."[27]

Lord Hillsborough, secretary of state for the colonies, viewed the circular letter as a seditious challenge and ordered the Massachusetts Assembly to rescind it. When they refused to comply, Governor Francis Bernard dissolved the legislature. Nevertheless, the colonists resorted once again to nonimportation as they had done during the Stamp Act dispute, forcing Britain to eliminate most the Townshend Duties in 1770.

Determined to demonstrate that Parliament had a right to tax the colonies, Prime Minister Lord North insisted that the tax on tea remain in place. Accordingly, colonists generally refused to buy it. This left the British East India Company with warehouses of unsold tea, which served as one of many factors threatening it with insolvency. The Tea Act of 1773 sought to solve this problem by granting the East India Company a monopoly on tea sales to the colonies while maintaining the duty of three pence by giving exporters in Britain a rebate on the taxes paid there. This would enable the East India Company to sell its higher-quality tea to the colonists even more cheaply than smuggled tea, while retaining Parliament's right to tax the colonies. In response, on December 16, 1773, Bostonian Sons of Liberty perpetrated their "Destruction of the Tea," later immortalized as the Boston Tea Party, by throwing 342 chests of East India Company tea worth £9,000 into Boston Harbor.[28] Parliament viewed the act as wanton destruction of private property and a blatant disregard of its authority. It responded with the Coercive Acts, seen by American patriots as "Intolerable," thus pushing the colonists toward revolution.

The patriots maintained their constitutional objections to Parliamentary taxation without their consent during the next two years of crisis, which culminated in the Declaration of Independence. In direct response to the Intolerable Acts, patriots in Massachusetts issued the Suffolk Resolves on September 9, 1774. These resolves recommended that local tax collectors "and all other Officers who have Publick monies in their Hands, to retain the same, and not to make any Payment thereof to the Province or County Treasurers, until the Civil Government of the Province is placed upon a constitutional Foundation."[29] Since Britain had altered Massachusetts's charter, the government was no longer constitutional in the patriots' eyes, and therefore they refused to fund it. This was an example of internal taxation without consent for an individual colony.

Following the outbreak of hostilities at the battles of Lexington, Concord, and Bunker Hill, the Second Continental Congress drafted *A Declaration by the Representatives of the United Colonies of North-America* in early July 1775. In it, the colonists argued that Parliament was "stimulated by an inordinate passion for a power not only unjustifiable, but which they know to be peculiarly reprobated by the very constitution of that kingdom." The Congress declared: "[Parliament has] undertaken to give and grant our money without our consent, though we have ever exercised an exclusive right to dispose of our own property." The colonists continued to adhere to their principle of direct representation by claiming, "Not a single man of those who assume it, is chosen by us; or is subject to our control or influence." The Congress maintained that Parliament sought to reduce its tax burden by having the Americans pick it up. Finally, Congress characterized Britain's offer to let the colonies' assemblies raise their quota of imperial taxes as "an insidious manoeuvre calculated to divide" them and rejected what they saw as an effort "to extort from [them], at the point of the bayonet, the unknown sums that should be sufficient to gratify, if possible to gratify, ministerial rapacity."[30] Interestingly, the Declaration of Independence (1776) only made one mention of taxation among its grievances against King George III by noting, "For imposing taxes upon us without our Consent."[31] Although the patriots had a number of other constitutional disputes with Parliament over issues such as the right to trial by jury, protection against the quartering of troops in private homes, and the colonial assemblies' power of the purse over local royal officials, the interrelated issues of taxation, representation, and Parliamentary sovereignty formed the central crux of the imperial debate and justification for their rebellion.

By 1766, Parliament had clearly come to consider itself to have unlimited power over the entire British Empire and had embraced the doctrine of virtual representation. Proponents of virtual representation maintained that Parliament legislated on behalf of all George III's subjects. Therefore, it was of no consequence that some subjects, such as those living in "rotten boroughs" at home or colonies abroad, did not directly elect MPs, because Parliament still represented their interests. Patriots, however, retained an older conception of the British constitution, one in which Parliament had no authority over the American colonies. Their only allegiance was to the Crown, and that was a conditional one. Once the Crown removed the colonists from its protection, they were free to declare independence. The colonists proved to their satisfaction that King George III and Parliament had violated their natural rights, thus becoming tyrants by definition and justifying their rebellion. However, their principled stance ignored Grotius's advice, "By the Law of charity (we have showed other where) the prosecution of right is rather to be omitted, seeing, that by law, the life of man ought to be more esteemed (among Christians especially) than our Goods."[32] Many of the thirty thousand Continentals, an untold number of American militiamen, and nearly one hundred thousand European soldiers who died in the war would probably have agreed with Grotius considering the minimal injuries the colonists actually suffered before the war.[33]

When Parliament passed the Stamp Act in 1765, the colonies were only paying £1,800 annually.[34] Although Parliament did seek a thirtyfold increase, £60,000 annually with the Stamp Act, this amount would only cover seventeen percent of the £350,000 required to keep ten thousand regulars in the colonies. More importantly, the colonists' tax burden paled in comparison to that of those living in England.[35] Following the Seven Years' War, Britons in the home islands paid an average of twenty-five shillings annually versus the colonists' six pence of imperial taxes, which translates to fifty times the colonists' tax rate.[36] The patriots, of course, claimed that it was the principle rather than the amount which mattered, based on their Whiggish fears of a tyrannical plot.

The colonists freely expressed these fears in the documents they used to justify their actions. In *A Declaration by the Representatives of the United Colonies of North-America* the Second Continental Congress proclaimed, "Parliament was influenced to adopt the pernicious project [taxation], and assuming a new power over them, have in the course of eleven years, given such decisive specimens of the spirit and consequences attending this power, as to leave no doubt concerning the effects of acquiescence under it." The outcome in the patriots' minds was their enslavement. The patriots' fervent belief in a British conspiracy against them was also on full view in the Declaration of Independence. This time the Continental Congress maintained that "a long train of abuses and usurpations, pursuing invariably the same Object, evinces a design to reduce them under absolute Despotism" and that "the history of the present King of Great Britain is a history of repeated injuries and usurpations, all having in direct object the establishment of absolute Tyranny over these States."[37] The patriots did not rebel in 1775 only because of what Great Britain had actually done to them but also because of their fears of what they thought the British would do next. They said as much in the *Olive Branch Petition* (1775) when they wrote, "They [the colonists] were alarmed by a new system of statutes and regulations adopted for the administration of the colonies, that filled their minds with the most painful fears and jealousies," but George III refused to even receive the petition, thereby bolstering colonial perceptions of his tyranny.[38] Even though the colonists' constitutional and conspiratorial claims were questionable justifications of the American Revolutionary War, the patriots' claim that they acted in self-defense demands closer inspection.

American patriots believed that Britain began the war at the battles of Lexington and Concord on April 19, 1775, and that as a result they were justified in defending themselves with military force. The leading international jurists of the day—Grotius, Pufendorf, and Vattel—all viewed defensive wars as a legitimate undertaking. If the Americans could prove the British started the hostilities, it would serve as one of the few ways they could justify their rebellion as a nonstate actor. In *A Declaration by the Representatives of the United Colonies of North-America* (1775) they wrote of "the arms" they had "been compelled by [their] enemies to assume," while they maintained, "Against violence actually offered, we have taken up arms. We shall lay them down when hostilities shall cease on the part of the aggressors, and all danger of their being renewed shall be removed, and not before." They also appealed to the international community: "We exhibit to mankind the remarkable spectacle of a people attacked by unprovoked enemies, without any imputation or even suspicion of offence." The *Olive Branch Petition* noted, "Your Majesty's Ministers, persevering in their measures, and proceeding to open hostilities for enforcing them, have compelled us to arm in our own defence." Finally, in the Declaration of Independence, the delegates claimed, "[King George] has abdicated Government here, by declaring us out of his Protection and waging War against us."[39] Once again, however, the historical facts raise serious questions regarding the patriots' interpretation of events.

No one will ever know who fired the first shot at Lexington, but it is irrelevant to who bears the blame for the fighting. The British troops were on their way to Concord to prevent the outbreak of hostilities by seizing the weapons rumored to be there. Lexington militiamen, believing that they had a right to defend themselves, were not about to let their weapons be seized. When Major John Pitcairn's advance guard of 238 regulars met Captain John Parker's roughly sixty to seventy militiamen on the green, he ordered them to disperse. Despite their noncompliance, Pitcairn never ordered his men to fire on the militiamen, instead commanding that they should be surrounded and disarmed. When the firing began, Pitcairn's men responded on their own initiative, killing eight colonists and wounding nine others. The only casualty for the British was one soldier who was shot in the thigh. If this small skirmish had been the only action of the day, it would not have amounted to much more than another "Boston Massacre," which was also a police operation by the British army that turned deadly when armed, angry colonists confronted them.[40] Unfortunately, that was not the case.

After arriving in Concord and destroying whatever war material they could find, the British cut down and burned the town's liberty pole. The fire spread to the nearby courthouse, and the town's militiamen who had been watching from above the North Bridge mistakenly believed the British were burning the entire town. This prompted them to attack, and the New England militiamen harried the British troops all the way back to Boston. When the British had finished running their gauntlet, 73 were dead, 174 had been wounded, and another 26 were missing. On the American side, only 49 had died, 39 were wounded, and 4 were missing.[41] The colonists followed up this assault by laying siege to the city of Boston with an Army of Observation. The patriots further escalated the conflict when the Second Continental Congress adopted the Army of Observation as the Continental Army on June 14, 1775, and made George Washington its commander. By this action, the Congress transformed a regional rebellion into a continent-wide civil war. Four days later, the New England troops enticed the British to attack them by fortifying Breed's Hill. The final aggressive act the colonists made prior to the Declaration of Independence was the invasion of Canada. The Americans hoped to wage a war of liberation and make Canada the Fourteenth Colony.[42] At a minimum, it seems reasonable to classify the patriots' actions as something more than mere "self-defense."

The War of Independence arguably failed the *ius ad bellum* requirements that war be declared by a legitimate authority and only be undertaken as a last resort. Most of the early political actions were the result of ad hoc organizations such as the Sons of Liberty, Committees of Correspondence, Nonimportation Associations, and Committees of Safety, whose claims to representing the entire community were tenuous at best. Actions of the colonial legislatures and various congresses the colonists employed throughout the imperial crisis—Stamp Act Congress, First Continental Congress, Second Continental Congress—are arguably more legitimate. Perhaps these bodies even constitute the "inferior magistrates" required by Calvin and other early Reformers.

By any measure, the War of Independence was not a war of last resort. The British were still willing to make compromises through the summer of 1776. Parliament proposed the Conciliatory Resolution in February 1775, which offered to allow the colonies to tax themselves as long as they contributed "their proportion to the common defence." The Continental Congress rejected this offer. When Admiral Lord Richard Howe and General William Howe arrived in New York City at the head of thirty-two thousand troops in July of 1776, they came not only as military commanders but also as peace commissioners. They were authorized to settle the issue of taxation under the terms of the Conciliatory Resolution, as well as grant pardons and remove trade restrictions.[43] Unfortunately for Lord Howe, the Americans declared independence eight days before he arrived.

British-born revolutionary propaganda writer Thomas Paine's *Common Sense* (1776) addressed the final two *ius ad bellum* requirements, right intent and reasonable hope for success. Using heavy doses of natural law and selective historical examples, he characterized the institution of monarchy as inherently oppressive and warlike. Paine contended that America should be governed by a republic, which would ensure its liberty, peace, and economic freedom. Although both his logic and evidence suffered flaws, his reasoning was profoundly popular with patriots and sold nearly five hundred thousand copies. Paine also addressed the likelihood of American success in a war against Britain. He contended, "It is not in numbers, but in unity, that our great strength lies; yet our present numbers are sufficient to repel the force of all the world. The Continent hath, at this time, the largest body of armed and disciplined men of any Power under Heaven." Although he conceded Britain's vast naval superiority, Paine averred that America could build its own fleet in time. Paine also acknowledged the patriots' need for foreign support declaring, "Under our present denomination as British subjects, we can neither be received nor heard abroad: The custom of all courts is against us, and will be so, until, by an independence, we take rank with other nations."[44] While *Common Sense* suggests the Americans did have a right intent, Paine's military arguments represent wishful thinking. The only chance the patriots had of winning the War of Independence was to gain foreign support. Even though France covertly provided over 75 percent of the Continental Army's weapons and ammunition up to 1777, and openly involved French armies and naval forces following the Treaty of Alliance in 1778, thereby tipping the balance of the war in the patriots' favor, the outcome of the contest was always precarious and could have easily resulted in a British victory through exhaustion.[45]

Whether or not the Patriots met the *ius ad bellum* requirements to justify the War of Independence is largely a matter of partisan perspective, since both sides could avail themselves of contemporary philosophies to support their claims. Nevertheless, the Continental Army conducted itself in an exemplary fashion, not only strictly adhering to *ius in bello* criteria but frequently exceeding the eighteenth-century "customs and usages of war."[46] The Continental Army's commander in chief, George Washington, was especially sensitive about his reputation as a Southern aristocratic gentleman, and he and his fellow officers were adamant that their conduct in the war should do them honor. This punctilious concern with the rules of war was not merely a personal matter, however, for by conforming to the Enlightenment ideals of humanity the Continental Army bolstered the legitimacy of its cause.[47]

Generally speaking, warfare in the eighteenth century was more chivalrous and limited than the laws of war required. The Swiss jurist Emmerich Vattel noted, "At the present day, the Nations of Europe almost always carry on war with great forbearance and generosity. These dispositions have given rise to several commendable practices which exhibit often a high degree of courtesy."[48] Vattel, of course, was referring to the numerous conventions European armies adhered to, such as using white flags to prompt a truce, engaging in parleys with the enemy both prior to and during battles, granting the honors of war to armies defeated in a siege, caring for wounded enemies, and using paroles and exchanges to expedite the return of prisoners of war (POWs).[49]

POWs were an issue by which commanders could demonstrate their humanity and enhance their honor simultaneously both by how they captured the enemy and then by their subsequent treatment of the prisoners. On July 16, 1779, Continental brigadier general Anthony Wayne led 1,200 men in a nighttime assault on roughly 700 British regulars at Stony Point. Although his men relied exclusively upon their bayonets in the attack, they not only captured the fort but, contrary to the laws of war, they spared the lives of 543 men in the garrison. This stood in stark contrast to the Paoli Massacre committed by British major general Charles Grey's men two years earlier when they caught Wayne's unit in a similar night ambush and slaughtered at least 150 Americans. After learning of Stony Point, British vice admiral Sir George Collier observed, "The laws of war give a right to the assailants of putting all to death who are found in arms; justice is due to all and commendation should be given where it is deserved. The rebels had made the attack with a bravery they never before exhibited, and they showed at this moment a generosity and clemency which during the course of the rebellion has no parallel."[50] There can be no greater compliment than a sincere one from a mortal enemy. Furthermore, unlike the British, who produced numerous examples of refusing to give quarter to American troops trying to surrender, there were only two noteworthy cases where Continentals exercised such brutality. The first was during the battle of Germantown on October 4, 1777, when the Continental soldiers sought revenge for the Paoli Massacre and their officers unsuccessfully "exerted themselves to save many of the poor [British] wretches who were crying for mercy."[51] The second instance occurred in early 1781 when Lieutenant Colonel "Light Horse Harry" Lee's Legion executed eighteen British dragoons just before they retreated across the Dan River.[52]

While demonstrating humanity by granting quarter to a vanquished foe on the battlefield certainly enhanced a commander's honor, how the victor treated his foe after capture was no less important. Historians estimate the British captured 18,158 American POWs during the war, and of that number nearly 8,500 (47 percent) died from cruelty and neglect.[53] Although British POW deaths were tiny in comparison, the treatment of prisoners was a constant source of complaints and accusations between the two sides. Regarding prisoners, the most egregious example of the Americans acting in bad faith was the revocation of the Convention of Saratoga, which had granted parole to the 5,895 British and Hessian soldiers who surrendered following the Battle of Bemis Heights on October 17, 1777.⁵⁴ While Washington agreed that it would be foolish to parole the enemy army, ultimately the Second Continental Congress bears the blame for this breach of trust. Washington was, however, directly involved in a dispute over retaliation against POWs. The Associated Loyalists captured New Jersey militiaman Joshua Huddy and hanged him in April 1782. In response, the Americans threatened to execute Captain Charles Asgill. Concerned with unleashing a vicious spiral of reprisals at this late stage in the war, Washington wrote to British lieutenant general James Robertson, "I am as earnestly desirous as you can be, that the war may be carried on agreeable to the Rules which humanity formed and the example of the politest Nations recommends & shall be extremely happy in agreeing with you to punish every breach of the Rule of War within the spheres of our respective Commands."⁵⁵ Due to diplomatic pressure from France, the Continental Congress freed Asgill, who returned home safely, and both sides backed away from any further reprisals.

The Continental Army was no less upright in its treatment toward inhabitants who did not participate in the fighting, religiously adhering to the principle of discrimination between active participants in the war and innocent bystanders.⁵⁶ The Continental Army did the best it could to protect both their persons and property against military violence. While inhabitants certainly got caught in the crossfire in a number of battles which took place in urban areas—such as New York, Germantown, Savannah, Newport, and Charlestown, to name a few—the Continental Army never targeted anyone who was not resisting them with military force. In addition, Washington admonished his troops to win the inhabitants' support by scrupulously paying for all of the supplies they requisitioned. When his men failed to live up to his expectations, Washington was a strict disciplinarian. He approved 194 courts-martial convictions, whose typical punishment consisted of a £50 fine and two hundred lashes.⁵⁷

Despite all of this humane and honorable conduct, the Continental Army could be brutal at times, which brings into question if it adhered to the *ius in bello* principles of limited objectives and proportionate means. The two most challenging episodes of the war regarding these criteria were the burning of New York City in 1776 and John Sullivan's campaign against the Iroquois in 1779. As Benjamin Carp has compellingly shown, patriot arsonists set fire to New York City less than a week after the British captured it, even though Congress had prohibited Washington from burning the town.[58] On the eve of the American War of Independence, New York City had a population of approximately twenty-five thousand. Various panics after the start of fighting in 1775 had caused mass exoduses. Roughly eight thousand inhabitants fled in 1775 fearing a British assault, and over ten thousand more evacuated in 1776 as the British conquest loomed. When the British actually landed, there were probably only five thousand souls in the city.[59] The good news for the British was that they did not need to find accommodations for the entire army of twenty-four thousand, since many of them were still in the field on active campaign and the remainder could be dispersed to cantonments in Staten Island and Long Island. Therefore, they initially only needed to find space for the roughly fifty-six hundred soldiers in New York City proper. Unfortunately for the British, the relative ease of finding quarters for the initial garrison evaporated on the night of September 21, 1776, when the Great Fire consumed at least 493 of the 4,000 inhabitable buildings within the city.[60] While fire is an inherently indiscriminate weapon, the facts that there were as many British troops in the city as inhabitants at the time and that nearly half of the city's structures were vacant mitigates the patriots' use of fire. Furthermore, military necessity justified burning the town to prevent the British from using it as a base of operations.

The other notorious example of Continental brutality was Major General John Sullivan's expedition against the British-allied Iroquois. The Wyoming Valley and Cherry Valley Massacres, in June and November 1778, respectively, pressured Washington to contend with the threat along the frontier. In response, he sent Sullivan and Brigadier General James Clinton with four thousand troops to invade Iroquoia. Washington instructed them, "The immediate objects are the total destruction and devastation of their settlements, and the capture of as many prisoners of every age and sex as possible.... Parties should be detached to lay waste all the settlements around, with instructions to do it in the most effectual manner, that the country may not be merely overrun, but destroyed."[61] Sullivan and Clinton did not disappoint their commander in chief, for by the end of September they had burned 160,000 bushels of corn, fatally damaged thousands of fruit trees, and destroyed up to forty Iroquois and allied villages. How can this atrocity be reconciled with the Continentals' previous restraint and the rules of war? The answer is twofold. First, as Wayne Lee has noted, by 1779 Native Americans were firmly fixed as "barbarians" in the Anglo-American mind, and the humane protections of war did not apply to "savages" who violated them.[62] Second, according to long-standing Anglo-American patterns of colonial warfare, military necessity dictated that the best way to secure the frontier was to engage in a "feedfight," which would eliminate the Iroquois's ability to conduct raids.[63] In this case, however, the British at Fort Niagara provided foodstuffs to the Iroquois, and the raids continued. Nevertheless, the atrocities on the frontier escaped censure because the victims were beyond the pale of *ius in bello* protections and therefore did not tarnish the commanders' honor.

The final category of just war doctrine, *ius post bello*, is only briefly discussed here because it is a recent invention that had no contemporary parallel in 1783 when the United States of America signed the Treaty of Paris with Great Britain. America arguably failed in this category because of the American interests which led them to sacrifice any serious effort to restore the Loyalists to their lands or punish belligerents who violated *ius in bello*. Article V of the treaty declared, "Congress shall earnestly recommend it to the legislatures of the respective states to provide for the restitution of all estates, rights, and properties, which have been confiscated belonging to real British subjects." None of the plenipotentiaries to the treaty believed Congress could or would enforce this fig leaf to cover British shame. Instead, seventy-five thousand Loyalists fled the U.S. in search of a better life rather than endure the penury and servitude promised them by the peace treaty.[64] Article VI of the treaty granted immunity to all parties in the conflict, proclaiming, "There shall be no future confiscations made nor any prosecutions commenced against any person or persons for, or by reason of, the part which he or they may have taken in the present war."[65] This excused the conduct of such infamous figures as Lieutenant Colonel Banastre Tarleton for his Waxhaws Massacre and Major General Benedict Arnold for his treasonous plot to sell West Point and his subsequent service in the British army, where he engaged in a number of destructive raids against Connecticut and Virginia.

For those inclined to be generous, the treaty did attempt to reconcile the Anglo-American relationship by making considerable territorial and economic concessions. Nevertheless, interest had to guide the newborn nation's diplomacy through the peace negotiations, because the U.S. was too fragile to do otherwise.

As the definitive Treaty of Paris neared ratification, one of its key architects, Benjamin Franklin, wrote to a friend, "May we never see another War! for in my Opinion *there never was a good War, or a bad Peace.*"[66] Although Franklin's pacific sentiments were noble, they were also ironic, because the Continental Army had arguably fought an unjust war in a just manner to secure an unjust peace. While the patriots had valid constitutional complaints against the British ministry, as well as the support of Protestant resistance theology to justify their rebellion, the actual injuries they sustained did not meet the *ius ad bellum* criteria to resort to arms. Furthermore, the colonists' initial military actions—the ambush at Concord, siege of Boston, and invasion of Canada—were offensive rather than defensive measures due to the colonists' fears of conspiratorial designs to reduce them to slavery. Despite this, the Continental Army not only heeded but exceeded eighteenth-century customs of war on the battlefield and in their treatment of prisoners, because its commanders sought personal honor and legitimacy for the cause. The patriots, however, produced an unjust peace treaty because it was not in American interests to punish belligerents who committed atrocities or ensure that Loyalists received compensation for their losses.

NOTES

1. Hugo Grotius, *The Illustrious Hugo Grotius of the Law of Warre and Peace: With Annotations, III Parts, and Memorials of the Author's Life and Death*, ed. and trans. Clement Barksdale (London, 1655), 411.

2. For two recent exceptions to this trend, see John Keown, "America's War for Independence: Just or Unjust?," *Journal of Catholic Social Thought* 6, no. 2 (2009): 277–304; Gregg Frazer, "The American Revolution: Not a Just War," *Journal of Military Ethics* 14, no. 1 (2015): 35–56.

3. Thucydides, *The Landmark Thucydides: A Comprehensive Guide to the Peloponnesian War*, ed. Richard Crawley and Robert B. Strassler (New York: Free Press, 1996), 43.

4. For a good overview of the development of Calvinist resistance theory see Quentin Skinner, *The Foundations of Modern Political Thought*, vol. 2, *The Age of Reformation* (Cambridge: Cambridge University Press, 1978).

5. Sydney Ahlstrom, *A Religious History of the American People* (Garden City, NY: Doubleday, 1975), 1:426.

6. John Locke, *Two Treatises of Government: In the Former, the False Principles and Foundation of Sir Robert Filmer, and His Followers Are Detected and Overthrown. The Latter, Is an Essay Concerning the True Original, Extent, and End of Civil-Government. By John Locke, Esq*, 4th ed. (London: 1713), 300–301.

7. Bernard Bailyn, *The Ideological Origins of the American Revolution*, Enl. ed. (Cambridge, MA: Belknap Press of Harvard University Press, 1992), 43.

8. Stanley Elkins and Eric McKitrick, *The Age of Federalism: The Early American Republic, 1788–1800* (Oxford: Oxford University Press, 1995), 7. ("Ministry," as used in this quotation, refers to the prime minister and the heads of the government's major departments.)

9. Bailyn, *Ideological Origins of the American Revolution*, 144–59; Pauline Maier, *From Resistance to Revolution: Colonial Radicals and the Development of American Opposition to Britain, 1765–1776* (New York: Knopf, 1972), 183–91.

10. Jonathan Mayhew, *A Discourse, Concerning Unlimited Submission and Non-Resistance to the Higher Powers: With Some Reflections on the Resistance Made to King Charles I. And on the Anniversary of His Death: In Which the Mysterious Doctrine of That Prince's Saintship and Martyrdom Is Unriddled: The Substance of Which Was Delivered in a Sermon Preached in the West Meeting House, in Boston, on the Lord's Day after the 30th of January, 1749–50* (Boston, 1750), 28.

11. John Adams to William Tudor Sr., April 5, 1818, in *The Adams Papers Digital Edition*, ed. C. James Taylor (Charlottesville: University of Virginia Press, Rotunda, 2008–17). The other pamphlet Adams referred to was *A Vindication of the Conduct of the House of Representatives of the Province of Massachusetts Bay* (Boston, 1763).

12. Abraham Keteltas, "God Arising and Pleading His People's Cause," quoted in John Fea, *Was America Founded as a Christian Nation? A Historical Introduction* (Louisville: Westminster John Knox Press, 2011), 110.

13. Fred Anderson, *Crucible of War: The Seven Years' War and the Fate of Empire in British North America, 1754–1766*, 1st ed. (New York: Knopf, 2000), 562.

14. Anderson, *Crucible of War*, 574. The new enforcement measures included Vice Admiralty Courts and writs of assistance.

15. James Otis, *The Rights of the British Colonies Asserted and Proved*, vol. 1, no. 2, in *A Collection of the Most Interesting Tracts . . . On the Subjects*

of Taxing the American Colonies, and Regulating Their Trade (London, 1766–67), 63.

16. Otis, *Rights of the British Colonies*, 92.

17. Mark Mayo Boatner and Harold E. Selesky, eds., *Encyclopedia of the American Revolution: Library of Military History*, 2 vols. (Detroit: Charles Scribner's Sons, 2006), 2:1104–6.

18. Daniel Dulany, *Considerations on the Propriety of Imposing Taxes in the British Colonies: For the Purpose of Raising a Revenue, by Act of Parliament . . .* ([Annapolis] North-America: Printed by a North-American [Jonas Green], 1765), Early American Imprints, series 1: Evans, 1639–1800, 11, https://www.readex.com/content/early-american-imprints-series-i-evans-1639-1800.

19. Patrick Henry, *Virginia Resolves* (1765), quoted in Robert Middlekauff, *The Glorious Cause: The American Revolution, 1763–1789* (New York: Oxford University Press, 1982), 79–83.

20. "Benjamin Franklin and the Stamp Act Crisis," Digital History, ID 152, accessed January 5, 2017, www.digitalhistory.uh.edu/disp_textbook.cfm?smtID=3&psid=152.

21. Pitt is quoted by John Dickinson in one of his *Letters from a Farmer, in Pennsylvania*, available in *The Writings of John Dickinson* (Philadelphia: Historical Society of Philadelphia), 1: 333.

22. Edmund S. Morgan and Helen M. Morgan, *The Stamp Act Crisis: Prologue to Revolution* (Chapel Hill: University of North Carolina Press, 1995), 119–21.

23. Continental Congress, *Authentic Account of the Proceedings of the Congress Held at New-York, in Mdcclxv, on the Subject of the American Stamp Act* (London [?], 1767), 5–8.

24. "The Declaratory Act," March 18, 1766, Constitution Society, accessed February 16, 2017, http://www.constitution.org/bcp/decl_act.htm.

25. Jack P. Greene and J. R. Pole, eds., *A Companion to the American Revolution* (Malden, MA: Blackwell, 2000), 138–39.

26. Dickinson, *Letters from a Farmer, in Pennsylvania*, 59.

27. "Massachusetts Circular Letter to the Colonial Legislatures," Avalon Project, accessed January 3, 2017, http://avalon.law.yale.edu/subject_menus/18th.asp.

28. Alfred Fabian Young, *The Shoemaker and the Tea Party: Memory and the American Revolution* (Boston, MA: Beacon Press, 1999), 42–45, 99–107.

29. *At a Meeting of the Delegates of Every Town and District in the County of Suffolk, On Tuesday the Sixth of September, at the House of Mr. Richard Woodward of Dedham, and by Adjournment at the House of Mr. Daniel Vose of Milton, on Friday the Ninth Instant . . . A Committee Was Chosen to Bring in a Report to*

the Convention, and the Following Being Several Times Read and Put Paragraph by Paragraph, Was Unanimously Voted, Viz. . . ., ed. William Thompson and Joseph Warren ([Boston:] Printed by Edes and Gill, 1774), in Early American Imprints, series 1: Evans, https://www.readex.com/content/early-american-imprints-series-i-evans-1639-1800.

30. *A Declaration by the Representatives of the United Colonies of North-America*, Avalon Project, accessed January 14, 2017, at http://avalon.law.yale.edu/18th_century/arms.asp.

31. G. B. Tindall and D. E. Shi, *America: A Narrative History*, 9th ed., 2 vols. (New York: W. W. Norton, 2012), 1:A61–A65.

32. Grotius, *Illustrious Hugo Grotius*, 516.

33. John E. Ferling, *Whirlwind: The American Revolution and the War That Won It* (New York: Bloomsbury, 2015), 325–26.

34. Morgan and Morgan, *Stamp Act Crisis*, 23.

35. Alvin Rabushka, *Taxation in Colonial America* (Princeton: Princeton University Press, 2008), 772, 814, 856, A3. This dramatic difference in taxation narrows when the taxes the colonists' own assemblies imposed on them are added, but the English were still paying at least twice as much as the most heavily taxed colonists. For example, in 1774/75 Massachusetts' citizens paid a total of £10,312.10.0, or 12s. 6d. per capita. In 1775 Pennsylvania's total direct taxes were £24,509 or an average of 1s. 9d. per capita for its 276,873 inhabitants. Meanwhile, South Carolinians only paid 2s. 1d. on average for all of their taxes, both colonial and imperial, in 1775.

36. Frazer, "Not a Just War," 37.

37. Declaration of Independence, in Tindall and Shi, *America: A Narrative History*, 1:A61.

38. Tindall and Shi, *America: A Narrative History*, 1:A61.

39. "Journals of the Continental Congress—Petition to the King; July 8, 1775," Avalon Project, accessed January 27, 2017, http://avalon.law.yale.edu/18th_century/contcong_07-08-75.asp; Tindall and Shi, *America: A Narrative History*, 1:A63.

40. David Hackett Fischer, *Paul Revere's Ride* (New York: Oxford University Press, 1994), 184–201.

41. Robert A. Gross, *The Minutemen and Their World*, 25th anniversary ed. (New York: Hill and Wang, 2001), 122–32.

42. Mark R. Anderson, *The Battle for the Fourteenth Colony: America's War of Liberation in Canada, 1774–1776* (Hanover, NH: University Press of New England, 2013), 345–54.

43. Ira D. Gruber, *The Howe Brothers and the American Revolution* (Chapel Hill: University of North Carolina Press, 1972), 32.

44. Thomas Paine, *Thomas Paine on Liberty: Including "Common Sense" and Other Writings* (New York: Skyhorse Pub., 2012), 49, 62.

45. John E. Ferling, *Almost a Miracle: The American Victory in the War of Independence* (Oxford: Oxford University Press, 2007), 181.

46. George Washington to Continental Congress Camp Committee, January 29, 1778, The Papers of George Washington, Digital Edition (Charlottesville: University of Virginia Press, Rotunda, 2008). This characterization does not apply to the militia forces who fought particularly savage campaigns against their Loyalist neighbors throughout the colonies, and especially in the South. See Mark V. Kwasny, *Washington's Partisan War, 1775–1783* (Kent, OH: Kent State University Press, 1996); Ferling, *Whirlwind*, 276–92.

47. John Fabian Witt, *Lincoln's Code: The Laws of War in American History* (New York: Free Press, 2012), 20–26.

48. Emmerich Vattel, quoted in Geoffrey Best, *Humanity in Warfare* (New York: Columbia University Press, 1980), 36.

49. Armstrong Starkey, *War in the Age of Enlightenment, 1700–1789* (Westport, CT: Praeger, 2003), 93.

50. Vice Admiral Sir George Collier, quoted in A. Starkey, "Paoli to Stony-Point—Military Ethics and Weaponry during the American Revolution," *The Journal of Military History* 58, no. 1 (1994): 23.

51. General Anthony Wayne, quoted in Harold E. Selesky, "Colonial America," in *The Laws of War: Constraints on Warfare in the Western World*, ed. George J. Andreopoulos, Michael Howard, and Mark R. Shulman (New Haven: Yale University Press, 1994), 84.

52. Charles Royster, *Light-Horse Harry Lee and the Legacy of the American Revolution* (New York: Knopf, 1981), 36.

53. Ferling, *Almost a Miracle*, 428.

54. Richard M. Ketchum, *Saratoga: Turning Point of America's Revolutionary War* (New York: Henry Holt, 1997), 437.

55. George Washington to James Robertson, May 4, 1782, *The Papers of George Washington, Digital Edition* (Charlottesville: University of Virginia Press, Rotunda, 2008).

56. Stephen Conway, *A Short History of the American Revolutionary War* (London: I.B. Tauris, 2013), 120–21. The terms "civilian" and "noncombatant" are anachronistic to the eighteenth century.

57. For policy toward inhabitants see Holly A. Mayer, *Belonging to the Army: Camp Followers and Community during the American Revolution* (Columbia: University of South Carolina Press, 1996), 41–42. For courts-martial results, see Witt, *Lincoln's Code*, 22.

58. Benjamin L. Carp, "The Night the Yankees Burned Broadway: The New York City Fire of 1776," *Early American Studies: An Interdisciplinary Journal* 4, no. 2 (2006): 471–511.

59. For New York's total population before the war and at the start of the occupation, see Oscar Theodore Barck Jr., *New York City during the War for Independence: With Special Reference to the Period of British Occupation*, Studies in History, Economics, and Public Law 357 (New York: Columbia University Press, 1931), 74–75. For the waves of emigration, see Ruma Chopra, *Unnatural Rebellion: Loyalists in New York City during the Revolution* (Charlottesville: University of Virginia Press, 2011), 46.

60. Thomas Jefferson Wertenbaker, *Father Knickerbocker Rebels: New York City during the Revolution* (New York: C. Scribner's Sons, 1948), 101.

61. George Washington to John Sullivan, May 31, 1779, The Papers of George Washington, Digital Edition (Charlottesville: University of Virginia Press, Rotunda, 2008).

62. Wayne E. Lee, *Barbarians and Brothers: Anglo-American Warfare, 1500–1865* (Oxford: Oxford University Press, 2011), 214.

63. John Grenier, *The First Way of War: American War Making on the Frontier, 1607–1814* (Cambridge: Cambridge University Press, 2005), 22–24.

64. Maya Jasanoff, *Liberty's Exiles: American Loyalists in the Revolutionary World* (New York: Knopf, 2011), 6.

65. "The Paris Peace Treaty of September 30, 1783," Avalon Project, accessed February 1, 2017, http://avalon.law.yale.edu/18th_century/paris.asp.

66. Benjamin Franklin to Josiah Quincy Sr., September 11, 1783, Founders Online, National Archives, last modified December 28, 2016, http://founders.archives.gov/documents/Franklin/01-40-02-0385.

THREE

The War of 1812

Jonathan Den Hartog

O that the King and President were both here this moment to see the misery their quarrels lead to. They surely would never go to war without a cause that they could give as a reason to God at the last day, for thus destroying the creatures that He hath made in his own image.
—*An American widow after her husband died at the Battle of Lundy's Lane, 1814*[1]

President James Madison had decided the United States' situation was untenable. On June 1, 1812, he delivered an official message to Congress, recommending a declaration of war with Great Britain. In the message, he recounted the flash points between the two nations. Great Britain had been stopping American ships on the open ocean to look for runaway British seamen. British ships had been patrolling American coasts and enforcing a blockade, keeping the U.S. from trading with all countries.

The U.S. had responded with conciliatory gestures, which had all been rebuffed. Madison concluded that the British conduct amounted to no less than "on the side of Great Britain, a state of war against the United States."[2] In the face of existing naval violence, the only question was how the U.S. would respond. As Madison posed the question, the country faced the choice of "whether the United States shall continue passive under these progressive usurpations, and these accumulating wrongs, or, opposing force to force in defence of their national rights, shall commit a just cause into the hands of the Almighty disposer of events."[3] Congress deliberated on the question for two weeks, with strong resistance to a declaration of war coming from the Federalist minority. Still, by June 18, both houses of Congress had passed the war declaration. All that was left was for President Madison to make a formal declaration of war the next day. In the declaration, Madison called on Americans to support the government as it pursued "the last resort of injured nations" and sought "a speedy, a just and honorable peace."[4]

President Madison clearly believed the U.S. entry into the War of 1812 was just—so just that he could call on divine aid in support. But was he justified in making that claim? And on what grounds could he make that determination? These are the questions I take up in this chapter. Through careful ethical reflection based on classical just war principles, we shall be able to gain a better understanding of rights and wrongs in the War of 1812.[5] I pay special attention to evaluating the causes of the war, the conduct and costs of the war, and the conditions at the end of the war. This follows the traditional division of just war reasoning to examine the justice of going to war (*ius ad bellum*), just conduct in war (*ius in bello*), and just relations after the war (*ius post bellum*). Where possible, I bring in voices from the war itself to demonstrate how contentious and debated the war was in its own time. Many of these voices were critical of the war, and to my mind those voices that questioned the justice and prudence of the war had the stronger argument, both logically and morally. I conclude the chapter with some suggestions for how understanding the War of 1812 might contribute to policy making in the present. Any wisdom taken from reflecting on the past, though, must be contextual. There is no formula to be followed, only the priority to value prudence in matters of state—in itself a lesson President Madison would have done well to learn.

I approach these considerations as a historian of the early American republic, but I realize that writing about the War of 1812 through the lens of the just war ethical tradition will strike some readers as transgressing several intellectual borders. First, this chapter by necessity has to be interdisciplinary, bringing together the insights of historical scholarship and ethical analysis.[6] Second, this chapter will not only intentionally ask what occurred in the early nineteenth century and what contemporaries had to say about it, but it will also seek to apply moral categories to this interpretation and even seek to draw lessons for contemporary policy makers. This approach may seem anathema to some historians, who fear that the presentist concerns could bias my historical evaluation and would argue that historical scholarship is not suited to address such claims. Yet other historians have been articulating good grounds to bring self-conscious moral reflection to the study of historical topics.[7] With due caution, then, I begin this chapter by making historical claims about the War of 1812 and then analyze the evidence from the perspective of the just war tradition, seeking to give proper respect to both historical scholarship and normative ethical reflection on events.

JUST CAUSES OF THE WAR OF 1812?

To understand America's path to the War of 1812, it is necessary to begin with the presidency of Thomas Jefferson (1801–9). Jefferson confronted a world defined by the titanic struggle between Great Britain and Napoleonic France. The first years of the nineteenth century witnessed a brief peace, during which time Jefferson was able to negotiate the purchase of the Louisiana Territory. After 1803, conflict between Britain and France resumed, and it would last until Napoleon's final defeat in 1815. In this setting, the U.S. attempted to maintain its neutrality, even as Jefferson and his secretary of state, James Madison, expressed overt hostility to Great Britain, as a residual outlook from the American Revolution.[8]

The American defense of neutrality stumbled upon two key issues: trade and impressment. The Americans asserted a right to free trade, regardless of the source of the goods they were trading. Also, they sought to trade with both warring parties simultaneously, despite the desire of each combatant nation to limit the trade of the other. As the war between Britain and France intensified, both warring powers sought to control neutral trade, leading in 1807 to strong restrictions on trade by the British and French governments.

Simultaneously, because American and British definitions of citizenship differed, the two nations clashed over the right of impressment of sailors. The British viewed citizenship as permanent, with subjects holding "indefeasible allegiance," meaning that there was no legal way to escape the duties of British subjects to serve their country in its hour of need.[9] By contrast, the U.S. welcomed naturalization of immigrants to America and made it easy for immigrants to be naturalized. This opportunity was particularly popular for British sailors seeking to escape the Royal Navy and join America's merchant ships. In fact, not only did American captains encourage these sailors to join them, but a brisk trade in counterfeit naturalization documents flourished along the American coast, as well as overseas.

Facing an existential threat, chronically undermanned, and seeking support for global naval operations, the British sought to increase their crews by reclaiming former British sailors whom they found aboard U.S. ships. Although the U.S. did not object to the British searching merchant ships in British ports, it did object to the British stopping the same merchant ships on the open seas. Further, there was little test of whether the impressed sailors were, in fact, British subjects or simply wrongly accused Americans. It should be pointed out, however, that this U.S. claim was not accepted by any other European power; the British interpretation was not unusual or extraordinary.[10]

The issues of trade and impressment came to the fore during Jefferson's second term. In 1807, the USS *Chesapeake* left Norfolk, Virginia, heading for the Mediterranean, carrying several British deserters as crew. Waiting for it was the HMS *Leopard*, which fired upon the *Chesapeake*, forced her to surrender, boarded her, and seized the British sailors. This exchange fueled a great deal of American hostility toward Britain, and the affair itself was not resolved until years later.[11] Although Jefferson could have pushed the controversy to war at that point, he responded by addressing the issue of trade, which he believed was primary. Jefferson decided to declare an embargo on all American shipping, believing that the trade pressure placed on both Great Britain and France would force them to change their policies. The Embargo of 1807 was a disaster in the U.S., destroying America's maritime economy, creating great dissatisfaction with the government, and promoting American smuggling, while failing to influence the European powers.[12]

These two issues continued into James Madison's presidency. Jefferson's total embargo was replaced with the Non-Intercourse Act, which limited the trade restrictions solely to Britain and France. The government even offered a carrot to the warring parties with Macon's Bill No. 2, which promised that the trade restrictions would be lifted on the first of the two nations to rescind their trade policies, leaving the embargo upon the laggard combatant. Even with these maneuvers, the U.S. had failed to sway either Great Britain or France by early 1812. Put together, the issues of trade and impressment would create a powerful shorthand and slogan for going to war: "Free Trade and Sailors' Rights." Captain David Porter of the USS *Essex* initially raised a banner with that motto in 1812, and the phrase powerfully captured the motivation of many Americans.[13]

In addition to "Free Trade and Sailors' Rights," a powerful dimension of national expansionism was also at work. Congressmen from the western states and President Madison looked outward in several directions for the opportunities a war might provide. Most inviting was the prospect of Canada. Geographically, Canada was separated from Britain by the Atlantic Ocean while it shared a border with the U.S., suggesting ease for American troop movements and difficulty for the British in maintaining supply lines. Further, the Anglo-French population of Canada was small, and policy makers believed they could be easily overwhelmed by superior American numbers. These forecasts would prove to be horribly wrong, but before the war commenced, they proved a tempting allurement to battle. At the same time, war offered the possibility of easier expansion westward. Frontiersmen chafed at the resistance they encountered from the indigenous tribes, many of whom easily crossed the porous border with Canada to receive support and encouragement from the British. Just in the years surrounding 1812, an alliance of various tribes was forming under the leadership of Shawnee chief Tecumseh and his brother Tenskwatawa, a religious leader known as the Prophet. Although General William Henry Harrison had defeated Tecumseh at the Battle of Tippecanoe in 1811, resistance from the alliance remained strong. A defeat of the British would strip the tribes of the support they needed to rebuff American advances westward. Finally, war could also open Florida to American conquest, which would consolidate American territory, deal with raids from tribes living in Florida, and shut off an escape route for runaway slaves. Without a doubt, these expansionist impulses helped justify the assent that leaders gave to going to war in 1812.

Finally, the country went to war as a result of specific choices made by individual leaders. Definite pressure toward war was exerted by the group of Congressmen which came to be known as "War Hawks." These Congressmen—mostly young and from the South and West and including figures such as Henry Clay of Kentucky, John C. Calhoun of South Carolina, and Felix Grundy of Tennessee—actively pressured President Madison to accede to war. They saw the war as a chance to defend the nation's "honor" against insults and to strengthen the country's position in the West and on the high seas. They were aided by public opinion—especially in the areas of the South and West they were representing—that favored the war. These regions felt the pressure of attacks from various Native American tribes and imaginatively identified with sailors from the coast. Political passions and the press of public opinion also weighed on President Madison.[14] Ultimately, the decision for war lay with him. Although an insightful political theorist in the *Federalist Papers* and a keen strategist in the House of Representatives, Madison was less successful as a party head. Lacking charisma and force, he often operated in the presidency alone. Under pressure from the press and the War Hawks for war, he assented to it, drawn by the prospect of Canada and his personal antipathy to the British. He not only delivered his war message, but he pushed Congress for the declaration of war, over Federalist objections. Thus, the responsibility for the war finally falls on Madison. At the time and since, critics of the War of 1812 have called it "Mr. Madison's War," and that is appropriate: the war is inseparable from Madison's decision making.[15]

With this background, we can evaluate America's entry into the War of 1812 according to *ius ad bellum* (justice in going to war) principles. Did American claims justify the full effort of going to war? Although American claims cannot be dismissed entirely, they do not appear to meet several significant *ad bellum* benchmarks. First, it is very hard to argue that America had just cause to declare war on Great Britain as a matter of self-defense. To be sure, pro-war Americans viewed the retaking of naturalized American sailors on the high seas as an act of war, a violation of American sovereignty. However, the legal standing of these sailors was, in fact, disputed, raising questions of citizenship and the law of nations. Since other European powers did not see those aggressions as an act of war, it seems hard to justify by the standards of international justice as understood in the early nineteenth century. As well, although many Americans blamed the British for encouraging attacks from Native Americans on the frontier, the British had not officially ordered those attacks. Further, ownership of the land on the frontier was itself disputed. As a result, this conflict was primarily between the western tribes and the American government, not the British. In neither case was there an obvious need to attack the British in a claim of self-defense. Ironically, after the Americans declared war and invaded Canada, the British and Canadians *were* justified in claiming a right to self-defense, repelling American attacks, and even advancing into American territory.

Second, the war was clearly not a measure of last resort. America and Britain had bumped along for years without resolving the issues of impressment and trade, and although they were uncomfortable, there is nothing to suggest they could not have gone on in similar fashion. Further, to think those issues had to be solved exactly in 1812 betrayed a lack of understanding of the world situation, particularly the constraints Britain faced while struggling with Napoleon. Instead, with both nations taking positions that needed to be argued through, this would have been an ideal time to appoint a diplomatic commission with representatives from both nations. This strategy had served American diplomacy well earlier in its history. In 1794, when America and Britain had previously been in danger of going to war, President Washington sent Chief Justice John Jay to London to deal with the British directly. As part of the Treaty of Amity and Commerce that Jay brought back—popularly known as the Jay Treaty—a commission was set up to investigate improper seizures of American shipping.[16] Had this more pacific strategy been taken, it might have worked.

Finally, we know that war was unnecessary because, in the summer of 1812, the British government unilaterally moved to rescind the orders in council that had caused such offense, and they did so before the Americans declared war. Due to the time needed for an Atlantic crossing, news of the repeal reached the U.S. after Congress had voted to declare war. With the news, however, Madison did not immediately suspend military operations but instead pushed forward with his plans for the invasion of Canada. Had "Free Trade and Sailors' Rights" been the only concern, Madison could have seized that opportunity to stand down, without dragging the country through several more years of fighting. On the other side, even after the American declaration of war, the British held back until it was clear that the Americans were dedicated to continuing the war.[17]

A just war also entails the necessity of some prospect for success. On this point, American policy makers were either blind or delusional in their claims that the nation had the wherewithal to start a fight with one of the strongest powers on earth. Even a Britain distracted by the Napoleonic Wars could not simply accept American aggressions or allow the American republic to undercut its naval policies, which Britain saw as essential for its survival. For the American navy, the last major building project had occurred during the John Adams administration (1797–1801), so the U.S. was forced to fall back on privateers, just as in the American Revolution.[18] The army was little better. Because Jefferson and Madison's Democratic-Republicans possessed a strong suspicion of a standing army in peacetime, they had cut federal expenditures for the army, which in 1812 numbered just seven thousand men in total. In the absence of a ready army, military planners hoped to make extensive use of state militia units. These plans faltered when some militia units fought poorly, other units refused to cross into Canada, and New England governors—especially Caleb Strong of Massachusetts—resisted requests to place state militia under regular army control. Further, President Madison declared war with no army staff structure in place. Finally, in an era when financing armed conflict was becoming a greater challenge, the U.S. was in the process of closing the first Bank of the United States, the creation of Alexander Hamilton that had provided financial stability for the past twenty years. In the face of Britain's financial and naval juggernaut, the American standing was pitiable. Choosing to go to war at that point was choosing to do so with very little prospect of success.[19]

A DEBATED WAR

From its declaration, the war created a great deal of disagreement and debate across the nation. It received support primarily from members of Madison's Democratic-Republican party. The party had a strong base in the Southern states, and these areas rallied for the war effort. Thomas Jefferson reported to Madison from Monticello that the declaration of war was "entirely popular here," the only regret being that it had not been made as soon as Canada was open for campaigning in the spring.[20] Many western frontiersmen welcomed it, seeing in the war a chance to deal with aggression by indigenous peoples. Sailors who hoped to see their rights defended supported it across the Atlantic seaboard.

However, the war was questioned from its very beginning. One telling rebuke came from the Old Republicans, or "tertium quids," men who claimed to be upholding the principles of republican simplicity and self-government but who aligned with neither the Democratic-Republicans nor the Federalists. They questioned whether this new war was in the spirit of the American Revolution and in line with a republic that protected its citizens but maximized liberty through its minimal activity. The most articulate defender of this position was John Randolph of Roanoke, Virginia. When the war was being considered, Randolph denounced it. He decried the possibility of "[a] war not of defense, but of conquest, of aggrandizement, of ambition; a war foreign to the interests of this country, to the interests of humanity itself."[21] In addition to questioning the merits of the war, he charged that fighting it was contrary to the spirit of the Constitution. The government, according to Randolph, "was not calculated to wage offensive foreign war—it was instituted for the common defense and the general welfare."[22] In both statements, Randolph was condemning the war as an offensive, aggressive war, one not fought in just self-defense.

From the other political direction, the strongest opposition came from the Federalist party. Hailing primarily from New England and the Mid-Atlantic states, the Federalists represented those interests of Atlantic trade that had been hurt with the previous embargoes and that would be hurt even further with a war. Further, for New Englanders, any attack launched from Canada or at the Atlantic seaboard would largely hurt them. Thus, the Federalists had understandable reasons for opposing the war. As the war progressed, they also became the voice of dissatisfaction with the conduct of the war. Federalists demonstrated electoral gains during the war in their own right. In other areas, such as New York, the Federalists "rebranded" themselves to appear as tickets such as the "Peace and Commerce Party," allowing for electoral success while avoiding the possible stigma of the "Federalist" moniker. Federalist opposition to the war would culminate in the Hartford Convention (discussed below).[23]

Federalist opposition was not only an expression of self-interest, however, as the Federalists' leaders also made moral objections to the war. These received most eloquent expression in a pamphlet drafted by Josiah Quincy and James Bayard. Titled *An Address of the Minority to Their Constituents, on the Subject of War with Great-Britain*, the public declaration was signed by thirty-four Federalists in the House of Representatives. This declaration gained wide attention first as a pamphlet and then as an address published in newspapers across the country. These Federalists made relevant points which history has only confirmed.

Most importantly, these Federalist leaders insisted that the abuses suffered by the U.S. did not rise to the level of justifying war. "It appears to the undersigned," they insisted, "that the wrongs, of which the United States have to complain, although in some aspects very grievous to our interests, and in many humiliating to our pride, were yet of a nature which, in the present state of the world, either would not justify war, or which war would not remedy."[24] Neither occasional abuses by the British on the high seas nor the present conflicts with indigenous nations were sufficient to fully justify going to war. Further, the problems that did exist could not be solved by war. The authors granted, "If war would compensate any of our losses, or remove any of our complaints, there might be some alleviation of the suffering, in the charm of the prospect," but they denied that any help of this sort could come.[25] Measures such as invading eastern Canada could do nothing to address problems either on the seas or on the frontier. They also made the related point that "honor" was also not a sufficient justification for war, charging, "Is national honor a principle, which thirsts after vengeance, and is appeased only by blood, which, trampling on the hopes of man, and spurning the law of God, untaught by what is past and careless of what is to come, precipitates itself into any folly of madness, to gratify a selfish vanity or to satiate some unhallowed rage?"²⁶ The honor to which the War Hawks appealed was an unreliable basis for making decisions about warfare.

Further, these Federalists questioned the dangers the country faced by starting a war it was not prepared to win. The national government had demonstrated no foresight in preparation. The authors admitted, "It would be some relief to our anxiety, if amends were likely to be made for the weakness and wildness of this project, by the prudence of the preparation, but in no aspect of this anomalous affair can we trace the great and distinctive properties of wisdom." The government as a whole, with Madison at its head, had demonstrated a lack of prudence in stepping toward the possibility of war. Instead, the authors found "headlong rushing into difficulties, with little calculation about the means, and little concern about the consequences."²⁷ The failure to grasp consequence was damning to these Federalists. A desire for war was not enough; the government had done nothing to ensure military success, as was evident to the Federalists in the paucity of buildup in both the naval and land forces. Further, one of the great consequences was that the war might endanger the U.S. itself. These Federalists emphasized the still tenuous bands of union and wanted instead to strengthen the U.S. internally. Because the American republic was still "experimental," it should not be tested, or "hastily precipitated into situations, calculated to put to trial the strength of the moral bound, by which they are united."²⁸ Preserving "time" for the union should be the greatest goal, instead of endangering the union or promoting divisions through waging a war.

Debates over the justice of the war and objections to it carried over from the political realm into the religious realm.²⁹ New England's Congregationalist ministers agreed with Federalist leaders about the errors of the war. From their pulpits they proclaimed the war as unjust and unjustifiable, even to the point of urging people not to fight. In their sermons, New England ministers laid out significant reasons for opposing the war. First, they saw it as an offensive war, rather than defensive war. Because the U.S. initiated the war, it could not be justified. "A wicked, offensive war may be expected to draw down uncommon judgments of God on the land," warned Elijah Parish.³⁰ The president of Yale College, Timothy Dwight, bemoaned the fact that "a great part of our countrymen believe the war in which we are engaged, to be unnecessary and unjust."³¹

Second, clergy worried that the war was not prudent, because the U.S. was unprepared. Third, the war would bring great moral evils to the land, which would consequently do great damage to the state, since morals and politics were linked. It was therefore incumbent on ministers and people alike to resist moral degradation and promote repentance and upright lives.[32] Fourth, the ministers worried about the connections with France such a war would produce. To make such an alliance would be to side with God's enemies, the unbelieving French, against Britain, the defender of Protestantism. "God forbid," Elijah Parish declared, "that the sons of New-England should enlist in this war of atheism against christianity; this war of vice against virtue; this war of Anti-Christ against the prince of peace."[33] With such words, ministers not only rejected the justice of the war but even laid out reasons, grounded in Scripture and New England religious culture, to resist America's fighting the war.

Some ministers, on the other hand, supported the war. Not surprisingly, many of them hailed from Democratic-Republican areas such as the South and the West and emerged from populist denominations such as the Baptists.[34] Even in New England, though, some voices spoke for the war, such as John H. Stevens, minister of Stoneham, Massachusetts. As the state's citizens attended church services in honor of the state's April 1813 Fast Day, Rev. Stevens delivered a very different message than was heard from many Federalist pulpits. Instead, he offered a ringing endorsement for the war. Drawing on the story of Deborah and Barak in Judges 4 and 5, Stevens drew extended parallels between the condition of the ancient Israelites and the U.S. in 1813. Just as the sins of Israel had brought oppression from the Canaanites, so American sins had brought military oppression from Britain. Stevens did not hesitate in denouncing American sins, such as lack of gratitude, pride, profanity, intemperance, lying, gaming, Sabbath breaking, and inordinate love of money.[35] The British oppression had caused death and suffering for many American sailors, over America's diplomatic, peaceful protests. Stevens set out his own criteria for a just war:

> To make a war just and righteous, and have it approved by heaven, the injuries must be many and great, and long persisted in, they

must be without any just provocation; and the injured nation must make all suitable exertions, amicably and peaceably, to obtain redress of their grievances. Now I believe in my heart, all this is true of our nation; . . . hence the inference is clear as the sun in the firmament of heaven, that the war, in which our nation is engaged, is a just and a righteous war, and that God approves of it.[36]

Although he was using rhetorical shortcuts, Stevens was insisting that the war was a defensive reaction against unjust assaults and that the U.S. fought it as a last resort. But, rather than seeing this as a debatable point, he believed the conclusion was forthrightly clear. If the war was obviously just, it bore God's approval. Further, anyone who questioned the war or failed to support it wholeheartedly—as was the case with Federalist Governor Caleb Strong of Massachusetts[37]—was actually resisting God's will! Only repentance and corporate unity in support of the war could bring God's blessing and military success. The success that Stevens desired and anticipated, however, was extremely slow in coming, as the war limped along for the next two years.

These debates continued throughout the war. Many Northerners increasingly complained as the war dragged on, with neither success nor resolution, and they blamed President Madison for the war's continued mismanagement.[38] This lack of enthusiasm during the war enflamed Southern and Democratic-Republican sentiment against their opponents. By the end of the war, then, the war had exacerbated differences within the nation. As a result of this discord, the American republic was itself threatened. Although it was never pushed to the breaking point, the union and its republican institutions were seriously challenged. The union, which the founding generation realized was experimental and a work in progress, was endangered by confronting a war that lacked popular consensus. Madison was making a dangerous wager that only became clear as the war progressed—perhaps by the time a British raid actually burned Washington, DC.[39]

Most powerfully, the discord created by the war birthed the Hartford Convention. New England Federalists, distressed at the progress of the war, convened the convention in late 1814. They decried both President Madison's incompetence and the constitutional ease by which he had led the country into war and impinged on the rights of the individual states. Although later Democratic-Republican polemics tarred the Federalists with secessionist and separatist impulses, the Hartford Convention deserves better understanding. As the historian James Banner has pointed out, the convention was actually dominated by moderates. Although there were a few New England firebrands calling for radical action, the convention was managed by Federalist leaders who sought to channel regional grievances into constructive responses.[40] The end result was a series of recommendations for constitutional amendments that the convention believed would make war less likely, protect the rights of the states, and reduce the power of Southern slaveholders in government.[41] The Hartford Convention reveals the deep political concerns created by the war. Unfortunately for the convention—and the nation's response to it—the representatives of the convention arrived in Washington, DC, simultaneously with the news of Gen. Andrew Jackson's victory at New Orleans and the peace treaty from Ghent. Rather than using the opportunity to reflect on constitutional principles, the Democratic-Republicans turned the convention into a political cudgel for partisan purposes. The conflict over the convention thus produced at least as much bitterness as the convention itself expressed.

JUST CONDUCT IN THE WAR?

Even as the war was debated, the military campaigns raged from the summer of 1812 through January 1815. The war should also be evaluated on how American participants followed *ius in bello* (justice in the midst of war) principles. In particular, we should ask about whether the levels of violence were proportional, how civilians were treated, and how surrendered soldiers and prisoners of war were treated. In this evaluation, the Americans certainly do not escape censure, but they seemed to have attempted to define just standards, even if the armies did not always adhere to those standards.

In regard to proportional violence, we should acknowledge that although the War of 1812 was of smaller scale than some other American wars, it still involved much violence and suffering for those fighting in or affected by it. Thus, many soldiers did lose their lives. As calculated by the historian Donald Hickey, although the official reports suggest

2,260 American soldiers and 2,700 British soldiers died in combat, the total casualties of the war were much higher, perhaps 15,000 deaths for the Americans, 10,000 for the British, and 7,500 for the various indigenous tribes.[42] Naval engagements followed expectations for the law of the sea, even when the American vessels were privateers. On land, both American and British officers were concerned about the escalating levels of needless violence, but they often decried it in vain. A large element of this violence had to do with the fact that both the British and the Americans fought with indigenous allies, and these allies proved extremely difficult to control, enacting levels of violence that Anglo-American officers deemed unacceptable. The clearest example of needless violence occurred with the frontier practice of scalping enemies. Although both sides claimed the other side started the practice, by the end of the war, not only Native Americans were practicing scalping but many American irregular units were, too. In response to violence by Native Americans, the U.S. forces most likely to commit comparable violence were the Kentucky militia companies that served in Canada, along the western frontier, and in Louisiana. Their "long knives" brought their own dread to the British and their indigenous allies. These frontiersmen were often motivated by memories of violence inflicted on the Americans, such as at Fort Mims (where men of the Creek nation had burned American soldiers alive in buildings and killed those who surrendered) or the Raisin River Massacre (where dozens of wounded American prisoners were burned or tomahawked to death).[43]

In dealing with civilians, American officers were usually able to protect the lives of Canada's white inhabitants; their livestock and property, however, were a different story. The American ideal was to protect civilian property, so as to persuade the Canadians to join the American cause. The American general James Wilkinson proclaimed to his troops, "It will be the pride and glory of this Army to conquer[,] not to destroy. Its character, its honor, and that of the American people are intrusted, deeply intrusted, in its magnanimity, its forbearance, and its sacred regard of private property."[44] However, Wilkinson's ideals were not enforced on the American troops—especially the militia companies—who encountered Canadian civilians. Plundering occurred throughout the war, a prime example being the systematic plunder of York after its capture in 1813. Further, the Americans destroyed a significant amount of property.

They burned many farms, buildings, barns, grain mills, and settlements, with Moraviantown being one of the most notable. There, a Moravian mission had gathered peaceful, neutral Native Americans into a community, but it was totally destroyed by Kentucky forces intent on revenge against any indigenous groups.[45]

As to the treatment of prisoners, the Americans behaved scrupulously well. They continued the "policy of humanity" Americans had put into practice in the American Revolution, immediately accepting the surrender of opponents.[46] The Americans sent some Canadian militia forces home, contingent on their promise that they would not return to battle until their service was officially exchanged for American prisoners. For those soldiers held as prisoners, American treatment was exemplary. Prisoners were able to hire themselves out for wages far above an infantryman's regular pay. American provision for British prisoners also surpassed their ordinary rations. The prime American prison in Pittsfield, Massachusetts, was a model of humane treatment. By contrast, Americans were treated much worse, with many of them shipped across the Atlantic to the large British prison of Dartmoor, where conditions deteriorated to the point of a prison riot, which could only be quelled by British arms.[47] Thus, although much violence and even retaliatory violence occurred, the American practice of war in 1812 at least took just war principles as ideals, even if they were not always followed in reality.

A JUST PEACE?

A final marker of just war has to be a consideration of the state of justice after the war (*ius post bellum*). How do the conclusion and the aftermath of a war speak to its character? Applying these concerns to the War if 1812 allows us to address issues of peacemaking. The American delegation, including John Quincy Adams, Henry Clay, and Albert Gallatin, met with the British in the city of Ghent, in the Low Countries. Negotiations began in August 1814. With the British defeat of Napoleon earlier in the year and with British successes in America, the initial British demands were for a harsh peace, involving a separate state for indigenous tribes between the Ohio River and the Great Lakes (consisting of up to 250,000 square miles), accession of much of Maine to

Canada, free British navigation on the Mississippi River, and eliminating American ships on the Great Lakes. Due to American military recovery, American diplomatic savvy, and the return of Napoleon from his first exile, American diplomats were able to argue for a more equitable peace. The end result was the Treaty of Ghent, signed on Christmas Eve, 1814. The Treaty of Ghent largely restored the *status quo antebellum*, with the British returning the American territory they had occupied and the Americans returning the Canadian. The treaty addressed neither the issue of neutral rights nor the issue of impressment, and it left other sticky points of dispute to be solved later.[48]

If the Treaty of Ghent produced an acceptable peace that merely returned to the *status quo antebellum*, this reveals a significant perspective on the justice of the war. The war neither increased nor decreased just relations between the parties involved; it merely restored a working, if imperfect, relationship. The problems of neutral shipping rights during European wars and of British impressment of American sailors lessened in importance, not because of America's fighting of the War of 1812, but because of the final defeat of Napoleon at Waterloo in 1815. A greater sensitivity to British difficulties and appreciation of the extremities in which the Napoleonic Wars had placed Britain should have tempered American eagerness for war. The war President Madison led the nation into did nothing to solve the problems he had pointed to at the outset.

An American appreciation of the war as a mistake for which the nation should be grateful for the opportunity to escape without greater harm, however, was short-circuited by the Battle of New Orleans, in which Gen. Andrew Jackson defeated Gen. Edward Pakenham in January 1815. The battle was fought after the Peace of Ghent had been signed but before news of it reached American shores. The victory allowed Americans to celebrate and then remember the war as a triumph, a success it had never been in actuality. Although valuable as a military victory, the Battle of New Orleans clouded Americans' assessment of the war and allowed political leaders and ordinary citizens to put the war behind them without grappling with its meaning or significance. As Paul Gilje encapsulates it, "Madison decided to declare victory regardless of the reality.... He began the great lie that the United States had won the war."[49]

The War of 1812 figures less in public memory than other wars, and much of it remains murky. Still, there is much in the American experience two hundred years ago to guide policy makers in the present.[50] First, the bar for going to war must be kept very high. Technological advances may make war appear "easier" or less personal, and hence cheaper, but because of the moral weight of war fighting—and because of modern warfare's greater capacity for destruction—the rush to war should be resisted. Put another way, the test for *ius ad bellum* (justice in going to war) must remain stringent. Thus, policy makers should constantly challenge each other as to the basic questions of going to war. In this light, war should be fought only as a last resort, after all reasonable diplomatic means have been exhausted—as was not the case with the War of 1812. Further, possibilities of success must be calculated realistically, not inserting optimism or ideology. Concomitantly, emotion is not enough to justify war. There remains a consistent temptation to be swayed by passions in foreign policy. This danger, documented as early as Thucydides in the Peloponnesian War, threatens to pull nations into wars they do not need to fight. Statesmanship needs to stand before and resist passions that might demand unjust war. Whether such passions come from an individual, a party (such as the War Hawks), or the population at large, they cannot by themselves justify war on their own and may, in fact, cloud the moral reflection about going to war.

Second, war fighting must involve prudence. Prudence, as the virtue of the statesman in Aristotle's terms, involves applying practical wisdom situated for the conditions at the time and place. It is applied wisdom, knowing what is appropriate given the multitude of factors present. But prudence also realizes that there is no one-size-fits-all formula for warfare. Outcomes and developments can never be predicted ahead of time or reduced to a simple formula. Prudence involves not only seeking the best path to success but simultaneously avoiding catastrophic failures. The wise pilot of the ship of state not only charts a path forward but avoids the shoals and rocks that could capsize his craft.[51] A valid criticism of President Madison in the War of 1812 is that he failed to demonstrate prudence in the moment. Approaching the war, he miscalculated the costs of the war and the risks into which he was taking the country. He viewed the rewards (especially the acquisition of Canada) as easier to obtain than they actually were. As the country faltered in 1814 through renewed British attacks, it approached a breaking point, and it was saved only through deft diplomacy at Ghent and Jackson's victory at New Orleans. The War of 1812 was thus an example of a gamble that nearly proved disastrous.

Finally, although popular passion is not enough to justify a war, the successful prosecution of a war requires the support of its citizens. This element of war fighting is a particular challenge in republics such as the U.S. Here, the first challenge is building a consensus that going to war is justified, but then the greater need is to sustain that commitment to a war over the length of time needed to complete it. Although many Americans demonstrated support for the War of 1812 when it broke out, that enthusiasm waned significantly as Canada proved more difficult to conquer than had been promised, as the naval victories proved inconclusive, and as British troops increasingly raided on American soil. Further, when popular support in a conflict is not forthcoming, it should provide a great incentive to evaluate the war. The Hartford Convention was a strong signal of condemnation for the War of 1812 from the entire region of New England. The war's ending and Jackson's victory allowed President Madison to escape the full consequences of his unpopular war.

Altogether, the War of 1812 instructs most keenly in how not to pursue a war. In ignoring questions about the justice of going to war and the prudence of conducting a war once started, President Madison placed the U.S. on an extremely dangerous footing, one that put the nation itself at risk. The end result of moral and ethical reflection on the War of 1812 should be to caution us against going to war when the justice of the cause is disputed and when adequate provisions have not been made to fight the war to a successful conclusion. Warfare is not a game, and national standing should not be gambled with lightly. With these ideas in mind, however, the War of 1812 can go from a war many Americans would like to forget to one which can teach practical wisdom in the present.

NOTES

1. Quoted in Alan Taylor, *The Civil War of 1812: American Citizens, British Subjects, Irish Rebels, and Indian Allies* (New York: Knopf, 2010), 405.

2. James Madison, "War Message to Congress," June 1, 1812, in *The War of 1812: Writings from America's Second War of Independence*, ed. Donald Hickey (New York: Library of America, 2013), 8.

3. Madison, "War Message to Congress," 8.

4. James Madison, "Proclamation of War," June 19, 1812 in Hickey, *War of 1812*, 36, 37. For three outstanding general treatments of the War of 1812, see J. C. A. Stagg, *Mr. Madison's War: Politics, Diplomacy, and Warfare in the Early American Republic, 1783–1830* (Princeton: Princeton University Press, 1983); Taylor, *Civil War of 1812*; Donald Hickey, *The War of 1812: A Forgotten Conflict*, bicentennial ed. (Urbana, IL: University of Illinois Press, 2012).

5. One essay that approaches the war with similar questions is Ralph Beebe, "The War of 1812," in *The Wars of America: Christian Views*, ed. Ronald Wells (Grand Rapids: Eerdmans, 1981), 25–43. The present essay, by contrast, brings in more recent and more extensive scholarship on the War of 1812, addresses the details of the War more fully, and takes the just war tradition more seriously.

6. For an overview of the just war tradition, see the introduction to this volume.

7. Discussion of the place of moral reflection in history over the past several decades can be traced back to John Higham, *Writing American History: Essays on Modern Scholarship* (Bloomington: Indiana University Press, 1970), 147–55. More recently, see Grant Wacker, "Understanding the Past, Using the Past: Reflections on Two Approaches to History," in *Religious Advocacy in American History*, ed. Bruce Kuklick and D. G. Hart (Grand Rapids: Eerdmans, 1997), 159–79; Michael Kugler, "Enlightenment History, Objectivity, and the Moral Imagination," in *Confessing History: Explorations in Christian Faith and the Historian's Vocation*, ed. John Fea, Jay Green, and Eric Miller (Notre Dame, IN: University of Notre Dame Press, 2010), 128–52; and Jay Green, *Christian Historiography: Five Rival Versions* (Waco, TX: Baylor University Press, 2015), 86–97.

8. This paragraph and the following ones are synthesized from Stagg, *Mr. Madison's War*, and Hickey, *War of 1812*, as well as George Herring, *From Colony to Superpower: U.S. Foreign Relations since 1776* (New York: Oxford University Press, 2008), 114–27, and Donald Hickey, *Don't Give Up the Ship!: Myths of the War of 1812* (Urbana, IL: University of Illinois Press, 2006), 12–47.

9. Herring, *From Colony to Superpower*, 116.

10. Herring, *From Colony to Superpower*, 116.

11. See Spencer Tucker and Frank Reuter, *Injured Honor: The Chesapeake-Leopard Affair, June 22, 1807* (Annapolis, MD: Naval Institute Press, 1997).

12. Although Ralph Beebe praises Jefferson's restraint and believes that his strategy of economic pressure would have succeeded had it been pursued patiently, the evidence argues against such an optimistic interpretation. Other conditions, not Jefferson's embargo or the modified policy under Madison, did much more to secure American interests. Beebe, "War of 1812," 30–35.

13. On the phrase, see Paul Gilje, *Free Trade and Sailors' Rights in the War of 1812* (New York: Cambridge University Press, 2013).

14. On these points, see Nicole Eustace, *1812: War and the Passions of Patriotism* (Philadelphia: University of Pennsylvania Press, 2012), ix–xvii, 36–75; Steven Watts, *The Republic Reborn: War and the Making of Liberal America, 1790–1820* (Baltimore: Johns Hopkins University Press, 1987), 63–92.

15. J. C. A. Stagg's significant history of the war is rightly titled *Mr. Madison's War*. Madison's role can also be traced in various biographies of the president, such as Garry Wills, *James Madison* (New York: Times Books / Henry Holt and Company, 2002).

16. For the outlines of Jay's diplomacy, see Samuel Flagg Bemis, *Jay's Treaty: A Study in Commerce and Diplomacy*, 2nd ed. (New Haven: Yale University Press, 1962).

17. Donald Hickey, *Don't Give Up the Ship!*, 36–46.

18. On lack of naval preparation, see Stephen Budiansky, *Perilous Fight: America's Intrepid War with Britain on the High Seas, 1812–1815* (New York: Knopf, 2010).

19. Herring, *From Colony to Superpower*, 127–28.

20. Thomas Jefferson to James Madison, June 29, 1812, in *The War of 1812: Writings from America's Second War of Independence*, ed. Donald Hickey (New York: Library of America, 1813), 44.

21. John Randolph, speech of December 10, 1811, quoted in *John Randolph of Roanoke*, by David Johnson (Baton Rouge: Louisiana State University Press, 2012), 143.

22. Randolph, speech of December 10, 1811, 144.

23. See Philip Lampi, "The Federalist Party Resurgence, 1808–1816: Evidence from the New Nation Votes Database," *Journal of the Early Republic* 33 (Summer 2013): 255–81.

24. Thirty-four members of the U.S. House of Representatives, "An Address of the Minority to Their Constituents, on the Subject of War with Great-Britain," in Hickey, *War of 1812*, 50.

25. Thirty-four members of the U.S. House of Representatives, "Address of the Minority," 51.

26. Thirty-four members of the U.S. House of Representatives, "Address of the Minority," 51.

27. Thirty-four members of the U.S. House of Representatives, "Address of the Minority," 52.

28. Thirty-four members of the U.S. House of Representatives, "Address of the Minority," 50.

29. The best, though a partially flawed, account of religious responses to the War of 1812 is William Gribbin, *The Churches Militant: The War of 1812 and American Religion* (New Haven: Yale University Press, 1973), especially 1–60. For the larger context of Federalist ministers commenting on the war, see Jonathan Den Hartog, *Patriotism and Piety: Federalist Politics and Religious Struggle in the New American Nation* (Charlottesville: University of Virginia Press, 2015), 45–69.

30. Elijah Parish, *A Discourse, Delivered at Byfield, On the Annual Fast, April 8, 1813* (Newburyport, MA, 1813), 17.

31. Timothy Dwight, *A Discourse, in Two Parts, Delivered July 23, 1812, on the Public Fast* (New Haven, 1812), 49.

32. Dwight, *Discourse, in Two Parts*, 12–13, 50, 52–53.

33. Parish, *Discourse, Delivered at Byfield*, 22.

34. Gribbin, *Churches Militant*, 61–77.

35. John Hathaway Stevens, *A Discourse, Delivered in Stoneham, (Mass.) April 8, 1813: Being the Day of the State Fast* (Boston, 1813), 8–10.

36. Stevens, *Discourse, Delivered in Stoneham*, 18.

37. On Caleb Strong, see Den Hartog, *Patriotism and Piety*, 70–72, 79–92.

38. Samuel Eliot Morison, "Dissent in the War of 1812," in *Dissent in Three American Wars*, by Samuel Eliot Morison, Frederick Merk, and Frank Freidel (Cambridge, MA: Harvard University Press, 1970), 1–32.

39. Robert Watson calls the War of 1812 "America's first crisis." See his *America's First Crisis* (Albany, NY: Excelsior Editions of the State University of New York Press, 2014). The talk of disunion which the crisis provoked is analyzed in Elizabeth Varon's *Disunion! The Coming of the American Civil War, 1789–1859* (Chapel Hill: University of North Carolina Press, 2008), 31–50.

40. James Banner Jr., *To the Hartford Convention: The Federalists and the Origins of Party Politics in Massachusetts, 1789–1815* (New York: Knopf, 1970).

41. See "Report of the Hartford Convention," in *The American Republic: Primary Sources*, ed. Bruce Frohnen (Indianapolis: Liberty Fund, 2002), 447–57. The character and motivation of the Hartford Convention are also detailed in Theodore Dwight, *History of the Hartford Convention, with a Review of the Policy of the United States Government, Which Led to the War of 1812* (New York, 1833).

42. Hickey, *Don't Give Up the Ship!*, 297–99.

43. Taylor, *Civil War of 1812*, 204–14; Hickey, *Don't Give Up the Ship!*, 53–55.

44. James Wilkinson, quoted in Taylor, *Civil War of 1812*, 284.

45. Taylor, *Civil War of 1812*, 214–17, 244–45.

46. David Hackett Fischer, *Washington's Crossing* (New York: Oxford University Press, 2004), 375–79.

47. Taylor, *Civil War of 1812*, 371–76; Gilje, *Free Trade and Sailors' Rights*, 262–75.

48. Herring, *From Colony to Superpower*, 129–33.

49. Gilje, *Free Trade and Sailors' Rights*, 279. On the Battle of New Orleans, see Robert Remini, *The Battle of New Orleans: Andrew Jackson and America's First Military Victory* (New York: Viking, 1999); Walter Borneman, *1812: The War That Forged a Nation* (New York: HarperCollins, 2004), 271–304. For the political uses of the Battle of New Orleans, see Joseph F. Stoltz III, *A Bloodless Victory: The Battle of New Orleans in History and Memory* (Baltimore: Johns Hopkins University Press, 2017).

50. It should be noted that this approach was also taken by several scholars at the Brookings Institution think tank, although their conclusions came to differ significantly from the proposals I put forward. See Pietro Nivola and Peter Kastor, eds., *What So Proudly We Hailed: Essays on the Contemporary Meaning of the War of 1812* (Washington, DC: The Brookings Institution Press, 2012).

51. Much has been written on the classical virtue of prudence. For but one example from the twentieth century, see Yves Simon, *Practical Knowledge*, ed. Robert Mulvaney (New York: Fordham University Press, 1991), 1–78.

FOUR

James K. Polk and the War with Mexico

Daniel Walker Howe

The U.S.-Mexican War is a forgotten war. Hardly anyone remembers it or calls attention to it nowadays. The Mexicans don't like to remember it because they lost. Americans don't like to remember it, either; it contradicts our image of western expansion as a peaceful, democratic movement led by ordinary families in covered wagons. Today, my wife and I live in Los Angeles, named by the Mexican settlers who founded it in the eighteenth century. The reason why our home is in the U.S., and not still in Mexico, is the Mexican War.

MANIFEST DESTINY

The war with Mexico was largely the work of a single person: James Knox Polk, president of the U.S. Polk had narrowly won a hard-fought election in 1844 by campaigning for the acquisition of Texas and all of what was then called the Oregon Country. Once in the White House, Polk compromised the Oregon Question, agreeing with Britain to partition the vast Oregon Country. Canada got what is now British Columbia, and the U.S. got what is now the states of Washington, Oregon, and Idaho.

Texas posed a very different kind of issue from Oregon. By the time of Polk's inauguration, his predecessor, John Tyler, had already signed a joint resolution of Congress offering Texas statehood in the Union, so the annexation of Texas no longer remained an open question. Although Mexico still claimed Texas as part of her republic, in fact Texas had waged a successful revolution and had been independent since 1836; all the major powers had recognized Texan independence. The U.S. probably could have occupied the former Mexican province of Texas peacefully; Mexico would have been unlikely to do more than protest.

Mexico was in no condition to go to war with the U.S.; the Mexican government had been virtually bankrupted by the dictator Antonio de Santa Anna, now no longer in office. But Polk's plans for U.S. expansion were not confined to Texas and Oregon. Secretly, he nursed a more grandiose ambition, one that had not been discussed in his election campaign: the acquisition of California.

The U.S. expanded enormously during the administration of James K. Polk. To look at a map of U.S. expansion and add up the areas of Texas annexation, the Mexican cession, and the partition of Oregon, it appears that Polk acquired more land for his country than any other president—more than Thomas Jefferson, who obtained the Louisiana Purchase, and even more than Andrew Johnson, the president who obtained Alaska from Russia. However, Polk should probably not be credited with all of Texas, as he generally is. President Tyler signed the bill offering Texas statehood three days before the expiration of his term in office. Tyler and his secretary of state, John C. Calhoun, had worked very hard to achieve the acquisition of Texas. Subsequently, the proposed statehood was approved by the voters in Texas. The newly independent Texas claimed a vast additional area, thinly populated by Native Americans and Mexican settlers. Polk went to war over the disputed boundary of Texas. It might be fairer, therefore, to credit the little-known President Tyler with the smaller version of Texas (Texas as it was when part of Mexico), and Polk with the disputed area.

Contemporaries often explained and justified the expansion of the U.S. in the 1840s in religious and moral terms. Americans of the time sometimes claimed that the westward expansion of the U.S. simply realized its "Manifest Destiny"—that is, its plain, obvious destiny. In their frame of reference, American expansion implemented God's plan. Their religious argument went like this: just as ancient Israel had a providential mission to nurture ethical monotheism, so the modern U.S. had a providential mission to nurture democratic government. In present-day terms, of course, the U.S. of the 1840s practiced a strictly limited democracy, since it enslaved millions of people and denied the suffrage to women, to most blacks even if free, and to tribal aborigines. Nevertheless, contemporaries both at home and abroad regarded the U.S. as a democracy, and its citizens celebrated democracy as a national ideal.

The term "Manifest Destiny" was first used in July 1845, a few months after Polk's inauguration that March. It appeared in an article on the Texas issue in New York's *Democratic Review* and soon became widespread.[1] That article appeared unsigned, but it has usually been credited to the prominent journalist John L. O'Sullivan. O'Sullivan envisioned expansion as a peaceful process: settlers establishing family farms. He would later criticize Polk's decision to achieve expansion by going to war and would therefore lose his position as a prominent Democratic party spokesman. The expression "Manifest Destiny" has also been attributed to Jane Storm, an ardent expansionist who wrote anonymously or under a gender-neutral pseudonym (C. Montgomery). She would later serve as a spy for the U.S. in Mexico during the war.[2]

Despite the appeal of the slogan "Manifest Destiny," imperialism did not in fact command a consensus among Americans. The two political parties of the day, Democrats and Whigs, divided on the issue. Polk's Democratic party, followers of Andrew Jackson, enthusiastically embraced national expansion. The Whig party, on the other hand, conceived of American development more in terms of qualitative economic improvement than quantitative expansion of territory. As Henry Clay (for many years the leader of the Whig party) wrote to a fellow Kentuckian, "It is much more important that we unite, harmonize, and improve what we have than attempt to acquire more."[3] To Whigs, national *improvement* meant building economic infrastructure, industrial development, public education, and moral reforms like restrictions on the abuse of alcohol. The historian Christopher Clark has distinguished between the two partisan goals, explaining that the Democrats, such as Polk, pursued America's "extensive" development, and the Whigs, such as Clay, its "intensive" development.[4]

GEOPOLITICAL CONTEXT

President Polk, a scrupulously observant Presbyterian, went to church every Sunday without fail. There was more to his foreign policy formation, however, than a religious belief in America's Manifest Destiny. His geopolitical strategy was also shaped by his deep-seated, visceral distrust of Britain. Polk had been nurtured in politics by Andrew Jackson and was perceived by everyone at the time as Jackson's protégé. Polk inherited Jackson's profound suspicion of British motives. The mid-nineteenth century, of course, witnessed an enormous British Empire growing larger all the time. Polk not only saw Britain as a rival in the Oregon Country; he also feared the British might take California from Mexico, if the U.S. didn't do it first.

Historians have searched British government papers in this period and have found no evidence that the British really pursued the acquisition of California. However, the British government did take an active interest in Mexican affairs, looking out for the interests of British private investors, including British holders of Mexican government bonds. In the 1830s and '40s the Mexican government ran perennial deficits. Wealth in Mexico was concentrated in a small class of landowners, who contrived to avoid much taxation. The largest landholder of all, the Roman Catholic Church, was exempt from taxation.

To finance its perennial deficits, the Mexican government sold "deferred land bonds." "Deferred" meant that payment of interest on the bonds was postponed. Upon maturity, the bonds could be cashed in for government-owned land in Mexico. The Mexican government did not make the bonds available to U.S. citizens because they worried about encouraging American settlers—that was a mistake they had made in Texas. British capitalists did not seem to pose such a danger. Mexico hoped to persuade British investors to buy deferred bonds for land in California, and further hoped that such a stake in California real estate might somehow legitimate the Royal Navy defending California against any U.S. takeover. Lord Aberdeen's government rejected the whole idea.[5] Discussion of the proposal shows that Polk's interest in California had already been discerned by foreign diplomats, if not yet by much of the American public.

POLK'S DIPLOMACY

The southern boundary of Texas, when it had been part of Mexico, had been the Nueces River. However, since their revolution, the Texans had claimed the Rio Grande as their southern boundary. After the annexation of Texas to the U.S., Polk decided to send an army, under the command of General Zachary Taylor, into the disputed area between the Nueces and the Rio Grande. U.S. lieutenant colonel Ethan Hitchcock, serving in General Taylor's Army, wrote this in his diary: "We have not one particle of right to be here. It looks as if the government sent a small force on purpose to bring on a war, so as to have a pretext for taking California and as much of this country as it chooses." Colonel Hitchcock was right.[6]

Much of the disputed area consisted of grassland, cattle-ranching country. However, Polk's invasion was motivated not only by a desire for the area itself but, even more, by his desire for California. At the same time that Polk ordered his army into the disputed area, he was also sending an emissary named John Slidell to Mexico City, charged with negotiating the purchase of the Texan disputed area for $2 million, the purchase of New Mexico for $5 million, and the purchase of California for $20 million. The presence of General Taylor's army at the Rio Grande might intimidate the Mexicans into selling part of their national territory (even though they had consistently refused to consider doing so in the past). Alternatively, the invasion might provoke a war which Polk knew the U.S. would win. Meanwhile, Polk was also sending word out to California that if the American settlers there would start a Texas-style revolt against Mexican authority, the U.S. would welcome it and help them out. Although he could not be sure which of these three plans would bear fruit, the president figured that, one way or another, he could probably take California home.

If Polk had a preference among the three scenarios, it might well have been for war. He structured Slidell's diplomatic mission in ways that made it very difficult for the Mexicans actually to receive and negotiate with him. He appointed Slidell "minister plenipotentiary" to Mexico, meaning that his reception by Mexican authorities would constitute a resumption of full diplomatic relations with the U.S. Mexico had severed diplomatic relations in protest against the annexation of Texas. President José Joaquin Herrera, a moderate reformer, had recently offered to negotiate about Texas, but not to resume full diplomatic relations. Polk appointed as the second-ranking member of the negotiating team a man named William S. Parrott, whom the Mexicans knew to have been a U.S. spy and had declared unacceptable as an emissary.[7] If the Mexicans refused to negotiate at all with Slidell and Parrott, Polk could add this to his list of grievances to justify going to war.

Divining Polk's motives sometimes has to be done by inference. He was an unusually private man, who kept his goals and political plans to himself. James K. Polk had only two confidants, the first being his wife, Sarah. Sarah Polk was a thoroughly political woman, whom James had married at Andrew Jackson's prompting. The other person Polk trusted was George Bancroft, whom he made secretary of the navy. This represented a crucial position, because the navy had to be prepared, even before any declaration of war, to capture California.

Bancroft carried out Polk's wishes to perfection. In June 1845, almost a year before the U.S. declared war on Mexico in May 1846, Secretary Bancroft ordered Captain John D. Sloat of the U.S. Pacific Fleet, in the event of war with Mexico, to "at once possess [himself] of the port of San Francisco, and blockade or occupy such other ports as [his] force [might] permit."[8] When war came, Sloat obeyed Bancroft's order with alacrity and captured Monterey (then California's capital) on July 7, 1846, proclaiming California part of the U.S. without waiting for a treaty to confirm it.

George Bancroft was a New England intellectual with a German PhD, the greatest American historian who lived in the nineteenth century. Bancroft and Polk seemed an unlikely pair. But Bancroft shared Polk's vision of America's Manifest Destiny to expand. It expressed Bancroft's version of the romantic nationalism that he had acquired in Germany. Bancroft also shared Polk's suspicion and jealousy of the British Empire. After the California naval campaign had been prepared, Polk sent Bancroft off to be his emissary to Great Britain. The Oregon Question had not yet been resolved, making this a critically important post. For his part, Bancroft had always dreamed of being the American minister in London, so he felt happy to trade a cabinet post for his next job.

Letters between Polk and Bancroft provide historians with valuable insights into Polk's policies; so do Bancroft's later memories. Polk also kept a diary while he was in the White House, which was not published until 1910. Polk seems to have expected that posterity would read the diary, so although the diary contains much valuable evidence, especially about what went on in Cabinet meetings, he was rather guarded in what he revealed there.[9] A rare statement of Polk's purposes comes from a private conversation Bancroft remembered long afterwards. "There are to be four great measures of my administration," the recently elected Polk confided to his friend. Slapping his thigh, Polk enumerated the resolution of the Oregon Question with Britain, the acquisition of California, the reduction of the tariff, and the establishment of an independent federal treasury with no ties to a central bank.[10] Polk achieved all of these objectives in the single term that he served, a stunning record of accomplishment. Three of the measures had figured in the recent election campaign. California, however, did not engage the American public until the *Washington Union*, a newspaper controlled by the Polk administration, began to encourage its acquisition in June 1845.[11]

In Mexico City, President Herrera refused to receive Slidell upon his arrival. Before long, however, Herrera was overthrown by a conservative coup that installed an army officer named Manuel Paredes. The new President Paredes and his officials realized all too well that their armed forces were unprepared for a major war, that their treasury was empty, and hopes for foreign aid illusory. Yet, whoever was their president, the public opinion of the Mexican ruling classes overwhelmingly demanded resistance to the insulting, bullying *yanquis*. So, like Herrera, Paredes refused to negotiate with Slidell, who told President Polk: "A war would probably be the best mode of settling our affairs with Mexico."[12] Slidell then returned to the U.S.

POLK'S WAR

General Taylor's army had to advance all the way across the disputed area to the Rio Grande before it could prompt violent resistance on the part of the Mexicans. The future general Ulysses Grant, then a second lieutenant in Taylor's army, described the process in his *Memoirs*: "We were sent to provoke a fight, but it was essential that Mexico should commence it. It was very doubtful whether Congress would declare war, but if Mexico should attack our troops, the Executive [that is, the American President] could announce, 'Whereas, war exists by the act of, etc.,' and prosecute the contest with vigor."[13] For a while it seemed that the invasion of the disputed area, which had failed to intimidate the Mexicans into selling territory, might also fail to provoke a war. The Mexican army watched but made no move to confront Taylor's army. In May 1846, President Polk became impatient and prepared a message to Congress asking for a declaration of war on two grounds: (1) Mexico had failed to make interest payments on $2 million in debts to U.S. bondholders. This was a weak justification for war, particularly since several U.S. states had defaulted on larger sums to foreign creditors just a few years before. (2) Mexico had refused to negotiate the sale of its territory. This was an even less legitimate ground for war.

But just as the president was about to send his message to Congress, word arrived that a Mexican force had finally ambushed an American patrol in the disputed area. Now Polk could make his message to Congress much stronger. The Mexicans, the president wrote, had "passed the boundary of the United States, . . . invaded our territory and shed American blood on American soil." Polk declared, "War exists by the act of Mexico herself, notwithstanding all our efforts to prevent it."[14]

When Polk's war message arrived at the Capitol, leaders of the Democratic majority in the House of Representatives attached a statement recognizing the existence of war with Mexico to an appropriation of $10 million for the troops at the front. Thus, they made it harder for the Whig minority to vote against war without also voting against support for the troops. On the key vote to join the two together, the Democratic leadership prevailed, 123 to 67. Once the two measures were combined, they passed 174 to 14, with 35 abstentions. The opposition of the old Federalist Party to the War of 1812 had seemingly led to its demise; the Whigs of the 1840s had no desire to repeat the Federalists' mistake. The fourteen irreconcilables, led by ex-president John Quincy Adams, all represented safe Whig constituencies. The abstainers, remarkably, included twenty-two Democrats.

Reluctance to embrace Polk's war with Mexico was stronger in the Senate. There, Whig opponents were joined by John C. Calhoun, now a senator from South Carolina. Calhoun had been an active agent in acquiring Texas, but felt no enthusiasm for California. Texas, which had legalized slavery, would strengthen its influence in Congress when annexed. But California, Calhoun foresaw correctly, would not embrace the cause of slavery. The South Carolinian feared that acquisition and statehood for California would tip the balance of power in favor of the free states. He was right.[15]

Initial votes in the Senate indicated that the war party commanded about 26 votes; the peace party, 20. Senators pointed out that, actually, Mexico had not declared war on the U.S. (She never did; the Mexican government simply resisted invasion.) Even some Democrats (including Thomas Hart Benton of Missouri and John Dix of New York) expressed doubt about Mr. Polk's War. Yet once the decision for war had been linked to supporting the troops, the senators went along with it, 40 to 2, with 3 abstentions. On May 13, 1846, Polk had the war he wanted.[16]

Critics of Polk's administration, both in his own time and since, have often accused him of waging his aggressive war out of a desire to expand slavery. As a Tennessee slaveholder, secretive about his purposes, Polk left himself open to this suspicion. That he compromised with Britain over Oregon while offering no compromises to Mexico might seem to confirm it. However, on balance, evidence seems to point rather in favor of the president's objectives being geopolitical rather than proslavery. Polk was primarily interested in expanding U.S. power all the way to the Pacific and checkmating the British Empire. His loyal subordinate George Bancroft claimed to be opposed to slavery in theory, while the opposition of Calhoun, undoubtedly the strongest supporter of slavery in American political life at the time, reminds us that if Polk did hope to expand slavery by taking over California, he misjudged the consequences of his policy.

Once engaged, the U.S. armed forces achieved extraordinary military success in winning a war across vast continental distances, in the face of formidable geographical barriers and a hostile population. Winning the war consumed two years, which seems short to us; we have become used to wars that last much longer than that. But their war took longer than the Polk administration had expected. One of the reasons why the president had been ready to provoke war was his belief that victory would be easy and quick and inexpensive. As things turned out, the conquest of Mexico cost the U.S. about thirteen thousand lives and a hundred million dollars, not counting pensions to veterans and widows. Far more soldiers died of disease than from enemy action. In relation to the numbers engaged, the war in Mexico was the deadliest war the U.S. has ever fought, because about one American soldier in ten died during its two-year span.

The American public followed the events of the war with the greatest interest. The new electric telegraph (demonstrated publicly in May 1844) facilitated the spread of news, and the eagerness of the newspapers to feed the public hunger for information from the battlefront encouraged more and more telegraph wires to be strung. Mexico had no telegraph lines; messengers therefore needed to carry the news across the Gulf to New Orleans, and then it could be telegraphed from there. The telegraph reached New Orleans before the railroad did, even though the railroad had been invented much earlier.

Although the papers were reporting U.S. victories, the American public did not by any means support the war unanimously. Opposition to the war appeared at once and increased as the war continued. Divisions over the war reflected party politics. The Whig party rallied opponents of the war in both North and South. Whigs believed the president had contrived an unjust war. They did not share Polk's enthusiasm for territorial expansion because they foresaw that North and South would quickly fall to quarreling over whether to introduce slavery into the newly acquired territories. A proposal to ban slavery in any lands that might be taken from Mexico, called the Wilmot Proviso, attracted much support in the North, and repeatedly passed the House of Representatives, but could never pass the Senate. In the midterm congressional elections of 1846–47 (each of the states held its own congressional election, at various different dates), the opposition Whigs gained seats and won control of the House of Representatives.[17]

Once the newly elected House took office, opposition to "Mr. Polk's war" (as its critics termed it) and its territorial conquests found voice in a young Whig congressman from Illinois named Abraham Lincoln. On December 22, 1847, Lincoln challenged Polk's claim that the war began on U.S. soil. With the logical organization characteristic of him, Lincoln ticked off his points: the spot where the armed clash took place was not really "American soil," but had been a part of Mexico recognized by treaty in 1819; its local population remained loyal to Mexico and fled when the U.S. Army approached; the U.S. citizens whose blood the Mexicans shed were soldiers in an invading army.[18] A month later Lincoln followed up this speech with another, even stronger, denunciation of Polk. In this address, Lincoln complained that Polk's justification for war was, "from beginning to end, the sheerest deception." Polk needed to remember that he sat "where Washington sat"—and that Washington was famous for telling the truth.[19]

While Lincoln was delivering his denunciations of President Polk for waging aggressive war, secret negotiations were already in progress to bring the war to an end. The American negotiator, Nicholas Trist, arranged a treaty of peace contrary to the instructions of President Polk. By the Treaty of Guadalupe Hidalgo, Mexico conceded to the U.S. California, the larger version of Texas, and everything in between. But President Polk had wanted to wait until the Mexicans had suffered longer under U.S. occupation before making peace; he expected they would then be willing to cede even more territory to the U.S.

Trist reached the opposite conclusion, that time was not on his side. A moderate political faction had come to power in Mexico, eager to end the war and turn its attention to long-deferred political and financial reform. Trist, on the scene in Mexico, understood this and chose to make peace while he could, lest a faction of populist irreconcilables called *puros* come to power. Some *puros* intended never to make peace, but to wage guerrilla warfare until the *yanquis* tired and went home without getting what they came for. Since communication with the White House took many weeks, Trist felt justified in relying on his own judgment rather than the president's. Polk was furious at Trist and had him arrested for disobeying orders, but reluctantly concluded that he would settle for Trist's treaty. (Trist had made the treaty attractive to Polk by providing that the U.S. should pay only fifteen million dollars for the lands taken; Polk had been willing to pay twenty million.) When the Senate learned about the treaty, they went ahead and ratified it. Although not prosecuted, Nicholas Trist received no salary for the period when he negotiated the Treaty of Guadalupe Hidalgo. Only many years later, after Abraham Lincoln had become president, did Trist receive his back pay.[20]

IN RETROSPECT

How should Americans today look back on President Polk's role in making war with Mexico? There is no doubt that the U.S. benefited enormously from his territorial gains, beginning with the discovery of gold in newly acquired California. Historical interpretations of Polk's presidency and his war with Mexico have varied across the generations, sometimes influenced by more recent events. Polk died three months after leaving the White House. For the rest of the nineteenth century and into the early twentieth, mainstream historians followed the Whig Party's interpretation and described Polk as waging aggressive war.[21]

The dominant attitude of historians toward President Polk changed around the time of the First World War. Historians then decided that it seemed a good thing that the U.S. was so powerful, and some began to give credit to Polk for making it that way. The belated publication of Polk's diary in 1910 provided his perspective on events. Justin H. Smith's two-volume work, *The War with Mexico*, published in 1919, manifested the new perspective.[22] An ambitious undertaking, based on extensive study of manuscripts, Smith's history celebrated President Polk and American Manifest Destiny. Mexican society and politics were corrupt and inefficient, concluded Smith; Mexico did not deserve to control Texas, New Mexico, or California. What seemed to some historians America's aggression, Smith believed, was in a larger sense progress. Justin Smith won the Pulitzer Prize for history in 1920.

But Smith's interpretation was challenged in the 1960s by a monumental biography of Polk written by Charles Sellers. In the first volume, dealing with Polk's prepresidential career, Sellers shows sympathy for the young politician as the spokesman for small farmers. In the second volume, however, dealing with Polk's presidential campaign and early presidency, Sellers is sternly critical of his subject's imperialist designs and the means by which he provoked war with Mexico while professing to seek peace. A third volume, originally planned to complete the account of Polk's presidency and the Treaty of Guadalupe Hidalgo, was never written.[23]

In the past half century, historical treatments of President Polk and his war have included both moral criticism and exoneration in terms of historical views of progress. Particular historians emphasize one side or the other; there is no consensus. I shall not undertake a detailed assessment of the historiography, but at least two fine historians—Thomas M. Leonard and Sam W. Haynes—have sought to take account of moral criticism while retaining sympathy for Polk and his aims.[24] Two particularly original approaches to the issues are those of Joseph Wheelan and Amy Greenberg.[25]

Our present volume is intended to consider America's wars in the light of the just war tradition. This tradition, which originated long before the war with Mexico, clearly condemns going to war for the purpose of acquiring territory. By this measure, the decision of the U.S. (more specifically, the decision of President Polk) to invade Mexico was clearly unjust. Many Americans deplored it at the time as unjust; in so evaluating it today we are not applying inappropriate standards of the present to an earlier time. If there were a contest to identify the most clearly unjust war the U.S. has ever launched, the war against Mexico would be a strong contender. As to the issue of *ius post bellum*, the Treaty of Guadalupe Hidalgo looks legitimate only by comparison with the greater territorial ambitions of President Polk. For decades after the war, the property rights of the formerly Mexican, now U.S., citizen inhabitants of the acquisitions were often breached.

There remains to consider *ius in bello*—whether the conduct of the American forces waging the war and occupying Mexican lands conformed to prevailing standards of justice. Their behavior varied a lot. Under the lax command of General Zachary Taylor in the Rio Grande theater of operations, illegitimate incidents occurred, for example the massacre of between twenty and thirty Mexican civilians by Arkansas volunteers in revenge for the killing of one of their own number.[26] Volunteers from Texas sometimes perpetrated reprisals for alleged Mexican crimes committed a decade earlier during the Texan revolution. In general, volunteer units were more prone to misconduct against civilians than soldiers in the regular U.S. Army.[27] Insurgencies occurred in both California and New Mexico after their initial occupations by U.S. forces. In Taos, New Mexico, sixteen captured insurgents were court-martialed for treason and murder, and hanged. Secretary of War William Marcy revoked their convictions, recognizing that they could not commit treason because they did not owe allegiance to the U.S.—yet all save one of the sentences had already been carried out.[28]

On the positive side, however, General Winfield Scott's occupations of Veracruz, Puebla, and Mexico City applied even-handed military justice to both U.S. military and Mexican civilian populations.[29] Scott was an informed student of military policy and understood the practical as well as ethical advantages of a just occupation. He assigned a guard outside every Catholic Church in occupied areas to prevent sacrilege by U.S. Protestant vandals and avoid alienating the local population. His occupation of Mexico City proved so efficient and benign that some middle-class citizens even came to hope that he would remain and govern their city indefinitely.[30] Back in Washington, the Polk administration wanted Mexican civilians to experience a harsh occupation, hoping they would then press their government to make peace and cede territory, and so preferred Taylor's laxity to Scott's law and order. The Polk administration wanted customs duties and taxes to continue to be collected, but turned over to the U.S. Army to defer the costs of occupation. Scott did in fact remit the duties, but not the taxes, which he allowed the local authorities to continue to spend on community upkeep. The wisdom of Scott's approach was vindicated by Trist's success in obtaining an advantageous peace treaty, but Polk eventually relieved Scott of his command and brought prolonged court-martial proceedings against him for political reasons. (Scott was a Whig.)[31]

President Polk's legacy involves not only the giant territories and resources his war conquered but also the way he went about pursuing his aims. Americans at the time could be already fully aware that Polk's methods in bringing on war with Mexico would have durable implications for national political life. Daniel Webster, a prominent Whig and former secretary of state, addressed the subject in its larger significance:

> Ordering the army to the Rio Grande was a step naturally, if not necessarily, tending to provoke hostilities, and to bring on war. . . . This whole proceeding is against the spirit of the Constitution, and the just limitations of the different departments of government. . . . No power but Congress can declare war; but what is the value of this constitutional provision, if the President of his own authority may make such military movements as must bring on war? . . . It was, as it seems to me, an extension of executive authority, of a very dangerous character.[32]

Polk did indeed pioneer a development in American constitutional practice that has gradually strengthened the presidency at the expense of congressional authority in war making and foreign policy generally. Webster's concerns remain as relevant today as when he voiced them in December of 1846.

NOTES

1. "Annexation," *Democratic Review*, vol. 17 (July 1845), 5.

2. Linda Hudson, *Mistress of Manifest Destiny: A Biography of Jane McManus Storm Cazneau, 1807–1878* (Austin: Texas State Historical Association, 2001), 60–62. This attribution is questioned in Robert D. Sampson, *John L. O'Sullivan and His Times* (Kent, OH: Kent State University Press, 2003), 244–45.

3. Henry Clay to John J. Crittenden, December 5, 1843, in *The Papers of Henry Clay*, ed. Robert Seager II (Lexington: University Press of Kentucky, 1988), 9:898.

4. Christopher Clark, *Social Change in America: From the Revolution through the Civil War* (Chicago: Ivan R. Dee, 2006), 205–6.

5. George L. Rives, "Mexican Diplomacy on the Eve of War with the United States," *American Historical Review* 18 (January 1913): 275–94.

6. Ethan Hitchcock, journal entry for March 26, 1846, in *Fifty Years in Camp and Field*, by Ethan Allen Hitchcock, ed. W. A. Croffut (New York: G. P. Putnam's Sons, 1909), 213.

7. Charles Sellers, *James K. Polk, Continentalist* (Princeton: Princeton University Press, 1966), 331.

8. Sellers, *James K. Polk*, 227.

9. James K. Polk, *The Diary of James K. Polk during his Presidency, 1845 to 1849*, ed. Milo Milton Quaife, 4 vols. (Chicago: A. C. McClurg & Co., 1910).

10. Polk's words and gestures, as Bancroft remembered them, are quoted in Sellers, *James K. Polk*, 213.

11. *Washington Union*, June 2 and 6, 1845.

12. John Slidell to James K. Polk, December 29, 1845, *Correspondence of James K. Polk*, ed. Wayne Cutler and James Rogers II (Knoxville: University of Tennessee Press, 2004), 10:449–50. On Mexican public opinion, see Timothy Henderson, *A Glorious Defeat: Mexico and Its War with the United States* (New York: Hill & Wang, 2007).

13. Ulysses S. Grant, *Personal Memoirs*, ed. Mary and William McFeely (first published 1885; New York: Library of America, 1990), 50.

14. *A Compilation of the Messages and Papers of the Presidents*, ed. James D. Richardson (Washington, DC, 1901), 4:442–43.

15. Ernest M. Lander, *Reluctant Imperialists: Calhoun, the South Carolinians, and the Mexican War* (Baton Rouge: Louisiana State University Press, 1980), 6–10, 62–63.

16. *Congressional Globe*, 29th Congress, lst session, 794–804.

17. See John H. Schroeder, *Mr. Polk's War: American Opposition and Dissent, 1846–1848* (Madison: University of Wisconsin Press, 1973).

18. Abraham Lincoln, "'Spot' Resolutions in the House of Representatives," in *Collected Works of Abraham Lincoln*, ed. Roy P. Basler (New Brunswick, NJ: Rutgers University Press, 1953), 1:420–22.

19. Abraham Lincoln, "Speech in the United States House of Representatives: The War with Mexico," in *Works of Abraham Lincoln*, 1:433, 439.

20. See Robert W. Drexler, *Guilty of Making Peace: A Biography of Nicholas P. Trist* (Lanham, MD: University Press of America, 1991).

21. For example, see James Schouler, *History of the United States under the Constitution*, 7 vols., esp. vol. 4 (New York, 1889).

22. Justin Harvey Smith, *The War with Mexico*, 2 vols. (New York: Macmillan, 1919).

23. See note 7.

24. Thomas M. Leonard, *James K. Polk: A Clear and Unquestionable Destiny* (Wilmington, DE: Scholarly Resources, 2001); Sam W. Haynes, *James K. Polk and the Expansionist Impulse*, 2nd ed. (New York: Longman, 2002).

25. Joseph Wheelan, *Invading Mexico: America's Continental Dream and the Mexican War, 1846–1848* (New York: Carroll & Graf, 2007); Amy S. Greenberg, *A Wicked War: Polk, Clay, Lincoln, and the U.S. Invasion of Mexico* (New York: Knopf, 2012).

26. An eyewitness account is in Samuel Emery Chamberlain, *My Confession: Recollections of a Rogue*, ed. William H. Goetzman (Austin: Texas State Historical Association, 1996; written 1855–61), 132–34.

27. On atrocities committed in this war, see Paul Foos, *A Short, Offhand, Killing Affair: Soldiers and Social Conflict during the Mexican-American War* (Charlotte: University of North Carolina Press, 2002).

28. Stephen G. Hyslop, *Bound for Santa Fe: The Road to New Mexico and the American Conquest, 1806–1848* (Norman: University of Oklahoma Press, 2002), 381–402.

29. Scott quoted his orders in *Memoirs of Winfield Scott, Written by Himself* (New York, 1864), 2:392–96, 540–46.

30. See John Eisenhower, *Agent of Destiny: The Life and Times of General Winfield Scott* (New York: Free Press, 1997), 307–8.

31. See Allan Peskin, *Winfield Scott and the Profession of Arms* (Kent, OH: Kent State University Press, 2003), 194–205.

32. Daniel Webster, "Public Dinner at Philadelphia," speech delivered on December 2, 1846, in *Writings and Speeches* (Boston: Little, Brown, 1903), 4:31–32.

FIVE

The Fractured Union and the Justification for War

Gregory R. Jones

The manner in which scholars understand the American Civil War is often contextualized in the "sectional crisis," a long process of distancing between the "North" and the "South." Of course, the primary issue between those two sections of the Union was the determination of the right to own slaves. Northern states began outlawing slavery in the late eighteenth century, but those in the South, with their reliance on plantation agriculture—namely cotton, tobacco, and rice—needed slave labor to preserve their profits. Of course, volumes of historical essays and books have explored these topics in far greater depth than is prudent here, but this context helps scholars better understand why, in fact, so many thousands of Americans on both sides of the Mason-Dixon Line felt the need to go to war with one another. Both sides could find justification for their actions by a variety of interpretations of natural and moral law, but when it comes to the time-honored tradition of just war, an ever-evolving doctrine with deep roots in Western historical tradition, the waters become ever murkier. Is it possible that both the Union and the Confederacy were fighting just wars? If not, which side was in the right? If so, what does it mean that both sides in the conflict fought a just war? This essay asserts that the justification to go to war existed for the necessity to preserve the Union but that, as the war grew increasingly brutal, the justification for how the war was conducted and its aftermath were not justified.

The just war tradition gives scholars a vocabulary for discussing the complex developments of the Civil War. The elements of the tradition of just war, that of *ius ad bellum, ius in bello,* and *ius post bellum,* are interlocking moral criteria for understanding the complexities of war. They become central to breaking down a full understanding of the conflict due to the way that they help to illuminate complex concepts like motivations, combat conduct, and restoration of peace after the war. Further, because the mission of the Civil War changed as the war evolved in the minds and hearts of many Americans, including President Abraham Lincoln, it is evident that justification itself was a malleable concept. Yet, realizing the importance of the just war tradition in the context of the Civil War, we will find it helpful to have a way to better deconstruct how the circumstances of the devastating fratricidal conflict changed for the politicians, preachers, soldiers, and supporters who experienced the war.

A just war is not only about creating conditions of peace but also, just as importantly, about creating the conditions of justice. Explaining the systemic nature of slavery, Eugene D. Genovese writes, "Slavery, while it bound the South economically, granted it the privilege of developing an aristocratic tradition, a disciplined and cohesive ruling class, and a mythology of its own."[1] When folks talked of the "southern way of life," they meant more than just the institution of slavery; they meant also the economic and social system that revolved around plantation life and that held some Americans in bondage. For abolitionists confronting the brutality of slavery, the ownership of other humans was such a grave injustice that it superseded the need for peace. The rationales that John Brown gave for his attacks on proslavery advocates in Kansas and the federal arsenal in Virginia both speak to the view that justice is more important than peace. This is also why some characterize Brown as being a terrorist, even though in his mind he was acting out of a place of justice and conscience.

Harry S. Stout, a preeminent scholar of religious history and the American Civil War, provides a brief discussion of the intersection of the just war tradition and the Civil War in his book *Upon the Altar of the Nation: A Moral History of the Civil War*. In it, Stout explores a number of important elements of combat, confession, and compromise that characterized the war. His explanation of the postwar conditions, considerations, and justifications of the war seem particularly prudent here. "Such was the case with the American Civil War, in which each of two considerable populations came to the conclusion that war was their last best option. With this conviction, each side joined the battle convinced that its cause was just and that God was on its side."[2]

For Southerners, the election of someone they considered to be an abolitionist president, after several years of harsh sectional conflict over slavery, was itself an act of aggression. For Northerners, watching rebel militiamen occupy federal fortifications across the South (not just Fort Sumter in Charleston, South Carolina) was enough to get their blood boiling. When it came to justification, both believed themselves in the right. When the Union and Confederacy rallied two strong and diverse armies to fight one another, the emphasis on all being "right" in the fight helped to spur the war on to its brutal battles and contested conclusion.

Ronald D. Rietveld examines the intersection of Christianity and the American Civil War in Ronald Wells's edited volume *The Wars of America: Christian Views*. There, he discusses many of the moral issues of that war, including slavery. Rietveld concludes that the soldiers and their supporters on both sides of the conflict considered the pain of the war worthwhile, hoping that it would make the nation better in the end. But in order to get there, several moral controversies had to be settled. Rietveld explains that some in the mid-nineteenth-century world desired to make the world a better place through missions, science, the arts, and ultimately the American democratic experiment. To fracture the Union would hinder one of those central goals for thousands of Americans.[3]

Rietveld also highlights the significance of the perceived moral weight of slavery as it influenced the nation. What was once dismissed as the South's "peculiar institution" became an important national crime against humanity when viewed through the frame of African American human rights. Rietveld writes, "For most northern Protestants the issue was no longer focused alone on whether a local institution, though sinful, should be endured, but whether the nation could endure having southern iniquity pressed upon the entire country."[4] The man who was charged with dealing with that iniquity, carrying the torch of abolitionists before him, was the "redeemer president" himself, Abraham Lincoln.

According to Rietveld, it was Lincoln's own transformation that provides a looking glass for scholars grasping to understand the evolving nature of Americans' moral struggle during the Civil War. Rietveld explains that Lincoln understood both the need for atoning sacrifice—cued by John Brown's martyrdom on the Virginia gallows trying to incite slave rebellion—and the call for reconciliation and reunion. Without a heart for reconciliation, the war for the Union could not have been a just war. Allen C. Guelzo writes, in his masterful book *Abraham Lincoln: Redeemer President*, that the sixteenth president was a politician, not an intellectual; an Enlightenment thinker; and a classical liberal with a focus on liberty.[5] Lincoln's motivation was always the preservation of the Union. Lincoln's own wrestling with the war, especially *in bello* considerations such as the brutality of fighting, reflected a national feeling of a desire for justice that outweighed the weight of the violence needed to secure it.[6]

BACKGROUND FOR THE WAR

In the context of the Civil War, the future of slavery seemed irreconcilable between Northerners and Southerners. Despite repeated efforts to compromise in 1820, 1850, and 1854, the relative weight of slave and free states in the House of Representatives and the Electoral College continued to cause controversy.[7] President Lincoln and his supporters hoped that a legislative solution might be viable rather than the "last resort" of war. He famously even considered the schemes of the American Colonization Society, members of which wanted to transport African Americans to the continent of Africa, even though virtually all of them were born in the U.S. It was a fascinating proposed solution to a major regional and national problem. But despite these attempts to abolish slavery through diplomatic and legislative means, Southern slaveholders insisted on maintaining their right to own slaves. It took radical abolition and ultimately the force of the Union Army to free the slaves.[8] Even then it took several more decades to attain the type of justice that Brown and his radical abolition supporters such as Frederick Douglass,

William Lloyd Garrison, Thomas Wentworth Higginson, Samuel Gridley Howe, Theodore Parker, Franklin Benjamin Sanborn, Gerrit Smith, and George Luther Stearns had envisioned.[9]

Long before the shots began flying in 1861, there were complicated uncertainties during the sectional crisis, the time of division between North and South leading up to the Civil War.[10] The late 1840s brought the Mexican-American War and substantial territorial gain for the U.S. Not only did that war provide territory for the nation, but it also brought experience for a wide range of West Point–educated American soldiers. Those men found themselves often on opposite sides of the Civil War of the 1860s. One might say that the *post bellum* state of the Union following the Mexican-American War was fundamentally broken, especially with the transfer of a vast tract of land from Mexico to the U.S., which allowed the fervent debates of the sectional crisis to become ever more heated. As that residual effect in the aftermath of the war began brewing another war, thousands of slaves remained in bondage, hoping for an alleviation of their trouble.

But before the graybacks and bluebellies ever set foot on the battlefields of Virginia, violence erupted in other places across the Union. Most importantly, the bloody fields of Kansas became a dangerous fighting ground in the years leading up to the Civil War. One particular firebrand, John Brown, took to Kansas to represent the free-labor ideology in the face of proslavery advocates. Brown, some of his sons, and a few of his fellow abolitionists took a violent stand in the 1850s in Kansas as part of what is called "Bleeding Kansas." The fighting that transpired there, including a savage slaying of five slavery supporters at the Pottawatomie Creek Massacre by Brown and his associates, set the stage for a violent conflict over the issue of slavery. What many people failed to realize, though, was just how deep the conflict seeped into the consciousness of the nation. It was not merely a difference of political opinion. Rather, it was a fundamental disagreement on how to understand citizenship and freedom in the U.S.[11]

After the violence in Kansas, Brown remained an important historical figure as he began to plot a raid on the federal arsenal in Harper's Ferry, Virginia. His plan involved using the arms inside the arsenal to equip freed slaves with weapons of war, so that they might carry out their own war for liberation. It was an outrageous endeavor that seemed irrational to many people, but Brown found six important radical abolitionists to bankroll and support his efforts. In 1859, Brown carried out his plan and attacked the arsenal. He was not successful and some of his party were killed in the attack, and Brown found himself imprisoned and facing a death sentence for treason. He was later executed for his crime, allowing his legacy to live on as that of a martyr to the cause of abolition. In fact, as the Civil War began, Union soldiers sang, "John Brown's body lies a'mouldrin' in the grave, but his soul goes marchin' on," as they themselves marched into battle. Brown's legacy was that of a catalyst, sparking the Union war effort. For Brown and his abolitionist supporters, slavery was a violation of human rights and demanded intervention on behalf of the slaves.[12]

America's antebellum slavery took the French *Code Noir* (black code) to new levels, solidifying a race-based slavery that ensured people with dark skin would find slavery nearly inescapable, except for those few who purchased their freedom, were manumitted, or escaped. This race-based slavery became a defining feature of American life in the early nineteenth century. Even citizens living in Northern states, where abolition thrived, commented on the "peculiar institution" of Southern slavery. Very few people were willing to take action or attempt to help the slaves who had been in bondage for so many generations. Rather, the collective prosperity of the antebellum era seemed to obscure the vision of the American people to the extent that only religious zealots, such as John Brown and Henry Ward Beecher, or progressive philosophers, such as Frederick Douglass and Anna Elizabeth Dickinson, spoke loudly for abolition. Many others pocketed profits from direct or indirect slave trading, concocting beliefs of racial inferiority to justify the subjugation of an entire race of people. By the time the sectional crisis evolved to a point of actual, literal violence, thousands of people had a vested interest in maintaining the institution of slavery. It was a massive money-maker, despite its dubious moral status.

UNION AND CONFEDERATE JUSTIFICATIONS FOR GOING TO WAR

There was a regional context to the interpretations of Christian teachings surrounding slavery—namely, a division of North and South. While some scriptures from the Bible instructed slaves to be faithful to their masters, others pointed to the equality of all humans. Further, and perhaps fitting in the language of American civil religion, the Declaration of Independence proclaims that all men are "created equal." The differing opinions of interpretation on both scripture and the Declaration were the key elements to the fight between Union and Confederate soldiers years later. Notable Southern ministers such as Robert Lewis Dabney and James Henry Thornwell provided extensive proslavery arguments drawn from the Bible.

When the guns fired upon Fort Sumter in the spring of 1861, the Union fractured. It was not a neat and tidy split merely of North and South. Rather, communities fractured between abolition and slave. Church denominations, several of which had split in the decades leading up to the war, also found themselves broken and working on redemption. Communities, counties, and states split in their own unique ways around political, class, and even sometimes racial lines. These divisions in mid-nineteenth-century American life were powerful. Those communities, then, generated the soldiers who fought the war itself. They were the communities that sent off thousands of dollars of support for their volunteers as well.

Eventually the ideological divisions of the Union regarding slavery were mirrored within the South itself, but in the early stages of the war, the Confederacy was relatively unified around their cause of independence. The Confederate perspective before the war was fairly straightforward; politicians, farmers, and common folk in the Confederacy all saw the contested election of 1860 as a touchstone for secession. It was, in many ways, a kind of referendum on the issue of slavery. The election of the free-labor candidate, running on the Republican ticket, Abraham Lincoln, was, from the Southern perspective, a clear indication that abolition was coming soon.[13]

For his part, Lincoln had made it clear that he abhorred slavery, but that he did not plan to eliminate it in the South. In a speech in Peoria, Illinois, in 1854 he said, "Slavery is founded in the selfishness of man's nature—opposition to it in his love of justice. These principles are an eternal antagonism; and when brought into collision so fiercely, as slavery extension brings them, shocks, and throes, and convulsions must ceaselessly follow."¹⁴ He, like other Republicans, had indicated that slavery should not be permitted to spread further west into the territory gained in the Mexican-American War, but he did not support altering the rights of the American citizens living in the South. Yet those same Southerners believed that Lincoln had the confiscation of their property and abolition of slavery as a top priority of his presidency. The moral pressure was heavy due to a variety of opinions on the legal and moral legitimacy of slavery.¹⁵

Numerous Southerners had offered theoretical defenses of slavery in the antebellum era based on scripture, natural rights, and theories of white racial superiority, but the step from defending slavery as an institution to actually fighting for its survival was an enormous one. There was a fundamental moral clash between Southern slaveholders' belief in their right to own slaves and slaves' belief in their right to be free. Although not every Union soldier supported an abolitionist war, many did under the auspices of the very same Christianity that the Confederate soldiers utilized to defend slavery. There was no special revelation for the slaveholders, and an attempted biblical cover-up for an unjust economic scheme is fodder for an entirely different discussion. To put it bluntly, as Bertram Wyatt-Brown does, "The southern clergy ... consider[ed] slavery a condition of life like death and taxes—not to be celebrated but to be borne stoically and practiced humanely."¹⁶

The election of Lincoln did not carry quite the same weight for Northerners that it did for their Southern brethren before the attack on Fort Sumter. Rather, for many in the North, the 1850s had been a time of great prosperity. New railroads were crossing the country, with many communities seeing significant economic growth through commerce and sharing an overall upbeat perspective in economic terms. Social factors, such as Harriet Beecher Stowe's novel *Uncle Tom's Cabin*, had tugged on the heartstrings of many people in the antebellum North, who then voted more along abolitionist lines. But even as the abolition cause grew in importance, desire for abolition was far from universal in the North. In fact, many thought that Lincoln's election meant internal improvements of railroads and infrastructure far more than any sort of moral purge of the sin of slavery. John Brown and his supporters were in the minority among Yankees, not the majority.

Lincoln's electoral significance was different in each region of the nation.[17] As historian George Rable writes, "The legitimate election of Lincoln, the attempt of a minority to defy the will of a majority, and the southern attack on the flag all buttressed the idea that the Federal government and the northern people had right on their side."[18] For Southerners, quickly identifying as Confederates, the election of Abraham Lincoln marked a direct attack on the so-called Southern way of life. It meant that for Southerners, the justification for going to war was to preserve their own way of life, one that relied upon slavery, which they believed they could defend with the same Bible that justified the war. In fact, once the Union Army crossed the Mason-Dixon Line, Southerners believed they held the moral high ground for the rest of the war. The nation's later identity was forged in the fiery furnace of the Civil War. Advocates in both North and South turned the Civil War into a crusade more than a just war. The Civil War was not caused by religion, but religion certainly played an intensifying role.[19]

SEEKING JUSTICE IN THE MIDST OF CIVIL WAR

With rapidly modernizing technology, the early years of the Civil War saw significant casualties and a need to regulate the conflict on gentlemanly or, at very least, "civil" grounds. Historian D. H. Dilbeck makes a compelling argument in his book *A More Civil War: How the Union Waged a Just War* that the remarkable reality of the American Civil War was that the armies showed such restraint in midst of such utter devastation. Dilbeck's argument focuses particularly on the Union Army, but shows how elements like a westernized conception of civility and Francis Lieber's code for the conduct of armies helped to provide the rules of engagement for soldiers.[20] Lieber was a German-American scholar who sought to make sense of moral conduct in war. As a veteran of the Napoleonic wars, he wrote extensively in the nineteenth century about the need for restraint in war. His code, "Instructions for the Government of Armies of the United States in the Field," was signed by President Abraham Lincoln in April 1863.[21] A shorter name, simply "The Lieber Code," was frequently used. Soldiers followed this code to varying degrees in the latter part of the war as a moral guide for interactions with the enemy, civilians, and slaves.[22]

The Lieber Code was one of the most important developments determining moral conduct in the American Civil War. This code, a sort of amalgamation of key ideas about how soldiers should conduct themselves in war, emerged as an effort to curb the cycle of violence that characterized total war. The code became an internationally relevant and influential document, published in newspapers and explicitly addressed by officers as a means to control their troops.[23] As soldiers found themselves in conflict with ever-more-violent enemies, the lines of combatant versus noncombatant began to blur. Soldiers on both sides targeted homes, families, and especially the supplies of the opposing army. To the extent that General William Tecumseh Sherman targeted civilians and their property in his "March to the Sea," he was in violation of the rules of war. The targeting of civilians is very far from the kind of "just" war proposed by St. Augustine and the other Christian thinkers whose other writings seemed to resonate so powerfully with the soldiers of the North and South.[24]

One such example of unethical wartime violence that crossed the line from "war" into something even more barbaric came at Fort Pillow in Tennessee. Typically, when a soldier surrenders, his captors take him away. There, via the rules of war, he is to be cared for, at least minimally, until he can be detained for the duration of the war. In the case of Fort Pillow, however, a number of African American soldiers were fighting in the Union Army. Perhaps unsurprisingly, the Confederate soldiers capturing the fort demanded the surrender of the Union soldiers occupying it. After their surrender, Confederate soldiers massacred the surrendering black soldiers. Details of this story are contested, but there is little doubt that a horrific massacre occurred, something that undoubtedly breached the ethics of war. No one was ever charged for what happened at Fort Pillow, but the event remains one of the most significant actions outside of the laws of war.[25]

Proper conduct in the Fort Pillow circumstance would have been for the Confederate soldiers to take the soldiers, black and white, as prisoners of war. Michael Walzer writes, "Surrender is an explicit agreement and exchange; the individual soldier promises to stop fighting in exchange for benevolent quarantine for the duration of the war; a government promises that its citizens will stop fighting in exchange for the restoration of ordinary public life."[26] The failure of the conquering troops at Fort Pillow to fulfill this promise made the cycle of violence and mistrust increase in the Civil War. No longer were black Union soldiers willing to surrender in battle, instead preferring to press on and fight even more fiercely.[27] Fort Pillow also helped to influence General Ulysses S. Grant's policy not to exchange prisoners with the Confederacy, shifting the overall strategy of the war to attrition and away from Napoleonic victory.[28]

The just war tradition insists that military forces should attack military objectives, but from the beginning of the Civil War both sides targeted civilians.[29] For instance, when General Thomas J. "Stonewall" Jackson left the fields of First Bull Run, he did not merely retreat back to the Confederate capital in Richmond to build trenches and wait for Yankee attack. He formed his army and began marching, so quickly in fact that it became known as Jackson's "foot cavalry." Jackson used the speed of his infantry to effectively target the Shenandoah Valley as early as the spring of 1862. There the Confederates found supporters as well as those opposed, and all civilians found themselves receiving similar treatment from Jackson's men; animals and foodstuffs were taken for the good of the Confederate cause. Jackson, a devout Christian, regularly referenced his faith as a motivation and an encouragement to his soldiers. If the godly General Jackson ordered violence on civilians, who were his soldiers to question him? As Harry Stout observes, "As God's first warrior hero, Jackson's embrace of wholesale violence and Christian faith embodied the civil religions of both nations' leaders and commanders."[30]

Later in the war, General William T. Sherman reasoned that as long as Confederate armies could continue to live off of the land, including the ample "breadbasket of the Confederacy" in the Shenandoah Valley, those soldiers could stay in the field year after fighting year.[31] Sherman's solution focused on limiting the ability of the common people of the South to provide resources, willfully or not, to the Confederate Army.[32] Michael Walzer makes the explicit connection when he writes, "The Shenandoah valley was laid waste in the American Civil War, and the burning of farms on Sherman's March through Georgia had, among other purposes, the strategic goal of starving the Confederate army."[33] Burning farms and stealing resources prevented the rebel army from capturing those much-needed supplies for themselves.

If Sherman's reasoning for the "March to the Sea" was to regain territory lost by the sovereign U.S., he might have had solid justification for his attack. However, by the latter part of the war, the aims of the war had shifted with the subjects of emancipation and redefining American citizenship. But regardless of motive, Sherman's "March to the Sea" is an example of how even the Union Army committed acts that violated just war principles and helped to perpetuate an even longer cycle of violence that carried over into the violence of the Reconstruction Era through voter intimidation, the rise of the White League and Ku Klux Klan, and especially the proliferation of lynching. To put it into perspective, Stout writes that for Sherman, "the cause was just and indeed holy, but the conduct profane and disconnected to God and the suffering Savior. Sherman's religion was America, and America's God was a jealous God of law and order, such that all those who resisted were reprobates who deserved death."[34] According to Dilbeck's research, common Union soldiers saw the destruction of Sherman's infamous "March to the Sea" as welcome retribution for the Southern instigation of the war. Union soldiers "rejoiced" when Southern civilians in Georgia and South Carolina faced the "hard war" that their instigation had caused.[35]

Scholars have spilled much ink on the subject of total war because it was and still is such a hotly contested issue.[36] But it is important to remember that total war, by definition, is about more than merely targeting civilians by burning homes or stealing property for the purpose of winning victory in violent conflict. According to James Turner Johnson in his authoritative *Just War Tradition and the Restraint of War: A Moral and Historical Inquiry*, the cause in a total war must be ultimate, and there must be general popular support for the belligerent nations, a full mobilization of economic and manpower resources, and finally a disregard of the restraints on war. Of course, there were total wars at various points in history, including the example of the English Civil War, but on the topic of America's Civil War, Johnson elaborates on his definition with considerable precision: "The American Civil War, to which Lieber's works were in immediate reaction, was a national war in the more general sense of scope, scale and impact upon the belligerent populations, combatant and noncombatant alike. Both South and North endeavored, in different ways, to make the war intolerable for the civil population of their opponent as a means of drying up support for the armed forces and thereby shortening the war."[37]

The most significant Union effort to attack the noncombatant base of Confederate ability to fight was Sherman's devastating march, first cutting across Georgia from Atlanta to Savannah, then thrusting northward through the Carolinas. Johnson adds that Sherman's work changed the nature of the war. "Sherman's achievement made this war a total war, at least in its effect upon the South."[38] It also meant that there was a new precedent for the way that a war might work to target, for the sake of justice, the common people of a place. The specific targeting of civilian property, especially food and the ability to produce food, was central to the mission of putting down the Southern rebellion. Without this tactic the war might have continued even longer. It stands to reason, then, that the original strategy proposed in 1861 by the aged General Winfield Scott, dubbed the "Anaconda Plan," similarly targeted the "people" of the Southern rebellion. According to Scott's plan, in addition to fighting with the open-field tactics of Napoleonic war, the Union Navy would establish a blockade preventing European and especially British supplies from aiding the Confederacy in their move for independence. This "anaconda" would make its way up the Mississippi River via gunboats, effectively cutting the rebellious states in half and squeezing the life out of the rebellion itself. It was a strategic plan to attain clear military goals, but when put in conversation with the much-maligned plan of Sherman's March, it seems a similar targeting of the livelihood of ordinary people. This is why scholars must keep in mind Johnson's distinction that total war includes "general popular support" of belligerent nations; had the Southern people resisted the rule of Confederate leaders both in their home states and then in the Confederate capitol of Richmond, perhaps the war would not have become a total war. It was not, in fact, until the fall of 1864 that the tide began to turn toward surrender. Once the common soldiers of the Confederacy began to desert for home, it was only a matter of time for the fledgling nation to crumble with it.[39]

General Sherman's infamous observation that "war is hell" often comes across as trite. Who would know more about how hellish war could be than one of the hell hounds himself? Bringing an interesting twist to this description, Michael Walzer writes, "The sentence 'War is Hell' is doctrine, not description; it is a moral argument, an attempt at self-justification." Taken out of context, this statement could seem to show that Walzer strongly opposes Sherman's actions, but a bit earlier in his book *Just and Unjust Wars* he writes, "The experience of war as hell generates what might be called a higher ambition; one doesn't aim to settle with the enemy but to defeat and punish him and, if not to abolish the tyranny of war, at least to reduce the probability of future oppression."[40] The purpose of Sherman's March to the Sea was to make sure the Union won total victory in the South. The Union leadership did not want any lingering opportunities for "future oppression" of the former slaves or of the common people of the South. This moral angle on Sherman shows more than just a pride-filled, overly ambitious agenda for personal glory. It shows that Sherman's decisions, like those inglorious calculations of General Grant later in the war, were made with an interest in ending the war in a finalizing way. This, among other reasons, is why the U.S. has not experienced another civil war; the first and only one was sufficiently brutal as to ensure there would not be another.

Although it might be easy for us to look back on the brutality of the Civil War and stand in judgment of it, the people who lived through it saw it as a necessity. To them, the ends justified the means. In the words of one African American soldier who had a personal stake in the outcome of the war, "We prefer a disturbed liberty to a quiet slavery."[41] Because Southern slaveholders had proven themselves unwilling to give up slavery as political compromise, the use of force was the only way to restore what many abolitionists and their supporters deemed "justice" through emancipation.

No war is fought in a thoroughly just manner, yet the Civil War has more than its share of unjust tactics. Fort Pillow and Sherman's March to the Sea are only two of the most prominent instances of unjust strategies that come out of this conflict. Perhaps such an outcome is inevitable in a war that breaks apart families and pits brother against brother, particularly when each participant believes that God is on their side.

SEEKING JUSTICE AFTER THE CIVIL WAR

Once the guns fell silent at Appomattox Court House in April 1865, the difficult work of reconstructing the American South began. Of course, both Congress and the president intended to accomplish that great task in a number of ways, but it is important that scholars acknowledge that President Lincoln began thinking about reconstruction, and more importantly reconciliation, long before the fighting ceased. It was central to his thinking that the *post bellum* reality of the Civil War not be one that further debilitated the South, but rather one that restored it to a level of strength that would enable it to contribute again to the larger health of the Union. For many reasons, Lincoln did not want to see the South leave the Union in the first place; her valuable contributions to national economic and social character were certainly factors in Lincoln's reasoning.

Unfortunately, John Wilkes Booth assassinated Lincoln at Ford's Theater in Washington City in April 1865, thereby altering the course of whatever Lincoln had planned to reconstruct the Union. Instead, his vice president, Andrew Johnson, took the reins of power. Johnson, an antislavery Tennessean, had much to consider in the rebuilding of the South. The radical Republicans occupying Congress had their own plans for the country as well. This essay cannot consider in detail presidential and congressional reconstruction plans, but suffice it to say that the conflict over how to restore the peace was one that seemingly no one took lightly. The marquee problems that needed to be solved were the four million newly freed slaves awaiting their own "new birth of freedom" following emancipation, the physical restructuring of Southern cities destroyed in the fighting, and the substantial psychological rebuilding of the iconic Southern mind.

Taken together, the task of *post bellum* work in the former Confederacy was monumental, perhaps even impossible. The most significant aspect of *post bellum* life in the American South was the failure of emancipation for African Americans. Slavery was officially abolished with the Thirteenth Amendment to the U.S. Constitution, but the de facto slavery that developed in the region rendered the sacrifice of the Civil War nearly meaningless. Guelzo rebuts this argument in his book *Lincoln's Emancipation Proclamation* by asserting that no slave freed by the Emancipation Proclamation went back to a state of actual slavery.[42] If the whole point of the war was to keep the Union together, Guelzo points out, then the soldiers had accomplished their goal. But contra Guelzo, if the purpose of the war was, indeed, to end slavery without qualification throughout the Old South, then it failed because a new version of slavery emerged under the guise of the Reconstruction South.⁴³ As millions of Americans toiled on cotton fields and in big houses across the South, they found themselves out of options for a place to go. Many did not have the means, skills, or transportation to leave the region. Those who did found themselves rejected and discriminated against in their new homes in the Upper South, the North itself, and even in the West. Life for the sharecroppers and laborers of the black South was not a whole lot easier after the war than before, although Guelzo is correct that no one ended up in de jure slavery ever again.

J. Michael Martinez argues persuasively that the intensification of the black codes and the enforcement arm of the Ku Klux Klan actually made life worse after the war.⁴⁴ The former Confederates who donned the white robes of the KKK rode through the night, terrorizing the homes of African Americans in the South well into the middle of the twentieth century. Angry former Confederates and their white supporters destroyed crops, killed animals, and even lynched black people, causing a reign of terror that followed the end of "Reconstruction" and made the region a difficult place for blacks to live. Though freedom was a sweet respite for the former slaves, the weight of oppression took many more decades to fully remove.⁴⁵

It is ultimately unclear who was responsible for putting the postwar world in position to be successful. What more could Union officials have done to create a just and lasting peace? The Confederate leadership certainly wanted to establish what it considered to be a just and lasting peace, offering the chance to settle for peace and Confederate independence throughout the conflict. From the Confederate perspective, then, it was really a Union problem to insist that the war go on. Why not end the war, allow the Confederacy its freedom, and move on as two separate nations with two distinct ways of life?

From the Union perspective, highlighted by President Lincoln himself, it was the supreme charge of the U.S. Constitution to maintain the Union at all costs. To disrupt the Union itself, regardless of whatever issue might divide citizens from each other, was to contradict the years of hard work the founders and other Americans had done. So when

Congress and President Lincoln both sought to establish ways to rebuild the South in the wake of the war, they planned not only to rebuild the infrastructure but also to restore social order, issuing pardons for former Confederate officials and creating an entire organization—called the United States Bureau of Refugees, Freedmen, and Abandoned Lands, or "the Freedmen's Bureau" for short—dedicated to helping African Americans transition from a life of dependent slavery to a life of independent freedom. These constructs took time to build and develop. Additionally, Reconstruction mandated that the Union take care of hundreds of thousands of Union veterans, in various levels of fitness and capability, and help them work their way back into their ordinary lives. There was not much more the U.S. government could do without infringing the rights of citizens. The fact that there was very little tangible resistance in the American South until after the end of the occupation by Federal soldiers in 1877 is a testimony not only to the restraint of the occupiers but to a society that was willing to embrace healing in the wake of a brutal, schismatic war.

Students of the Reconstruction era quickly point out that by some accounts the Civil War never really ended. Of the thousands of Confederate soldiers who walked home in the spring of 1865, many had never desired to be a part of the Union again. The festering animosity continued well into the late nineteenth century, especially in the years when Republican-appointed government officials dominated state and national legislatures. For the former Confederates, seeing black politicians in states like South Carolina was the exact fulfillment of their "worst nightmare." These realities exacerbated the differences between the two sides, so that in 1877, when the election of Rutherford B. Hayes resulted in a backroom negotiation for national power, the Jim Crow era in Southern life really began to take hold. There in the postwar and post-Reconstruction world, the so-called Southern way of life that held African Americans in bondage reemerged as strong as it had been in the antebellum world. One might say that in this way, the *post bellum* conditions of the Civil War fell short of the restoration of justice and peace called for by the just war tradition. Although the Reconstruction Amendments made their way into the American Constitution, the de facto racism and destruction of black rights meant that the war, although militarily successful, failed its eventual goal for full and total abolition of codified slavery.

THE AMERICAN CIVIL WAR presented a moment when people were attuned to their significance in a larger narrative. Writers like Walt Whitman reflected regularly on the scenes of their lives. Even common farmers felt the need to write diaries or journals to document their part in the larger event of the war. Yet we find ourselves asking about the real significance of the war. What difference did it actually make? How can just war principles sharpen our focus on the meaning of the Civil War?

Maybe the best way to get at answering that question could come from Lincoln's own perspective on the war. Putting it succinctly, Guelzo writes, "Between the word of abolition and the deed of emancipation falls the ambiguous shadow of Abraham Lincoln."[46] Lincoln's reluctance to enter the war in the first place shows the restraining nature of just war thinking with great clarity. Lincoln knew that war was no small thing, yet from his perspective the Confederacy had forced his hand. After all, one of the main justifications for just war is to preserve a country's borders. The Confederacy had carved itself out from the borders of the U.S.; Lincoln, by that defense, had every right (including right authority as the freely elected president of a sovereign nation) to use military force to preserve the borders. Had the same claim been made to Southern lands by an outside nation, there would have been no doubt of a legitimate cause to go to war. As Johnson explains, "Preservation of the Union at all costs was the rationale enunciated by Lincoln in the American Civil War, and in spite of considerable political opposition this helped to produce a method of waging war that devastated the South as a means of subjugating the Confederacy."[47]

But as the war continued, Lincoln's idealistic hope that the war would end quickly did not come to fruition. Instead, he saw his most prized generals languish in defeat against the stalwart Confederates fighting to defend their homes. Lincoln reluctantly pushed forward an agenda of emancipation because he knew it was the central issue for the war, but also because he knew that adding an influx of free black and newly freed former slaves would support the war effort in unprecedented ways. As Rietveld observes, freedom for blacks was not equality, but it was not slavery either. Rietveld writes pointedly, "As a result of the Civil War, this nation experienced a 'new birth of freedom.' The process of birth, however, was accompanied by great pain and agony."[48]

The cost of war, in lives and limbs, is sometimes oversimplified in the history books, but it permeated life after the war with after-effects that resonate over a century and a half later. For men and women who might struggle with the notion of a just war ever being possible or important in society, consider Daniel M. Bell's observation that "loving and seeking justice for our neighbors in times of war is inextricably connected to how we love and seek justice for our neighbors in our everyday lives in times of peace."[49] This sentiment helps to identify and assess the work of those abolitionists who felt compelled to move toward violence. It was, for them, about more than fighting for the Union. Fighting for the liberation of slaves was a way to pursue "justice for our neighbors," and war was the only solution after the end of a horrifyingly inefficient time of attempting compromise. When Southern political officials refused to budge on the issue of slavery—which actually was the issue of the citizenship and human rights of African American people—they put themselves in the position of being oppressors. Any defense of the Southern way of life or slavery as a whole fails to consider that human rights were being systemically, massively violated throughout the American South. When abolitionists and their sympathizers stood up to that power, they took on a violent position which might seem contrary to the gospel but which accorded with just war reasoning in that by their violence they sought to right an injustice, bringing the human right of freedom to four million people who had that right taken from them for four hundred years. As Harry Stout more succinctly puts it, "I believe [it is] reasonable . . . to conclude that the right side won *in spite of itself.*"[50]

So, was the Civil War a just war from the Union or Confederate perspective? No war is entirely or purely a just war. Rather, wars can be placed on a continuum of injustice. In that sense, the Civil War was not a fully justified war for either side. Both found themselves acting in ways that were ethically questionable, occasionally taking actions that were absolutely brutal and inhumane toward their opposition. Although neither the Union nor the Confederate Army fought a "just war," the motivation for justice in freeing enslaved people remains a powerful legacy for four years of fractured union.

NOTES

1. Eugene D. Genovese, *The Political Economy of Slavery* (Hanover, NH: Wesleyan University Press, 1989), 34.
2. Harry Stout, *Upon the Altar of the Nation: A Moral History of the Civil War* (New York: Viking Press, 2006), xiv.
3. Ronald D. Rietveld, "The Civil War," in *The Wars of America: Christian Views*, ed. Ronald Wells (Grand Rapids, MI: Eerdmans, 1981; repr., Macon, GA: Mercer University Press, 1991), 93.
4. Rietveld, "Civil War," 102.
5. Allen C. Guelzo, *Abraham Lincoln: Redeemer President* (Grand Rapids, MI: Eerdmans, 2009), 21.
6. Rietveld, "Civil War," 110.
7. For a clear explanation of the North and South regional divide, consider Allen C. Guelzo, *Fateful Lightning* (Oxford: Oxford University Press, 2012), 48–49.
8. For more on slavery as a capitalist system, see Eugene D. Genovese, *The World the Slaveholders Made* (New York: Pantheon Books, 1969), x, 14–17.
9. For more on Garrison et al., see Guelzo, *Fateful Lightning*, 49.
10. For an excellent discussion of the myriad key issues during the sectional crisis, see Allen C. Guelzo, *Lincoln and Douglas: The Debates That Defined America* (New York: Simon and Schuster, 2008), xxv.
11. For more on the conditions in Kansas during the sectional crisis, see Guelzo, *Lincoln and Douglas*, 18–19.
12. Tony Horwitz, *Midnight Rising* (New York: Henry Holt and Company, 2011), 113–25.
13. For more on the context of Lincoln's election, see Michael Burlingame, *Abraham Lincoln: A Life* (Baltimore: Johns Hopkins University Press, 2008), 558–626.
14. Abraham Lincoln, "Peoria Speech, October 16, 1854." The speech is conveniently available from the website of the National Park Service, U.S. Department of the Interior, accessed September 3, 2016, https://www.nps.gov/liho/learn/historyculture/peoriaspeech.htm, which reproduces the speech from vol. 2 of *The Collected Works of Abraham Lincoln*, ed. Roy P. Basler (Springfield, IL: Abraham Lincoln Association, 1953; New Brunswick, NJ: 1953), also available online at https://quod.lib.umich.edu/l/lincoln/.
15. Abraham Lincoln to Horace Greeley, August 22, 1862, *Lincoln's Writings: The Multimedia Edition*, website of House Divided: The Civil War Research Engine at Dickinson College, accessed June 27, 2016, http://house

divided.dickinson.edu/sites/lincoln/letter-to-horace-greeley-august-22-1862/.

16. Bertram Wyatt-Brown, "Church, Honor, and Secession," in *Religion and the American Civil War*, ed. Randall M. Miller et al. (Oxford: Oxford University Press, 1998), 91.

17. James M. McPherson, *For Cause and Comrades: Why Men Fought in the Civil War* (Oxford: Oxford University Press, 1998), 128–29, 146, 176–78.

18. George Rable, *God's Almost Chosen Peoples: A Religious History of the American Civil War* (Chapel Hill: University of North Carolina Press, 2010), 53.

19. J. Daryl Charles and Timothy J. Demy, *War, Peace, and Christianity* (Wheaton, IL: Crossway, 2010), 154–56.

20. D. H. Dilbeck, *A More Civil War: How the Union Waged a Just War* (Chapel Hill: University of North Carolina Press, 2016), 3–11.

21. Francis Lieber, "Instructions for the Government of Armies of the United States in the Field," website of The Avalon Project, Lillian Goldman Law Library, Yale Law School, accessed September 3, 2016, http://avalon.law.yale.edu/19th_century/lieber.asp.

22. John Fabian Witt, *Lincoln's Code: The Laws of War in American History* (New York: Simon and Schuster, 2012), 2.

23. Witt, *Lincoln's Code*.

24. Stout, *Upon the Altar of the Nation*, xv.

25. Brian Steel Wills, *The River Was Dyed with Blood: Nathan Bedford Forrest and Fort Pillow* (Norman: University of Oklahoma Press, 2014).

26. Michael Walzer, *Just and Unjust Wars: A Moral Argument with Historical Illustrations*, 4th ed. (New York: Basic Books, 2006), 177.

27. James Turner Johnson, *Ethics and the Use of Force: Just War in Historical Perspective* (Burlington, VT: Ashgate, 2011), 143, 146.

28. James Turner Johnson, *Just War Tradition and the Restraint of War: A Moral and Historical Inquiry* (Princeton: Princeton University Press, 1981), 297, 312.

29. Walzer, *Just and Unjust Wars*, 190, 196.

30. Stout, *Upon the Altar of the Nation*, 73.

31. Wesley Moody, *Demon of the Lost Cause: Sherman and Civil War History* (Columbia: University of Missouri Press, 2011), 22–34.

32. Moody, *Demon of the Lost Cause*, 2.

33. Walzer, *Just and Unjust Wars*, 171.

34. Stout, *Upon the Altar of the Nation*, 371.

35. Dilbeck, *More Civil War*, 140–50.

36. Stout, *Upon the Altar of the Nation*, 139–49.

37. Johnson, *Just War Tradition*, 247.

38. Johnson, *Just War Tradition*, 247.

39. Mark Weitz, *More Damning than Slaughter* (Lincoln: University of Nebraska Press, 2005).

40. Walzer, *Just and Unjust Wars*, 31–32.

41. Lewis James as quoted in Chandra Manning, *What This Cruel War Was Over* (New York: Knopf, 2007), 197. Manning's volume is the best single-volume work on the centrality of slavery to the purpose and outcome of the war.

42. Allen C. Guelzo, *Lincoln's Emancipation Proclamation* (New York: Simon and Schuster, 2004), 8.

43. Douglas A. Blackburn, *Slavery by Another Name* (New York: Anchor Books, 2008), 7. For the authoritative account see C. Vann Woodward, *The Strange Career of Jim Crow*, 3rd rev. ed. (New York: Oxford University Press, 1974), 6–8.

44. J. Michael Martinez, *Carpetbaggers, Cavalry, and the Ku Klux Klan: Exposing the Invisible Empire during Reconstruction* (Lanham, MD: Rowman & Littlefield, 2007), 3–5.

45. Gaines Foster, *Ghosts of the Confederacy* (Oxford: Oxford University Press, 1988).

46. Allen C. Guelzo, *Abraham Lincoln as a Man of Ideas* (Carbondale: Southern Illinois University Press, 2009), 101.

47. Johnson, *Just War Tradition*, 268.

48. Rietveld, "Civil War", 114–15.

49. Daniel M. Bell Jr., *Just War as Christian Discipleship: Recentering the Tradition in the Church Rather than the State* (Grand Rapids, MI: Brazos Press, 2009), 20.

50. Stout, *Upon the Altar of the Nation*, xvi.

SIX

Just War and the Spanish-American War

Timothy J. Demy

The Spanish-American War of 1898 was the first international conflict the U.S. had fought with a foreign power since the Mexican War of 1846–48.[1] The war with Spain was short-lived—April 25 to August 12, 1898—three months, two weeks, four days. But at the end of the war and on the eve of a new century, the U.S. was decidedly an international power.

By the time the U.S. entered into conflict with Spain on the island of Cuba, ninety miles south of America's southern border, armed conflict and insurrection known as the Cuban War of Independence or the Spanish-Cuban War had already been occurring there for three years. That was itself a renewal of long-standing unrest after the "Ten Years' War" of 1868–78 and "The Little War" of 1879–80 on what the Spanish mistakenly termed "the ever faithful isle."[2]

The Spanish-American War was called "a splendid little war" by then Secretary of State John Hay, but was it a "just little war"? Its brevity and surrounding circumstances, when set against the backdrop of the era, do indeed make it a bit of a curiosity to most Americans with respect to America's military history, and yet small wars and conflicts have been a steady drumbeat in the nation's history of warfare from King Philip's War (1675–78) to the Invasion of Grenada (1983) and Operation Just Cause in Panama (1989–90).[3] Notable also for this study is the Philippine-American War (1898–1902), which arose in the aftermath of and as a direct result of the Spanish-American War.

To what extent at the time of the war did American politicians, citizens, and soldiers believe that they were ethically justified in going to war with Spain? And what can we say of the justice or injustice of America's participation in the war? What benefit, if any, can we derive from thinking about the war in light of the just war tradition? In this question the scholar is a bit like the referee who has the benefit of instant replay to evaluate a judgment call and also to overturn it (except that we have no ability to change the tragedy of the war). Brevity in war is never guaranteed, and though desired, it should not be something that trumps other ethical considerations for the employment of force.

Americans are now more than a hundred years removed from the war, and the passage of time should allow for a reasoned consideration of the war with respect to the just war tradition. History is about what happened in the past, what people think happened in the past, and what historians and others write about what happened in the past. Facts can be difficult enough to determine, but when one begins to assess and evaluate those facts, the truth can be difficult to discern. In his seminal treatise *On War (Vom Kriege)*, the great nineteenth-century Prussian military strategist and general Baron Carl von Clausewitz wrote of the "fog of war" that occurs in the midst of battle. Military historians and military ethicists routinely find themselves in a different "fog of war" as they study the precursors of a conflict, the actual conflict itself, and the postconflict environment. So, too, is it with the Spanish-American War and the just war tradition.

AN UNCERTAIN MEMORY

To the extent that most Americans know anything today of the Spanish-American War, it is likely limited to five fuzzy ideas: (1) the battleship USS *Maine* blew up in Havana Harbor, Cuba; (2) Teddy Roosevelt heroically led a group of soldiers called the "Rough Riders" (1st Volunteer

Cavalry Regiment) on a charge up San Juan Hill; (3) U.S. Navy rear admiral George Dewey had a naval victory of some sort at Manila Bay in the Philippines; (4) the present-day U.S. presence and military base at Guantanamo Bay has something to do with the war, and (5) there is a scene in the 1969 American western film *Butch Cassidy and the Sundance Kid* in which Butch considers the viability of surrendering to officials if they will drop all robbery charges against him and let him enlist to fight in the war. Regrettably, apart from the sinking of the *Maine*, none of those things helps in studying the justice of the war, nor is all of it completely accurate.

Interestingly, from the contemporary vantage point one finds in the conflict many components of subsequent American wars. These consist of but are not limited to regime change, insurgency, election-year politics, humanitarian intervention, occupation, exaggerated reports, massive suffering and death, prospects of civil war, questions of new nationhood, economic interests, forced removal of civilians from villages, religious overtones, journalistic sensationalism, European power plays, legal and illegal arms shipments, and questions of U.S. troops serving under foreign command.

One thing the brief war clearly demonstrates is the complexity and gravity of the political decision-making process by Congress and the president in any potential conflict. Writing of President William McKinley's challenges, the historian John L. Offner observes: "At home it was congressional partisan politics, economic and business concerns, religious and moral views, deeply rooted cultural biases, and unexpected events that inflamed American patriotism; abroad it was U.S. interests in Cuba, failed diplomatic efforts to get Spain to withdraw from Cuba, and relations with Europe's Great Powers."[4]

Before war was declared, American citizens knew of the ongoing conflict in Cuba between insurgent Cubans and Spanish military forces, but there was little objectivity in the sources from which they derived their knowledge.

In the lead-up to the war both Spain and the U.S. were involved in political brinksmanship with respect to what the Spanish would or would not do regarding their military operations and political actions in Cuba. However, once American lives were lost in Havana Harbor, the winds of war shifted.

JUST WAR THOUGHT AND AMERICA'S DECISION TO JOIN THE CONFLICT (*IUS AD BELLUM*)

Unlike the considerations for some protracted wars, most of the just war considerations for the Spanish-American War pertain to the decision to go to war. Once war was declared, the duration of the conflict was short, and much of it involved naval warfare in which concerns for noncombatants and proportionality were far less a factor than they would have been in ground warfare.

The four-year-old battleship USS *Maine* entered Havana Harbor on Tuesday morning, January 25, 1898, for what was designated an official and courtesy call and with full permission of Spanish authorities. The extended port visit was the first for the U.S. Navy since it had suspended port calls in Cuba after the outbreak of armed rebellion in 1895. Sailors and officers were allowed ashore in small groups, and for three weeks there was little indication of unrest as the *Maine* rested calmly at buoy 4 in the harbor. Then, on the evening of February 15 at 9:40, a tremendous explosion aboard the warship caused excessive fires and flooding such that attempts at damage control were performed in vain for the quickly sinking ship. The commanding officer, Captain Charles Sigsbee, shifted from his attempt to save the ship to attempts to save survivors.

Of 328 enlisted crew members, 250 died at the scene, 8 died later from wounds, and 54 were injured. Of the officers, 2 of the 22 were killed. Early on February 16, in a telegram sent to Sigsbee's senior officer at Key West, the *Maine*'s home port, Sigsbee stated, "Public opinion should be suspended until further report."[5] Although a Court of Naval Inquiry was established immediately, the press and the public were not as patient as Sigsbee desired, and the loss of the *Maine* became the final factor—as will be seen below—in an equation of war between the U.S. and Spain. Although the declaration of war did not come until after President McKinley and Congress received the navy's report, the public had few qualms about the decision to go to fight, and many did not believe it necessary for the naval investigation to be complete before doing so.[6] Indeed, some called for war long before the *Maine* sank. The Court of Naval Inquiry determined that the *Maine* had been sunk by the detonation of an external mine that subsequently caused the detonation of the ship's forward magazines. The later inquiries that would question and reject that analysis were still in the future, and many Americans believed the ship's sinking was ample justification for war. Once the findings were released (and leaked by the press before President McKinley could give them to Congress), diplomacy was sinking as fast as had the *Maine*.

In the calm waters of Havana Harbor naval diplomacy had become a naval disaster, and simmering sentiments for war against Spain on behalf of Cuban rebels boiled over as the U.S. opted for war rather than peace and a continuation of the status quo. By 2:10 a.m., on February 16, Joseph Pulitzer's newspaper *New York World* had word of the tragedy, and it broke the story that morning. Similarly, William Randolph Hearst learned of the story and instructed staff at his newspaper, "There is not any other big news. Please spread the story all over the [front] page. This means war."[7] And so it did. But there were other factors in the equation as well. Several factors are commonly thought important in the decision to go to war with Spain, the sinking of the *Maine* being the last.

What were the other factors? What was known at the time? What was "ground truth" before the sinking of the *Maine*? Few would have disagreed with Offner's assessment: "The essential ingredient was the deplorable condition of Cuba."[8] This condition was the result of years of fighting harsh policies of the governing Spanish authorities and military leaders. This in turn leads to consideration of the *first factor in 1898—the military successes of the insurgents.*

Years of conflict and unrest had devastated the island. The rebels who were seeking independence (and had been since 1868) were well organized and had broken out of the mountainous eastern part of the island and carried the second rebellion, which had begun in 1895, westward to the central and western provinces that were the heart of the island's agricultural economy. This second rebellion started during the second term of President Grover Cleveland (1893–97), whose administration saw little political benefit in overturning the political order in Cuba. However, "the Cuba question" would not go away politically and would be inherited by the President McKinley when he took office in March 1897. Poorly equipped Cuban insurgents attacked the economy rather than the better-equipped Spanish soldiers. The Cuban economy was predominantly agricultural and based on sugarcane as the primary cash crop. This also affected the U.S., where between 1897 and 1901, Cuban sugar exports to the U.S. accounted for 17 percent of all sugar imported to the U.S.[9] Any attack on this industry was bound to gain American attention. Rarely numbering more than twenty-five thousand and always operating in small groups, the insurgents "burned sugar cane fields and mills and destroyed railroads, telegraph lines, and other property. They sought to turn Cuba into an economic desert, thereby making the island unprofitable and convincing Spain to leave."[10] This affected outside investors in the U.S. and, for some political leaders, also ignited negative memories of other revolts and rebellions in the region's history as well as memories of the prejudices and effects of the recent American Civil War and Reconstruction era.

But of greater significance was the overall adverse effect the Spanish-Cuban conflict was having on the U.S. economy. Offner notes: "In 1895, the United States was suffering a severe depression that cut industrial production and employment and depressed agricultural prices, resulting in domestic unrest seen in strikes, riots, and protest marches. The Cuban wartime economic devastation added to the slump in some important U.S. businesses."[11] Trade with Cuba dropped by more than two-thirds, and import-export business leaders petitioned the administration to pressure Spain to bring the conflict to an end. Countering this, however, some American investors in Cuba condemned the rebels and favored peace but with a Spanish victory. Thus, U.S. business interests were divided but alarmed. However, for most Americans, the revolutionaries were seen as underdogs in an unfair fight. And they were meeting with success.

Earlier, during the Ten Years' War, Spanish forces had been able to contain the rebels to Cuba's eastern mountains. Now that containment was gone. Rebels attacked wealthy sugar and tobacco plantation owners. The Spanish Army responded by sending two hundred thousand troops to Cuba, as well as arming local volunteers. Under the leadership of Spanish general Valeriano Weyler (1838–1930), known as "the Butcher" because of his harsh methods of dealing with the insurgents, Spain achieved some success against them. But no victory was in sight for Spain. Weyler had hoped to defeat the insurgents in decisive battles but was unable to do so. This emboldened the rebels such that they rejected any overtures that provided for anything short of full independence. They would not accept autonomy under Spain, and Spain would not accept full independence. Both sides rejected a political middle-ground solution.

A *second factor* in the decision for war was the *brutal campaign carried out by Spanish forces against insurgents and insurgency sympathizers.* Unable to defeat the rebels in battle, General Weyler issued "reconcentration" orders on October 21, 1896, requiring the removal of Cuban peasants from their villages to cities and towns controlled by Spanish military garrisons. In so doing he was separating the rebels from sympathizers who provided them with food. Once the peasants, *reconcentrados*, were removed, Spanish troops burned the villages, razed the crops, and killed the cattle, causing agricultural production and foreign trade to plummet.[12]

Peasants were forcibly marched to the relocation areas designated to protect them, but upon their arrival, government authorities were unprepared to deal with the new population, and concerns for shelter, disease, sanitation, and food overwhelmed the peasants and authorities. Death and disease soon followed, and the event, receiving wide attention in the American press, became a public relations disaster for the Spanish. In early 1895 the population of Cuba was about 1,600,000, but during the war approximately 240,000 Cubans died from disease and starvation.[13] "While Weyler's order may have made sense from an amoral operational perspective, as the British and Americans resorted to similar schemes in South Africa, the Philippines, Malaya, and Vietnam, it generated a humanitarian and public relations disaster."[14] There were legitimate and exaggerated accounts of the suffering, and both fueled the call by many Americans for resolution or intervention.

American newspapers daily carried stories of the plight of the *reconcentrados*. A lead article in the *New York World* on May 17, 1896, proclaimed, "Blood on the roadside, blood in the fields, blood on the doorsteps, blood, blood, blood. The old, the young, the weak, the crippled, all are butchered without mercy."[15] A week earlier the same paper had carried a story characterizing Spanish policy as "murder by starvation" and declared "the extermination of a people" to be imminent.[16]

In June 1897 former congressman William Calhoun embarked on a fact-finding mission for the incoming McKinley administration and reported, among other things, that the "countryside outside the military posts was practically depopulated. Every house had been burned, banana trees cut down, cane fields swept by fire, and everything in the shape of food destroyed. I did not see a house, man, woman or child, a horse, mule, or cow, nor even a dog. . . . The countryside was wrapped in the stillness of death and the silence of desolation."[17] Calhoun told McKinley that neither side was willing to compromise and that although the U.S. could remain inactive and wait for the Cubans and Spanish to battle until exhausted, such inaction would do nothing to alleviate the suffering of the *reconcentrados*.[18] With reports such as this, calls for action by the U.S. on humanitarian grounds increased. What in the twenty-first century would become known as the "Responsibility to Protect" ("R2P") as adopted by the U.N. in 2005 was being voiced as legitimate grounds for war by many in the U.S. The responsibility to protect is a recent construct in international relations and international law arising out of the late twentieth century and early twenty-first century. An attempt to prevent humanitarian crises, the doctrine holds that there are no geographical boundaries for such responsibility and that when a state is unable or unwilling to prevent such a crisis, other nations are obligated to intervene on behalf of those in distress.[19]

The McKinley administration sought a diplomatic resolution with an American message to Spain that strongly condemned the condition of the *reconcentrados* and demanded Spain end its policies of brutality. McKinley gave an ultimatum of three months after which the U.S. would begin to intervene. While his emissary was en route to Spain, an anarchist assassinated the Spanish prime minister, and within a few weeks a new party took control of the government. The new party was more amenable to reforms in Cuba and moved toward autonomy that was to begin January 1, 1898. McKinley modified his stance and pressured Spain to accept the involvement of the American Red Cross in distributing food and clothing to Cubans. However, Cuban rebels rejected autonomy and continued to press for full independence even though an autonomous government began functioning on January 1, 1898. Twelve days later, riots broke out in Havana, and though the riots were quickly put down by Spanish authorities, there was concern that future outbreaks might harm U.S. citizens.[20] This was one reason McKinley sent the USS *Maine* to Havana Harbor. He wanted to move slowly and cautiously with respect to Cuba in hopes of avoiding intervention and conflict.

To the extent that Americans had an opinion of Spain, it was largely negative. They associated Spain with the Inquisition of earlier centuries and a cruel and decadent monarchy. Anti-Catholic sentiment was also strong, and Americans saw the conflict as the latest iteration of people in the New World throwing off the tyranny of the Old World.[21] The Protestant-Catholic religious framework in the American understanding of Spain's presence in Cuba was very strong and helped set the mood for American intervention as part of a larger theological plan of God.[22] In 1896–98, Americans read much about the plight of Cuban revolutionaries and about civilian noncombatants. This was due in part to the third and fourth factors in the equation of the U.S. going to war—good organization on behalf of the political arm of the rebels and sympathetic press in the U.S.

A *third factor* in the decision for war, then, was *a well-organized political campaign in the U.S. by the insurgents.* In 1892 Cuban nationalist José Martí (José Julián Martí y Pérez, 1853–95) founded the Cuban Revolutionary Party (Partido Revolucionario Cubano) with a goal of absolute independence for Cuba. The party advocated armed struggle against Spain and encouraged all Cubans to join the liberation fight. It was a key unifying force for veterans of the Ten Years' War and appealed to all classes and races of Cubans for support. Although Martí had reservations about U.S. interests in Cuba, he strategically placed the party headquarters in New York City, close to some of the nation's leading newspapers, and also had an office in Philadelphia and established a legation in Washington, DC. He spent many years before the war coordinating and mobilizing support for an independent Cuba among expatriates and other sympathizers in the U.S., Central America, and the West Indies.[23] The party raised funds, held "Sympathy Fairs," and engaged in an extremely successful media campaign of information warfare against the Spanish.[24] The solid political structure of the party and its methodical and persistent public relations campaign ensured that the plight of Cubans and the struggle for independence were never far from the front pages in the American press, and articles did not hesitate to draw parallels between the earlier struggle of American colonists against the British and the struggle of colonial Cuba against Spain. Such parallels, coupled with other events and perceptions, gave a sympathetic audience to the Cuban independence struggle and also prepared popular opinion for the call to arms against Spain.

A *fourth factor* in the decision for war was *a pro-Cuban leaning in much of the American press*—mainstream and otherwise.[25] Though much has been made of the sensationalism of the "yellow press" of the era (a term likely stemming from yellow ink), the press did reflect a bias for the rebels, and coverage of the conflict in Cuba was widespread. On February 9, 1898, the *New York Journal* published private correspondence of a Spanish official disparaging McKinley and the idea of autonomy for Cuba. In response, McKinley asked the Republicans in Congress to ask the State Department to release consular reports on Cuba. The reports were extremely graphic and critical of conditions in Cuba, and their release would provide justification for U.S. intervention.[26] However, before they could be released, the *Maine* exploded, providing the fifth and final factor in the equation for war.

With respect to the just war tradition, the usual elements of the *ius ad bellum* portion of the construct were present in the Spanish-American War. On both sides a legitimate authority formally declared war; and the U.S. had a very reasonable hope and expectation of success, recognized an overall proportionality of good over evil in the action, undertook the war with a good intention—namely, to bring about peace with justice (and also issued specific statements of nonterritorial war aims with respect to Cuba)—and viewed the decision to go to war as a last resort.

From the just war perspective, the primary historical question for this conflict is that of the legitimacy of the intervention by the U.S. on behalf of the Cubans. The just war tradition has long accepted the permissibility of intervention on behalf of those who are unable to defend or help themselves. But such intervention is not required. As Jean Bethke Elshtain notes: "Approaching humanitarian intervention through a just war lens means that such interventions, or their possibility, must be subjected to intense scrutiny and cannot be played out simply by appealing to compassion or to doing the 'right thing.' The just war tradition acknowledges the tragedy of situations in which there may be a 'right thing' to do on some absolute standard of justice, but no prudent or decent way to do it."[27] Elshtain also reminds all concerned, "No one can intervene militarily without getting blood on his hands."[28] Interestingly, Michael Walzer's 1977 landmark study of the just war tradition, *Just and Unjust Wars: A Moral Argument with Historical Illustrations*, declared: "Clear examples of what is called 'humanitarian intervention' are very rare."[29] He does acknowledge that there are instances of humanitarian intervention with "mixed motives," and he provides the cases of Cuba in 1898 and Bangladesh in 1971 as two examples. Walzer is, however, critical of the course and conclusion of the intervention in Cuba, and views it as a just endeavor poorly executed.[30] Indeed, at the time, the motives were mixed, but the suffering of the *reconcentrados* was a central concern of the McKinley administration.

On humanitarian intervention as a legitimate action in the just war tradition, James Turner Johnson acknowledges the viability of intervention but, like Elshtain, is wary of it, considering it a fragile concept as currently understood and applied in international affairs. Yet of its applicability within the just war tradition he writes:

> First, humanitarian assistance to the victims of conflict may be imposed by intervention even against the will of the conflicting parties, and there is *prima facie* obligation to do this.
>
> Second, intervention may involve the use of military force if this is necessary to achieve the purposes that justify the intervention....
>
> Third, both the provision of humanitarian aid and intervention by force may go forward even when they are not neutral in their effects on the conflicting parties. In practice, such assistance may favor one party against the other up to the point of *de facto* belligerence on the part of the intervening forces.[31]

The just war tradition does not view intervention as a disqualification for just war. Intervention is permitted, although just war proponents are wary of it and it has the potential of becoming a first resort rather than a last resort.

JUST WAR AND THE ONE HUNDRED DAYS OF U.S. CONFLICT ENGAGEMENT (*IUS IN BELLO*)

On April 11, 1898, President McKinley told Congress, "[I have] exhausted every effort to relieve the intolerable condition of affairs which is at our door"; he was therefore requesting authorization to intervene in

Cuba's conflict to protect Cuban citizens and "endangered American interests."[32] Congress consented and passed a joint resolution acknowledging Cuban independence and forswore any intention to annex Cuba. Congress also gave the president authorization to use any military force he deemed necessary. Spain responded by severing diplomatic relations with the U.S., and McKinley implemented a naval blockade on April 22, 1898, and issued a call for 125,000 volunteer soldiers on April 23, 1898, to augment the small U.S. Army. On the same day, Spain declared war on the U.S., and on April 25, 1898, the U.S. Congress voted to go to war with Spain. As the war unfolded, it was fought in two theaters—the Pacific (Philippines and Guam) and the Caribbean (Cuba and Puerto Rico)—with the major sites being the Philippines and Cuba.

Less than one week after the U.S. declared war, on May 1, 1898, it fought its first battle with Spain in Manila Bay, Philippines. By attacking the Spanish in the Philippines the U.S. was showing that more was at stake than disaster relief in the form of food and medicine. The American response would be robust and seek to be decisive. In this naval engagement the American Asiatic Squadron under the command of Commodore George Dewey (1837–1917) engaged and defeated the Spanish Pacific Squadron under command of Admiral Patricio Montojo (1839–1917). In about six hours, beginning at 5:40 a.m., Dewey's force destroyed all of the Spanish ships in Manila Bay. Spanish casualties were 167 dead and 240 wounded, and U.S. casualties were 8 or 9 wounded. Dewey then captured the small Manila Bay island of Cavite and blockaded the city Manila, the capital and most important city in the Philippines, while awaiting more forces (ground troops) to capture the city. On June 30, ten thousand troops of the U.S. Army VIII Corps known as the Philippine Expeditionary Force arrived under the command of Major General Wesley Merritt. On August 13 (unaware that a cease-fire agreement had been signed between Spain and the U.S.), U.S. forces attacked the city (in the war's last battle), in alliance with ten thousand Filipino nationalist troops under the command of General Emilio Aguinaldo y Famy, who had formally proclaimed independence and the Republic of the Philippines on June 12.

On June 10, U.S. Army troops landed at Guantanamo Bay, Cuba, and additional forces landed near Santiago on June 22 and June 24. Spanish Army forces were isolated and defeated, and shortly thereafter, on July 3, the Spanish Caribbean squadron was defeated in a naval battle off Santiago de Cuba as the Spanish attempted to break out of the American naval blockade consisting of five battleships (the *Indiana*, *Iowa*, *Massachusetts*, *Oregon*, and *Texas*) and a number of smaller ships but were overwhelmed by superior U.S. firepower. At the end of a four-hour naval battle the Spanish lost all of their ships through sinking or scuttling, and 323 of their men had been killed, 151 wounded, and 1,720 taken prisoner. The U.S. had one killed and one wounded.[33]

The ground campaign in Cuba did not go as smoothly as the naval campaign. Logistics, disease, flawed planning, lack of coordination, and miscalculation all affected the operational tempo of the fighting ashore. Fighting with pro-independence rebels led by General Calixto García, American forces engaged entrenched Spanish forces on July 1 in assaults at the Battle of El Caney and the Battle of Kettle Hill and San Juan Hill on the outskirts of Santiago. After these battles the advances and gains stopped, and U.S. forces decided to besiege Santiago rather than attack it—especially after General Shafter, commander of U.S. forces in Cuba, learned of the naval victory.[34] During the siege, fighting and losses continued due to combat and disease. The Americans permitted civilians to evacuate the city, and more than twenty thousand left and moved to El Caney, about four miles to the northeast, creating additional humanitarian needs. Some prisoners of war were also exchanged, and others released.[35] The siege continued until negotiations for capitulation of Santiago de Cuba could be completed with Spanish commander General José Toral y Vásquez, who surrendered to Shafter on July 17.

Toral y Vásquez surrendered after negotiations between the commanders and in consultation with leaders in Washington, DC, and Madrid. Significantly, the agreement allowed refugees to return to the city and provided humanitarian relief through the American National Red Cross via the relief ship *State of Texas*. In the aftermath, disease—primarily malaria and yellow fever—began to debilitate American forces, and this sped up the removal of many troops from Cuba, although soldiers in African American units were not immediately removed.

On many occasions during the brief days and weeks of fighting combatants on both sides tried to minimize damage and casualties and fight in accordance with accepted standards of conduct and perhaps even excessively exaggerated notions of honor. Combat was brutal, but both sides understood that it was governed by laws and limits.

On July 26, the adversaries began to discuss peace, and on August 12 they signed a cease-fire agreement. The war ended officially four months later on December 10, 1898, with the signing of the Treaty of Paris.

JUST WAR THOUGHT AND THE AFTERMATH OF THE CONFLICT (*IUS POST BELLUM*)

In the immediate aftermath of the conflict the military aspects in Cuba went smoothly. Repatriation of Spanish troops back to Spain was arranged, and transport was provided on Spanish ships with attention given to rations, space, and comfort of the troops. Likewise, in the Philippines the defeated Spanish were treated professionally. Less successful was the political transition. In both former Spanish colonies the U.S. refused to grant immediate full independence, and this created resentment among the civilian population and former insurgents.

In Cuba, the American occupying military government quickly established relief efforts, administrative reforms, and public works projects creating jobs and restoring and improving social services. The occupiers took particular interest in public health and education programs. Although transition to independence was not immediate, the cause for originally going to war loomed large in the collective military, social, and political American conscience, and the transition did progress and the final goal was never in doubt. Not so in the Philippines, where the situation quickly deteriorated into a new conflict wherein Filipino opposition to the Spanish was replaced with Filipino opposition to the U.S. and a very vivid reminder of Clausewitz's dictum "In war the result is never final."[36]

The U.S. had done little postwar planning, and evidence of the lack of preparation quickly arose. In the Philippines, this led to three years of unexpected conflict with Filipino nationalists in what became the Philippine-American War. By the time a formal end to fighting was declared on July 4, 1902, by President Theodore Roosevelt, more than 4,000 American troops had been killed and 2,800 wounded in the

Philippines, out of a total troop presence of 126,000 soldiers. The insurgents had lost between 16,000 and 20,000 people, the countryside was devastated, and an estimated 200,000 civilians had died. Sporadic guerrilla resistance also continued in remote parts of the archipelago for another five years.[37]

Throughout the conflict "brutality governed both sides as the fighting drew on and frustration escalated."[38] Especially brutal were the atrocities committed on the island of Samar.[39] For a variety of political and cultural reasons imbued with strong religious overtones of benevolence and destiny, the U.S. did not anticipate the insurgency that arose in the Philippines in the aftermath of the Spanish-American War.[40] Because of distance, lack of communications from the U.S., and inadequate knowledge of the Philippines on the part of Americans, the American citizens knew little of what was occurring there, and when they found out, many simply understood it as an aberration that would soon cease.[41] As a result, there arose a tragic irony in that the very problem that had developed in Cuba because of Spanish policies and that the U.S. had sought to stop there was now being repeated in the Philippines by the U.S. In fact, in April 1899, one New York publication observed, "The war of 1898 'for the cause of humanity' has degenerated . . . into a war of conquest, characterized by rapine and cruelty worthy of savages."[42]

BEFORE, DURING, AND AFTER the conflict with Spain there was concern for an unfolding humanitarian disaster among the Cuban civilian population. This was not the sole political interest of the U.S., but it was a dominant and oft-repeated one. It was written of frequently and prominently in government correspondence and the public press. Although conditions certainly were exaggerated by some citizens, politicians, and reporters, many Cuban citizens suffered and had to endure intolerable conditions. American motives for going to war were mixed (as is always the case in any conflict and with any entity engaged in conflict), but humanitarian intervention was a major and, for many, the predominant reason. From the outset American politicians stated that Cuban independence was part of the desired end-state.

An ethical evaluation of any conflict will yield one of four conclusions—that it was an unjust war fought unjustly, an unjust war fought justly, a just war fought unjustly, and a just war fought justly. Victors and vanquished will always argue the last of the options—that it was a just war fought justly. Yet ethical valuations are first and foremost those of individuals and the individual conscience. As with a stone cast in a still pond, the ripples may be many but the single stone is the cause. Military ethicist Thomas Grassey (a former colleague of mine at the U.S. Naval War College) often reminded students that good ethical decisions and determinations are based upon "all things considered." He noted: "Ethics is the study of what is the right thing to do, here and now, given the limitations of time and knowledge, all things considered. 'Right' of course must be defined with care."[43] What then might have been the just war ethicist's verdict at the time, and what is the call today?

The outcome of the war with respect to the U.S. as a rising international power should be viewed separately from the ethics of the war. That discussion is for political scientists, international relations experts, and historians of the late nineteenth and early twentieth centuries. For those interested in the ethics of war, the Spanish-American War was a just war. However, its aftermath was such that it excluded those for whom it had been fought and, in turn, generated further conflict in the Pacific theater of the war.

The ramifications of any war are many, often tragic, and occur on multiple levels. For that reason, no war should be entered into lightly or viewed as being like a game of chess. From the viewpoint of the Christian ethicist, war inevitably entails the suffering and death of individuals created in the image of God, and every war, just and unjust, is a tragedy.

The Spanish-American War reminds all who study ethics, history, and war that no war is final in the sense that time continues to move forward, and as it does, so too do the actions of political leaders as well as the consequences of those actions.

In February 1899, *McClure's Magazine* published a poem by Rudyard Kipling titled "The White Man's Burden: An Address to the United States," which welcomed the U.S. to the imperial enterprise. For some readers, the poem became an instant rallying point for anti-imperialism. For others, it was just the opposite. Debate about the poem and its meaning became controversial in itself. The poem also appeared in the London *Times* on February 4, 1899, two days before the U.S. Senate debate about annexation of the Philippines.[44] The ambiguity of the poem made it amenable to both sides of the annexation debate; however, most

Americans at the time received the poem favorably. Regardless of how one viewed the rise of the U.S. in the international arena of the new twentieth century, few people could have imagined the bloodshed that was over the horizon as the U.S. ship of state boldly sailed ahead.

NOTES

1. For excellent studies of the war see David F. Trask, *The War with Spain in 1898* (New York: Free Press, 1981); Albert A. Nofi, *The Spanish-American War, 1898* (Conshohocken, PA: Combined Publishing, 1996).

2. Interestingly, Russell F. Weigley's landmark study *The American Way of War: A History of United States Military Strategy and Policy* (Bloomington: Indiana University Press, 1973) mentions the war only briefly, and then only with respect to naval aspects and the thought of admiral and geostrategist Alfred Thayer Mahan, whose work *The Influence of Sea Power upon History, 1660–1783* (Boston, 1890) received worldwide naval attention and acclaim.

3. See, for example, Max Boot's *The Savage Peace: Small Wars and the Rise of American Power* (New York: Basic Books, 2002).

4. John L. Offner, "McKinley and the Spanish-American War," *Presidential Studies Quarterly* 34, no. 1 (March 2004): 50. See also his work *An Unwanted War: The Diplomacy of the United States and Spain over Cuba, 1895–1898* (Chapel Hill: University of North Carolina Press, 1992).

5. Telegram from Charles Sigsbee, cited in Douglas Carl Peifer, *Choosing War: Presidential Decisions in the Maine, Lusitania, and Panay Incidents* (New York: Oxford University Press, 2016), 18.

6. The Naval Court of Inquiry (often called the Sampson Court or Sampson Board after the name of its senior member) convened on February 21, 1898, and adjourned on March 21, 1898, formally providing its findings to President McKinley on March 24, 1898, after briefing him earlier on March 19, 1898.

7. William Randolph Hearst, cited in Peifer, *Choosing War*, 19.

8. Offner, "McKinley and the Spanish-American War," 50.

9. Rob Shafer, "Cuban Sugar," in *The Encyclopedia of the Spanish-American and Philippine-American Wars*, ed. Spencer C. Tucker, 3 vols. (Santa Barbara, CA: ABC-CLIO, 2009), 1:161.

10. Offner, "McKinley and the Spanish-American War," 51.

11. Offner, "McKinley and the Spanish-American War," 51.

12. Offner, "McKinley and the Spanish-American War," 51.

13. Offner, "McKinley and the Spanish-American War," 51.
14. Peifer, *Choosing War*, 27.
15. Cited in Peifer, *Choosing War*, 27. See also, John Lawrence, *Tone, War and Genocide in Cuba, 1895–1898* (Chapel Hill: University of North Carolina Press, 2006).
16. Cited in *Choosing War*, 27.
17. Cited in *Choosing War*, 27–28.
18. Offner, "McKinley and the Spanish-American War," 52.
19. See Charles Homans, "Responsibility to Protect: A Short History," *Foreign Policy*, online edition, October 11, 2011, http://foreignpolicy.com/2011/10/11/responsibility-to-protect-a-short-history/.
20. Offner, "McKinley and the Spanish-American War," 54–56.
21. Offner, "McKinley and the Spanish-American War," 52.
22. See John Edwin Smylie, "Protestant Clergymen and American Destiny: II. Prelude to Imperialism, 1865–1900," *Harvard Theological Review* 56, no. 4 (October 1963): 297–311.
23. On the life and work of Martí, see Alfred J. López, *José Martí: A Revolutionary Life* (Austin: University of Texas Press, 2014).
24. Peifer, *Choosing War*, 24–25.
25. Peifer, *Choosing War*, 26.
26. Offner, "McKinley and the Spanish-American War," 56.
27. Jean Bethke Elshtain, "Just War and Humanitarian Intervention," *Proceedings of the Annual Meeting of the American Society of International Law* 95 (April 4–7, 2001): 1.
28. Elshtain, "Just War and Humanitarian Intervention," 2.
29. Michael Walzer, *Just and Unjust Wars: A Moral Argument with Historical Illustrations* (New York: Basic Books, 1977), 101. Subsequent editions of the work have not changed this statement.
30. Walzer, *Just and Unjust Wars*, 102–4.
31. James Turner Johnson, *Morality and Contemporary Warfare* (New Haven: Yale University Press, 1999), 111.
32. William McKinley, "War Message to Congress, 1898," Digital History website, 2016, www.digitalhistory.uh.edu/disp_textbook.cfm?smtID=3&psid=1373.
33. Spencer C. Tucker, "Santiago de Cuba, Battle of," in *Encyclopedia of the Spanish-American and Philippine-American Wars*, 2:575–77.
34. Trask, *War with Spain in 1898*, 286.
35. Trask, *War with Spain in 1898*, 286–87.
36. Carl von Clausewitz, *On War*, ed. and trans. Michael Howard and Peter Paret (Princeton: Princeton University Press, 1976), bk. 1, chap. 1 (p. 80).

37. Joseph Smith, *The Spanish-American War: Conflict in the Caribbean and the Pacific, 1895–1902* (New York: Longman, 1994), 225.

38. Matthew McCullough, *The Cross of War: Christian Nationalism and U.S. Expansion in the Spanish-American War* (Madison: University of Wisconsin Press, 2014), 133.

39. See Brian M. Linn, "The Struggle for Samar," in *Crucible of Empire: The Spanish-American War & Its Aftermath*, ed. James C. Bradford (Annapolis, MD: Naval Institute Press, 1993), 158–82.

40. In addition to McCullough's work on religious overtones and motivations, for the Philippines, see Susan K. Harris, *God's Arbiters: Americans and the Philippines, 1898–1902* (New York: Oxford University Press, 2011).

41. McCullough, *Cross of War*, 138.

42. *The Nation* (New York), April 20, 1899, cited in Smith, *Spanish-American War*, 224.

43. Thomas Grassey, personal correspondence with author, March 16, 2009. Used with permission.

44. Harris, *God's Arbiters*, 129, 145. Harris's chapter "The White Man's Burden," 129–53, provides an excellent analysis of the poem's public and political reception in Britain and the U.S.

SEVEN

The Great War, the United States, and Just War Thought

Jonathan H. Ebel

This chapter examines the unlikely intersection of a trio of terms—just war thought, the Great War, and the U.S.—any two of which are an odd match. The relationship between just war thought and the Great War in history and historiography is strained at best. One can argue that because Germany moved first on the Western Front, France had just cause to defend itself from invasion in 1914, and on that basis one can make a compelling case that the French government would have been practically and morally remiss to do otherwise. From the perspective of the allied powers, the British entry into the war, to assist France and to work for the liberation of Belgium, was also just. Germany had violated Belgian sovereignty on its way to violating French sovereignty. Yet it is also true that these causes, however just, quickly eroded in a deluge of old animosities, imperial designs, and pornographic propaganda. The old enemies of restraint in warfare—Manichaean worldviews and holy war rhetoric—encouraged combatants to inflict and absorb losses grossly out of proportion with tactical and strategic goods. Beating back an invading army, a matter of existential urgency for any nation, may raise the threshold for proportionality to the point that the loss of one million lives or more is justifiable. But in the context of Great War–era France, one must also confront questions of ongoing intention (e.g., were French commanders only interested in restoring to France lands occupied by the Germans?) and proportionate means (e.g., could French and British commanders have accomplished their tactical and strategic goals with less loss of life?).

Today historians write of the "pity" of the Great War, describe it as a "religious crusade," and observe that the "fundamental tragedy of the First World War was that what was to a very large extent an old-style 'war of policy' to readjust the balance of power in Europe . . . became seen, because of mass participation and mass propaganda, as a total war between incompatible and mutually exclusive cultures, when in fact it need have been nothing of the kind."[1] To be sure, combatants justified their involvement in the war frequently and passionately, but one would be hard pressed to argue that they sought justice in more than its narrowest and most self-serving sense. The Great War is more at home as "Exhibit A" in the hall of mindless wars than in a discussion of the principled application of the just war tradition.

The U.S.'s relationship to the Great War is also awkward. The place that the war occupies in national culture, politics, and civil religion is undeniably, if also understandably, small. America's involvement in the war was brief. Congress declared a state of war with Germany on April 6, 1917. Small numbers of American soldiers entered combat in November of that year, but it wasn't until May of 1918, six months before the armistice, that there was a substantial American presence on the Western Front. Compared to most other combatant nations, the U.S. lost few soldiers: 116,516 dead, 204,002 wounded, with just over 56,000 killed in combat. These are large numbers, to be sure. (American combat deaths in the Great War approach the number of soldiers killed in Vietnam and occurred in the space of one year, not ten.) The losses were crushing for the families that bore them. But they represent less than 1.5 percent of casualties among the Allied Powers and not even 1 percent of the total casualties among all combatants. More importantly for purposes of explaining America's Great War amnesia, the noble aims that animated so many Americans were left unrealized. The allies gutted Wilson's plan for peace. The U.S. Senate rejected the League of Nations. Within fifteen years, the world was sliding from bad to worse to hellishly violent. The Great War challenges the faith many Americans maintain in our collective ability to know the world and to shape it in our image.

Finally, as a historical matter, the relationship between just war thought and the U.S. is decidedly mixed. Just war discourse has been established in the U.S. since the 1960s, a legacy of the work of people like Paul Ramsey, Jean Bethke Elshtain, James Turner Johnson, and Michael Walzer. Today, the just war tradition has many advocates in the military and in the academy, provides a common though contested framework for considering the moral dimensions of war, and is undeniably influential at the *in bello* level. The landscape was different in the Progressive Era. Just war thought was not an easily identifiable public presence. Evidence of American theological reflection on war and the exercise of power in the world dates to the early colonial period and can be traced through America's martial history. As James Turner Johnson has noted, from the time of the Civil War forward American thinkers were concerned about restraint in war, at least when the enemy troops were white men.[2] But these war-related ruminations and *in bello* concerns did not lead to a consistent concern for justice in the waging of war, much less an embrace of just war thinking. The self-evident justice of a pax Americana—wherever, whenever, and however it could be established—was often sufficient salve for the consciences of white Americans.

There are, however, more than historical oddities where these three mismatched terms meet. As I will argue, Woodrow Wilson's address to Congress requesting a declaration of war with Germany is shot through with evidence of just war thought. In that speech he repeatedly referenced six *ad bellum* criteria and relied on a reasoned, sober casuistry as the foundation for his lofty rhetoric. Wilson's opponents in Congress countered that the causes the president invoked masked the unrighteous intentions of powerful financial interests, and that because Wilson had his thumb on the scales of international justice, entry into the war was not a last resort. Wilson won the day, and the U.S. and its allies won the war. Yet the peace that American soldiers made possible fell far short of Wilson's hopes. The chasm separating *ad bellum* rhetoric and *post bellum* reality presents a significant challenge to just war traditions. If just war thought distinguishes itself from other approaches to war by its concern for justice in war and in peace, and by its position that state actors have a duty to work for and safeguard justice, what are the implications when a just war (or a war perceived as just) increases injustice exponentially? America's involvement in the Great War offers a cautionary tale with regard to the epistemological and agential presuppositions woven into just war thinking.

By the same token, American opponents of involvement in the war have little cause to rest comfortably on their side of history. Their arguments against intervention, arguments that had been aired elsewhere long before the Senate debates of April 1917, proceed from a perfectionist view of global politics and of justice and lead very quickly to no place in particular. For good reasons history has not been kind to the authors of the Great War, Woodrow Wilson included. But in considering the justice of American involvement in the war, we do well to recall that by intervening in the conflict Wilson and the American military helped create an opportunity for peace and justice where none existed previously, and to ask whether Wilson bears responsibility for the world's many failures when faced with that opportunity.

AN UNJUST WAR FOR AN UNJUST WORLD

When Congress authorized a declaration of war with Germany in April 1917, the U.S. joined a war already in progress. What began on the Western Front in 1914 with the German invasion of Belgium and France had by 1917 settled into a frustrating and bloody stalemate. The awful tragedy that the war became was evident to one prominent European observer in November of 1914. He wrote, "On every side the dread phantom of war holds sway: there is scarce room for another thought in the minds of men. The combatants are the greatest and wealthiest nations of the earth; what wonder, then, if, well provided with the most awful weapons modern military science has devised, they destroy one another with refinements of horror."[3] According to this writer, the war was consuming minds and bodies, upending reason, and corrupting faith. Modern instruments of power were directed not toward brotherhood and progress, but toward enmity and destruction. The distraught author of these words was born Giacomo della Chiesa in 1854. In September 1914 he emerged from the papal conclave as Pope Benedict XV.

Before looking at Wilson's war address and responses to it, I will consider briefly a wartime encyclical of Pope Benedict XV, spiritual leader of between 17 and 20 percent of Americans in 1917 and of large numbers of soldiers on both sides of the war. Pope Benedict's *Ad Beatissimi Apostolorum* reminds us of three important facts. First and most basically, the U.S. entered a war that by 1917 had a well-established moral trajectory. Already in 1914 Benedict was appalled by the "refinements of horror" and saw insufficient concern for justice (and for God) on all sides. For Benedict XV, the Great War was unjust, a tragedy, long before Verdun, the Somme, Gallipoli, or Passchendaele. Second, the bellicose nationalisms and holy war frameworks so common in Europe were not the only lenses through which citizens and soldiers viewed the war. Pope Benedict stood close to the Great War and condemned it fiercely. *Ad Beatissimi Apostolorum* is a searing jeremiad, condemning the warring nations for violating God's law, calling them back to righteousness, and describing the war as a sign of spiritual and political breakdown.

Finally, context matters when it comes to evaluating war. Pope Benedict had interests on all sides of the war, including above and beyond it. For Benedict, no shot fired on the Western Front was only a shot for good. Each shell that exploded added to the tragedy. Without a nation-state to defend or imperial loyalties to demonstrate and with Catholics in uniform on both sides of every front, it stands to reason that Benedict would condemn the entire enterprise and the era that spawned it. Yet three years later, when similar arguments emerged from critics of Wilson and American intervention in the war, they sounded less noble, even a bit provincial. Benedict had no tools at his disposal for shaping the war, much less bringing it to an end. The U.S. did, which of course does not mean that it was morally required to use them, but it does—along with three years of fighting and dying—cast a haze of irresponsibility over congressional opponents' demands to let the fires burn themselves out.

Benedict XV issued *Ad Beatissimi Apostolorum* in November 1914, just two months into his papacy. By that point it was apparent to him that his beloved community, both the Catholic Church and western Christendom more generally, had fractured in horrific ways. French

Catholics and German Catholics were killing each other; Austrian Catholics and Italian Catholics were doing the same. Almost all of European Christendom was murderously aflame. "Who would imagine," he asked, "they are all one common stock, all of the same nature, all members of the same human society? Who would recognize brothers whose Father is in heaven?" Benedict XV addressed the Great War directly in his encyclical but placed the conflict in a broader constellation of social and theological problems, in effect treating the war as the product of other sins. God's people had veered away from God's word, he proclaimed, and were reaping a whirlwind of chaos, violence, and tragedy.

In *Ad Beatissimi Apostolorum*, Benedict eschewed the casuistry of just war thought and adopted instead impassioned, covenantal tones. It is as if the question of the war's justice had such an obvious answer that any clear-eyed person could see it. To Benedict, the fundamental reality of the Great War was that it was an affront to God and to God's church. Yet the encyclical is not entirely disengaged from the just war tradition. The critiques Benedict developed and aimed at the modernizing West undercut the possibility of a just war by eviscerating claims of just cause, right intention, proportionality, and even legitimate authority. The pontiff saw disorder, disobedience, and corruption wherever he looked. Europe's leaders and soldiers could tell themselves that the conflict was just and that the suffering of the moment would lead to a more righteous world, but the state of society and of humanity demonstrated that these were delusions. The Great War was no struggle to save the world, Benedict argued. As he read the signs of the times, "the end of civilization would seem to be at hand."

Corruption and disorder were evident to Benedict in the hatreds proliferating between and within combatant nations. This spirit, he noted, was in direct violation of the Christian requirement of brotherly love, which flowed forward through history from Golgotha. "As [Christ] was hanging from the cross, He poured out His blood on us all, whence being as it were compacted and fitly joined together in one body, we should love one another, with a love like that which one member bears to another in the same body." This is the condition to which Christians were committed by virtue of their faith. In their lives however, brotherly love was tragically absent. "Race hatred has reached its climax," Benedict wrote, and "peoples are more divided by jealousies than by frontiers; within one and the same nation, within the same city there raves the burning envy of class against class; and amongst individuals it is self-love which is the supreme law over-ruling everything." In the midst of an epidemic of hatred, how could the intentions of a nation be just? With jealousy and self-love dividing society, how could similar engines of injustice *not* operate across national boundaries?

Benedict was also concerned that political and social authority were under attack and that the order and harmony that pleased God had been displaced by chaos and discord. He reminded his audience that, in the words of Paul to the Romans, "Whatever power then is exercised amongst man, whether that of the King or that of an inferior authority, it has its origin from God." This is a surprising statement from a pontiff distressed about war in Europe (the armies battling each other were, presumably, obeying authority figures), but the image he painted of the war is not one of legitimate authorities calling citizens to the justified defense of society. Instead, he described a disordered expression of violence on the battlefield and in the social and economic order. "There is no limit to the measure of ruin and slaughter; day by day the earth is drenched with newly shed blood, and is covered with the bodies of the wounded and of the slain."

As Benedict saw things, the war zone "slaughter" was matched in senselessness by un-Christian class conflict on the home front. He wrote, "And so the poor who strive against the rich . . . not merely act contrary to justice and charity, but also act irrationally, particularly as they themselves by honest industry can improve their fortunes if they choose." Evidence of the breakdown of authority could also be found in the church itself. Respect for the hierarchy and trust that it was working for the good of all was not, on his account, abundant enough. And so Benedict called for an end to dissent and disobedience in the church. The duty of the pope, he wrote, was to teach and command. "The duty of others is to harken to him reverently when he speaks and to carry out what he says."

Benedict then addressed a third sin of the Christian West, "desire for money," which was fueling the war, corrupting people, eroding values, and erasing restraint. This was relevant to the war as an indictment both of motives (regardless of stated intentions, the combatants were likely fighting for material gain) and of means (leaders and generals were willing to do anything to enrich themselves and their governments). Building quickly from 1 Timothy 6:10 ("For the love of money is the root of all evil") to a jeremiadic crescendo, Benedict wrote, "Once the plastic minds of children have been molded by godless schools, and the ideas of the inexperienced masses have been formed by a bad daily or periodical press, and . . . there has been instilled into the minds of men . . . that it is here, here below that he is to be happy in the enjoyment of wealth and honor and pleasure: what wonder that men . . . break down whatever delays or impedes their obtaining it." How could the society Benedict described, intently focused as it was on this world and on material gain, wage war for a just and durable peace? Even those who claimed otherwise were surely motivated by, in his words, "wealth and honor and pleasure."

Benedict XV was clearly heartbroken over social divisions, class strife, and the war that grew out of them. When he looked out on the world in November 1914, he saw chaos caused by disobedience and reparable not by violence legitimately conceived and properly directed, but by a return to God's will for the world. Shift the eyes of men and women to the "eternal goods" and "supernatural truths," diminish their "striving after the empty goods of the world," he argued, and "little by little social unrest and strife will cease." Benedict did not see justice anywhere in the war except, perhaps, in the justice of the suffering it brought to a disobedient, forgetful, careless people. He did not call on the faithful to fight for a just peace. Rather, he encouraged Christians to end the plague of war by embracing an older, orderly, more loving life.

Benedict XV expressed through his ecclesiastical office and in a theological register what many soldier-poets saw in the Great War: tragedy, confusion, disorder, and the breakdown of society. The apocalyptic tones of his 1914 encyclical are not out of line with the war's devastating, ongoing consequences for Europe and the Middle East. He also converges with modern secular historians, who tend to see very little justice in the war and a great deal of vindictiveness, greed, industrial violence, and rank stupidity. One recent work says of Benedict, "Throughout his papacy, [he] spoke and acted as modern observers might have expected a Christian leader to do."[4]

A RIGHTEOUS NATION AND A JUST INTERVENTION

Woodrow Wilson was also a Christian leader. Presbyterianism was almost as dear to him as Catholicism was to Benedict. Yet two and a half years after *Ad Beatissimi Apostolorum*, Wilson presented Congress with a compelling case for the justice of America's entry into the war. He directed the eyes of the nation to German viciousness on the high seas and German subterfuge in matters of diplomacy. He also described in soaring terms the greater cause America would serve by defeating Germany. Wilson's rhetoric, combined with his insistence on connecting American involvement in the war to the task of world redemption, make it easy to see his war address as a purely emotional appeal, an effort to preach a crusade. Like any good political speech, Wilson's war address appealed to emotions. He wrote in the penultimate section, "But the right is more precious than peace, and we shall fight for the things which we have always carried nearest our hearts—for democracy, for the right of those who submit to authority to have a voice in their own governments, for the rights and liberties of small nations, for a universal dominion of right by such a concert of free peoples as shall bring peace and safety to all nations and make the world itself at last free."[5] Critics note that these lofty phrases work better as poetry than as policy. Yet the speech was also logical and casuistic, indicting Germany for its violations and arguing that the U.S. must stand for justice. Even the rhetorical flourishes have overtones of just war thought. The notion that "the right is more precious than the peace," for instance, is one way of stating a central premise of just war traditions: the temporary violence of a just war is preferable to the enduring violence of an unjust peace.

The words Woodrow Wilson spoke before Congress on April 2, 1917, were calibrated to move America toward war, but he faced a challenging task in his address. Wilson was the leader of a racially and ethnically diverse nation. His constituency had many connections to the war, but had not for the most part been touched by it. Wilson had to justify entry into a war that posed no obvious threats to American security and brought no consistent danger to the lives of the vast majority of

Americans. What was at risk, Wilson argued famously, was liberty, decency, and the possibility of democracy. So he spoke capaciously, steered clear of the prejudices that reigned at so many other moments in his life, and appealed to the sense of civic duty and international responsibility that he hoped Americans felt.

Those listening to Wilson and those who read his speech could have been forgiven for thinking him a hypocrite as he called Americans to defend freedom abroad while he actively worked against freedom at home. Wilson was, like many men of his era and social origin, toxically racist and deeply distrustful of Catholicism. Born in 1856 to a proslavery southern Presbyterian minister, he would have been more at ease with racial and religious prejudices than others, and those prejudices would have been more difficult for argument or experience to eradicate. This does not mean that we should forgive Wilson, but does suggest that in evaluating him we do well to keep in mind words written by Reinhold Niebuhr in 1956: "We are all, whatever our pretensions, the children of our day and hour."[6]

In her recent study of the role religion played in Wilson's political thought, historian Cara Burnidge describes his negative views of Catholicism. Wilson believed that the Roman Catholic Church and its hierarchy shackled believers mentally and spiritually and encouraged forms of government antithetical to American principles. Burnidge quotes a letter that Wilson wrote while in law school in which he argued of Catholicism, "Its strength is used to exalt its power above the civil power, and its influence to unfit its adherents for intelligent or patriotic citizenship."[7] Given the persistence of anti-Catholic sentiments in Wilson's life, it is remarkable the extent to which his summons to war service—which generally qualifies as a high expression of "patriotic citizenship"—owes a debt to just war thought and the Catholic intellectual tradition. In arguing for America's involvement in the war, he repeatedly addressed six common *ad bellum* criteria: legitimate authority, just cause, right intention, proportionality, reasonable chance of success, and last resort. And while calling Germany to account for repeated, egregious violations of the principles of proportionate means and noncombatant immunity, he reassured Americans that their soldiers would adhere to the highest standards of *in bello* justice.

Wilson took little for granted in building the case for war, not even the legitimacy of his exercise of authority. From the outset of his address Wilson made it clear to the assembled senators and congressmen that he cared about and was acting in accordance with the Constitution. "There are serious, very serious, choices of policy to be made," he announced, "which it was neither right nor constitutionally permissible that I should assume the responsibility of making." He was no emperor, no Kaiser ordering troops into battle to settle personal scores or to satisfy blood lust. Wilson would act as commander in chief once a war had been declared, but first Congress had to make the declaration. Whatever concerns elected representatives or citizens might have had about Wilson's case for war, he was at least respectful of law and process. His words and his presence in the chamber stated this clearly.

Wilson then took up the question of just cause, describing at length Germany's "warfare against mankind." The Imperial German government, he lamented, had resumed unrestricted submarine warfare against shipping in the Atlantic. "Vessels of every kind, whatever their flag, their character, their cargo ... have been ruthlessly sent to the bottom without warning and without thought of help or mercy for those on board." This violation of international law was bad enough. Worse still were the casualties, "the wanton and wholesale destruction of the lives of noncombatants, men, women, and children, engaged in pursuits which have always ... been deemed innocent and legitimate." By pointing to German behavior on the high seas, Wilson recalled both the *Lusitania* sinking and his restraint in the face of public pressure to declare war. He thus subtly assured listeners, as he did at many other moments in the address, that the U.S. saw entry into the war as a last resort and was at the brink of war because Germany refused to discriminate between combatants and noncombatants *in bello*.

Maintaining international order, upholding the rule of law, and protecting the defenseless from violence is a solid troika of just causes. But Wilson buttressed his case further by addressing directly concerns that America's cause might be, at some level, unjust. "We have no selfish ends to serve," he announced. "We desire no conquest, no dominion. We seek no indemnities." And later in his address: "We act without animus, not in enmity towards a people or with the desire to bring any injury or disadvantage upon them." Of course, it is always possible that a leader is using a just cause as a pretense for an unjust conflict. Wilson assured listeners that this was not the case, and that his intentions in war—and the nation's intentions as well—would be right and proper. Far from a deceitful rush to war, the decision to fight against Germany would be "made with a moderation of counsel and a temperateness of judgment befitting our character and our motives as a nation." In the end, though, Wilson wanted it known that a declaration of war from Congress was not the beginning of hostilities with Germany, but rather a formal recognition of "the status of belligerent which has been thrust upon [the nation]."

Wilson also used his speech to announce that he was prepared to take every reasonable and legal measure to bring the war to an end. Fighting had consumed Europe since the late summer of 1914 with little progress and much dying on all sides. To change this, the U.S. needed to commit fully to the war effort. He thus called for the "organization and mobilization of all the material resources of the nation," "the immediate and full equipment of the Navy," "the immediate addition to the armed forces of . . . at least 500,000 men . . . chosen upon the principle of universal liability," and the "granting of adequate credits" both to the U.S. government and to the "governments now at war with Germany." All of these measures would, in the language of just war thought, create a reasonable chance of success.

The course that Wilson described for the nation was, in his words, "serious, very serious," and would certainly lead to losses of men and material. This is the nature of war. But in Wilson's eyes and in the eyes of millions of Americans as well, the potential costs were proportionate to the good he hoped war would achieve. The struggle itself—the thing toward which his casuistry was directed—was bigger than any one nation-state. It was a struggle between value systems and styles of governance. It was a struggle in which freedom itself hung in the balance. "Our object now," he explained, "is to vindicate the principles of peace and justice in the life of the world as against selfish and autocratic power and to set up amongst the really free and self-governed peoples of the world such a concert of purpose and of action as will henceforth ensure the observance of those principles." He continued, "Neutrality is no longer feasible or desirable where the peace of the world is involved and the freedom of its peoples, and the menace to that peace and freedom lies in the existence of autocratic governments backed by organized force which is controlled wholly by their will, not by the will of their people." The American blood that would be shed and the sorrow that would spread through American homes, towns, and cities had to be weighed against not just the rule of tyranny in a few far-off places, but against its contagion-like spread into a peaceful and peace-loving world.

At various points in his address Wilson alluded to the notion that war was a last resort, that other methods of confronting Germany had been tried and had failed. Having stayed distant from the war for as long as he did, and having for years frustrated American preparedness advocates, he had no difficulty making the case for last resort. Wilson did, however, remind Congress of his previous appearances before them, previous agreements with Germany, and the "moderation of counsel" that guided him and the whole nation. On Wilson's account, America's leaders were approaching the war as reasonably and as reluctantly as any nation had approached war before.

Wilson sprinkled references to *in bello* criteria throughout his address, mostly to demonstrate the perfidy of militant Germany. He described German submarine warfare as a "cruel and unmanly business," which demonstrated a "reckless lack of compassion or of principle." As noted earlier, he decried the targeting of "noncombatants" and of those "engaged in pursuits . . . innocent and legitimate," reporting that "there [had] been no discrimination" between types of ships or national origins. For those worried that involvement in the war would debase America's young men through coarsening violence or that, loosed from the restraints of home and peace, American soldiers might also prove to be "cruel and unmanly," Wilson argued that the young men going off to war embodied the same nobility of motive that suffused the nation. "Just because we fight without rancour and without selfish object, seeking nothing for ourselves but what we shall wish to share with all free peoples, we shall, I feel confident, conduct our operations as belligerents without passion and ourselves observe with proud punctilio the principles of right and of fair play we profess to be fighting for." A righteous nation would field a righteous army, willing to fight and die and win by the rules. In light of this case for the justness of American involvement in the Great War, Woodrow Wilson noted that noninvolvement was no longer an option for the U.S. "God helping her," he concluded, "she can do no other."

President Wilson's address to Congress and to the nation combined a legalistic argument that at least paralleled just war thought with emotional appeals based on familiar civil religious themes. According to Wilson, justice, history, and the divine were all calling America forward into the fight against an "irresponsible government which has thrown aside all considerations of humanity and of right and is running amuck." The case that he made was compelling, coherent, and ultimately convincing enough to bring a declaration of war. There was, however, resistance and debate in the Senate, featuring forceful refutations of Wilson's characterization of the international situation and of America's agenda in the war. From a just war perspective, the most interesting of these was put forward by Senator George W. Norris of Nebraska. Norris argued famously that the war was "unholy and unrighteous," that U.S.'s neutrality was a sham, and that Wilson had not done nearly enough to avoid entering the war.

Imbedded in Norris's assessment were two significant just war critiques. First, while he conceded that protecting freedom of navigation on the seas was just cause for war, he argued that America did not intend to fight for full freedom of navigation. Germany had indeed "flagrantly violated in the most serious manner the rights of neutral vessels and neutral nations," but Great Britain was every bit as guilty of the same violations. "The only difference," he argued, "is that in the case of Germany we have persisted in our protest, while in the case of England we have submitted." According to Norris, U.S. actions betrayed an anti-German agenda. American biases were shaped, he continued, by love of money. "We have loaned many hundreds of millions of dollars to the Allies in this controversy. While such action was legal and countenanced by international law, there is no doubt in my mind but the enormous amount of money loaned to the Allies in this country has been instrumental in bringing about a public sentiment in favor of [entering the war]." Taking a page from Pope Benedict's *Ad Beatissimi Apostolorum*, he upbraided those who looked at the war and saw financial opportunity. "Their object in having war and in preparing for war is to make money. Human suffering and the sacrifice of human life are necessary, but Wall Street considers only the dollars and the cents. The men who do the fighting, the people who make the sacrifices are the ones who will not be counted in the measure of this great prosperity . . ."⁸

Second, Norris argued that because the U.S. had not been truly neutral, war was not a last resort. Where the shipping restrictions were concerned, he noted, the U.S. could have acted differently, defying both Germany and England or protesting but respecting both. Better yet, he suggested, "We might have refused to permit the sailing of any ship from any American port to either of these military zones" and used an embargo to pressure the combatants to rethink their policies and the war more generally. Indeed, Norris offered that if the U.S. were truly neutral in its actions, the war would end quickly, as England would no longer be able to count on American supplies.

Senator Norris's primary interlocutors were the legislative and executive branches of the U.S. government. His call was for a deeper consideration of the nation's motives in the war, a more neutral neutrality, and a return to nonviolent approaches to ending the war. This was, no doubt, an earnest call issued by a man who wanted to spare his constituents and the nation the human and material costs of war. Yet for two reasons Norris's protests, though meaningful, are less than convincing from a just war perspective. First and most basically, his critiques presuppose a world in which it is possible to have no interests in war beyond the defeat of an enemy, and they require that before entering war a would-be combatant nation try every possible means short of war. This is one way to read just war thought, but it is out of synch with the tradition's many insights about the fallenness of the world, the sinfulness of humanity, and the real dangers of appeasement and/or inaction. Second, though at moments Senator Norris sounds like Pope Benedict XV, he is far less in touch than the pontiff was with the war as an ongoing human tragedy. As I read Norris, his case against intervening in the war was based on the hope that the fighting and dying would end somehow and that the consequences of that ending, whatever shape it took, would reflect back at the U.S. the neutrality that it showed European combatants. There are good reasons to doubt that either of these results—the expeditious end of the war, a postwar Europe hospitable to American values and concerns—would have come about had the U.S. done nothing.

Looking back from a vantage point sixty years in the future, Michael Walzer saw different reasons to critique Wilson and America's entry into the war. He argued that to the extent that Wilson's case for war relied upon the possibility of an unchecked "aggressor moving from one triumph to another, or . . . a radical increase in the incidence of aggression"—to use Wilson's words, "an irresponsible government which . . . is running amuck"—that case rested "uneasily on imaginings about which there is no general agreement and which often look painfully implausible after the fact." Walzer continued, "It seems very strange today . . . that any conceivable outcome of World War I could have been thought to pose a universal threat to peace and freedom (or a greater threat than was posed by the actual outcome)."[9] As Walzer and Senator Norris suggest, the fires in Europe might well have burned themselves out with no armed involvement from the U.S. Exhausted empires and battered nations might then have found a sustainable peace among the ashes. It is also possible that an ongoing war would have warped and distorted societies and their moralities into things even more grotesque than what emerged in Germany and Russia in the 1930s. History does not allow mulligans or let us run multiple scenarios to see which approach actually maximizes justice. But looking back not from Norris's or Walzer's worlds, but from ours—a world that now knows Rwanda, Syria, Sudan, and Srebrenica—we may wish to temper our estimates of human appetites for peace and our hopes that justice will, somehow, find a way.

Pope Benedict's words failed to steer the combatant nations toward peace. Senator Norris's did not persuade his colleagues in the Senate to reembrace neutrality. Wilson did not have the benefit of Walzer's hindsight, but American force did help bring a stop to four years of killing. Two million American soldiers and the promise of at least another two million gave renewed energy to the beleaguered allies. When the spring fighting season arrived in 1918, American troops played a pivotal role in halting the last German offensive and launching the series of counteroffensives that led Germany to sue for peace. The U.S. Army did not single-handedly save the day and, tactically speaking, was far from flawless in waging the war. But it was instrumental in bringing a horrific situation to a close.

ON HIS WAY TO THE Paris Peace Conference in 1919, President Wilson visited the Vatican and was received there by Pope Benedict XV. The visit, a first for a sitting president, seems to have been polite but, according to several accounts, was not especially comfortable. These were, after all, two men whose personal roles in the world were diverging and whose offices were changing rapidly as well. Circumstances were pulling the U.S. toward more frequent and more robust armed interventions in the world at the same time that they were pushing the papacy into a primarily ecclesiastical sphere of influence. Not only that, but each man had his own reasons—religious reasons—to be suspicious of or at least concerned about the other. Yet there they were, President Wilson carrying the flag of righteous, armed peacemaking into the presence of Pope Benedict, who had tried and failed to use the force of his religious office to establish peace.[10]

Pope Benedict XV and President Wilson saw the Great War differently. In Benedict's eyes the war was destructive, fratricidal, and unjust. In Wilson's analysis circa 1917, America was justified in entering the war both because of the relative moral strength of the allies and because of the dangers posed by Germany and by German-style aggression. It was important to Wilson to bring the war to an end and to see that the ending favored those who could be trusted to shape the *post bellum* world properly. This, however, is where he fell short. Wilson's fellow victorious leaders found ways to punish Germany into poisonous resentment. His chosen mechanism, the League of Nations, failed utterly in the U.S. before failing tragically in Europe. The power structures that the victors erected in Africa and the Middle East inscribed injustices that fester to this day.

In light of the chasm between war aims and outcomes, it makes sense to ask why a war effort that seemed just to Wilson and to much of the nation he led brought so much injustice into the world, and what the implications might be for just war thinking. To be sure, just wars do not ensure just outcomes. But since outcomes are particularly important in just war thinking, it is not unfair to ask if tragic outcomes in any way implicate the just war tradition as a form of statecraft. When it comes to the specifics of American involvement in the Great War, just war thinkers can argue in at least three ways that there are no negative implications. One could argue (a) that Wilson did not think within the tradition, (b) that he thought within the tradition but reached the wrong conclusion, or (c) that just war thinking is shielded from responsibility for *post-bellum* injustice by the dizzying array of contingencies and unknowns that follow war. I do not find the first of these historically satisfying, and the third is not morally satisfying. One cannot commit oneself to establishing a more just peace through war only to turn from such concerns when the shooting stops.

The second proposition—that Wilson reached the wrong conclusion about the war—raises questions of epistemology—how we know, evaluate, and judge—that challenge the very foundations of just war thinking. Was Wilson wrong in his assessment of the combatants? Was Benedict right that there was no virtuous side and no justice in the war? If Wilson was wrong, how could he have been more right? And if Benedict was right about the thoroughgoing injustice of the war, what do we make of his epistemology when it comes to the peace? The hierarchical order that Benedict described as the sine qua non of peace in Europe was shot through with injustices and violence that he either did not see or understood as an expression of God's will. The class and race struggles against which he railed were clearly distasteful to him, but the quietism and acquiescence that he preached in *Ad Beatissimi Apostolorum* were hardly recipes for justice.

Or perhaps the problem was not primarily epistemological—one of equating peace with justice, overestimating virtue, or underestimating vice—but was rather a problem of agency. Wilson may have been clear-eyed as to the justice of American intervention. He may have harbored intentions that were more or less free from the sins of which Benedict accused the modernizing West. He may also have found that in spite of a reliable knowledge of the good, he could not bend history to a morally acceptable shape. Did America join the war too late to alter its moral trajectory and shed too little blood to generate sufficient moral urgency on the home front? Was the problem really one of insufficient leverage? Or is the problem the very notion that something like sufficient leverage exists and can be deployed reliably in a world of contingency and accident and willful turns toward darkness?

The Great War and its aftermath are an enduring challenge to the epistemological and agential foundations of the just war tradition. Assuming that one can know enough, well enough to deem a cause just, to appraise honestly one's intentions, and to measure accurately the proportionality of hoped-for goods and certain evils, to what extent does the evaluation of a decision to wage war depend upon outcomes that will always fail to match our ideals? I end with this question not to imply that wars (or any state actions, for that matter) can only be justified by guaranteed outcomes. This would be to sacrifice engagement on the altar of contingency. Rather, I wish to take seriously Jean Bethke Elshtain's statement that "just war 'theory' is not philosophically abstracted from the doing of it."[11] To me, this means looking upon the failure to forge a just world—or even a tolerably peaceful one—out of the ashes of the Great War not as an indictment of Wilson and the specifics of America's just intervention, but as a reminder that humility and faithful introspection, qualities organic to the just war tradition, must suffuse all stages of conflict. And as an indication that Benedict XV, helpless to stop the slaughter, was prophetic in seeing the war not as the defense or culmination of civilization, but as something closer to its end.

NOTES

1. Michael Howard, "*Temperamenta Belli*: Can War Be Controlled?," in *Just War Theory*, ed. Jean Bethke Elshtain (New York: New York University Press, 1992), 28–29.

2. James Turner Johnson, "Contemporary Warfare and American Efforts at Restraint," in *From Jeremiad to Jihad: Religion, Violence, and America*, ed. John Carlson and Jonathan Ebel (Berkeley: University of California Press, 2012), 233–49.

3. Benedict XV, *Ad Beatissimi Apostolorum*, encyclical, November 1, 1914, website of the Holy See, http://w2.vatican.va/content/benedict-xv/en/encyclicals/documents/hf_ben-xv_enc_01111914_ad-beatissimi-apostolorum.html. All subsequent quotations of Benedict XV come from this encyclical.

4. Philip Jenkins, *The Great and Holy War: How World War I Became a Religious Crusade* (New York: HarperOne, 2014), 65.

5. Woodrow Wilson, "War Message," 65th Cong., 1st Sess., Senate Doc. No. 5, Serial No. 7264, at 3–8, *passim* (1917), last modified May 28, 2009, https://wwi.lib.byu.edu/index.php/Wilson's_War_Message_to_Congress. All subsequent quotations of Wilson come from this document.

6. Reinhold Niebuhr, *Leaves from the Notebook of a Tamed Cynic* (Louisville, KY: Westminster John Knox Press, 1990), 1.

7. Cara Burnidge, *A Peaceful Conquest: Woodrow Wilson, Religion, and the New World Order* (Chicago: University of Chicago Press, 2016), 28.

8. George Norris, statement to the Senate on April 4, 1917, *Congressional Record*, 65th Cong., 1st Sess., vol. 55, pt. 1, pp. 212–13, last modified July 7, 2009, https://wwi.lib.byu.edu/index.php/Senator_Norris_Opposes_U.S._Entry_into_the_War. All subsequent quotations of Norris come from this document.

9. Michael Walzer, *Just and Unjust Wars: A Moral Argument with Historical Illustrations* (New York: Basic Books, 1977), 238.

10. Joseph McAuley, "When Presidents and Popes Meet: Woodrow Wilson and Benedict XV,'" *America Magazine*, September 4, 2015, http://americamagazine.org/content/all-things/pope-and-president-benedict-xv-and-woodrow-wilson-are-there-any-catholics-here.

11. Jean Bethke Elshtain, "New Preface," in Elshtain, *Just War Theory*, xiii.

EIGHT

The United States and Japan in the Second World War

A Just War Perspective

Kerry E. Irish

> One who justifies the wicked
> and one who condemns the righteous
> are both alike an abomination to the Lord.
> —*Proverbs 17:15 (NRSV)*

On December 7, 1941, Imperial Japan attacked the U.S. at Pearl Harbor, Hawaii. The very next day President Franklin D. Roosevelt told the American people that December 7 would forever "live in infamy."[1] Congress quickly declared war on Japan. Adolf Hitler then led Germany, already at war with Great Britain and the Soviet Union, into war with the U.S. The vast majority of Americans believed, and today most Americans still believe, their unwanted war with the Axis powers was a justified and necessary response to evil acts and intentions on the part of

Germany, Japan, and Italy. Nevertheless, some scholars have defended the Japanese decision for war by arguing that the Land of the Rising Sun struck a blow in self-defense and in support of subjugated Asian peoples. Since just war doctrine allows for preemptive strikes in just such a situation, the question arises as to which of the belligerent powers were waging a just war? While the answer to the question is more complex than many Americans suppose, there can be no doubt that the salient historical facts support the traditional American view that their war was a just response to Japan's unprovoked attack and Germany's declaration of war.

Historians, especially in recent years, have attempted to tell the story of the Pacific war with little or no reference to moral issues. But such a telling of the war denies readers an answer to a rational and human question: who should bear the lion's share of the moral blame for the most destructive war in history? Just war theorists agree that in order for a war to be morally acceptable, a nation must have a just cause. Second, the war must be declared by its recognized political leadership. Third, there must be a reasonable chance to win the war. Fourth, a nation must have a just intent for peace. And fifth, the use of force must be a proportional response to the provocation.

Since the U.S. declared war by authority of its own long-established political system, that condition is met. And since Americans leaders believed they would win any war with Japan and did so, its prospects of success are established. This leaves three elements of the question for more in-depth analysis. The mere fact that the U.S. was attacked does not absolve it from the charge of waging an unjust war if the American government provoked the attack. The fourth point regarding intent for peace is easily demonstrated in terms of declared purpose, but subsequent behavior must be shown to have supported the declared intent. This is a significant point of contention.[2] And finally, did the U.S. respond to the Japanese attack with a proportional use of force?

ORIGINS OF WORLD WAR II IN THE PACIFIC

In regard to the origins of the war between the U.S. and Japan, were the Japanese justified in striking the blow at Pearl Harbor because the

Americans had forced them into this desperate decision? If so, the Germans may also be praiseworthy in coming to the aid of their Asian ally.[3] A survey of Japanese history in the Far East is thus in order.

In the mid-nineteenth century, Japan quite rationally resisted the Western imperial powers' attempts at forced trade until U.S. commodore Matthew Perry, in command of a formidable naval squadron, entered Tokyo Bay in 1853. His steamships belched black smoke into the peaceful air, and his well-armed diplomacy "opened" the land of the shoguns. The arrival of the Americans and Europeans initiated two decades of economic, social, and political turbulence in Japan that resulted in the Meiji Restoration of 1868. Under Emperor Meiji the Japanese decided to fight fire with fire. Impressed with Western military prowess, the Land of the Rising Sun set out to become a modern industrial military power capable of defending itself from further encroachment and, ultimately, able to insist on fair and equal treatment at the hands of their imperial tutors. Their success in this endeavor was astonishing. Unfortunately, the Japanese were not content to establish their proper and peaceful place amongst nations, but further desired to emulate the rapacious Western empires of the day as they sought to divide China amongst themselves. The Japanese victory over China in 1895 strengthened the imperialist impulse among the people of Japan. Over the next fifty years the Japanese maintained a steady course in the Pacific: adding to the empire whenever time, chance, and military superiority made success likely.

But the Western powers were not inclined to give up their empires upon the asking. When the Boxer Rebellion enveloped China in 1900, they all sent troops to protect their interests. Japan, too, contributed to the restoration of peace and profits. The Americans now took the lead in establishing a new vision for China. Following its twin pillars of freedom and capitalism, the U.S. proposed that the imperial powers refrain from further carving up the vast domain of China and recognize the territorial sovereignty of the tottering Han dynasty. Furthermore, the Americans proposed the startling notion that trade in China be free of imperial divisions: that is, that all nations have access to the markets of China irrespective of the existing spheres of influence. The imperial powers would have laughed at this idealism had it not been for the fact that Great Britain was prepared to make good the new policy.

The American Open Door policy was a complicated and controversial idea. Historians have argued over its intent almost since its inception. In the recent Spanish-American War (1898), the U.S. had liberated Cuba from the Spaniards but placed a cloud of American hegemony over the island. Furthermore, the Americans annexed the Spanish colony of the Philippines. Filipinos, along with many Americans, quite properly wondered at this strange interpretation of the word "freedom." The political backlash against new manifestations of empire, along with a sincere friendship for the people of China, and an even greater love for profit, led to the Open Door policy. Eventually, that policy took on a life of its own, a development its formulators did not envision; indeed, they had no intention of firing a shot in the interest of the Open Door. However, as time passed, the policy became a doctrine, a statement of the American vision for not only for China but also the world: free trade and self-determination.

The Japanese were less ambivalent and more aggressive in the eastern Pacific. They coveted Korea and Manchuria, as did the Russians, and in 1904 launched a surprise attack on the czar's fleet at Port Arthur, Manchuria. After humiliating the arrogant Russians, Japan annexed Korea, and then expanded its commercial interests in Manchuria at the expense of the Chinese, not to mention the Manchurians. In 1931, the Japanese occupied all of Manchuria. The Rising Sun was rapidly ascending.

The next target was China itself. By 1937, Adolf Hitler's Nazi state had alarmed Europe, the U.S. had deeply buried itself in isolationist neutrality legislation, and the Great Depression had weakened Western interest in the Far East. Emboldened, the Japanese struck northern China in July of that year, thus beginning the Pacific war—the Asian theater of World War II. This aggressive and brutal act brought Japan into direct conflict with the American Open Door policy.

As we have seen, the Open Door had become the American vision for China. In 1922 it received formal acknowledgment as part of the Washington Naval Treaty, and it was further ensconced in international law as part of the utopian Kellogg-Briand Treaty of 1928. Japan signed both documents. However, the U.S. still had no intention of fighting for the Open Door. The whole point of the treaties was to make war less likely, not to assert the point at which the U.S. would go to war. Consequently, when Japan invaded China in 1937, President Franklin

Roosevelt sent only paltry aid to China and a polite note of protest to Japan. Shortly thereafter, the Japanese emphatically announced that the Open Door was closed.[4]

The Japanese were well aware of pan-Asian resentment of Western imperialism. Thus, they rationalized their own aggressive behavior on the pretext of expelling the Western powers from Asia. In order to garner both the sympathy and support of other Asian nations, they promulgated the Greater East Asia Co-Prosperity Sphere (GEACPS) while presenting themselves as liberators. In 1939, Prime Minister Fumimaro Konoe declared Japan's purpose in China was to "save China from her traditional fate as the 'victim of the imperialistic ambitions of the occidental powers.'"[5] Indeed, many Asians, though decidedly not the Chinese, greeted the Japanese in that spirit.

The truth is that Japan was a brutal and callous overlord. In the summer of 1937, the Japanese army in and around Nanking engaged in an orgy of rape and murder. Even the Japanese admit that forty thousand Chinese civilians died; the more accurate number is over two hundred thousand.[6] Unfortunately, the events in Nanking were not unique. Koreans were sent throughout the empire to work as laborers, and thousands of Korean women were also sent abroad to satisfy the sexual appetites of Japanese soldiers. In an effort to feed their army in the Philippines, the Japanese took rice from Vietnam and starved a million Vietnamese to death.[7] The Co-Prosperity Sphere was so blatantly mere propaganda that many who had welcomed the Japanese turned violently against them. Burmese leader Ba Maw grew deeply disillusioned with what he called "the brutality, arrogance, and racial pretensions of the Japanese militarists."[8] Saburo Ienaga has written, "To call Japan's disgraceful and bloody rampage a crusade for liberation is to stand truth and history on their heads."[9]

The U.S. had also followed the course of empire in the first half of the twentieth century. The Filipinos and Hawaiians were the two most prominent peoples subjugated and held against their will. The Americans fought a bloody war against Filipino nationalists at the turn of the century to maintain their possession of the archipelago. But the crown of empire always sat uneasily on the American brow. For the next thirty years, Americans argued and vacillated over the fate of the Philippines. Meanwhile, the U.S. proved a relatively benign master. Though the

Americans insisted on economic advantages in the Philippines, schools and hospitals were built, malarial swamps drained, land reform initiated, and a modicum of self-government granted. Then, in 1929, President Herbert Hoover, determined to be a "Good Neighbor," revised American foreign policy along more friendly lines. His successor was still more determined to retreat from imperialism. Franklin Delano Roosevelt signed the 1934 Tydings-McDuffie Act, which promised independence to the Filipinos in 1944. America was in the process of dissolving its empire. Historian David Fromkin captures the thrust, or more properly, the retreat, of American foreign policy in the late 1930s: "The United States should have been mobilizing its armed strength to defend American democracy. But instead—paradoxically—Americans sought safety in showing the world that they had disarmed and in trusting the outside world to therefore leave them alone."[10] While Americans would have preferred to remain sonorously out of the coming war, Roosevelt was well aware that the U.S. could not survive in a totalitarian world. Thus, world events forced FDR's hand; he gradually decided to risk war with Japan rather than see the Japanese empire control China, the rest of the Far East, and most of the Pacific Ocean.

Three factors were preeminent in the president's change of mind. First was the surprising ability of Chiang Kai-shek's Chinese Nationalist forces to hold out against the Japanese army. Second, with Germany preeminent on the continent by June 1940 (the fall of France), colonial possessions of the conquered European nations lay exposed like low-hanging fruit to Japan. The Japanese took the French colony of northern Indochina that summer. Third, it seemed wise to Japanese leaders to ally themselves with the Germans in July of that year; hence the Tripartite Pact. It was this Japanese decision to identify with Hitler's hordes that convinced Americans Japan was the Asian Germany. Now Roosevelt decided that China might play a key role in safeguarding American interests in the Far East. In 1938, the Open Door had appeared dislodged, discarded by the master builders of the Japanese Empire; in 1941, Roosevelt saw an opportunity, with Chinese help, to rehang that door. Chiang was more than willing to be helped.[11]

Thus, FDR haltingly moved the American people toward confronting the Axis powers. Some historians have thus blamed Roosevelt for the war because he had gradually reduced trade with Japan in selected industrial and military products, and then turned off the oil spigot to the Land of the Rising Sun in the late summer of 1941. The president had been loath to do this for fear that Japan would indeed begin a major war. Once the Japanese realized the Americans had cut off their oil imports, they would have to decide on war or peace concessions. But the Japanese had created this dilemma for the American president. They had allied themselves with Germany and Italy, and they had moved their forces into southern Indochina in July 1941 as an obvious step toward the oil of the Dutch East Indies. Moreover, American oil was fueling the Japanese war machine, which was killing Asians daily. Thus, Roosevelt decided that the time had come to deny Japan oil. The U.S. was merely responding to the aggressive moves Japan had made in the western Pacific.[12]

Unfortunately, the Japanese persuaded themselves the Americans were an aggressive Pacific power. A Japanese High Command paper formally reviewed at a September 6, 1941, imperial conference proclaimed that the American vision was "to dominate the world" and, in so doing, "prevent [the Japanese] empire from rising and developing in East Asia." The paper concluded that Japan must initiate a preemptive war to "ensure its preservation," or "lie prostrate at the feet of the United States."[13] As we have seen, there was no basis for this view. Nevertheless, most Japanese leaders believed in a fiction they called the "ABCD" encirclement.[14] The ABCD label stood for the American, British, Dutch, and Chinese hostile surrounding of Japan. Historian Akira Iriye, in explaining the origins of the Pacific war, gives much credence to this alleged encirclement. Iriye goes on to describe the coming of the war in morally sterilized terms. For Iriye, the war was a great power conflict the Japanese were wrong to wage not because they were aggressive imperialists, but because they could not win and were mistaken in their belief that their empire could not prosper in an American-dominated Pacific world.[15] For Iriye, the ABCD encirclement gave Japanese leaders but two alternatives—war or submission to the U.S.: "Resistance [war] would at least safeguard the nation's honor, whereas submission would mean nullifying the achievements of the past ten years, to go back to the 1920s which had been defined by an American-led world order. An American imposed peace, in other words, was considered less desirable and honorable than a Japanese initiated war."[16] Though Iriye seems unconcerned about the moral questions the coming of the war raised, even he admits the Japanese were the aggressors. Then, too, just writing the ABCD acronym on paper implied more strength and purpose to the cooperation between those four powers than existed before the attack on Pearl Harbor.

Surely it is absurd to argue that the Chinese were part of an encirclement of Japan when in 1937 Japan had invaded a China that was already wracked by a civil war between the nationalists and Communists. It is still more irrational to believe the Dutch were a threat to the Japanese as Hitler's panzers had rolled over that unfortunate nation in the spring of 1940. Then there was Great Britain. The British were a colonial power with substantial interests in the Far East. But they had barely survived the Battle of Britain in the fall of 1940 and were desperate for American aid and intervention. The British were in no position to threaten the Japanese in 1941. Indeed, Dutch and British forces in the Far East were completely inadequate to the task of defending their interests from Japan. These and France's colonies were the proverbial "low-hanging fruit."[17]

Finally, we have already observed how the Americans were in retreat in the western Pacific. The U.S. would have liked nothing more than to bury its isolationistic head in the sand of its beaches, rather than bury its sons in the sands of Iwo Jima. The whole idea that the only course open to Japan was war or acquiescence to ABCD dominance was absurd. Indeed, Japanese aggressive moves in China in 1937 and Indochina in 1940 and 1941 all quickly followed events in America and Europe that suggested to Japanese leaders they might move with impunity.[18] The Japanese did not act in self-defense but rather in a concerted, aggressive, and freely chosen attempt to build an unassailable and self-sufficient empire. The chief of the Japanese Bureau of Military Affairs declared in 1941, "Japan must be guaranteed freedom of control in the Greater Far East sphere, both in relation to its security and defense and in relation to future expansion." Gerhard Weinberg summarized the Japanese view as follows: "If the Americans would accept all prior Japanese conquests and also help her future expansion, they might be allowed to live in peace."[19] The Japanese militarists were so committed to the empire that they risked war with the U.S. even though they knew the chances of winning that war were slim; as Eri Hotta has written, "As long as there was the slightest chance of success, it [the war] was a gamble worth taking."[20]

Thus, the Japanese decision for war was itself immoral on the basis that the war was unlikely to succeed.

So, imperialism was the guiding light of Japanese leaders for decades. The method for achieving this empire was diplomatic and military opportunism. Their aggressive moves in the five years before Pearl Harbor followed developments in Europe or the U.S. which suggested their potential adversaries were either preoccupied or uninterested in the Far East. Japanese belief that the European War provided them with an opportunity is what lay behind the attack on the American fleet in Hawaii, not the fear of "ABCD" encirclement.

JAPANESE CONDUCT OF THE WAR

Unfortunately, the war the Japanese fought and the empire they administered were as brutal as their intentions were selfish. From the beginning of the war in China, Emperor Hirohito publicly espoused contempt for international law and the Chinese people. The emperor declared that since there was no clear government in China, his military personnel were not bound by any legalities in their treatment of civilians and prisoners of war. Japanese soldiers took full advantage of their emperor's indulgence. Nanking experienced the most infamous but by no means a singular fate. The "Rape of Nanking" went on for three months as Japanese soldiers killed and raped the Chinese people and sacked the city. These soldiers knew their emperor's heart.[21] Indeed, Hirohito's order and the behavior it suggested were an outgrowth of a Japanese military tradition that was harsh even on its own members. The warrior code of Bushido required death before dishonor. Thus, the Japanese Field Service Code forbade an imperial soldier to surrender even if badly wounded. It read, "Never give up a position but rather die." On the next page the order was repeated, "Do not give up under any circumstances." And as if the message had not been adequately sent, "After exerting all of your powers, spiritually and physically, calmly face death rejoicing in the hope of living in the eternal cause for which you serve."[22] Unfortunately, the code's equally frequent injunction that soldiers treat noncombatants humanely so as to avoid disgracing the imperial army was far too often ignored.[23] Finally, the Japanese experimented with biological weapons on captured prisoners of war and used them in China.[24] The just war tradition cannot be made to show that Japan's Pacific war was morally waged.

While it was the Japanese attack on Pearl Harbor that brought the U.S. into the Second World War, the conflict between the Land of the Rising Sun and China would almost certainly not have led the Japanese to war with the U.S. were it not for the war in Europe. It is necessary, therefore, in considering who is at fault for this horrific conflict, to examine events in Europe.

ORIGINS OF WORLD WAR II IN EUROPE

The origins of the war in Europe may be found, at least in part, in the follies that attended the Treaty of Versailles, which ended the First World War. In losing that conflict, Germany was punished far more harshly than the German people believed just, and far more harshly than American president Woodrow Wilson had advocated in his "fourteen points" and "peace without victory" speeches.[25] When the new, postwar democratic German government signed the treaty, it submitted to requirements that it make massive reparations payments, admit guilt for the war, and accept the relegation of Germany to third-rate status in the family of nations. What the treaty did not do was provide for an occupation of Germany which might have made a German resurgence more difficult. Ultimately, Versailles moved many Germans to seek revenge, without making their day of vengeance impossible. In the early 1930s, Adolf Hitler's Nazi party rose to power on this emotion combined with the Great Depression's fresh wounds. Then, too, Hitler's calling card was race. He persuaded the German people—and it wasn't particularly difficult—that their Aryan blood made them the master race. Thus, the majority of Germans believed it was particularly galling that the best of men were forced to endure a subservient existence because of the injustice of Versailles.

In 1933, Germans elected Hitler chancellor. He moved quickly to silence his opposition and end the unpopular German experiment in democracy. By 1936, he was ready to test the resolve of the Versailles victors in enforcing the treaty. In that year, Germany left the League of Nations and openly violated the Treaty of Versailles when Hitler remilitarized the Rhineland—German territory largely between the Rhine River and France, Belgium, and the Netherlands.

Most Europeans believed, and some were even sympathetic to, the notion that Hitler merely hoped to redress wrongs stemming from the Versailles Treaty. But Hitler never imagined a peaceful Europe; he knew his plans for domination of Central Europe and for acquisition of vast living space in Eastern Europe would engender war.[26] Indeed, in November 1937 he laid out his general plan of aggression for his war minister, Werner von Blomberg, and the service chiefs of the army, navy, and air force. He broached the subject by casually remarking that "force with its attendant risks . . . [is] the basis of the following exposition [on the necessary wars of aggression]."[27]

After amalgamating Austria into the German Reich in 1938 using the convenient excuse that Austrians spoke German and most of them desired to be part of Germany, Hitler used the same argument for the Sudetenland of western Czechoslovakia. Der Fuehrer actually hoped that his demand for the Sudetenland would be rebuffed and that war would ensue.[28] But at Munich in the fall of 1938, British prime minister Neville Chamberlain and French leader Edouard Daladier, the former proclaiming "peace in our time," signed off on the deal. Hitler was disappointed. Chamberlain eventually shouldered the opprobrium of being the architect of appeasement, but he was by no means the only culprit. Historian Michael Burleigh notes, "Appeasement is indivisibly associated with Chamberlain, its most obdurate proponent, although many rats had to get off the sinking ship in order to leave the captain in such splendid isolation."[29] In March 1939, Hitler, now too strong to be easily corralled, stormed into the rest of Czechoslovakia, where few Germans lived. The whole world now beheld Hitler's true colors: a twisted black cross on a field of blood.

Great Britain and France, caught ill prepared and still less willing to believe what had been obvious for some time, now arose from their stupor and guaranteed Poland's borders against a German invasion. But Poland was virtually indefensible. In March 1939, Hitler decided that war must decide Poland's fate. Negotiations could not be allowed to deny him a military victory and the end of Poland as an independent state. Hitler hoped and believed that Great Britain and France would do nothing to aid Poland, but was prepared to accept a war with the

Western powers if they proved to have more resolve than they had heretofore mustered. The war began on der Fuehrer's target date: September 1, 1939. For Hitler, war with Britain and France was only a relatively minor matter of timing. The ultimate target, of course, was the Russian leviathan. But the war against Joseph Stalin's country was to be the last step in the domination of Europe. Indeed, the Molotov-Ribbentrop agreement of late August 1939 was designed to ensure that Hitler would not have to worry about his Eastern Front while crushing his Western foes. The pact called for the division of Poland between the Soviet Union and Germany and had the attending impact of lulling the Russians into a false sense of security while assuring Poland's fate.[30] With the German invasion of Poland, Great Britain and France declared war on Hitler's Reich.

Obviously, Germany's cause does not rise to the threshold that just war principles posit. Indeed, the more appropriate question is to what degree Great Britain, France, and even the U.S. bear some responsibility for allowing Adolf Hitler to launch such a devastating aggressive war. But answering that question is not the object of this survey. Adolf Hitler's Germany must bear the lion's share of the moral responsibility for the coming of World War II. A brief survey of German behavior in waging the war will only confirm this view.

GERMAN CONDUCT OF THE WAR

Three days after the German invasion of Poland commenced, Hitler granted a general amnesty, much as Hirohito had done two years before, for any German military personnel convicted of crimes against Polish civilians.[31] In order to be sure his Polish pogrom was carried out, der Fuehrer gave responsibility for pacification behind the German lines to the master butchers of the Waffen-SS with instructions to "depopulate parts of Poland."[32] Joseph Goebbels, Hitler's minister of propaganda, described his intent for Poland as "annihilation," an ironically accurate description given the nature of most of his propaganda work. On August 22, a few days before the German invasion of Poland, at a military conference at the Berghof, one of Hitler's generals cryptically recorded der Fuehrer's thoughts: "Destruction of Poland in the foreground. The aim is elimination of living forces, not the arrival at a certain line."[33] Thus, the Germans put into operation a clandestine program of slaughter. Historian Niall Ferguson has aptly described the German and Japanese conduct of their war: "The brutal methods the Axis powers used to build their empires swiftly turned living space into killing space."[34]

THE U.S. AND THE ORIGINS OF THE EUROPEAN WAR

The question arises, was the U.S. aid to Britain morally just, given that this aid may have triggered Hitler's declaration of war? The fascist powers forced Franklin Roosevelt to face a world on the precipice of an abyss. In one of his Fireside Chats, FDR described the choice the American people faced as one between good and evil.[35] Given the nature of Hitler's regime, the American president had no moral path open to him but to lead his people to war. As Ernest Hemingway reminded Americans in 1940, English poet John Donne powerfully expressed the notion of our common humanity in the seventeenth century. It was this egalitarian ideal the fascist powers disdainfully rejected. Donne wrote: "No man is an island, entire of itself; every man is a piece of the continent, a part of the main. . . . Any man's death diminishes me, because I am involved in mankind, and therefore never send to know for whom the bell tolls; it tolls for thee."[36] Now, in the twentieth century, the very idea that all people shared this inherent equality was deep in the throes of its greatest crucible.

The path to FDR's decision had been long and uncertain. The American people had grown disillusioned with their crusade to make the world safe for democracy shortly after the Great War's end in 1918. Ironically, writers like Hemingway had played no small part in that development. In 1922, the Americans had scuttled a good deal of their navy in the Washington Naval Treaty, in 1928 they signed the sophomoric Kellogg-Briand Treaty, which sought to ban war by stuffing the muzzles of tanks and artillery with pen and paper, and in the mid-1930s, Congress, thinking as much of the last war as they were the next one, passed neutrality legislation that suggested the U.S. would do little to help the victims of Nazi aggression. Now the bell tolled.

After the fall of France in June 1940, Great Britain faced the Nazi hordes alone. That fall British pilots turned back German airmen in the angry skies over their island home. But the war bankrupted Britain. Prime Minister Winston Churchill wrote a pleading letter in December to President Roosevelt in which he explained in detail that his treasury was empty. He wrote, "I do not believe that the Government and people of the U.S. would find it in accordance with the principles which guide them to confine the help they have so generously promised to such munitions of war and commodities as could be immediately paid for."[37] In response, FDR decided to lend or lease aid to Great Britain—no payment required. In explaining the program to the American people he used a homely metaphor. He described a neighbor's house burning, the neighbor desperate for help. Would you not lend him a garden hose?, the president asked.[38] Of course, most Americans answered. The bill passed in March 1941. Lend-Lease (officially "An Act to Promote the Defense of the United States") marked a momentous move on the global chessboard; for FDR's brainchild was a decidedly un-neutral act and meant the risk of war.[39]

As Churchill contemplated his epistle to Roosevelt in November 1940, news from the north Atlantic was as dark and troubling as a winter tempest. German U-boats, now running like packs of wolves, sank over 350,000 tons of British merchant shipping in October, far surpassing their earlier efforts.[40] For Churchill, American aid in the battle against German submarines was essential. What sense did it make to send England supplies if that aid rested harmlessly at the bottom of the Atlantic? In the winter of 1940/41 the wolf-packs seemed sated, but the respite was short-lived; from March to June 1941 the British lost more than a million tons. In April, FDR moved more chess pieces; he approved the transfer of an aircraft carrier, three battleships, and other smaller warships from Pearl Harbor to the Atlantic. The reinforced American navy assumed defense of Iceland and in September began escorting the merchant ships of all nations.[41] German naval commander Erich Raeder implored Hitler to declare war on the U.S. After all, the Americans had certainly provided provocation. Hitler demurred; he had his hands full with the invasion of the Soviet Union. Nevertheless, both sides now risked war in the Atlantic. Roosevelt himself admitted as much in a Fireside Chat on September 11, 1941. Describing the U-boat menace in the

Atlantic, he told the American people, "But when you see a rattlesnake poised to strike, you do not wait until he has struck before you crush him."[42] In fact, the snake struck quickly. In October, German U-boats torpedoed the American destroyer Kearney, and three days later sank the USS *Reuben James*, killing 115 American sailors. Now Roosevelt demurred. Though Hitler and Roosevelt refused to acknowledge it, their navies were at war in the Atlantic.[43] So, the U.S. followed a course of action in 1940 and 1941 that provided more than enough cause for Germany to justly declare war in December 1941, unless Germany's own immoral acts in Europe justified American behavior. This, of course, is precisely what these pages have shown.

AMERICAN CONDUCT OF THE WAR

In reviewing the origins of the war in both Europe and the Pacific, we have seen how the Axis powers immorally launched and conducted their wars. What then of the American conduct of war? No nation engaged in total war avoids moral lapses. And no aspect of American policies during the Second World War has received as much criticism as the strategic bombing campaign which culminated in the dropping of the atomic bombs on Hiroshima and Nagasaki.[44] Then, too, America's own hypocrisy regarding racism must be examined.

An important question is whether just war doctrine condones all or some aspects of strategic bombing. For our purposes, strategic bombing may be divided into four categories: daylight high-altitude bombing of industrial and military targets, bombing of urban areas primarily to kill civilian defense workers and destroy their homes which contain cottage industries, any mode of bombing primarily intended to kill civilians and engender terror, and, finally, nuclear bombing. Just war thinking asserts a principle of discrimination between combatants and noncombatants. But the latter are defined as "not involved in harming, or helping to harm us."[45] Thus, it would seem that civilian workers engaged in war-related industries may reasonably be classified as combatants. Bombing designed to cripple such industries falls within the parameters of just war conditions even though the imprecision of such bombing resulted in many noncombatant deaths.

At the same time, American and British air forces engaged in bombing which was not primarily intended to destroy industrial-military targets but rather was intended to kill civilians. The German cities of Hamburg and Dresden were so attacked. In Japan, disappointing results of bombing industrial and military targets led to a change of strategy in March 1945. At that time, American general Curtis LeMay adopted incendiary bombing of Japanese cities.[46] This decision meant that the targets of American bombing were the people of Japan, not factories, not military installations. There can be no doubt that "a new stage of the air war had begun."[47] This decision was made even though Americans considered such bombing immoral in Europe. Tokyo's Shitamachi district was the targeted area. Though the Americans took measures to reduce civilian deaths, about eighty-eight thousand Japanese died in the Tokyo firebombing.[48]

Can such bombing be morally justified? This bombing campaign specifically targeted civilians, most of whom were not involved in war industries. Nor was there a reasonable mitigating hope that such bombing might end the war expeditiously. Indeed, most of the evidence gathered in the war suggested that bombing of urban areas to kill civilians did not destroy their will to resist, much less that of their nation's leaders. In retrospect, the *US Bombing Surveys* editors implied that the bombing of civilian targets in Japan had been counterproductive. They asserted that American bombing resources would have been more effectively directed at Japan's railroad transportation system and merchant fleet.[49] American brigadier general Bonner Fellers argued these raids were "one of the most ruthless and barbaric killings of non-combatants in all history."[50] Finally, Americans believed such bombing was immoral and said so in response to indiscriminate Japanese bombing in China in 1937.[51] And indeed, just war tradition does not justify the incendiary raids on Tokyo and several other Japanese cities in the spring of 1945.

Central to just war moral reasoning is that war should be conducted by means that are proportionate to the threat. Ironically, given their destructive capacity, but realistically because of it, the atomic bombs were the least morally objectionable option for ending the war available to American leaders. Although the bombs dropped on Hiroshima and Nagasaki in August of 1945 killed as indiscriminately as the incendiary raids the previous spring, their shock effect—a single bomb dropped from a single plane—had the potential of ending the war in short order. Indeed, this was the hope, if not the expectation, of American leaders. American secretary of war Henry Stimson grasped the distinction between the two bombing strategies. The difference lay not primarily in destructive capacity but in psychological impact on Japanese leaders.[52] None of the other possibilities for ending the war, including the resumption of firebombing, allowed for the hope that it might end in 1945.

The two most likely alternative scenarios were a D-Day-type invasion of the Japanese home islands, preceded by massive incendiary bombing, or a naval blockade of Japan that would eventually starve the Japanese into submission. Advocates of the first option usually argue that the casualties attendant to that choice would have been less than those occasioned by the nuclear bombs. There is no evidence for this assumption, and the most likely outcome is quite the opposite. Consider that in March, the month of the Tokyo firebombing, the U.S. dropped 13,800 tons of bombs on Japan. In July, just before surrender, the total was 42,700 tons—more than three times as much. With the activation of the U.S. Eighth Air Force, based on Okinawa, that total would rise to 115,000 tons per month.[53] Moreover, the Russians then would have been involved in the invasion, and Japan would have been conquered and divided in much the same way as Germany. An Allied invasion of Japan would have entailed the kind of suffering and death that attended the last year of the war on the Eastern Front of Europe, a campaign one scholar has aptly described as "Armageddon."[54]

The blockade option was actually preferred by Admiral Chester Nimitz, at least in part because he feared the U.S. Navy lacked the power to protect an invasion—another point against the invasion hypothesis. Many later advocates of the blockade option seem to believe that this method for ending the war would have been bloodless. But this is not at all so. As the blockade went on, the Japanese army in China would have continued its butchery there; meanwhile the Russians would have progressed through Manchuria and on into China. At the time of the dropping of the bombs, the Russian campaign in Manchuria had already cost four hundred thousand Japanese colonists their lives, nor were the Russians there to liberate Manchurians.[55] Moreover, the Japanese would not have simply acquiesced to an embargo; they still held nine thousand Kamikazes in reserve. The U.S. Navy would have taken a pounding as it attempted to enforce an embargo. Then, too, the embargo plan to "starve them out" was not hyperbole. In August 1945, the Japanese people were nearing starvation rations, but their leaders were not sharing in the hunger.[56] Finally, embargoes are notoriously ineffective in compelling a militaristic oligarchy to comply with the wishes of the blockaders. The most likely scenarios, had this option been chosen, were that the U.S. and its allies would have lost the will to enforce the embargo—leaving some form of the imperial government in place—or eventually resorted to an invasion. As it turned out, President Truman and his advisers' hopes were vindicated. The two bombs and the Soviet decision to declare war against Japan moved Emperor Hirohito to seek peace on American terms. The Americans made the bitter pill palatable by allowing the Japanese people to retain their emperor.

In addition to immoral strategic bombing, the Americans must be held accountable for their endemic racism. In the era of the Second World War, racism informed the national ethos of all of the major combatants to varying degrees. The U.S., of course, drank deeply from this poisonous well. In spite of the Declaration of Independence, most Americans did not believe that all men were created equal. People of color were inferior to whites, and the sons and daughters of former slaves were the most inferior and disadvantaged of all Americans. Indeed, racism in America was the nation's most intractable problem. Thus, when the Pacific war began, racism was an intrinsic aspect of the conflict on both sides.[57]

Americans believed their Japanese adversary to be both racially inferior and, quite ironically, diabolically clever.[58] Both nations were victims of their own racism from the beginning, which was the attack on Pearl Harbor. The Americans did not believe the Japanese had the ability to launch such a tactically difficult and devastating attack; the Japanese believed that just such an attack might so demoralize the inferior Americans that they would not fight.[59] Indeed, John W. Dower makes the point that Japanese racism may have been more extreme than German race hatred.[60]

It did not take long for the conduct of the Pacific war to degenerate into a barbarism unknown in the other theaters of the war except for several times and places on the German-Russian front. The Japanese attack on Pearl Harbor, far from demoralizing the Americans into submission, instilled a partially race-based rage that provided the Americans with a decided psychological motivation to revenge and victory. Add

Japanese mistreatment of prisoners of war and the emperor's soldiers' fanatic refusal to surrender as noted above, and the ingredients for a war of annihilation were omnipresent.[61] It did not take long for Americans to respond in kind. The idea that the Japanese soldier had to be killed, as opposed to captured, was well established during the Guadalcanal campaign of 1942–43. The U.S. Marines had a saying, "Remember Pearl Harbor—keep 'em dying."[62] This attitude amongst most American servicemen lasted for the duration of the war.

Sadly, American racism continued unabated at home. Black Americans, in spite of the nation's dire need of their services, continued to suffer the age-old racism and segregation of their American experience.[63] And racism also extended to Japanese nationals in America and their offspring. The saga of Japanese wartime internment in the U.S. is well known. John Blum, eminent historian of the American home front during the war, calls it "the most blatant mass violation of civil liberties in American history."[64] More than that, it made suspect the American commitment to the lofty goals of the Atlantic Charter—a world in which race did not matter. But Franklin Roosevelt and his successors took that commitment seriously, especially once the fighting had ended. Dower writes that the American occupation of Japan was "remarkably amicable and constructive."[65] And Fromkin, in one of the finer insights of American World War II historiography, writes:

> Observing the works of Nazi Germany . . . had the effect of reminding the United States of what it stood for. Americans told themselves, and others, that theirs was a country in which every person was as good as everybody else—a land tolerant of differences but conscious that beneath surface differences all were children of one God. . . . And, of course, that was not really true. . . . America was not of a piece with the picture of the United States that FDR summoned in the wartime years. That is why the creation of the image of magnificence [a prosperous and egalitarian nation] was so great an achievement—and why the decision to try to live up to it was so morally admirable.[66]

American conduct of the war often failed to live up to the standards of just war doctrine and to Americans' own deeply revered egalitarian ideals. But when compared to their adversaries, the Americans were vastly superior in moral conduct of the war and in their goals for the postwar world.

THE WORLD THAT WAS NOT

The racial theories of the Axis powers led to a war of annihilation as opposed to war between professional armies observing a commonly recognized code of conduct. Once one accepts the notion that other human beings are inferior, less human, then one is not far from the gas chambers of Belsen and Auschwitz or the rape of Nanking.[67] Most observers have argued that a Nazi victory would have been worse than the outcome that actually took place. The cost of such a peace would have been "horrendously high," and primarily paid by those left under Nazi rule. Germany's *Generalplan Ost* called for the deportation of fifty million people to Siberia.[68] Lest Americans think Hitler intended to let them live in peace, the evidence for his intentions to ring the bell for the New World is compelling.[69] It should go without saying that a Nazi victory would have meant extermination for the remnant of Europe's Jews.

The Japanese, similarly, planned to become the master race of Asia and the Pacific. Indeed, they had plans to rename much of the world to indicate Japanese hegemony.[70] As we have noted, the Japanese made a pretense, as the Germans did not, of liberating their Asian neighbors. But the reality the new overlords brought to their empire was hardly enlightened. The newly liberated people of Asia were instructed as to the magnificence of their new masters and their own good fortune.

> Nippon is the sun: protector of the land and provider of light to all beings on earth. The Nippon Empire will increase in power and importance, like the sun rising higher in the sky—this is eternal and is also the meaning of the term Nippon.
>
> In the creation of the world ... the first land was Nippon, Land of the Rising Sun. No one can challenge the sun—to do so is like the snow melting in the heat of the sun. Those opposing Nippon will undergo the same experience as the Snow.[71]

Korea's experience of being "liberated" by the Japanese early in the twentieth century suggests what was in store for a Japanese-dominated Pacific. In that tragically located nation, the Japanese smashed any harbingers of nationalism, denied Koreans the right to teach their own language in schools, enforced Shinto as the country's religion, and even insisted that Koreans adopt Japanese names. Meanwhile, co-prosperity eluded most Koreans; personal income hovered at 25 percent of the Japanese standard. Moreover, Japanese colonists were to avoid intermingling with the inferior races. Massive relocation of those people to inferior lands was planned. The Nipponese intended nothing short of apartheid and ethnic cleansing for the Pacific.[72]

THE WORLD THAT WAS

Given that the postwar world was not as irenic, democratic, and egalitarian as Americans hoped it to be, historians have too often neglected a careful telling of the Allied achievement in winning the Second World War. Led by Americans, that accomplishment was unprecedented, indeed breathtaking. Historian Gaddis Smith well remembers:

> Hitler was dead and Germany lay powerless under Allied occupation. The [Japanese] Emperor's decision to surrender meant that the landings on Japan would be bloodless. Italy had withdrawn from the war ... and was about to acquire a respected place among nations. Americans, virtually unaided, had beaten Japan in the Pacific while providing the leadership and more than half of the men for the attack on Hitler from the West. At the same time they had armed Britain, Russia, and China. Their diplomacy had preserved the great coalition, established the United Nations, and laid the foundation for peace in Europe and Asia.[73]

Further results of the war include the American decision to move away from unilateralism and isolationism toward internationalism and give the leading voice to basic human values of freedom, peace, and international cooperation that remain compelling to this day. Indeed, it seemed to most Americans that America might serve as the "Good Samaritan of the entire world."[74]

To that end the U.S. took the lead in founding the United Nations, the North Atlantic Treaty Organization, and the World Bank. FDR alone of the Allied leaders had a "world point of view," as opposed to a strictly nationalistic agenda. Roosevelt believed in a world that would willingly follow American values of freedom and democracy if given the opportunity. Thus, the American leader sought to provide the people of the world with a middle way between the totalitarianism of the left and the right. American goals in the war surpassed the defeat of the Axis powers and encompassed the ending of traditional colonialism; indeed, if the Americans had their way, the mercantile walls of empire would fall to the sound of American trumpets, and there would be no need for an Open Door as there would be no imperial wall upon which to hang it. Americans believed that the lesson of the Great Depression and the subsequent World War was that empires and tariffs had been major factors in the coming of the conflict. Thus, they envisioned a world in which freedom of trade, freedom of the seas, and freedom from war, upheld through the U.N., would be a blessing to all people.[75]

Even an old soldier like Douglas MacArthur, whose career had been molded on the American outpost of empire, the Philippines, gave eloquent voice to the new version of the old Wilsonian-American vision. At the surrender ceremony on board the USS *Missouri* in September 1945 he said, "It is my earnest hope and indeed the hope of all mankind that from this solemn occasion a better world shall emerge . . . a world founded on faith and understanding—a world dedicated to the dignity of man and the fulfillment of his most cherished wish—for freedom, tolerance and justice."[76] A Japanese diplomat, observing the surrender and hearing the American vision, wondered if "it would have been possible for us, had we been victorious, to embrace the vanquished with a similar magnanimity. Clearly, it would have been different."[77] Here, in these words, this Japanese statesman subtly but clearly enunciated why the American cause and purpose in the war was just: the American vision for the world was more egalitarian, merciful, and empowering of all the peoples. Indeed, MacArthur explicitly promised Japanese foreign minister Mamoru Shigemetsu that the "Supreme Commander has no intention of making slaves of the Japanese people."[78]

Throughout the war President Roosevelt led the world away from imperialism. In August 1941, he met with British prime minister Winston S. Churchill to discuss war goals should the United States become formally involved in the conflict as a British ally. Both leaders signed the Atlantic Charter, which reasserted FDR's "Four Freedoms." More specifically, the charter pledged the allies to fight for the restoration of self-government for the nations of the world who had lost it in the war, to eschew territorial gains, and, contrary to colonial practices of the era, to establish equal access to trade and natural resources.[79]

More importantly, the world the allied victors created after the war suggested the sincerity of the Western allies' proclamations. To the extent that Great Britain and the United States had it within their power, self-government was largely restored to nations that had felt the naked and brutal power of Axis domination. The United States established no new colonies among liberated peoples and kept its word to the Filipinos to grant independence. Indeed, the Americans generously helped rebuild the nations of Western Europe, while also energizing their own economy, with the Marshall Plan. Even vanquished Germany, Japan, and Italy experienced a magnanimous and generous peace along the lines of Roosevelt's hopes for the world. Within a mere seven years of the end of the war all three nations were once again independent and restored to full partnership in the open world commercial system. There were exceptions and mistakes along the way. American president Harry S. Truman approved of France reclaiming their empire in Indochina.[80] But by and large, where American will prevailed, the postwar world reflected American ideals of self-determination and free trade.

This is not to suggest that American corporations did not abuse their commercial opportunities in much of the world, and that the Cold War did not dramatically impact American foreign policy for the worse; they and it did. That said, as the second half of the twentieth century unfolded, the world gradually moved toward greater freedom in political institutions and trade. This would not have happened had the Axis powers emerged triumphant in the Second World War. Just before FDR died, he recognized that the war might accomplish this dream. In a perceptive moment—not uncommon for Roosevelt—he said: "It almost seems that the Japs were necessary evil in order to break down the old colonial system."[81] Nor did the president confine his anticolonial agenda to enemy nations. FDR repeatedly pressed Churchill, to the brink of weakening the wartime alliance, on the independence of India. Great Britain did regain much of its prewar empire, but grudgingly acquiesced in granting independence to many of its client states in subsequent years.

Though the Americans accomplished much, the world Franklin Roosevelt envisioned would not, indeed could not, arise from the ashes of World War II. Even though America had far greater power in 1945 than in 1918, even though our enemies were far more defeated than the Germany of the Great War, and even though Franklin Roosevelt was vastly more realistic than Woodrow Wilson in his hopes for the world, there are parallels between the American hopes for the peace subsequent to both wars, and between the failure to realize the one vision and the other. Indeed, American leaders now confident that the peace of the world necessitated American leadership found that the world would not entirely conform to the American vision.[82] As powerful as the United States was at the end of the war, it had neither the strength nor the will to insist the world follow its example. Then, too, America itself did not live up to its own highest ideals and aspirations. Indeed, the war helped us remember that failure. Just as the war ushered in revolution against colonialism and racism abroad, it would dramatically impact the latter at home.

In conclusion, the United States waged a just war against Germany, Japan, and Italy. The Americans responded in self-defense to the Axis powers that waged aggressive and immoral war in the hopes of creating imperial systems that would have enslaved most of the world. In their conduct of the war, American leaders generally upheld the recognized rules of war, though their enemies did not. But no major war is waged without moral failure on all sides. In the crucible of this catastrophic conflict, American leaders erred when they allowed the firebombing of largely civilian targets in Europe and Japan. However, the nuclear bombing of Hiroshima and Nagasaki was the least morally objectionable course open to the Americans in bringing the war to a close. No other option allowed for the hope that the war might end soon; no other option promised fewer casualties. Finally, in spite of America's own racism, the world system the Americans hoped to create provided far more freedom, equality, security, and prosperity to the people of the world than either the old colonial system or the fascist regimes.

NOTES

1. Franklin D. Roosevelt, War Message to Congress, December 8, 1941, *Congressional Record*, 77th Congress, 1st Sess., 9519.

2. For the view that the United States provoked the Japanese attack see Paul Schroeder, *The Axis Alliance and Japanese-American Relations* (Ithaca, NY: Cornell University Press, 1958), 200–204; Howard Zinn, *A People's History of the United States* (New York: Harper & Row, 1980), 398–416; David Kennedy, *Freedom from Fear: The American People in Depression and War, 1929–1945* (Oxford: Oxford University Press, 1999), 513, 514, 855; George Herring, *From Colony to Superpower: US Foreign Relations since 1776* (Oxford: Oxford University Press, 2008), 536; Walter LaFeber, *The Clash: A History of the U.S.–Japan Relations* (New York: W. W. Norton & Co., 2008), 212, 213.

3. Michael Quinlan and Charles Guthrie, *Just War: The Just War Tradition; Ethics in Modern Warfare* (New York: Walker & Co. 2007), 17.

4. Robert Dallek, *Franklin Roosevelt and American Foreign Policy, 1932–1945* (New York: Oxford University Press, 1979), 193.

5. Fumimaro Konoe, quoted in and translated by John Costello in *The Pacific War, 1941–1945* (New York: HarperCollins, 1981), 61.

6. Gerhard Weinberg, *A World at Arms: A Global History of World War II* (Cambridge: Cambridge University Press, 1994), 322.

7. Niall Ferguson, *The War of the World: Twentieth-Century Conflict and the Descent of the West* (New York: Penguin, 2006), 480.

8. Ba Maw, quoted in Ferguson, *War of the World*, 501.

9. Saburo Ienaga, *Japan's Last War: World War II and the Japanese, 1931–1945* (Canberra: Australian National University Press, 1979), 153–56.

10. David Fromkin, *In the Time of the Americans* (New York: Knopf, 1995), 339.

11. Youli Sun, *China and the Origins of the Pacific War, 1931–1941* (New York: St. Martin's Press, 1993), 133, 134, 136, 153, 157, 158, 159.

12. Eri Hotta, *Japan 1941: Countdown to Infamy* (New York: Knopf, 2013), 269, 270.

13. Paper issued by the Japanese High Command, quoted in Alvin D. Coox, "The Pacific War," in *The Cambridge History of Japan* (Cambridge: Cambridge University Press, 1988), 6:329, as quoted in Ferguson, *War of the World*, 490.

14. Robert J. C. Butow, *Tojo and the Coming of the War* (Princeton: Princeton University Press, 1961), 154, 224.

15. Akira Iriye, *The Origins of WWII in Asia and the Pacific* (New York: Longman, 1987), 176, 177, 178.

16. Iriye, *Origins of WWII in Asia and the Pacific*, 177, 178.
17. Ferguson, *War of the World*, 485.
18. Douglas Ford, *The Pacific War* (New York: Continuum, 2012), 37, 47.
19. Weinberg, *World at Arms*, 247–54.
20. Hotta, *Japan 1941*, 257.
21. Michael Burleigh, *Moral Combat: Good and Evil in World War II* (New York: HarperCollins, 2011), 18, 20.
22. *Field Service Code* (Tokyo: Tokyo Gazette Publishing House, 1941), 8, 9, 13. An English translation of this document is available upon request at the National Archives of Australia.
23. Field Service Code, 8, 16, 19.
24. Antony Beevor, *The Second World War* (New York: Little, Brown, 2012), 771, 772.
25. Woodrow Wilson to Congress, January 8, 1918, in *The Papers of Woodrow Wilson*, vol. 45 (Princeton: Princeton University Press, 1984), 534–39. Wilson to the Senate, January 22, 1917, in *Papers of Woodrow Wilson*, vol. 40 (Princeton: Princeton University Press, 1982), 536.
26. Weinberg, *World at Arms*, 20, 21.
27. Burleigh, *Moral Combat*, 32.
28. John Keegan, *The Second World War* (New York: Viking, 1989), 38, 39.
29. Burleigh, *Moral Combat*, 38.
30. Weinberg, *World at Arms*, 32, 33, 42, 43.
31. Burleigh, *Moral Combat*, 133.
32. Burleigh, *Moral Combat*, 123.
33. Christopher R. Browning, *The Origins of the Final Solution: The Evolution of Nazi Jewish Policy, September 1939–March 1942* (Lincoln: University of Nebraska Press, 2004), 15, quoted in Ferguson, *War of the World*, 397.
34. Ferguson, *War of the World*, 396, 475.
35. Herring, *From Colony to Superpower*, 524.
36. John Donne, "Meditation XVII," in *The Poems and Prose of John Donne* (Norwalk, CT: Easton Press, 1995), 227; Ernest Hemingway, *For Whom the Bell Tolls* (New York: Charles Scribner's Sons, 1940). Hemingway cites Donne in the front matter of *For Whom the Bell Tolls*.
37. Winston Churchill to Franklin Roosevelt, December 8, 1941, in *The Second World War*, vol. 2, *Their Finest Hour* (Boston: Houghton Mifflin, 1949), 558–67.
38. Franklin Roosevelt's press conference of December 17, 1940, in *The Public Papers and Addresses of Franklin D. Roosevelt*, 1940 volume (New York: Macmillan, 1941), 607.

39. Roosevelt's press conference of December 17, 1940, 604–15.

40. Williamson Murray and Allan R. Millett, *A War to Be Won: Fighting the Second World War* (Cambridge, MA: Belknap Press of Harvard University Press, 2000), 238.

41. Samuel Eliot Morison, *The Two-Ocean War: A Short History of the United States Navy in the Second World War* (Boston: Little, Brown, 1963), 35, 36.

42. Franklin D. Roosevelt, Fireside Chat of September 11, 1941, in *Public Papers and Addresses of Franklin D. Roosevelt*, 1941 volume (New York: Harper and Brothers, 1950), 390.

43. Murray and Millett, *War to Be Won*, 249.

44. For treatments of this topic see Stewart Ross, *Strategic Bombing by the United States in World War II* (Jefferson, NC: McFarland & Co., 2003); A. C. Grayling, *Among the Dead Cities: The History and Moral Legacy of the WWII Bombing of Civilians in Germany and Japan* (New York: Walker and Co., 2006).

45. Quinlan and Guthrie, *Just War*, 14, 38.

46. Burleigh, *Moral Combat*, 516.

47. Weinberg, *World at Arms*, 870.

48. Burleigh, *Moral Combat*, 516; John W. Dower, *War without Mercy: Race and Power in the Pacific War* (New York: Pantheon, 1986), 40.

49. *The United States Strategic Bombing Surveys* (Montgomery, AL: Maxwell Air Force Base, 1987), 39, 112.

50. Bonner Fellers, quoted in Dower, *War without Mercy*, 41.

51. Franklin D. Roosevelt's Quarantine speech of Oct 5, 1937, in *Public Papers and Addresses of Franklin D. Roosevelt*, 1937 volume (New York: Macmillan Co.), 406–11.

52. Burleigh, *Moral Combat*, 527.

53. *United States Strategic Bombing Surveys*, 86.

54. Max Hastings, *Armageddon: The Battle for Germany, 1944–1945* (New York: Knopf, 2004).

55. Burleigh, *Moral Combat*, 53.

56. Ienaga, *Japan's Last War*, 193, 194.

57. Dower, *War without Mercy*, preface, and consistently throughout the book.

58. Weinberg, *World at Arms*, 261; Gordon W. Prange, *At Dawn We Slept: The Untold Story of Pearl Harbor* (New York: Penguin Books, 1981), 582.

59. Kennedy, *Freedom from Fear*, 523; Weinberg, *World at Arms*, 261.

60. Dower, *War without Mercy*, 46.

61. Dower, *War without Mercy*, 36, 45, 46.

62. Dower, *War without Mercy*, 52, 36.

63. John Blum, *V Was for Victory: Politics and American Culture during World War II* (New York: Harcourt Brace Jovanovich, 1976), 182.

64. Blum, *V Was for Victory*, 155.

65. Dower, *War without Mercy*, ix.

66. Fromkin, *In the Time of the Americans*, 451, 452.

67. Ferguson, *War of the World*, 480.

68. Ferguson, *War of the World*, 469, 470.

69. See Norman Goda, *Tomorrow the World: Hitler, Northwest Africa, and the Path toward America* (College Station: Texas A & M University Press, 1998).

70. Ferguson, *War of the World*, 470, 471.

71. RvO IC 6262, NSIWD and International Military Tribunal of the Far East, 675A (document from the postwar criminal trial of Japanese war leaders), quoted in Van Waterford, *Prisoners of the Japanese in World War II* (Jefferson, NC: McFarland & Co., 1994), 26.

72. Wan-yao Chou, "The Kominka Movement in Taiwan and Korea: Comparisons and Interpretations," in *The Japanese Wartime Empire, 1931–1945*, ed. Peter Duus, Ramon Myers, and Mark Peattie (Princeton: Princeton University Press, 1996), 40–55.

73. Gaddis Smith, *American Diplomacy during the Second World War*, 2nd ed. (New York: McGraw-Hill, 1985).

74. Herring, *From Colony to Superpower*, 538, 539, 588, quotation from 594.

75. Herring, *From Colony to Superpower*, 545, 546, 549, 580.

76. Douglas MacArthur, *A Soldier Speaks: Public Papers and Speeches of General of the Army Douglas MacArthur* (New York: Praeger, 1965), 148, 149.

77. Kennedy, *Freedom from Fear*, 852, 853.

78. Geoffrey Perret, *Old Soldiers Never Die: The Life of Douglas MacArthur* (New York: Random House, 1996), 480.

79. *The Atlantic Charter: Official Statement on Meeting between the President and Prime Minister Churchill; August 14, 1941*, in *Public Papers and Addresses of Franklin D. Roosevelt*, 1941 volume (New York: Harper & Brothers, 1950), 314–17.

80. Herring, *From Colony to Superpower*, 618–20, 635.

81. Kennedy, *Freedom from Fear*, 853.

82. Herring, *From Colony to Superpower*, 555–64.

NINE

America's Ambiguous "Police Action"

The Korean Conflict

Laura Jane Gifford

Harry Brubaker, a twenty-nine-year-old lawyer from Denver, Colorado, was alone in a spot he had never intended to defend in a war he had not understood. In his home town at that moment the University of Colorado was playing Denver in their traditional basketball game. The stands were crowded with more than 8,000 people and not one of them gave a damn about Korea. In San Francisco a group of men was finishing dinner and because the Korean war was a vulnerable topic, they laid plans to lambaste it from one end of the country to the other, but none of them really cared about the war or sought to comprehend it. And in New York thousands of Americans were crowding into the night clubs where the food was good and the wine expensive, but hardly anywhere in the city except in a few homes whose men were overseas was there even an echo of Korea.

—*James A. Michener, The Bridges at Toko-Ri*[1]

James Michener's fictional chronicle of the Korean conflict reflects the ambiguity of American involvement on this East Asian peninsula between the end of World War II and the Korean armistice in 1953. An undeclared war fought by complicated networks of combatants, Korea remains essentially unresolved—more than sixty years after armistice documents were signed at Panmunjom. One of the earliest "hot war" conflicts of the Cold War, Korea illustrates the difficulty of assigning concrete parameters to a war which elements on both sides viewed in an emerging Cold War context extending far beyond the Korean peninsula itself. Korea also demonstrates the hazards inherent when conflicts hold very different meanings *within* coalitions. Was Korea about global politics, or was it a nationalist struggle? Was this war about East versus West, or was it about self-government? On whose terms should Korea be governed, and within what type of regional framework?

FOUNDATIONS: WHOSE KOREA?

While the Korean War itself was fought between 1950 and 1953, any analysis of U.S. involvement in the Korean conflict must start five years earlier, in 1945. In the closing days of World War II, American military officials tasked with developing a postwar order for the Pacific were confronted with an immediate problem: the Soviet Union, acting on its promise to join the conflict in the East following termination of hostilities in Europe, was entering the Korean peninsula. Despite a long history of cultural and political unity, Korea fell prey to Japanese colonization in 1910. Consequently, the Korean peninsula was one among many regions of the Far East that would require a postwar Allied administration to govern the transition from Japanese authority to self-rule. As many scholars have detailed, the U.S. was desperate to avoid large-scale Soviet involvement in Japan and its former territories; some have argued this was a significant factor in President Harry Truman's decision to drop atomic bombs upon Hiroshima and Nagasaki.

When word of the Soviets' entrance into Korea came to Brigadier General George Lincoln at 2 a.m. on August 11, 1945, the army's adviser to the State-War-Navy Coordinating Committee (SWNCC) knew he had to act quickly. James Dunn, a State Department official assigned to

SWNCC, informed Lincoln that the U.S. needed to move troops into Korea right away; the Soviets might be the U.S.'s erstwhile ally, but in an indication of just how shallow the wartime "alliance" truly was, SWNCC deemed a defense line against the Soviets in Korea to be imperative. Looking at a map of the peninsula, Lincoln focused in upon the 38th parallel—a convenient map marking, but a line with no political or cultural significance in Korea itself. Lincoln called in Colonels Charles Bonestreet and Dean Rusk, giving the men thirty minutes to confirm his decision or suggest an alternative. Bonestreet and Rusk confirmed Lincoln's judgment. This early-morning decision would become the Korean component of General Order Number One, the directive that determined to whom Japanese forces surrendered on August 15.[2]

The actions of the SWNCC had the result, then, of creating the geographic landscape of what would become the Korean conflict. At the committee's behest, Lincoln, Bonestreet, and Rusk *created* a divided Korea where none had previously existed. Even Japanese rule had preserved the territorial, if not the political, integrity of the Korean peninsula. On one level, this essay could end here. The U.S.'s decision to split the peninsula at the 38th parallel satisfied nobody in Korea, thus creating conditions that led to war. This conclusion, however, is unlikely to satisfy those seeking deeper analysis of the war itself and of U.S. actions during the conflict. Taking the 38th parallel division as the equivalent of an economic "sunk cost"—a fact of life that Koreans and their supporters simply had to deal with until political accommodation could be made— what then of the years 1950–53? Following brief explanation of the political situation prior to the outbreak of hostilities on June 25, 1950, this essay seeks to address each condition of both *ius ad bellum* and *ius in bello* before offering overall conclusions about the U.S.'s actions in Korea.

A DIVIDED STATUS QUO

While some postwar planners—and certainly the Korean people— envisioned the emergence of a unified Korea in the months and years following World War II, the development of Cold War tensions between the Soviets and the U.S. rendered unity infeasible. Of the various nationalist leaders active in and around Korean affairs circa 1945,

American interests coalesced behind Syngman Rhee, a U.S.-educated anti-Communist nationalist who had been a leader in the Korean independence movement since 1905, when Japan exercised nominal but not formal colonial control following the Russo-Japanese war. The Soviets, for their part, rather than supporting domestic leftists, preferred to underwrite the emergence of Kim Il Sung, a Soviet infantry school graduate and veteran of the World War II pan-Asian Soviet 88th Brigade, as leader in the North. By 1948, despite attempts by the U.N. Temporary Commission on Korea to hold unifying elections, the two halves of the Korean peninsula had established separate governments: the Democratic People's Republic of Korea (DPRK) in the north, and the Republic of Korea (ROK) in the south. Both the Soviets and the Americans "left" Korea, but in each case departure was a theoretical rather than an actual construct. The U.S. continued to provide civilian and military advisers and economic and military aid; the Soviets withdrew their troops but left all their equipment behind for the use of the Korean People's Army (KPA). Soviet sources have indicated that Moscow provided greater military assistance to the KPA in the late 1940s and early 1950s than that given to Mao's People's Liberation Army during the same period.[3]

George Kennan, who was just finishing up his term of service with the State Department's Policy Planning Staff at the time war broke out, viewed American withdrawal of forces from Korea in 1949 with little alarm. Not only did he suspect that the "ponderous burden of dependents, PXs and other housekeeping paraphernalia which the Pentagon at that time seemed to find indispensable for any American forces stationed abroad" had rendered Korea-stationed troops almost unfit for combat; he had also been assured by a high-ranking Air Force officer in 1948 that the U.S. Air Force could control any military operations on the Korean peninsula from Okinawa—there was no need for ground forces on-site.[4] While Truman administration critics, including some motivated by isolationism or by partisan politics, argued for reversing American foreign policy priorities, the administration privileged European concerns in an atmosphere characterized by postwar disarmament and increasing reliance upon atomic weaponry.[5] In January 1950, Secretary of State Dean Acheson omitted South Korea from his discussion of the American defense perimeter in Asia, fueling later claims that the

U.S. had "abandoned" Korea just as it had abandoned Chinese Nationalists the year before.[6]

RESPONDING TO AN INVASION FROM THE NORTH

For the state of South Korea, the question of just cause is answered quickly and easily. While ample evidence exists of provocation on both sides, the fact remains that North Korea invaded South Korea on June 25, 1950. In the wake of this invasion, South Korea was justified in mounting a defense of its territory. One might argue, as would many Koreans and some American officials (Kennan, for one[7]), that this was a civil conflict between two parts of one country, but it was, at the least, one country operating under two different "national" governments and with two separate fighting forces. Practically speaking, the two were separate, and one attacked the other. The other has the right, according to the just war tradition, to defend itself.

The question of whether the U.S. had the right to intervene on South Korea's behalf involves a different set of factors. Even if, as outlined previously, we set aside the U.S.'s role in creating the 38th parallel division, we must address whether the U.S. was justified in intervening. Kennan argued that in the absence of a peace treaty with Japan, Korea remained within the realm of the U.S.'s occupation responsibilities, even without resident troops.[8] U.S. officials moved quickly, however, to establish the American response to Korea as part of a U.N. action. This action sought to justify U.S. involvement in internationalist terms.

The global Cold War context in which American policy makers viewed the events of Korea led them to view intervention as essential, both for South Korea and for the free world as a whole. U.S. secretary of state Dean Acheson and others had deeply internalized the lessons of the 1930s: "Isolation was not a realistic course of action. It did not work and it had not been cheap." From the first hours following the North Korean invasion Acheson was convinced the attack had been "mounted, supplied, and instigated by the Soviet Union," but the proxy nature of the attack meant there was no *causus belli* against the Soviets. Equally plain, however, was that the invasion constituted an open challenge to the

U.S.'s internationally recognized position as protector of South Korea. To back away from the conflict would be "highly destructive of the power and prestige of the United States." Prestige, for Acheson, was more than window dressing; it was "the shadow cast by power, which is of great deterrent importance." In other words, immediate action was necessary to forestall a wider, more disastrous conflict later. The advice Acheson received from diplomat John Foster Dulles, just returning from a Korean side trip while engaged in the process of negotiating the Japanese peace treaty, reinforced his beliefs. "To sit by while Korea is overrun by unprovoked armed action," Dulles told Acheson, "would start a disastrous chain of events leading most probably to world war."[9]

Just cause? Certainly, in the minds of those making the decisions in the context of June 1950. Today, we understand that far from seeking wider war, Stalin took steps to avoid war with the U.S., inducing Mao and the Chinese Communists to take the leading role in supporting Kim Il Sung's North Koreans.[10] Stalin was no peacenik, but Korea was more a convenient opportunity than a central objective. Declassified Soviet documents indicate that while Stalin was pleased to see the U.S. embroiled in Korea, he viewed China and not the Soviet Union as North Korea's primary source of support. Like the U.S., the Soviets were preoccupied with Europe, and both powers would take steps throughout the war to limit the possibility of wider-scale conflict.[11]

While questions of proportionality in the conduct of the war will be discussed later, a proportionate response is also a factor in *ius ad bellum*. Was it a proportionate reaction for the U.S. to immediately become involved in the Korean conflict? As detailed above, U.S. policy makers viewed Korea in the context of a global Cold War struggle. In this context, given Soviet and Chinese Communist encouragement and material support for the North Korean invasion, the American response was proportionate. While the U.S.-imposed demarcation at the 38th parallel contributed to creating a flawed postwar order in Korea, in 1950 specifically it was the Communist powers that precipitated a "hot" conflict in the country. As a number of historians have observed, the basic issues over which Koreans were fighting were civil and revolutionary in nature.[12] This was a nationalist conflict. Outside powers really had no business in Korea. That said, they were there, and as the North Koreans had solicited—and gained—the support of "their side," the U.S. merely reciprocated. Historian William Stueck perhaps best sums up the situation by concluding, "However nationalistic the Koreans may have been—and they were intensely so—their fate was so closely tied to the designs of the U.S., the Soviet Union, and China that their ability to act independently was severely circumscribed."[13]

Kennan recalled that when data surfaced in late May and early June indicating armed forces of an unspecified Communist satellite were preparing for action, military authorities in Japan and in Washington replied that the biggest threat in Korea came not from the North, but from superior South Korean troops whom the U.S. must restrain from overrunning their deficient northern brethren.[14] As North Korean troops pushed rapidly into the South, the U.S. quickly realized that their estimates of South Korean troop strength were inaccurate. The first detachments of American troops sent to South Korea's aid provided ample evidence of deficiencies in the U.S. Army's troop strength, readiness, and equipment. There is no reason to suspect perfidy. American policy makers genuinely felt that a quick series of engagements would end the conflict. For their part, North Korea had convinced both the Soviets and the Chinese Communists that if the U.S. hadn't intervened in the Chinese civil war, it was hardly likely to involve itself in a small-scale conflict on the Korean peninsula. Kim's promises of quick success were instrumental in garnering his chief backers' support.[15] Perhaps the most eloquent statement on this subject comes from historian Peter Lowe, who notes: "Events in Korea revealed the extent of miscalculation and error by each state involved in the more fundamental decisions that led to the conflict and its escalation. But it also showed a maturity of judgment in appreciating the dangers of allowing matters to go too far."[16]

At the time of the North Korean invasion—June 25 in Korea, but June 24 across the international date line in the U.S.—President Truman was at home in Missouri. Acheson quickly recalled him to Washington and, meanwhile, dispatched instructions to the American ambassador to the U.N. to advocate for an international response. The U.N. Security Council passed a resolution on June 25 "calling for the immediate cessation of hostilities, withdrawal of North Korean forces south of the 38th parallel, and international assistance to the U.N. in carrying out the resolution." Two days later, the U.N. passed a second resolution recommending that U.N. members "furnish such assistance to the Republic of Korea as may be necessary to repel the armed attack and to restore international peace and security in the area."[17] The events of the intervening day, however, are paramount with regard to the U.S. response to the North Korean invasion specifically, and here the question of a public declaration of war becomes muddied. On June 26, Truman ordered U.S. naval and air forces stationed in Japan to attack the North Koreans south of the 38th parallel. In further demonstration of the integrated Cold War mind-set through which the U.S. viewed the conflict, he also sent the U.S. Seventh Fleet to patrol the waters between mainland China and Taiwan in an effort to forestall a feared attack on this remaining outpost of the Chinese Nationalist government. Truman did not seek a war declaration from Congress.[18]

Constitutionally, the president is commander in chief of the armed forces; on the other hand, Congress does retain the power to declare war. Truman circumvented this condition by declaring U.S. involvement in Korea a "police action." While this designation has been criticized since, at the time sources indicate many in Congress had little problem with the president's decision. Acheson records GOP senator Alexander Wiley of the Foreign Relations Committee, for example, as seeming to "express the consensus" when he commented that it was enough for him to know the U.S. was involved with force and that the president felt the level of force was adequate.[19] Congressional support for Korea at the outset has been masked somewhat by the furor with which many congressional representatives met General Douglas MacArthur's sacking several months later—but that is an entirely different issue.

While the U.N. resolutions of June 25 and June 27 quickly rendered the United Nations and not the United States the official "combatant," this was not the only avenue that might feasibly have been pursued. In fact, Kennan opposed U.N. involvement on two grounds: first, the Korean conflict related to the aftermath of World War II, which Article 107 of the U.N. Charter indicated was not a proper subject for the United Nations; and second, this was a civil and not an international conflict.[20] The latter rationale seems particularly dubious in light of frequent U.S. assertions that Korea was part of an interlocking set of Communist activities with global implications.

In the end, however, the war officially became a U.N. and not a U.S. conflict, and therefore the question of the United Nations' legitimate authority must be addressed. Article 42, Chapter VII of the U.N. Charter states that the Security Council "may take such action by air, sea, or land forces as may be necessary to maintain or restore international peace and security," should lesser measures fail. Article 51 grants member states the right to come to the collective self-defense of another state. Just war philosopher Richard J. Regan observes that the U.N. Security Council's involvement in Korea could be viewed either as endorsement of member states' collective actions (justification under Article 51) or as U.N. enforcement actions (justification under Article 42).[21] One of the Council's permanent members, the Soviet Union, was boycotting the Council at the time of the North Korean invasion. This action precluded the Soviets from vetoing the resolution. The boycott, however, was their decision. As such, it does not factor into the question of U.N. legitimacy.

Right intention will always be the trickiest qualification to answer. We cannot definitively enter the mind of Truman, Acheson, or other American policymakers. What evidence we can draw upon from memoirs and other documentation indicates that Truman and his cohort really did believe they were protecting the free world from insidious Communist expansion. As Truman later wrote, "Communism was acting in Korea just as Hitler, Mussolini, and the Japanese had acted ten, fifteen, and twenty years before.... If this was allowed to go unchallenged it would mean a third world war, just as similar incidents had brought on the second world war. It was also clear to me that the foundations and the principles of the United Nations were at stake unless this unprovoked attack on Korea could be stopped."[22] Truman may have been wrong. He, like Acheson and others, may have been blinkered by a tendency to discount the strength of nationalism and to view his world not only through a Cold War lens but through the lens of the previous war. His motives, however, were sincere.

A much stronger understanding of "right intention" is derived from considering ethicist Darrell Cole's analysis of how actions signal intention. By this standard, "investigation should begin by watching what the agent actually does."[23] American actions demonstrate mixed intentions in this regard. Acheson indicated that from the start, Truman intended to fight a limited engagement in Korea.[24] Structuring the U.N. response as a "police action" provided Truman with leeway to circumvent a congressional war declaration, but it also signaled intentions limited to restoring the prewar status quo. State Department Policy Planning staff favored North Korean withdrawal beyond the 38th parallel followed by a negotiated settlement.[25] On the other hand, historian Peter Lowe argues that in the military arena, personal political intentions would influence General Douglas MacArthur's far more bellicose strategy.[26] Such a conflation of personal, domestic concerns with the business of fighting a putatively defensive war mars the principle of "right intention." Consideration of MacArthur, however, brings us into *ius in bello*.

THE U.N. AT WAR: SHIFTING INTENTIONS

What can we determine about the justice of U.S.—and, by extension, U.N.—actions undertaken *during* the conflict? In considering *ius in bello*, we must address whether U.S. troops successfully exercised discrimination in target selection—including noncombatant immunity—and in proportionality. In both cases the principle of double effect must be observed: acts which have both a good and a bad effect are permissible *as long as* the bad effect is an unintended side effect, as long as it is proportional to the objectively good effect, and as long as there is no alternative way of achieving the good effect.[27] Here, unfortunately, the actions of U.S. troops fell short of the standard of justice. American policy makers did place restrictions upon hydroelectric plants along the Yalu River and other targets that could involve accidental bombing of either China or Siberia, though General Douglas MacArthur and his successors chafed against what they deemed provision of "sanctuary" for the Communists.[28] Even so, U.N. planes dropped more ordnance during the Korean conflict than the Allies used in the entire Pacific theater during World War II, including almost 10 million gallons of napalm. Koreans lost 1.2 million homes, more than 25,000 industrial plants, 9,000 schools, and more than 1,000 clinics and hospitals.[29] This level of destruction raises serious questions about whether the Allies respected the *ius in bello* principle of proportionality.

With regard to people, the racial component of this conflict played a significant role, as did KPA troops' own actions. U.S. troops faced a Korean enemy that favored guerrilla tactics. KPA troops infiltrated the general population of South Korea, creating conditions where distinguishing friend from foe became extremely difficult. The pervasiveness of the guerrilla problem in the summer of 1950 led U.N. commanders to issue orders preventing refugees from passing through U.N. lines, stating that those who attempted to do so would be fired upon.[30] Frustrating though KPA guerrilla tactics certainly were, American forces' tendency to conflate all Asians as looking alike contributed to questionable discrimination in target selection. Further, as Cole indicates, those engaging in just war are charged with taking due care to avoid harm to innocents, "regardless of whether or not the enemy has deliberately placed its own citizens in harm's way."[31]

When U.N. troops were forced to retreat from the 38th parallel to a small patch of territory on the southeast corner of the peninsula in the early days of the war, the size of the refugee population following them precipitated tremendously difficult decisions pertaining to double effect. As troops retreated across rivers such as the Naktong at Waegwan, hordes of refugees attempted to follow. Faced with the probability of KPA troops on their heels, U.S. soldiers felt forced to blow up bridges seemingly without regard for the thousands of civilian refugee casualties that resulted. Historians such as Stanley Sandler argue U.N. commanders had "no recourse" but to take such deadly action.[32] Perhaps better dissemination of information to refugees could have helped to curtail these tragedies. In the midst of a retreat, and given the infiltration problems detailed above, we must make certain allowances for those faced with making difficult decisions in confusing conditions and under severe time constraints. More troubling are incidents later in the war. During a U.N. retreat from Pyongyang, for example, U.N. forces destroyed many barges and ferries refugees were using to cross the Taedong River for fear refugees would block the path of retreat. Sometimes refugees were even strafed by ground or aircraft fire. U.N. forces did help evacuate refugees from the port of Chinnampo—twenty thousand of fifty thousand were saved. Such actions leave a decidedly mixed legacy.[33]

Next, we must consider the ends for which the war was fought. Debate over this question resulted in the greatest controversy of the war: the growing conflict between General MacArthur and President Truman, which led to MacArthur's dismissal on April 11, 1951. The U.N. Security Council resolution of June 25, 1950, referred specifically to restoring the authority of the 38th parallel. While South Korean president Syngman Rhee fervently advocated pursuit of a reunited Korea—under his administration—American policy makers were leery of stimulating a wider war, and allies such as Britain vigorously encouraged their caution.

Despite *ad bellum* statements of American and U.N. intentions with regard to the 38th parallel that indicated a limited objective, execution of these intentions was rife with confusion from the war's earliest days. Further, as the war continued, events demonstrated that civilian policy makers and some military officials were operating under different intentions. Two days after the outbreak of hostilities, Kennan confidently assured assembled NATO ambassadors in Washington, DC, that the United States intended nothing more than restoration of the preinvasion status quo. By the next day, however, Air Force officials were already pushing for authorization to operate beyond the confines of the 38th parallel.[34] Acheson's memoirs reflect policy makers' fraught thinking. If the second U.N. Security Council resolution governing the war effort, the resolution of June 27, referred to restoring "international peace and security in the area," might a reunited Korea be necessary to achieve this goal? In 1947, during the period of U.S. and Soviet occupation, the United Nations had called for "an independent, united Korean government." Behind this slogan lay the reality that the 38th parallel itself was the chief obstacle to peace and security. Despite the U.S. role in creating this barrier in 1945, Acheson placed blame for the 38th parallel as an international boundary upon the Soviets, who he argued viewed the line as a "wall around their preserve." Even so, the United States was unwilling to commit forces to the task of creating an independent and unified Korea at all costs. By September 1, the U.S. State and Defense Departments agreed, through the auspices of the National Security Council, upon a policy recommending a narrow interpretation of the June 27 resolution. The resolution was sufficient to authorize military operations north and south of the 38th parallel to repel the invasion and defeat invaders—as Acheson put it, "troops could not be expected . . . to march up to a surveyor's line and stop"—but not to pursue a reunited Korea.[35]

How, then, did U.N. troops wind up at the Manchurian border by late fall? First, General MacArthur's undeniable masterstroke of an invasion at the North Korean port of Inchon on September 15 transformed the conflict from a slogging defensive effort to a rapid and seemingly comprehensive triumph, with KPA troops on the run. On September 27, the Joint Chiefs of Staff (JCS) gave MacArthur limited authorization to forge his way north, effectively reframing *ad bellum* intentions, though he was instructed to submit his plans for future operations north of the 38th parallel to the JCS for approval. MacArthur's instructions from Washington were conditional upon the proviso that no significant Soviet or Chinese armed forces entered Korea and that neither country issued a threat of invasion if U.N. movement toward the north proceeded. MacArthur, while disgruntled by this interference from almost seven thousand miles away, submitted plans on the September 28. Unfortunately, however, the waters were muddied when the JCS instructions were followed two days later by an "eyes only" telegram from Secretary of Defense George Marshall to MacArthur: "We want you to feel unhampered tactically and strategically to proceed north of the 38th parallel." MacArthur viewed this as an open ticket: "Unless and until the enemy capitulates, I regard all Korea as open for our military operations," he replied. Acheson argued it was "inconceivable" that Marshall would have authorized MacArthur to violate JCS instructions that had been approved by Truman. "To me," the secretary of state later reflected, "the message seems directed toward soothing MacArthur's irritation at being required to submit his plan of operations [to the JCS].... His plan showed that he understood this perfectly." Regardless of Marshall's intent, the effect of his telegram was to legitimate MacArthur's sustained drive toward the Yalu River, even after China did issue a threat through Indian ambassador K. M. Panikkar on October 3 that if U.S. troops crossed the 38th parallel, China would enter the war.[36]

In retrospect, the explicit threat of Chinese intervention that reached Washington, DC, on October 3 should have halted U.N. troops at the 38th parallel. There are a number of reasons why this did not occur, ranging from the prosaic—U.N. forces had built up momentum—to the strategic, including a lack of faith in the Indian back channel through which information between Communist China and the United States had to pass in the absence of formal diplomatic relations. Furthermore, the United States assumed Mao, just one year removed from victory over the Chinese Nationalists, would not want to stretch his limited resources and risk becoming more dependent upon the Soviets than he already was. Finally, some American policy makers rationalized that failing to exert force against the Chinese Communists in Korea could encourage further Communist expansionism in Southeast Asia.[37]

The continued story of the Truman-MacArthur conflict has been well chronicled.[38] The significant question for this essay concerns what the fraught history of the 38th parallel reveals about the proportionality of U.S./U.N. military objectives. Manchurian and Siberian airstrips served as home bases for MiG flights over North Korea, but while U.N. planes engaged the fighters—often piloted by thinly disguised Soviets—MacArthur and his successors were prevented from striking across the North Korean border. "For the first time in military history," MacArthur lamented to his chief of staff, General Doyle Hickey, "a commander has been denied the use of his military power to safeguard the lives of his soldiers and safety of his army."[39] MacArthur and his supporters also favored arming Chinese Nationalist troops to open a second front against China emanating from Taiwan. "If we are not in Korea to win," lamented GOP minority leader Representative Joseph W. Martin to a Brooklyn audience in February 1951, "then this administration should be indicted for the murder of thousands of American boys."[40] General Clark suggested that had the United States decided "really to win the war," it would have made use of the atomic bomb.[41]

While the frustrations of MacArthur and his cohort are understandable, we must confront the reality that the North Korean invasion, however extensively it was supported by the Chinese and the Soviets, was a localized invasion within a context that Koreans viewed as domestic. The basic issues over which the war was fought were, as historian Bruce Cumings reminds, us, civil and revolutionary in nature.[42] Who would govern Korea? How would it be governed? Any actions that would extend the war beyond Korean borders would violate the principle of proportionality by creating a war larger than that which the initial aggressors envisioned. The key problem here is that from its inception, all outside actors viewed the war in the context of global Cold War strategy. Acheson's reflections demonstrate some consideration of Korea on its own terms. Most of the American discussion surrounding war outcomes, however, focused upon questions of regional or global influence. The United States took a Korean conflict and made it global. Extending the U.N. mission beyond the initial, restorative police action violated the principle of proportionality. That the Chinese and Soviets did so, also, does not lessen the United States' responsibility for this violation.

PRISONERS OF WAR

As outlined above in the discussion of discrimination in target selection and double effect, U.S. treatment of noncombatants sometimes strayed from the dictates of *ius in bello*, although conditions were such that extensive noncombatant losses were difficult if not nearly impossible to avoid. The prisoner-of-war question, however, quickly became a fraught issue for U.N. forces. While U.N. troops took few POWs prior to Inchon, by late fall of 1950 about 140,000 POWs fell under U.N. control. In January 1951, the vast majority of North Korean and Chinese POWs were transferred to an island south of the Korean mainland called Koje Do. The camp held an estimated 130,000 North Koreans and 20,000 Chinese, in addition to another 100,000 people classified as civilians and refugees, some of whom were DPRK functionaries.

Inadequate medical facilities and overcrowding plagued operations at Koje Do. In addition to disease, Koje Do bred dissent, with prisoners divided into pro- and anti-Communist populations. Violent outbursts at Koje Do precipitated the construction of two additional camps. Despite less crowded conditions, protests—and deaths—continued. While some have argued Communists ordered their own troops to surrender so they could incite camp inmates from within, historian Steven Hugh Lee concluded that poor camp living and security conditions were the most significant factors underlying the violence and death.[43]

Camp unrest, while significant, pales in comparison to the most crucial POW-related issue to impact the outcome of the Korean War. The question of POW repatriation effectively delayed the conclusion of the war by over a year and a half during two years of protracted armistice negotiations. It also touches upon suggestions in contemporary reappraisals of just war thinking that national and international laws must be observed where they do not fundamentally conflict with just war theory's other moral requirements.[44] The Geneva Convention of 1949 mandated a one-for-one exchange of war prisoners. As early as July 1951, however, the chief of psychological warfare of the U.S. Army suggested that for humanitarian and propaganda reasons the United States should consider a policy of "voluntary repatriation." In other words, if North Korean or Chinese POWs did not wish to return to their Communist homelands, they would not be forced to do so. By late 1951 this was the official U.N. position in the armistice negotiations that had begun in July.[45]

Between June 1950 and June 1951, 21,300 U.S. soldiers were killed, 53,100 were wounded, and 4,400 were declared missing or captured. In the next two years of the war—the years of the armistice negotiations, during which battle lines hardened into a stalemate—U.S. deaths numbered 12,300, wounded numbered 50,200, and missing or captured numbered 700.[46] Admiral C. Turner Joy, chief negotiator in the armistice talks, later argued that *"United Nations Command negotiators at Kaesong and Panmunjom were not in a position to deal from maximum strength, and well did the Communists know it* [emphasis Joy's]."[47] Joy believed power was the only language Communist negotiators understood, and like MacArthur, he averred that failure to strike directly at China prolonged the negotiations, causing "an unprecedented [American] breakdown before a show of force."[48] Despite Joy's admonitions, however, the central sticking point had been and remained the question of voluntary repatriation. Figures fluctuated regarding how many Communist POWs desired repatriation. On April 1, 1952, the U.N. Command informed the Communists that 116,000 of their 132,000 soldiers would be repatriated. Communist negotiators appeared satisfied with this figure. More extensive screening, however, revealed that only about 70,000 POWs desired repatriation, and 16,000 of 21,000 Chinese POWs refused to return to China. Hearing this, Communist negotiators rejected voluntary repatriation. Concerns persisted on both sides that Chinese Nationalist guards had intimidated POWs into refusing repatriation, and even U.N. commander general Matthew Ridgway suggested a new round of screenings. In the end, both sides stuck to their positions and negotiations dragged on into summer 1953.[49]

However unpalatable it might have been to contemplate returning POWs who did not desire to live under Communism, one-for-one, or "forced," repatriation remained the standard under international law. Did observing this law conflict with other, moral considerations of the just war tradition—a condition that would negate any need to observe this law? Further complicating matters was the reality that the United States was not an official signatory to the Geneva Convention. U.S. policy makers were not, then, legally bound to adhere to the standards, although a strong case could be made that U.S. advocacy of international agreements since the World War II years created a moral obligation. U.S. military leaders tended to advocate a speedy end to the war, and therefore accession to Geneva Law trumped any moral considerations. State Department policy makers, however, remained haunted by the fate of Russian POWs at the end of World War II who had requested asylum and were instead repatriated, often to face firing squads or life in the "reeducation camps" of the Gulag.[50] As frustrations mounted, arguments such as Joy's for expansion of the war gained increasing support in policy-making circles and among the American electorate. Korea was, of course, the "K" in Dwight Eisenhower's "C2K" campaign slogan of 1952. Even before Eisenhower took office, the Truman administration contemplated more aggressive steps to force an armistice. By spring 1953, the newly elected ex-general decided to expand the conflict to Chinese territory—and to use atomic weaponry—if Communists rejected the U.N. Command's final terms on the issue of voluntary repatriation.[51]

Ultimately, the North Koreans acceded to voluntary repatriation. Joy assigned credit for the armistice agreement to Eisenhower's willingness to expand the war.[52] Acheson, while not willing to grant specific credit to Eisenhower, concluded similarly that the U.S. presidential election, continuing battles, and ongoing heavy casualties were necessary to convince the Communists they could expect no better terms.[53] The United States was not the only major power to experience a change in leadership; Joseph Stalin died in March 1953. The turmoil of a political transition left the Soviets more willing to consider concessions, and Mao was less willing to follow a less authoritative Kremlin.[54] Syngman Rhee's continuing recalcitrance regarding a unified U.N. policy may also have influenced negotiations. Paul Nitze of the State Department's Policy Planning Staff cited Rhee's unilateral release of North Korean POWs held by his government into the general population as helping to break the POW impasse.[55]

ARMISTICE: *IUS POST BELLUM*?

The Korean armistice was signed July 27, 1953, in Panmunjom. It remains the defining document of the relationship between North Korea, South Korea, and the allied powers of the U.N. Command. No peace treaty has ever been signed, which means that technically speaking, a state of war continues to exist among the parties involved. American troops have remained stationed in South Korea since 1953. In a sense, there really isn't a *post bellum* Korea by which to assess *ius*.

To the degree we can discuss "postwar" conditions, we can safely state that South Korea's current economic status and level of political freedom far outshine those of North Korea—the most repressive society in the twenty-first-century world. Such justice, however, took several decades to fully emerge. Syngman Rhee's "postwar" regime struggled to keep pace with North Korean economic development in the years following the armistice, leading to a popular uprising and military coup in 1961 during which Major General Park Chung Hee took power.[56] South Korea's relationship with the United States, manifested in, among other things, support for the Vietnam War, and its rapprochement with Japan led to significant economic growth. Despite this growth, however, the state's permanent war footing and recurring incidents along the demilitarized zone did not encourage democratic government. Park was assassinated in 1979 by a fellow 1961 conspirator, Kim Chae-kyu, who then took power. Meanwhile, critics of the regime stepped up their criticism of human rights violations and demanded greater freedoms.[57] A growing student movement successfully forged relationships with mainstream citizens that culminated years later, in the summer of 1987, in a successful demand for democratic elections. On December 16, 1987, South Koreans elected No T'ae-u as the first democratically chosen president to govern South Korea after three decades of authoritarian rule.[58]

In conclusion, the question of justice in the Korean War remains as complicated as the conflict itself. American policy makers created a divided Korea in the first place. They did so in the context of growing concerns about Soviet power and expansion that would soon crystallize into the Cold War. By prioritizing global power considerations over the rights of a sovereign people with a long and unified history, the United

States played a significant role in creating the conditions that led to active war between 1950 and 1953.

Confining the discussion of "just war" in Korea to the years 1950 to 1953 produces a complex welter of conclusions. One can argue that from within their Cold War perspective, American policy makers truly believed they could satisfy the requirement of just cause. They were sincere. Within this same Cold War framework, the American response was also proportionate. The East struck first, and the West responded. Ample evidence exists to conclude that *both* sides in the global Cold War conflict viewed Korea in Cold War terms. Confusion comes, however, when we consider the war from a *Korean* perspective. In this context, the struggle for control of Korea was a civil, revolutionary conflict—a nationalist struggle—that was co-opted by both the Communist bloc and the West under the leadership of the United States. From this perspective, justice is far more difficult to find. Poor behavior by the Eastern Bloc may explain but not does legitimate poor behavior by the West.

The United States believed it had a reasonable expectation of success. The United Nations had a legitimate right to intervene under the U.N. Charter, but American involvement prior to June 27 is more fraught. President Truman did fail to secure a congressional declaration of war, but one could argue, first, that Congress effectively acquiesced in regarding U.S. involvement as a "police action" and, second, that the duration of involvement prior to the onset of U.N. oversight was so short and the situation so urgent that Truman's authority as commander in chief was sufficient to give him the right to send troops. The strength of U.S. control over the U.N. Command introduces yet another complication, but in the end the United Nations *was* the titular head of the effort, so the letter if not always the spirit of the law was respected. A strong argument exists for a moral obligation to accede to the request of the United Nations, even if it was a request the United States had forcefully advocated. With regard to right intention, not only do we have no reason to doubt American policy makers' sincerity, but the limited objectives policy makers asserted were commensurate with this principle—though shifting intentions as the war progressed complicated the initial *ad bellum* framework.

Attention to questions of *ius in bello* produce more complicated results. Violations of target discrimination and the doctrine of double effect were sometimes understandable but nonetheless present. The question of ends introduces the same problems found with regard to just cause, reflecting the danger of altering *ius ad bellum* intentions—and especially of contradictory intentions among policy makers. By proceeding beyond the 38th parallel, the U.N. Command under U.S. leadership took a Korean conflict and made it global. Again, shared responsibility with the Chinese and Soviet Communists for this reality may explain but does not legitimate U.S. actions. While North Korean and Chinese prisoners of war were treated much better than their U.N. Command counterparts, violations of *ius in bello* did occur. Finally, U.S. support for voluntary repatriation prolonged the conflict by a year and a half. Despite the deeply troubling questions State Department officials posed about "forced" repatriation, the lives of additional soldiers and civilians were lost.

On balance, then, even a constriction of our consideration to the years 1950 to 1953 produces troubling conclusions. While profoundly understandable within the Cold War context, the U.S. record in Korea was decidedly mixed, bringing into question the justice of this conflict. *Ius in bello* considerations, in particular, prompt concerns, as do policy makers' conflicting and often shifting statements of intention. Ultimately, however, we must return to the broader, deeper history of U.S. involvement in Korea. From the ashes of Japanese colonialism, the United States took a single, if deeply troubled, nation and split it in two. South Korea has flourished in the decades following armistice, and especially since democratic conditions were secured in the late 1980s. Even so, after almost seven decades Korea remains two nations, and peace remains elusive.

NOTES

1. James A. Michener, *The Bridges at Toko-Ri* (New York: Random House, 1953), 142.

2. William Stueck, *Rethinking the Korean War: A New Diplomatic and Strategic History* (Princeton: Princeton University Press, 2002), 11–12.

3. Sergei N. Goncharov, John W. Lewis, and Xue Litai, *Uncertain Partners: Stalin, Mao, and the Korean War* (Stanford, CA: Stanford University Press, 1993), 133.

4. George F. Kennan, *Memoirs, 1925–1950* (Boston: Little, Brown, 1967), 484.

5. Historian Richard Lowitt argues that the U.S. response to Communist expansion overall post-1945 was "handicapped owing to too rapid disarmament and to too great reliance on an atomic arsenal." Richard Lowitt, ed., *The Truman-MacArthur Controversy* (Chicago: Rand McNally, 1967), 2.

6. Acheson later defended himself by observing that he did not mention Australia or New Zealand, either, and both countries were indisputably under American protection. Furthermore, he argued, the first of all U.S. defense agreements signed post–World War II was signed with Korea (Dean Acheson, *Present at the Creation: My Years in the State Department* [New York: W. W. Norton and Co., 1969], 358). Nonetheless, Acheson became a particular target for criticism of the Truman administration's actions in the Far East.

7. Kennan, *Memoirs*, 490.

8. Kennan, *Memoirs*, 490.

9. Acheson, *Present at the Creation*, 376, 405, 407.

10. Goncharov, Lewis, and Litai, *Uncertain Partners*, 142–43.

11. Stalin's priorities are readily illustrated in his comment to Czechoslovakian president Klement Gottwald in August 1950 that "the United States of America is presently distracted from Europe in the Far East. Does it not give us an advantage in the global balance of power? It undoubtedly does." Donggil Kim and William Stueck, "Did Stalin Lure the United States into the Korean War? New Evidence on the Origins of the Korean War," North Korea International Documentation Project, Wilson Center, July 7, 2011, https://www.wilsoncenter.org/publication/did-stalin-lure-the-united-states-the-korean-war-new-evidence-the-origins-the-korean-war#sthash.hJ1R5JQM.bbBvmhU1.dpuf.

12. Bruce Cumings's *The Origins of the Korean War: Liberation and the Emergence of Separate Regimes, 1945–1947* (Princeton: Princeton University Press, 1981) was profoundly influential in developing historians' understandings of the Korean War as a nationalist conflict. Burton I. Kaufman also highlights this theme in *The Korean War: Challenges in Crisis, Credibility, and Command*, 2nd ed. (New York: McGraw-Hill, 1997). William Stueck argues that Cumings casts the United States as too ideologically rigid and the Soviets and Chinese as excessively flexible and defensive (*Rethinking the Korean War*, 6). Michael H. Hunt and Steven I. Levine emphasize that both the Soviets and the Americans failed to account for Korean nationalism (*Arc of Empire: America's Wars in Asia from the Philippines to Vietnam* [Chapel Hill: University of North Carolina Press, 2012], 131), and Peter Lowe joins them in this interpretation, concluding that "Left to her own devices, Korea would

probably have become a radical and very possibly communist state but one that would not have been subservient to the Soviet Union or China" (*The Origins of the Korean War*, 2nd ed. [London: Longman, 1997], 251). This is not a universal view; Stanley Sandler refers to historians' definition of the Korean War as a "civil war" as "the final irony of Korean history" (*The Korean War: No Victors, No Vanquished* [Lexington: University Press of Kentucky, 1999], 3). Sandler argues that because the great powers divided Korea in the first place, to call the war a "civil war" is an injustice. An injustice it was, but that does not diminish the fact that Korean leaders disagreed, fundamentally, upon the future direction of their country and solicited the backing of powerful allies to further their claims.

13. Stueck, *Rethinking the Korean War*, 66. Steven Hugh Lee essentially agrees with this interpretation in *The Korean War* (Harlow, England: Longman, 2001).

14. Kennan, *Memoirs*, 485.

15. Goncharov, Lewis, and Litai, *Uncertain Partners*, 141–42.

16. Peter Lowe, *The Korean War* (New York: St. Martin's Press, 2000), 5.

17. Lee, *Korean War*, 45.

18. Lee, *Korean War*, 45.

19. Acheson, *Present at the Creation*, 409.

20. Kennan, *Memoirs*, 490.

21. Richard J. Regan, *Just War: Principles and Cases* (Washington, DC: Catholic University Press of America, 1996), 25, 28.

22. Harry S. Truman, *Memoirs*, vol. 2, *Years of Trial and Hope* (Garden City, NY: Doubleday and Co., 1956), 333.

23. Darrell Cole, "War and Intention," *Journal of Military Ethics* 10, no. 3 (September 2011): 178.

24. Acheson, *Present at the Creation*, 416.

25. Lowe, *Origins*, 210.

26. Lowe, *Origins*, 82.

27. Paul Christopher, *The Ethics of War and Peace: An Introduction to Legal and Moral Issues*, 3rd ed. (Upper Saddle River, NJ: Pearson, 2004), 52.

28. Douglas MacArthur, *Reminiscences* (New York: McGraw-Hill, 1964), 365. In some cases, restrictions were lowered toward the end of the war as U.N. forces sought to apply extra pressure during armistice negotiations.

29. Hunt and Levine, *Arc of Empire*, 172.

30. Lee, *Korean War*, 142.

31. Cole, "War and Intention," 177–78.

32. Sandler, *Korean War*, 73.

33. Sheila Miyoshi Jager, *Brothers at War: The Unending Conflict in Korea* (New York: W.W. Norton, 2013), 145–47.

34. Kennan, *Memoirs*, 487.

35. Acheson, *Present at the Creation*, 445, 448–49, 452.

36. Acheson, *Present at the Creation*, 452–54.

37. Stueck, *Rethinking the Korean War*, 100–101.

38. In addition to the memoirs of key figures, strong coverage in general histories of the Korean War, and many MacArthur biographies of varying quality, notable contributions to the historiography of the Truman-MacArthur conflict include Lowitt's primary source collection *The Truman-MacArthur Controversy* and Stanley Weintraub, *MacArthur's War: Korea and the Undoing of an American Hero* (New York: Free Press, 2000).

39. MacArthur, *Reminiscences*, 370.

40. Lowitt, *Truman-MacArthur Controversy*, 37.

41. Mark W. Clark, *From the Danube to the Yalu* (New York: Harper, 1954), 3.

42. Cumings, *Origins of the Korean War*, xxi.

43. Lee, *Korean War*, 80–81.

44. Mark Evans, "Introduction: Moral Theory and the Idea of a Just War," in *Just War Theory: A Reappraisal*, ed. Mark Evans (New York: Palgrave Macmillan, 2005), 13.

45. Lee, *Korean War*, 86.

46. Acheson, *Present at the Creation*, 538, 652.

47. C. Turner Joy, *How Communists Negotiate* (New York: Macmillan, 1955), 166.

48. Joy, *How Communists Negotiate*, 163–64.

49. Lee, *Korean War*, 87.

50. Paul Nitze, *From Hiroshima to Glasnost: At the Center of Decision* (New York: Grove Weidenfeld, 1989), 115–16.

51. Rosemary Foot, *The Wrong War: American Policy and the Dimensions of the Korean Conflict, 1950–1953* (Ithaca, NY: Cornell University Press, 1985), 24.

52. Joy, *How Communists Negotiate*, 161–62.

53. Acheson, *Present at the Creation*, 696.

54. Hunt and Levine, *Arc of Empire*, 169–70.

55. Nitze, *From Hiroshima to Glasnost*, 116.

56. Jager, *Brothers at War*, 290.

57. Jager, *Brothers at War*, 416.

58. Jager, *Brothers at War*, 430.

TEN

Vietnam and the Just War Tradition

Mackubin Thomas Owens

In the history of American warfare, the conflict in Vietnam occupies a unique reputation as a particularly brutal and inhumane war. Critics have charged that it was unjust and characterized by war crimes, atrocities, and the disproportionate application of force. We know today that many of the most scandalous charges were part of a particularly effective Communist, especially Soviet, propaganda campaign. Of course, incidents such as the My Lai massacre seemed to validate the claims of the war's critics. However, an examination of Vietnam reveals that, contrary to the beliefs of many—if not most—Americans, the Vietnam War was for the most part conducted within the constraints of the law of war and the whole just war tradition.

It can be argued that Vietnam met both criteria of classical just war doctrine: *ius ad bellum*, the decision to go to war, and *ius in bello*, the conduct of war once that decision is made.[1] Of course, all decisions must be placed in their historical context.

In addition, it is necessary to apply prudence to the evaluation of actions in wartime. Different times and conditions may make one condition more important than another. Moreover, a reasonable judgment that a condition was met in a particular situation can be changed as a result of additional experience, information, or insight. Field Marshal Viscount Slim, in a delightful account of his early years in the British army, *Unofficial History*, provides an excellent example of the dilemma of the soldier who must react quickly and without much information:

> Then for the first time since I had left the Kotwali I had a moment to run over in my mind the action I had taken during the last half-hour. The soldier always knows that everything he does on such an occasion will be scrutinized by two classes of critics—by the Government which employs him and by the enemies of that government. As far as the Government is concerned, he is a little Admiral Jellicoe and this his tiny Battle of Jutland. He has to make a vital decision on incomplete information in a matter of seconds, and afterwards the experts can sit down at leisure, with all the facts before them, and argue about what he might, could, or should have done. Lucky the soldier if, as in Jellicoe's case, the tactical experts decide after twenty years' profound consideration that what he did in three minutes was right. As for the enemies of the Government, it does not much matter what he has done. They will twist, misinterpret, falsify, or invent any fact as evidence that he is an inhuman monster wallowing in innocent blood.[2]

Those who would judge the conduct of soldiers under the most difficult of circumstances must always remember what Slim says. And at this point it must be stressed that the just war doctrine places restraints on *all* belligerents, regardless of the justness of their cause. Even a cause that is universally recognized to be just does not justify use of any and all means.

JUST WAR IN VIETNAM

For its part, the United States has at one time or another been accused of violating all such standards during the Vietnam War. Critics of the U.S. claimed that its military committed atrocities in the ordinary course of combat and conducted a policy of genocide against the Vietnamese by means of the indiscriminate killing of civilians through bombing and other tactics.

For example, in 1967, Noam Chomsky wrote that "the Vietnam war is the most obscene example of a frightening phenomenon of contemporary history—the attempt by our country to impose its particular concept of order and stability throughout much of the world."[3] In Vietnam, according to Chomsky, the U.S. was waging "a criminal war." Likewise, anti-American groups like the Committee of Concerned Asian Scholars accused the U.S. of ignoring the constraints of the just war tradition in waging war. "The fact is that U.S. war crimes are an accepted and regularly used method of waging war in Indochina," they wrote.[4] According to Guenter Lewy, the charges included "the relocation of population and the creation of free-fire zones, the use of napalm and herbicides, and the treatment of prisoners."[5]

In order to go to war, the just war tradition teaches that competent authority, just cause, and right intention are necessary. Opponents of the Vietnam War claimed that the war was illegal and constituted a war of aggression and that, therefore, the U.S. was in violation of this tradition.

It has been claimed that the U.S. intervention lacked competent authority, that President Johnson conducted the war in violation of his powers under the Constitution. Early congressional opponents of the war, including Senators Wayne Morse (D-OR) and Ernest Gruening (D-AK), later joined by others, made this argument. But in fact, Congress passed the Gulf of Tonkin Resolution in August 1964, which constituted a de facto declaration of war.[6] Johnson and his successor enjoyed eight years of overwhelming congressional support. No one can deny that Congress gave its imprimatur to the war and did not withdraw it until after U.S. troops had left Vietnam.[7] The courts refused to challenge its legality. And the overwhelming majority of the American people accepted the legitimacy of the war. Even when public support withered, it was because people believed it was wasteful and accomplishing no useful purpose, not because they thought it illegal.

Opponents of the war charged that there was no just cause for the war since the U.S. allegedly was intervening in a civil war. But the war in South Vietnam was planned and coordinated by the Communist Party of North Vietnam. North Vietnamese records show that the 15th plenum of the Lao Dong party decided in 1959 to begin the armed struggle against the Saigon government. To support this decision, the North Vietnamese built the "Ho Chi Minh" Trails through Laos and Cambodia, in violation of those countries' neutrality, over which men and supplies moved long before the decision to land American combat units in 1965.[8] The North Vietnamese records, in fact, confirm the U.S. claim in justification of its action in Vietnam. South Vietnam was recognized in international law and diplomacy as an independent sovereign entity, possessing the right of self-defense against external aggression. Furthermore, the U.S. intervention was in keeping with Article 51 of the U.N. Charter, which recognizes the right of collective self-defense.

Opponents of the war cited the corrupt nature of the Saigon government in support of their charge that the regime was illegitimate and therefore did not provide just cause for American intervention. But even a corrupt government has the right not to be victimized by external aggression. And the legitimacy of the South Vietnamese government was far greater than opponents were willing to admit. For, while the support may have been minimal at times, the fact remains that the people *did* support the government. The false narrative that the Vietnam conflict was a civil war or revolutionary war should have been exploded during Tet 1968 when the "popular uprising" predicted by the Communists failed to materialize. It was precisely during that time that the southern insurgents, the Viet Cong, were effectively wiped out because "the people" did not join them.

Opponents of the war asserted that there could have been a peaceful settlement of the conflict without U.S. intervention. But this claim flies in the face of the evidence that the war was directed by the Communist government of North Vietnam. Also, many contemporary conflicts do not lend themselves to peaceful settlements until there is a military decision. Such was the case in Vietnam. There was nothing negotiable: Saigon wished to continue to govern South Vietnam; Hanoi wished to subjugate South Vietnam. If there was ever any doubt about this goal, it should have been dispelled by the disbanding of the National Liberation Front, the Viet Cong, by Hanoi shortly after its victory in the spring of 1975. Most of the Southern insurgents, who thought they were fighting for local autonomy, either were "reeducated" by the Communists or became refugees to the West or China.[9]

Opponents of the Vietnam War often claim that America had imperialistic designs on Southeast Asia. Of course, Vietnam's geographic position certainly made it one of only five or six countries in the world that were truly vital to U.S. interests at the time. The subsequent Soviet presence in Cam Ranh Bay attests to the strategic importance of Southeast Asia. But there was no gain of the sort "anti-imperialists" usually attribute to an imperialist enterprise.

At the same time, the U.S. went out of its way to avoid the impression that Vietnam constituted some sort of an anti-Communist crusade. The American attitude was summarized by Robert McNamara: "The greatest contribution Vietnam is making—right or wrong is beside the point—is that it is developing an ability in the United States to fight a limited war, to go to war without the necessity of arousing the public ire."[10] The late Harry Summers demonstrated in his book *On Strategy* the critical problem with this approach to war, but in any event it clearly indicates right intention on the part of the U.S.

Given that the cause was just, and in the light of the probability of success, were the expected costs and evils of the war proportionate to the good achieved by defending that just cause? On the basis of the information available to the decision makers at the time, it appears that the costs and evils were proportionate to the good. In retrospect, we can say the probability of success was overestimated, because the will of the North Vietnamese was underestimated, and that of the Americans overestimated. But given the information available at the time of the decision, the costs of the attempt to achieve a degree of success comparable to that achieved in the Korean War were proportionate to the end of avoiding a Communist victory. Certainly this judgment is vindicated in retrospect by the brutalities that have been subsequently inflicted upon all of Southeast Asia by the Communist conquerors.

Even many critics who maintain that the U.S. had a right to be in Vietnam believe that the U.S. military conducted the war in a particularly brutal way, violating the international laws of war or committing war crimes and crimes against humanity. These charges are very serious, yet few people who accept the conclusions of the critics understand what is actually at stake. The 1946 Judgment of the International Military Tribunal at Nuremberg defined war crimes as violations of the laws or customs of war. Such violations shall include, but not be limited to, murder, ill-treatment, or deportation to slave labor or for any other purpose of civilian population of or in occupied territory, murder or ill-treatment of prisoners of war or persons on the seas, killing of hostages, plunder of public or private property, wanton destruction of cities, towns, or villages, or devastation not justified by military necessity. Crimes against humanity are described as murder, extermination, enslavement, deportation and other inhuman acts committed against any civilian population, before or during the war, or persecutions on political, racial, or religious grounds.[11]

A candid observer examining U.S. conduct of the Vietnam War in light of the Nuremberg criteria would have to conclude that the U.S. generally executed the conflict within the guidelines of customary law, just war reasoning, and the positive law of war. Excesses and violations were usually treated as such. A close examination of the charges made against the U.S. in its conduct of the war reveals that they are mostly without substance.

FIRE POWER

No one can deny that Americans relied heavily on the use of fire power in Vietnam. Fire power is a part, for better or worse, of the "American way of war."[12] Americans traditionally have looked at soldiering as temporary, something to be gotten over as quickly as possible. Fire power is the American substitute for expending infantrymen's lives. While American commanders have been willing to accept heavy casualties at a given time and place, and while American soldiers have never lacked courage or been unwilling to face death, fire power has constituted the American alternative to producing a nation of soldiers and is designed to keep casualties relatively low.

But the use of fire power itself does not per se violate the positive law of war or the principles of just-war conduct. Richard A. Falk's charge that the "massive use [by Americans] of cruel tactics directed indiscriminately against the civilian population [was] in flagrant violation of the minimum rules of war" is simply untrue.[13] It was, after all, the Viet Cong and North Vietnamese Army who turned hamlets into battlefields. The Communist practice of "clutching the people to their breast" was a violation of the Geneva Convention of 1949, which prohibits a combatant from using members of a civilian population as a shield: "The presence of a protected person may not be used to render certain points or areas immune from military operations."[14] And while the Hague Convention IV (1907) prohibits the attack or bombardment of inhabited areas that are not defended, it is the general practice of states to treat a town occupied by a military enemy as a defended place, subject to attack. That the official U.S. position was to avoid the indiscriminate attack of civilians is indicated by a 1966 directive of the U.S. military command in Vietnam: "Firing on localities which are undefended and without military significance, is a war crime."[15] Clearly, the U.S. command attempted to abide by the principle of discrimination, but the method of fighting employed by the Viet Cong and the Peoples' Army of Vietnam (PAVN) made discrimination difficult in practice.

Furthermore, the ideological claim of the Vietnam Communists was that in a "peoples' war," there is really no such thing as a noncombatant. Such a belief makes it very difficult to abide by the principle of discrimination. General Giáp, as well as other advocates of people's war, maintained that the population as a whole were in effect soldiers, that the role of the people in a protracted war is essential, and that success in people's war required the total commitment of the whole population. In Vietnam, women and children often set mines and booby traps and engaged in other warlike actions against Americans. If the U.S. had taken Giáp seriously, it logically could have concluded that it had no need to concern itself with such just-war and law-of-war niceties as discrimination. Nonetheless, adherence to the principle of discrimination was the official U.S. position, and despite the severe difficulties of the Vietnam environment, most commanders and individual soldiers discriminated between civilians and the enemy when at all possible.

Interestingly, a major U.S.-Vietnamese effort to facilitate discrimination—the population relocation program and the concurrent designation of certain areas known to be hostile as "specified strike zones," a euphemism for free-fire area—was attacked by critics as itself a war crime. The reason for relocating certain parts of the South Vietnamese population was to enhance both the security of the population and the effectiveness of U.S. fire power. Though the population was more secure in these areas than in those contested by the Allies and the PAVN-VC, critics charged that such relocations were in violation of Article 49 of the Geneva Convention of 1949. But it should be noted that Article 49 not only *allows* the evacuation of civilians from a combat zone; it imposes a *duty* to effect such relocations. Article 49 refers to an "Occupying Power" in its prohibition against "mass forcible transfers, as well as deportations of protected persons from occupied territory to the Territory of Occupying Power or to that of any other country occupied or not."[16] The main intention of this article thus is to prohibit the deportation of subject populations for the purpose of employing them as forced labor, a practice followed by the Germans in World War II. But even if it is claimed that the U.S. was an occupying power, which it was not, Article 49 allows "total or partial evacuation of a given area if the security of the population or imperative military reasons so demand."[17] Since it can be argued that both requirements existed in many contested areas of Vietnam, even one who accepts the most unfavorable representation of the status of the U.S. under international law cannot claim that the U.S. violated Article 49 by relocating Vietnamese civilians.

While the U.S. attempted to adhere to the principle of discrimination in conducting the war, the issue of proportionality is far more troublesome. Although the U.S. Army's Law of Land Warfare, which governed the conduct of army and marine units in Vietnam, clearly states that "loss of life and damage to property must not be out of proportion to the military advantage to be gained,"[18] in practice disproportionate means were often employed. The reason for the frequent use of disproportionate means derives partly from the "American Way of War" described above, but also because in most combat situations a commander or an individual has to act on the basis of incomplete information, a point that Slim made in the situation described above. Doubtless American soldiers and unit commanders overreacted on many occasions and employed fire power out of proportion to military utility. But any judgment that a particular action was disproportionate must take into account the specific circumstances as seen by the decision maker *at that time*. A commander who overestimates the size of an enemy force and who, based on his overestimation, employs artillery and air support in an effort to reduce casualties to his troops is guilty perhaps of bad judgment, but not of war crimes. As stated in the *Hostages* case before the Nuremberg Tribunal:

> If the facts were such as would justify the action by the exercise of judgment, after given consideration to all the factors and existing possibilities, even though the conclusion reached may have been faulty, it cannot be said to be criminal. And further, it is our considered opinion that the conditions, as they appeared to the defendant at the time, were sufficient upon which he could honestly conclude that urgent military necessity warranted the decision made. This being true, the defendant may have erred in the exercise of his judgment, but he was guilty of no criminal act.[19]

Many authors have observed that the destructive U.S. search-and-destroy missions that eventually affronted the moral sensibilities of the American people resulted from a faulty strategic understanding. But this means that American conduct of the war was a strategic, not a moral, failure, a judgment confirmed by the ruling in the *Hostages* case. We shall return to U.S. operational strategy later in the chapter.

NAPALM AND DEFOLIANTS

One of the customary bases of just-war conduct is the prohibition of certain means. There has been a long history of attempts to outlaw certain weapons; unfortunately, effective weapons are not likely to be banned by international agreement without some overriding reason. The Hague Convention IV prohibits the use of "arms, projectiles, or material calculated to cause unnecessary suffering," a rule intended to achieve proportionality and humanity reflective of the intent of the law of war to avoid needless suffering. But according to the U.S. Law of Land Warfare, "What weapons cause 'unnecessary injury' can only be determined in light of the practice of states in refraining from the use of a given weapon because it is believed to have that effect."[20] Since the standard used has been whether a weapon causes suffering disproportionate to the military advantage it confers on its user, in practice no *effective* weapon has ever been banned because it causes "unnecessary suffering."

Such is the case with napalm. The international legal consensus, ratified by the practice of states, is that the use of incendiary weapons against military targets does not violate Article 23 of Hague Convention IV, as charged in 1971 by the International Commission of Inquiry into U.S. Crimes in Indochina. Napalm is particularly effective against troops in fortified positions, bunkers, caves, and tunnels, and in cases where close proximity to friendly forces prohibits the use of high-explosive fragmentation bombs. U.S. rules of engagement stated that "the use of weapons which employ fire, such as tracer ammunition, flamethrowers, napalm and other incendiary agents, against targets requiring their use is not violative of international law. They should not, however, be employed in such a way as to cause unnecessary suffering to individuals."[21] Yet, as in the case of fire power, much latitude generally was given to the commander on the spot in his decision to use napalm. The question then is not one of the legality of napalm, but of proportionality. As in the *Hostages* case, while the use of napalm may have indicated an error in judgment, it did not constitute a criminal act.

Concerning the use of herbicides and riot control agents, the situation is more complex. In 1966, the Communist countries criticized the U.S. for using chemical defoliants and tear gas in Vietnam. In the General Assembly of the United Nations, Hungary charged that the use of these chemicals in wartime constituted a violation of the Geneva Protocol of 1925 prohibiting "the use in war of asphyxiating, poisonous, or other gases, and bacteriological methods of warfare." At the time, the U.S. was not a party to the protocol, although it was generally accepted in the U.S. that the use of chemical or biological agents was prohibited by customary usage. To the Hungarian charges, the United States replied that the protocol did not apply to nontoxic gases or chemical herbicides. It was supported in this interpretation by Canada, Japan, the U.K., and Italy. While the debate over the interpretation of the protocol was still going on, President Nixon announced on November 25, 1969, that he would resubmit the protocol to the Senate for ratification. He reaffirmed

U.S. renunciation of the first use of lethal chemicals and announced the unilateral U.S. renunciation of biological warfare.

ATROCITIES

It is a common charge that Americans committed atrocities in Vietnam daily. For instance, John Kerry, a former U.S. senator and secretary of state during the Obama administration, leveled this charge during testimony before the Senate Foreign Relations Committee in April 1971.

> I would like to talk, representing all those veterans, and say that several months ago in Detroit, we had an investigation at which over 150 honorably discharged and many very highly decorated veterans testified to war crimes committed in Southeast Asia, not isolated incidents but crimes committed on a day-to-day basis with the full awareness of officers at all levels of command.... They told the stories at times they had personally raped, cut off ears, cut off heads, taped wires from portable telephones to human genitals and turned up the power, cut off limbs, blown up bodies, randomly shot at civilians, razed villages in fashion reminiscent of Genghis Khan, shot cattle and dogs for fun, poisoned food stocks, and generally ravaged the countryside of South Vietnam in addition to the normal ravage of war, and the normal and very particular ravaging which is done by the applied bombing power of this country.[22]

The revelation that a massacre of civilians had taken place at My Lai and had been covered up by the army seemed to confirm this view. Various "tribunals" and "inquiries" were established, and because of the testimony given at these events, it was generally accepted that U.S. atrocities were a matter of policy. Close examination of the records reveals that few of the witnesses at these tribunals gave specifics. But despite the absence of corroborating evidence, the media treated the atrocity stories with little circumspection. Allegations were repeated again and again to the extent that it became difficult, if not impossible, to determine the truth.

Again, there is no question that atrocities occurred. Between 1965 and 1973, 201 army personnel and 77 marines were convicted of serious crimes against Vietnamese. That many crimes either in war or in peace go unreported, combined with the particular difficulties encountered by Americans fighting in Vietnam, suggests that more crimes were committed than reported or tried. But even such a severe critic of American actions in Vietnam as Daniel Ellsberg rejected the idea that events like My Lai happened daily. "My Lai was beyond the bounds of permissible behavior, and that is recognizable by virtually every soldier in Vietnam. They know it was wrong. . . . The men who were at My Lai knew there were aspects out of the ordinary. That is why they tried to hide the event, talked about it to no one, discussed it very little even among themselves."[23] Indeed, it was a U.S. Army helicopter pilot interposing his aircraft between American soldiers and Vietnamese civilians during the massacre that helped end it.

The atrocities committed by Americans in Vietnam can be generally attributed to what the Greeks called *thumos*, or spiritedness, which manifests itself as righteous indignation or anger. The frustration of troops fighting under the most difficult conditions, against a frequently unseen enemy, the loss of friends to mines and booby traps, sometimes planted by ostensible noncombatants, led them on some occasions to vent their anger on Vietnamese civilians. While this does not excuse barbaric behavior, it does help explain it. And certainly the random violence of individual American acts is to be contrasted to the use of terror as a matter of policy by the Vietnamese Communists. Yet so widespread was the belief that Americans were conducting a barbaric war that many opinion makers refused to believe, despite the irrefutable evidence, that the wholesale slaughter of civilians in Hue during Tet was perpetrated by the Communists.

Those atrocities that were committed by Americans in Vietnam were, with the exception of My Lai, committed by individuals or small groups. All were in violation of standing orders. The U.S. rules of engagement were, according to Telford Taylor, formerly chief counsel for the prosecution at the Nuremberg trials and a critic of many aspects of U.S. Vietnam policy, "virtually impeccable."[24] Indeed they were so restrictive that they evoked a great deal of criticism from members of Congress appalled at the disabilities placed on American units. The evidence that Americans committed atrocities regularly as a result of operational policy is severely lacking.

BOMBING OF NORTH VIETNAM

Perhaps no aspect of the U.S. war in Vietnam has been as roundly attacked and condemned as the use of air power against North Vietnam. Opponents charged that the U.S. engaged in terror bombing on a scale unprecedented in the history of the world. The infamous Russell International War Crimes Tribunal accused American aviators of systematically and intentionally bombing medical facilities and other noncombatant targets. In May 1967, the tribunal concluded unanimously that "the government and armed forces of the U.S. are guilty of the deliberate systematic and large-scale bombardment of civilian targets, including civilian populations, dwellings, villages, dams, dikes, medical establishments, leper colonies, schools, churches, pagodas, historical and cultural monuments."[25]

Fortunately, the vicious anti-America bias of the tribunal (which led even Richard Falk, a vociferous critic of the war, to label it a "judicial farce") undermined its credibility.[26] But U.S. prestige was severely damaged by the reports of the respected *New York Times* correspondent Harrison Salisbury, which indicated that the United States was intentionally attacking civilians in the North—even though the facts were otherwise.[27] In his report on Nam Dinh, for instance, Salisbury created the impression that the U.S. was bombing a peaceful textile town with no military targets. Nam Dinh, however, was a major transshipment point for supplies and soldiers en route to the South. It also housed a large railroad yard, a major storage depot, a fuel dump, and a thermal power plant. It was ringed by anti-aircraft gun batteries and surface-to-air missile (SAM) launchers. As Taylor concluded, Salisbury's reports "fell far short of demonstrating any intent to cause civilian casualties."[28] Only after the damage to the U.S. cause had been done was it acknowledged that Salisbury's dispatches from Hanoi and Nam Dinh were based on unverified North Vietnamese claims.

During Rolling Thunder, the U.S. bombing campaign in North Vietnam from 1965 to 1968, the U.S. estimates are that 52,000 civilians were killed.[29] This figure, representing three years of bombing, must be compared to the 84,000 who were killed in only two nights of bombing against Tokyo in 1945. The relatively small number of civilian casualties in Vietnam can be attributed to the severe restrictions placed on U.S. flyers. Most if not all civilian casualties resulted from collateral effects, and none were intentional. Restrictions on bombing were tight, both in terms of targets authorized and rules of engagement. Restrictive approach angles and other tactical requirements designed to reduce civilian casualties led in many cases to the loss of American flyers. In March 1968, Air Force secretary Harold Brown requested that restrictions be lifted "so as to permit bombing of military targets without the present scrupulous concern for collateral civilian damage and casualties."[30] His request was denied, and the demand for maximum protection of the attacking aircraft was sacrificed to maintaining low levels of collateral damage.

The problem with air power from the standpoint of just-war conduct and the law of war is its inherent inaccuracy. Despite tremendous improvements in precision since World War II, errors were still possible. The North Vietnamese practice of dispersing targets of military importance throughout the country and close to civilian dwellings made collateral damage more likely. And much collateral damage resulted from heavy and sophisticated air defenses in North Vietnam—it is difficult to maintain perfect bombing accuracy when one is under attack by air defense weapons.[31]

While the charges against the U.S. conduct of Rolling Thunder were continuous and intensive, they were nothing compared to the vituperative attack on the so-called Christmas bombing of 1972. "Linebacker II" was a twelve-day bombing campaign to force North Vietnam back to the negotiating table. The evidence is overwhelming that the goal was achieved. The severe criticism evoked by this action constitutes a microcosm of the charges against U.S. use of air power during the whole Vietnam War. Hanoi charged that the bombing was an "escalation of genocide to an all-time high."[32] In only twelve days, the Vietnamese Communists continued, "the Nixon administration wrought innumerable Oradours, Lidices, Guernicas, Coventrys . . ."[33] Americans joined in the denunciation. *New York Times* columnist Anthony Lewis called the bombing not only "a crime against humanity" but "the most terrible destruction in the history of wars."[34] George McGovern, who had participated in the World War II air raids over Germany, called it "the most murderous aerial bombardment in the history of the world."[35]

These claims were dissected and refuted by W. Hays Parks in a seminal article for the *Air University Review*. A cursory examination of the chart from Parks's "Linebacker and the Law of War"[36] reveals the fatuousness of claims such as those sampled above (see table 1). Of course, some at the time recognized the exaggerated nature of the charges against the U.S. in connection with Linebacker II. The *Economist* of London wrote that the Hanoi death toll was "smaller than the number of civilians killed by the North Vietnamese in their artillery bombardment of An Loc in April [1972] or the toll of refugees ambushed when trying to escape from Quang Tri at the beginning of May." That was what made "the denunciation of Mr. Nixon as another Hitler sound so unreal."[37]

This account demonstrates that the bombing campaigns against North Vietnam evoked a great outcry of condemnation of the U.S. brutality. It also indicates that the claims of those who condemned U.S. actions were exaggerations, often bordering on hysterical. But the question remains: Was the U.S. bombing lawful? Was it proportionate? Fifty-two thousand people killed over three years, or thirteen hundred in twelve days, does not compare to eighty-four thousand killed in two days, but it is still a great number of people.

It seems clear from the evidence cited above that Americans did not intentionally attack civilians. The severe restrictions imposed by the rules of engagement and the testimony of those who flew the missions confirm this point. This being the case, the major claim of the opponents regarding illegality evaporates.

The standard of judgment in evaluating aerial warfare is the protocol on air war of the International Committee of the Red Cross (ICRC). The protocol, while not formally ratified, seems to have wide support and can thus be considered a part of international customary law. The principles of this protocol have been accepted by the U.S. Air Force in its Air Force Pamphlet 110–31, *International Law—The Conduct of Armed Conflict and Air Operations*. The protocol states that aerial attacks are to be restricted to military objectives, "which by their nature or use, contribute effectively and directly to the military effort of the adversary, or which are of a generally recognized military interest."[38] Such attacks are still constrained by the principle of proportionality between damage caused and military gain achieved. Continuing, the protocol forbids the direct attack of civilians; "however, civilians who are within a military

Table 1. Comparison of Collateral Civilian Casualties and Damage

Target/Attack	Date(s)	Bomb Tonnage	Dwellings Destroyed	Dwellings Destroyed Per Ton of Bombs	Civilian Deaths	Deaths Per Ton of Bombs
GUERNICA	26 Apr. 1937	40.5	271	6.69	1,654	40.83
GREAT BRITAIN	June–Dec. 1940	40,885	(not available)		23,002	0.56
COVENTRY	14 Nov. 1940	533	2,306	4.33	568	1.06
HAMBURG	24–30 July 1943	5,128.12	40,385	7.87	42,600	8.03
DRESDEN	14–15 Feb. 1945	7,100.5	78,000	10.98	25,000	3.52
TOKYO	9–10 Mar. 1945	1,665	173,182	104.01	83,793	50.33
LINEBACKER II	18–29 Dec. 1972	15,287.4	600	0.04	1,318	0.08

objective run the risk consequent upon any attack launched against this objective."[39] Moreover, the enemy does not gain immunity by locating military targets within populated areas. The civilian population cannot be used as a shield: "The civilian population or individual civilians shall never be used in an attempt to shield, by their presence, military objectives from attack."[40] Furthermore, it is generally agreed that the presence of a military force in a populated area, whether it is occupying it or passing through, deprives such a location of its status as an undefended place.

The moral doctrine which informs the customary law of war governing aerial warfare is the principle of the "double effect." The double effect is a means of reconciling the absolute prohibition against attacking noncombatants with the legitimate conduct of military activity. According to the double-effect argument, it is permitted to perform an act likely to have evil consequences—that is, the killing of noncombatants—if (1) the act is good in itself or at least indifferent, in this case that it is a legitimate act of war; (2) the direct effect is morally justified—that is, the attack of a legitimate military target; (3) the actor aims only at the acceptable effect and does not intend the evil effect, nor does he see the evil effect as a means to his end, however good; and (4) the good effect outweighs the evil effect.[41]

Clearly, the question of intentionality governs any use of the double-effect principle. The evidence supports the contention that U.S. aerial attacks against North Vietnam did not intentionally target civilians, that civilian deaths were the unfortunate collateral result of the North Vietnamese policy of locating military targets in close proximity to populated areas, and that therefore the principle of the double effect is applicable. I conclude that the bombing of North Vietnam did not violate the positive law of war or the constraints of just-war conduct.

COULD THE UNITED STATES HAVE WON IN VIETNAM?

It is an axiom of Vietnam War critics that the Vietnamese Communists were too determined, the South Vietnamese too corrupt, and the Americans incapable of fighting the kind of war that would have been necessary to prevail. According to the conventional view, Vietnam was indeed a "quagmire," a war the U.S. was destined to lose from the very outset.

Some important work of historical revisionism argues that this argument is wrong. The most persuasive work of this genre is Lewis Sorley's important 1999 book, *A Better War*.[42] In this work, Sorley examines the largely neglected later years of the conflict, concluding that the war in Vietnam "was being won on the ground even as it was being lost at the peace table and in the US Congress." As noted earlier, U.S. operational strategy emphasized the employment of lavish firepower and the attrition of PAVN forces in a "war of the big battalions": multibattalion, and sometimes even multidivision, sweeps through remote jungle areas in an effort to fix and destroy the enemy. Such "search and destroy" operations were usually unsuccessful, since the enemy could avoid battle unless it was advantageous for him to accept it. Sorley argues that although such tactics squandered four years of public and congressional support for the war, things began to change when General Creighton Abrams succeeded General William Westmoreland as commander of U.S. forces shortly after the 1968 Tet offensive, joining Ellsworth Bunker, who had assumed the post of U.S. ambassador to the Saigon government the previous spring, and William Colby, a career CIA officer who coordinated the pacification effort. Abrams's approach emphasized not the destruction of enemy forces per se but protection of the South Vietnamese population by controlling key areas. He then concentrated on attacking the enemy's "logistics nose" (as opposed to a "logistics tail"): since the North Vietnamese lacked heavy transport within South Vietnam, they had to preposition supplies forward of their sanctuaries preparatory to launching an offensive. Fighting was still heavy, but now North Vietnamese offensive timetables were being disrupted by preemptive allied attacks, buying more time to enable the South Vietnamese to fight without American assistance.

In addition, rather than ignoring the insurgency and pushing the South Vietnamese aside as General Westmoreland had done, General Abrams followed a policy of "one war," integrating all aspects of the struggle against the Communists. The result, says Sorley, was "a better war" in which the U.S. and South Vietnamese essentially achieved the military and political conditions necessary for South Vietnam's survival as a viable political entity.

Unfortunately, the specter of Robert McNamara has led analysts to overemphasize the early years of the war at the expense of the fighting after Tet 1968. All too often, the history of the war has been derailed over the question of when McNamara turned against the war and why he didn't make his views known earlier. But as Colby observed in a review of McNamara's disgraceful memoir, *In Retrospect*, by limiting serious consideration of the military situation in Vietnam to the period before mid-1968, historians leave Americans with a record "similar to what we would know if histories of World War II stopped before Stalingrad, Operation Torch in North Africa and Guadalcanal in the Pacific."

Sorley argues that to truly understand the Vietnam War, it is absolutely imperative to come to grips with the years after 1968. He contends that, far from constituting a mere holding action, the approach followed by the new team constituted a positive strategy for ensuring the survival of South Vietnam. Bunker, Abrams, and Colby operated from a different understanding of the nature of the war and applied different measures of merit and different tactics. They employed diminishing resources in manpower, materiel, money, and time as they raced to render the South Vietnamese capable of defending themselves before the last American forces were withdrawn. In the process, they came very close to achieving the goal of a viable nation and a lasting peace.

The defenders of the conventional wisdom have replied that Sorley's argument is refuted by the fact that South Vietnam did fall to the North Vietnamese Communists. They have repeated the claim that the South Vietnamese lacked the leadership, skill, character, and endurance of their adversaries. Sorley has acknowledged the shortcomings of the South Vietnamese and agrees that the U.S. would have had to provide continued air, naval, and intelligence support. But, he has contended, the real cause of U.S. defeat was that the Nixon administration and Congress threw away the successes achieved by U.S. and South Vietnamese arms. The proof lay in the 1972 Easter Offensive. This episode of armed *dau tranh* constituted the biggest offensive push of the war, greater in magnitude than either the 1968 Tet offensive or the final assault of 1975. The U.S. provided massive air and naval support, and some units of the South Vietnamese army (Army of the Republic of Vietnam [ARVN]) inevitably failed, but all in all, the South Vietnamese fought well. Then, having blunted the Communist thrust, they recaptured much of the territory that had been lost to Hanoi. Finally, so effective was the twelve-day "Christmas bombing" campaign (Linebacker II) later that year that the British counterinsurgency expert Sir Robert Thompson commented, "You had won the war. It was over." But three years later, despite the heroic performance of most ARVN units, South Vietnam collapsed against a cobbled-together PAVN offensive. What happened to cause this reversal? First, the Nixon administration, in its rush to extricate the country from Vietnam, forced the government of South Vietnam (the Republic of Vietnam [RVN]) to accept a cease-fire that permitted PAVN forces to remain in the south. Then, in an act that still shames the U.S. to this day, Congress cut off military and economic assistance to South Vietnam. Finally, President Nixon resigned over Watergate, and his successor, constrained by congressional action, defaulted on promises to respond with force to North Vietnamese violations of the peace terms.

We cannot say with assurance that South Vietnam would have survived after 1975. But its chances of survival were much improved by Abrams's approach. One wonders what would have happened had Westmoreland's tactics not, in Sorley's words, "squandered four years of public and congressional support for the war."

WHAT KIND OF FAILURE?

Did the U.S. conduct a just war in Vietnam? In terms of *ius ad bellum*, one's answer depends on one's view of the importance of resisting Communist aggression, or (which is the same thing) how one determines legitimacy. If one supports the republican principle of legitimacy, the Vietnam War was just. If on the contrary one advocates a revolutionary paradigm, U.S. intervention was unjust. The record of Communist regimes in meeting the material needs of their people, in recognizing and protecting human rights, and in providing the minimum requirements for fundamental human dignity certainly supports the former claim. Unfortunately, unlike the case of World War II and Korea, there was no agreement of the legitimacy of American involvement in Vietnam. This lack of consensus is the source of a paradox we face in trying to evaluate the Vietnam War. The paradox is that by the principles of *ius in bello*,

American conduct in Vietnam was far more just than in World War II or Korea. The violations in Vietnam of the basic principles of proportion and discrimination were the consequence of inadequate command-and-control efforts, not—as in World War II—the result of deliberate policies, such as the intentional direct attack of civilians. Furthermore, many just-war conduct violations in Vietnam were the result of the deliberate use of the population as a shield by the Communists. Yet the issue of disproportionate or indiscriminate use of force and the incidence of civilian casualties in combat areas has not been raised (until very recently) in critiques of World War II or Korea.

As William O'Brien points out, this means that "the conduct of the Vietnam war has been judged by a different, higher standard than that applied to the conduct of World War II and the Korean War."[43] Despite the substantial record of the U.S. command in attempting to alleviate combat practices that violated the principles of discrimination and proportion, the U.S. was constantly accused of committing war crimes. This leads to a dangerous approach in our evaluation of war. O'Brien writes: "To condemn the Vietnam war on ... *jus in bello* [conduct] grounds means that the *unintended* use of disproportionate and indiscriminate means in Vietnam is weighed more heavily than the *intended* use of such means in a more clearly justified war against Germany and Japan. Such a judgement seems to imply a sliding scale whereby a more just war in terms of *ends* may use more questionable means. Whereas a less just war in terms of ends is required to adhere more strictly to *jus in bello* standards" (emphasis added).[44] This implies that the end justifies the means, a principle which has never been accepted in the just war tradition. It moves us dangerously close to the holy war approach that characterizes the Marxist view of war. And it seems to deny the requirement that all belligerents, just defenders and aggressors alike, equally observe the restraints of just-war conduct. But adherence to objective standards of just war, both in terms of the decision to wage war and the conduct of war, is particularly necessary in the modern age, and no sliding scale can be admitted.

O'Brien continues, making a concise argument on behalf of the requirement for a doctrine of just war: "In view of man's imperfect nature and history, war is a perennial fact of human life. Accordingly, it is necessary and just to prepare for the eventuality of war when efforts to avoid it have failed. The preparation for war of the just and prudent person requires the formulation of moral presumptions and broad policy guidelines that should inform his decisions concerning recourse to war and its conduct."[45] Moral men are often required to fight in defense of both their political communities and the right way of life for human beings. But even given just cause, restraint in the conduct of war is important. War, after all, can never be an end, only a means. Thus, it is right that soldiers be taught and expected to restrain themselves, for without this restraint the ideas for which just wars are fought are negated. Clearly this restraint must be balanced against the requirements of military necessity. Soldiers cannot be required to commit suicide. In particular instances, right action cannot be determined, because of the requirement that decisions be made quickly and under pressure, with information obscured by the "fog of uncertainty" in war.

Given those arguments, and based upon an objective evaluation of the evidence (and personal experience), I would conclude that, in general, American forces fought the Vietnam War within the constraints established by the just war tradition. Excesses and violations were aberrations, not policy. With few exceptions, violators of the customary law, just-war conduct, and the positive law of war were recognized as such and punished accordingly. Authors have shown how our involvement in Vietnam constituted a strategic failure. It was not, however, a moral one.

NOTES

1. On the just war tradition, I have relied heavily on William O'Brien, *The Conduct of Just and Unjust Wars* (Greenport, CT: Praeger, 1981); James Turner Johnson, *Just War Tradition and the Restraint of War: A Moral and Historical Inquiry* (Princeton: Princeton University Press, 1981).

2. Field Marshal Viscount William Slim, *Unofficial History* (Westport, CT: Greenwood Press, 1959), 84–85.

3. Noam Chomsky, "On Resistance," *New York Review of Books*, December 7, 1967.

4. Committee of Concerned Asia Scholars, *The Indochina Story: A Fully Documented Account* (New York: Pantheon Books, 1970), 128.

5. Guenter Lewy, *America in Vietnam* (New York: Oxford University Press, 1978), 224.

6. Gulf of Tonkin Resolution, Pub. L. No. 88-408, 78 Stat. 384. Some legal scholars, while acknowledging that the Gulf of Tonkin Resolution did indeed authorize the president to take military action in Vietnam, nonetheless argue that Congress's action was still unconstitutional because as a "contingent" declaration, it delegated congressional power to the president.

7. The Gulf of Tonkin Resolution was repealed in January 1971.

8. On the decision of the 15th plenum of the Lao Dong Party, see Douglas Pike, *PAVN: People's Army of Vietnam* (Novato, CA: Presidio Press, 1986), 42–49.

9. Doan Van Toai, "A Lament for Vietnam," *New York Times Magazine*, March 29, 1981; Nguyen Cong Hoan, "Hearings Before the Subcommittee on International Organizations of the House Committee on International Relations," July 26, 1977, 145–67. See also Norman Podhoretz, *Why We Were in Vietnam* (New York: Simon and Schuster, 1982), 198–201.

10. Robert McNamara, cited in Harry Summers, *On Strategy: A Critical Analysis of the Vietnam War* (Novato, CA: Presidio Press, 1982), 18.

11. *International Military Tribunal (Nuremberg), Judgment of 1 October, 1946*, 58, The Global Campaign for Ratification and Implementation of the Kampala Amendments on the Crime of Aggression, http://crimeofaggression.info/documents/6/1946_Nuremberg_Judgement.pdf.

12. Russell Weigley, *The American Way of War: A History of United States Military Strategy and Policy* (Bloomington: Indiana University Press, 1960).

13. Richard Falk, introduction to *The Wasted Nation: Report of the International Commission of Enquiry into United States Crimes in Indochina*, ed. Frank Browning and Dorothy Forman (New York: Harper and Row, 1972).

14. Geneva Convention IV, Article 28, International Committee of the Red Cross, https://ihl-databases.icrc.org/customary-ihl/eng/docs/v2_rul_rule97.

15. MACV Directive 20-4, April 27, 1967 (Superseding MACV Directive 20-4, March 25, 1966), Section 3.c., Military Legal Resources, Library of Congress, http://www.loc.gov/rr/frd/Military_Law/pdf/RDAR-Vol-III Book1.pdf.

16. *Convention (IV) Relative to the Protection of Civilian Persons in Time of War*, Geneva, August 12, 1949, International Committee of the Red Cross, https://ihl-databases.icrc.org/ihl/webart/380-600056.

17. *Convention (IV) Relative to the Protection of Civilian Persons in Time of War.*

18. FM 27-10, *The Law of Land Warfare* (July 18, 1956), chapter 2, section 4.

19. *U.S. vs. Wilhelm List et al.*, in *Trials of War Criminals before the Nuremberg Military Tribunal* (Washington, DC: U.S. Government Printing Office, 1950), 11:1297.

20. FM 27-10, *Law of Land Warfare*, chapter 1, para. 34, 18.

21. FM 27-10, *Law of Land Warfare*, chapter 1, section 3, para. 36, 18.

22. John Kerry, "Vietnam War Veteran John Kerry's Testimony before the Senate Foreign Relations Committee, April 22, 1971," in a study module for an online course prepared by Dr. Ernest Bolt and Amanda Garrett at the University of Richmond, accessed April 11, 2018, https://facultystaff.richmond.edu/~ebolt/history398/JohnKerryTestimony.html.

23. Daniel Ellsberg, cited in *War Crimes and the American Conscience*, ed. Erwin Knoll and Judith McFadden (New York: Henry Holt, 1970), 130.

24. Telford Taylor, "Vietnam and the Nuremberg Principles: A Colloquy on War Crimes," in *The Vietnam War and International Law*, ed. Richard Falk (Princeton: Princeton University Press, 1969), 4:369.

25. John Duffett, ed., *Against the Crime of Silence: Proceedings of the Russell International War Crimes Tribunal* (New York: Simon and Schuster, 1970), 189.

26. Richard Falk, cited in Lewy, *America in Vietnam*, 312.

27. On Harrison Salisbury's reporting, see Lewy, *America in Vietnam*, 306–406.

28. Telford Taylor, *Nuremberg and Vietnam: An American Tragedy* (New York: Bantam, 1971), 141.

29. Mark Clodfelter, *The Limits of Airpower: The American Bombing of Vietnam* (New York: Free Press, 1989), 136.

30. *The Pentagon Papers: The Defense Department History of United States Decisionmaking on Vietnam* (Boston: Beacon Press, 1971), 4:261.

31. On Rolling Thunder, see Hays Parks, "Rolling Thunder and the Law of War," *Air University Review*, January–February 1982, http://biotech.law.lsu.edu/cases/nat-sec/Vietnam/Rolling-Thunder-and-the-Law-of-War.html.

32. *Pentagon Papers*, 4:261.

33. *DRVN Commission for Investigation of US Imperialists' War Crimes in Vietnam*, 7, 25, cited in Lewy, *America in Vietnam*, 413.

34. Anthony Lewis, "Vietnam Delenda Est," *New York Times*, December 23, 1972, http://vietnamwar.lib.umb.edu/warHome/docs/AnthonyLewisBombing1972.html.

35. George McGovern, NBC interview, December 26, 1972, cited in Martin Herz, *The Prestige Press and the Christmas Bombing 1972* (Washington, DC: Ethics and Public Policy Center, 1980), 42.

36. W. Hays Parks, "Linebacker and the Law of War," *Air University Review* 34, January–February 1983, 2–30.

37. "Use of Air Power," *Economist*, January 13, 1973, 15.

38. Javier Guisández Gómez, "Law of Air Warfare," *International Review of the Red Cross*, no. 323, June 30, 1998, International Committee of the Red Cross, https://www.icrc.org/eng/resources/documents/article/other/57jpcl.htm.

39. Gómez, "Law of Air Warfare."

40. Gómez, "Law of Air Warfare."

41. On the double effect, see, e.g. Thomas Aquinas, *Summa Theologiae*, II-II, q. 64, a. 7, New Advent, http://www.newadvent.org/summa/3064.htm#article7.

42. Lewis Sorley, *A Better War: The Unexamined Victories and Final Tragedy of America's Last Years in Vietnam* (New York: Harcourt Brace and Company, 1999).

43. O'Brien, *Conduct of Just and Unjust Wars*, 124.

44. O'Brien, *Conduct of Just and Unjust Wars*, 125.

45. O'Brien, *Conduct of Just and Unjust Wars*, 329.

ELEVEN

The First and Second Gulf Wars

Darrell Cole

The Greek historian Thucydides once argued that all war is caused by some combination of fear, honor, and interest.[1] These are the reasons peoples fight. We recognize these reasons in the U.S.'s decision to initiate the Gulf Wars. The U.S. fought the First Gulf War (GW1) for reasons of honor in living up to the treaty with Kuwait, and of interest in preserving stability in the Gulf region. The Second Gulf War (GW2) was fought for reasons of fear of Iraq providing terrorist groups with the means to attack the U.S. or its allies with weapons of mass destruction (WMD), of honor in striking at any political regime that would support elements that lent their power to the terrorist attacks on 9/11, and of interests in ridding the Gulf region of a destabilizing force. These are also the very reasons why GW2 spilled into Afghanistan. Fighting wars for reasons of fear, honor, and interest is what human beings do, but those reasons are not always just in themselves. The just war tradition demands a higher level of moral reasoning to justify the use of force. This chapter examines these reasons for the Gulf Wars in the light of what the just war tradition specifies as possible just causes for war. In addition to looking at both wars in terms of right authority, right intention, reasonable hope of success, and use of force as best means, I examine whether the combat tactics demonstrated, in the main, concern for causing more good than harm (proportion) and for protecting as far as possible innocent life (discrimination or noncombatant immunity). I conclude by examining how well the U.S. gave the conquered people their due in the aftermath of both wars.

IUS AD BELLUM

Right Authority

With respect to the U.S., there is no question that right authority was met in both Gulf Wars. In both cases Congress authorized President George H. W. Bush and then President George W. Bush to use force if they determined it to be necessary. And they did. True, those who tend to hold the legal positivist view of just war would find more justice in George H. W. Bush's decision to fight GW1 because his administration created an impressive international coalition (thirty-four nation-states) and received explicit authorization from the U.N. Security Council for the invasion. George H. W. Bush was able to do this because he was responding to a clear act of illegal aggression by Iraq when it invaded and annexed Kuwait in August 1990. George W. Bush's coalition efforts for GW2 were much smaller and much less successful. Still, the efforts were made, and the legal story is not as straightforward as critics would have it. President George W. Bush may not have had the full international blessing his father was granted in GW1, but he did have at least a partial blessing.[2] In any event, right authority in classical just war tradition terms was met with respect to the U.S. in both cases as the country's lawful political leaders of the nation held the responsibility for choosing to use force for the common good.

Just Cause

Were the causes just in both wars? The cause of GW1 was Saddam Hussein's act of aggression against Kuwait, the human rights abuses inflicted by Hussein's regime, and the U.S.'s duty to live up to the treaty with

Kuwait by expelling Iraqi forces and inflicting enough damage on Iraq's military to keep Hussein's territorial expansion desires dormant for a considerable time. This, in turn, would strengthen political and economic stability in the region. These are obvious elements of a just cause, and there has been little debate over the issue. The cause of GW2, however, was more complex and has been subject to considerable debate. In a March 17, 2003, televised speech from the White House, President George W. Bush stated four causes for GW2:

1. Iraq possessed weapons of mass destruction.
2. Saddam Hussein's regime was a threat to the region, to the U.S., and to the U.S.'s allies.
3. Iraq was aiding, training, and harboring terrorists.
4. The U.S. had a right to preemption, to "set a course of safety" instead of allowing the status quo to reach its deadly consequences for the region, the U.S., and its allies.[3]

The Bush administration has been attacked most vociferously over the claim that Iraq possessed weapons of mass destruction. In clarifying this issue we must distinguish what the administration and its main ally (the U.K.) thought they had good reasons to believe and what was actually discovered after the invasion. If there were good reasons to believe that Iraq did possess such weapons, it would be unfair and incorrect to judge the war unjust merely because no WMD were found. Were there good reasons? The answer may depend on what one wishes to count as a WMD. By most definitions of WMD, which include weapons such as anthrax, Iraq did possess them and in great quantities.[4] The Bush administration, however, led people to believe that Saddam Hussein was in the process of gaining nuclear weapons capabilities, and this was, to put it most generously, a misreading of the information that borders on incompetence. Critics such as Craig White have no intention of putting the matter so generously and accuse the administration of intentionally misleading the audience in an attempt to garner overwhelming support for the invasion.[5] However, it is important to point out that, even if this were true, we could not jump immediately to the conclusion that the war was unjust, only that President Bush "sweetened" the just cause category with misinformation. In other words, the great quantities of other WMD were just cause enough, and there was no doubt about the character of the regime that had proven its willingness to use WMD on its own people.

The Bush administration has also been roundly criticized for making too close a connection between Iraq and terrorism. White, for example, argues that the only known terror-training camp in Iraq was in the northeastern province and it was not controlled by Saddam Hussein.[6] However, it is necessary to delve more deeply into the motivations of the Bush administration. The August 2003 terrorist attack on the U.N. headquarters in Baghdad was seen by the administration as an attack on the very principles of the international system of nation-state relations. This attack took place in a nation-state led by a man who showed little compunction when he used chemical WMD on his own people and had stockpiled more for future use. To add to U.S. worries, Hussein desired nuclear weapons as a deterrent to intervention and as a possible weapon to use against any enemy. The administration was also keenly aware that Hussein was killing thousands of his own people while the previous Bush and Clinton policy of containment was in place.[7] A regime capable of such evil would surely not stop at cutting WMD deals with terrorists if it thought it could do so to its own advantage.

There is no doubt that Saddam Hussein posed a threat both to the region and to the U.S. and its allies. The only dispute concerns just how imminent the threat had become by the time the president decided to invade. How one answers that question will set the table for how one views the right to preemption, a right that is open to the governing authorities in the eyes of the classical just war tradition. If in principle we judge that an enemy's status quo will certainly lead to dire consequences for us, then we may use preemptive force to protect ourselves.[8]

Preemptive war is especially controversial because it is currently unlawful, but such wars could be necessary and just against enemies that have the potential to acquire or use WMD for terroristic purposes.[9] Were such concerns justified? Certainly Paul Wolfowitz, the deputy defense secretary under George W. Bush, was convinced that the U.S. was not going to be spared terrorist attacks. The U.S.'s best defense was to become more proactive in the fight against terror. By July 2002, the head of Britain's MI6, Sir Richard Dearlove, had concluded that the Bush administration wanted to remove Saddam Hussein because of the "conjunction of terrorism and WMD."[10] The U.S. was not confident that the U.N. could set a course of safety, and with good reason. The U.N. and Europe failed in Bosnia. U.N. Secretary General Kofi Annan admitted that the U.N. could not do its job of bringing peace and order to places as politically unstable as Bosnia. President Clinton responded by ordering air strikes on Serbian positions. In March 1999 NATO bombed Yugoslavia. These acts of force were carried out without a U.N. resolution. The U.S. and the U.K. knew such a resolution would never be forthcoming because Russia would veto it. Annan voiced his regret that the U.N. Security Council was not consulted but admitted that sometimes force must be used.[11] The problem here is that the U.N. was not created to deal with the dangers of nonstate actors and their attempts to acquire WMD or to influence rogue nations who possess WMD.[12] With no effective protection to be had from the U.N., the Bush administration decided to set its own course of safety with preemption.

Supporters of the invasion may also note the consequences of allowing the inspectors more time and not invading in a timely manner. The policy of containment had already been very costly both in financial terms (large number of troops employed in Saudi Arabia) and political terms (those same troops provoked unrest in the area because Islamic extremists resented their presence and stirred up action against the U.S.). One could argue further that the sanctions in place had begun to erode to such a degree that they were in fact ineffectual.[13] U.S. and U.K. troops had already gathered around the border, and Saddam Hussein was aware of all this. All he had to do was to give in a little (not substantially and certainly not permanently), the allied troops would have to leave, and he would achieve a great victory and be free to go right back to developing more WMD. Also, the U.S. would in the eyes of the Muslim world no longer be feared as a nation willing to back up its threats with actual force. The U.N. itself would have been rendered ineffectual in the eyes of Hussein and much of the Muslim world since everyone could see how easy it was to get around its requirements.

One may still question the necessity of GW2. Of course, the potential justice of a war is not exhausted by its necessity. Strictly speaking, no war is necessary because state leaders can always choose to capitulate to an enemy or do nothing to protect their people or others. Thankfully, few leaders will follow this path. However, because war brings so much misery, we rightly wish any recourse to it to be necessary in the sense that we simply must engage in it if we wish to achieve a desired and specific just state of affairs in a timely manner. Thus, we are always on the lookout for ways to help us distinguish some obviously necessary uses of force from those that are not so obvious. One popular way of doing this is well articulated by Richard Haass, who argues that wars of necessity involve "the most important national interests," while wars of choice involve lesser interests.[14] Haass admits to the subjective nature of the distinction, and he demonstrates little desire to work out any boundary markers, but he comes down squarely on the side of self-defensive wars as necessary and just while all other wars are unnecessary and, so, much harder to justify. Haass argues that GW2 was unnecessary because the U.S. could have modified Iraq's behavior without forcing a regime change. He may be right about that. Michael Walzer was certainly of the opinion that the U.S. could have achieved the disarmament of Iraq by extending the no-fly zone to cover all of Iraq, increasing the stopping and searching of all ships bound for Iraqi ports, adding more inspectors, bringing in U.N. troops, and applying pressure on France to build up its own troops and send them to Iraq.[15] The reply from an invasion supporter would be threefold: first, that the containment measures in themselves would prove ineffective; second, that France (and Russia) would never agree to send their own troops in Iraq; and third, that even if the combination of containment measures and the presence of U.N. and French (or Russian) troops would modify Hussein's behavior to some degree, the invasion would succeed in a more complete and lasting fashion than other options such as containment because it would effect a more permanent political change within the country. In the end, this is a judgment call, and it is one that we must allow those responsible for our safety to make.

War for Oil?

I would be remiss if I failed to point out that there has been a hot debate about an underlying cause of the Gulf Wars, a cause not made explicit by either president. Many believe that the reasons for both Gulf Wars are reducible to a war for oil. Andrew Bacevich ably argues for this view, and it needs to be considered because there is some truth to it which has a bearing on the justice of both Gulf Wars.[16] Bacevich traces the wars back to President Franklin Roosevelt's Middle East policy, in which the U.S. guaranteed security for Saudi Arabia in return for preferential treatment for oil contracts. When the Iranian revolution threatened the U.S.'s oil supply, President Carter responded by announcing that any threat to the Persian Gulf region is a threat to the vital interests of the U.S. and, as such, must be repelled by any means necessary, including military force. Every subsequent U.S. president has followed the Carter doctrine. Bacevich believes that Carter felt pressured to create this doctrine because it was the only way to preserve U.S. affluence. His basic idea is that American citizens have become so self-indulgent and inwardly empty that they refuse to make do with less, which is what a responsible energy policy would force upon them.

Bacevich's argument has merit, and his assessment need not be read as exclusive of other reasons for engaging in the Gulf Wars.[17] No moral assessment of the Gulf Wars can be complete if we ignore one of the very foundational reasons for U.S. interest in the Gulf region, which is oil. Bacevich rightly brings that reason into focus, but he ignores the genuine concern the U.S. has in rooting out terrorism and the basic ideological rift that exists between all liberal democracies and militant Islam. Bacevich also ignores the fact that U.S. concern about oil is about more than out-of-control consumerism (although it is about that too). Oil is power, and the U.S. does not wish to see that level of power in the hands of terrorists. Thus, any fair assessment of U.S. reasons for fighting two Gulf Wars must include the desire for affordable oil and the desire to protect itself and others from terrorism, which includes the desire to keep the Gulf region out of the hands of militant, terroristic, groups.

Fighting for a scarce resource is not necessarily an immoral act if that resource is required for the common good and has been contracted for in just terms. Consider the following analogy. If the U.S. was literally running out of water and contracted with Canada to provide us with the same, and part of the contract stipulated that we would come to Canada's aid when it was threatened by forces without or within, would this be a just contract? The answer is "yes," because water is clearly a resource that the common good cannot do without. Of course, oil is not as necessary as water, but that does not mean it is not necessary at all. How necessary must the scarce resource be before we can declare uses of force to protect our supply just? One thing is certain. Even if we may rightly argue that, given our present circumstances, oil is of such necessity that uses of force to protect our justly contracted supply are just, we still need a far-reaching energy policy that would make us less dependent upon oil, or at least upon the oil of others, for the lack of an energy policy less dependent upon Middle East oil reserves will lead us into more conflicts in the future.

Right Intention

Right intention means that we must always aim at advancing the good or avoiding evil by securing peace, punishing evildoers, and uplifting the good. Did the U.S.'s military goals meet these intentions? The answer is not as clear-cut as we would like. For one thing, it is hard to achieve the U.S.'s intended political goals in the Middle East with mere military force. General Rupert Smith has written that what Victor Davis Hanson once called "the western way of war," characterized by wars decided by huge, decisive battles, no longer exists.[18] Military force is effective in killing and destroying, and when those two things are useful for achieving a political goal, as they were, for example, in the two World Wars, then military force can be helpful in solving political problems. However, mere killing and destroying will not achieve our intended goals in the Middle East, where one of the main problems is trying to change the will of the people in places where the governing structures are being created and maintained in the face of guerrilla opposition. If we follow General Smith's advice, we must learn how to use the military to "win the clash of wills rather than the trial of strength."[19]

We can see what General Smith is getting at when we review the outcome of GW1, where, despite our overwhelming military victory, we did not meet all of our strategic goals. In fact, we failed to destroy much of the Iraqi military, which meant that we could not modify Hussein's behavior as much as we desired. Certainly we fell well short of weakening him to such a degree that he would be vulnerable to removal. If General Smith's analysis rings true, then what we saw in GW1 is a strategy that could certainly punish evildoers but could not secure lasting peace and so was less effective than it could have been in uplifting the good. In reply to this, a supporter of the limited intervention could argue, as, indeed, it was argued by the president and his national security adviser Brent Scowcroft in their published apologia, that the negatives of trying to run Iraq (an immediate collapse of the coalition, economic costs, additional troop casualties, and increased collateral damage) outweighed the positive of a new regime.[20]

One of President Bush's stated intentions in GW2 was to rid the country, the region, and the world of an evil regime and to replace it with a better one, which is certainly a clear intention of securing a lasting peace rather than merely punishing wrongdoing. Many of the president's critics fail to see just how liberal he was in his efforts. President Bush genuinely sought the change based on an age-old argument about liberal democracies being essentially peaceful regimes. As the Enlightenment philosopher Immanuel Kant once argued, if you want peace, set up democratic republics.[21] This is what Bush sought to do. This is why one of the main supporters of the Bush repudiation of containment, Robert Kagan, argued that President Bush was not a moral realist from the Kissinger school but a liberal in the classic sense.[22] As Thomas Ricks points out, Paul Wolfowitz repudiated the accepted doctrine of containment that had helped to bring democracy to South Korea and the Philippines. He believed all peoples were capable of democracy and that it was in the U.S.'s interest to spread democracy.[23] The intention here is certainly a good one.

One need not intend something malicious in order to fail to meet the criterion of right intention. We may also fail to meet that criterion by a faulty planning that reveals a lack of effort in thinking through the likely consequences of one's actions to the harm of others. The idea here is that evidence of right intention always means that, among other things, the likely consequences of one's actions as they bear on harm to others is thought out well enough that due concern can be noted in subsequent actions. So, wherever right intention is met we should be able to see a correlation between one's stated intentions and one's actions. This is exactly where the intentions of GW2 are suspect. The U.S. failed to field enough soldiers to keep the peace and establish good order. It is telling that GW1 was fought using the military principle of overwhelming superiority, with the U.S. fielding 500,000 troops to remove Iraqi troops from Kuwait. Under Rumsfeld's urging, overwhelming superiority was not adhered to in GW2, and the U.S. fielded only 150,000 troops, sufficient to remove Saddam Hussein from power but little else. This meant that with a force of less than a third of that used in GW1, the troops of GW2 would have to invade, occupy, and keep the peace. With so few troops to guard the borders, terrorists had little trouble making their way into Iraq to oppose the new government.

The U.S. also underestimated how bad the political structure had become in Iraq and how ill prepared the people were to take control of the governing process. With so few troops, America was not prepared to occupy for an extended time. Worse, the Iraqi army was disbanded because the U.S. did not wish to allow any Baath party members to share in the government. This meant turning out thousands of unemployed soldiers, many of whom were easy game for terrorist recruitment. Put simply, the military campaign was not planned in accordance with the stated political intentions. The Bush administration wanted to "change history," but it fielded an army woefully short of the number of troops required to get the job done. It was, indeed, as one of the detractors puts it, "a flawed plan for war and a worse approach to occupation."[24] Apparently, few Middle East experts inside the military were consulted on the war plan, which gives rise to the suspicion that Bush's main intention was to remove Hussein with, at best, the thought that his removal would be enough to bring about the democratic process. One of the supporters of the invasion, David Brock, has intimated that such a view was held by many of Bush's supporters, and they soon came to realize that such a view was nothing more than a "childish fantasy."[25] The strategic objective in Iraq was to bring about a democratic Iraq, which requires the willingness of the majority of Iraqi citizens. The military could not achieve this goal on its own. It is not made to do so. The goal of a democratic Iraq should have meant an extensively worked-out plan of occupation, the very thing so sadly lacking even on the evidence of the U.S. military itself.[26]

The Bush administration stated an intention to remove a dangerous presence from the Middle East and to change history by replacing that dangerous presence with a democratic regime but planned a strategy that had little chance of succeeding in the latter. Thus, the plan had less chance of securing a lasting peace and uplifting the good than it would have had if the planning had been more thorough. The cynic might reply that all the administration wanted to achieve was the removal of Saddam Hussein and his Baath party. But the actions of the administration do not support the cynical view. The amount of money and time spent by the administration (ill spent, actually) in trying to bring about order to postwar Iraq belies such a view. A harder, more realistic, interpretation of the facts is that the administration was simply inept, which, as Aquinas rightly reminds us, is a moral failure when so many lives are at stake. True, supporters of GW2 may wish to appeal to the doctrine of double effect, a moral tool first derived from Aquinas that enables us to draw distinctions between foresight and intention so that the foreseen (but unintended) evil outcome of our actions is not imputed to us as long as there are good intentions and the unintended evil effect is not a means to our intended good outcome. Surely no one would argue that the botched occupation was a means to any good sought. However, Aquinas persuasively argues that even when we do not intend the evil outcome of our actions, and the evil consequence serves as no means to the good we intend, we may still be guilty of evil if we do not show due care in our actions. Lack of due care is clearly evident in the planning of GW2.[27]

Reasonable Hope for Success

Right intention and reasonable hope for success are closely intertwined, for it is hard to see how we could have the former without the latter. The U.S.'s goal in GW1 was simply to get Iraq out of Kuwait, inflict enough damage on Iraq to take the sting out of its military tail for a while, and contain. The goal in GW2 was to eliminate the government of Saddam Hussein and replace it with a democratic one that would be stable and friendly to the U.S. The administration had every chance of meeting its goals in GW1 even if it did not actually succeed as well it desired. Measuring the likelihood of success in GW2 is harder to determine. On the one hand, there was every reason to believe that the U.S. would have little trouble in eliminating the dictatorship of Saddam Hussein and the ruling Baath party. On the other hand, creating a democratic regime in Iraq had to be seen as a long shot at best. However, even if those in the Bush administration believed that there was a good chance for success, that kind of success can only be determined after decades and would be partly determined by being supported by a successive number of presidential administrations (or, at least, not explicitly repudiated by them), much like Truman's Cold War policy. In any event, in order for the policy to succeed, America, at minimum, should not have pulled out of Iraq until the Iraqi people had a functioning government capable defending itself and its citizens. As George Packer points out, Iraq had been disintegrating for decades.[28] The invasion simply accelerated the process. If political victory is to be achieved in Iraq, it will be a process and not an event. The Obama administration's lack of support may mean that we will never know if the Bush administration's plan would have succeeded as intended. With the rise of ISIS it certainly looks like the early withdrawal was a disaster for the region. Whether or not we can ever undo the damage done to the region by two successive presidential administrations, the one by insufficient planning and the other by an untimely pullout, is something no one can predict at this point.

Use of Force as Best Means

The criterion of best means needs to be distinguished from the contemporary criterion of last resort. Last resort is very open to abuse by those who simply wish to counter any and all efforts of using force. However, there is a good point behind the criterion that we should not lose, and I have attempted to capture that in the concept of best means. The point is that we should not resort to force if peaceful means are available that will achieve what we want to achieve in a timely manner. "Best means" makes sure that we have taken the trouble to determine that the use of force in a particular case is the best or only way of achieving our goals in a timely manner. "Best means" was surely met in the GW1. Whether it was met in GW2 depends on how one looks at the goals of the administration. As a way to remove a dangerous threat to the region and to the U.S., the invasion was the best means available. As a way to protect the U.S. from terrorist attacks, the invasion was certainly the only way to achieve that goal in the short term. As a way of protecting the U.S. in the long run by creating a more peaceful and democratic state in the Middle East, the invasion may or may not have been the best means. Regime change is a drastic measure, and when one connects the slim likelihood of success to best means, one has a hard time arguing that regime change in Iraq was the best means. However, one must keep in mind that, according to the Kay Report of September 2004 (from a fact-finding mission headed by David Kay, which looked into possible WMD programs in Iraq), Saddam Hussein was still trying to acquire WMD.[29] Iraq may not have been an immediate threat, but it was an inevitable one.

IUS IN BELLO: DISCRIMINATION AND PROPORTION

Did the wars meet the criteria of proportion and discrimination? The U.S.'s concern with following international law, which has been shaped so largely by the just war principles of discrimination and proportion, meant that both wars in Iraq were fought with scrupulous attention to proportion and discrimination, particularly in the initial phase of GW2, at which point the administration knew that it lacked the popular international support it had in GW1. The air campaign in GW1 first destroyed Iraq's military and civilian communications systems and then caused havoc on Iraqi army positions and supply lines. A very high degree of precision was achieved with the new "smart bomb" technology, created with the specific purpose of meeting the moral commitment to discrimination and proportion. Those same concerns led General Franks to oppose a similar air campaign in GW2 because the Iraqi forces were so widely dispersed that proportion was not likely to be met (too much collateral damage). Thus, a very precise air campaign was devised that concentrated on military targets. U.S. scruples in the area are nowhere better seen than in the U.S.'s decision to risk failing in an important mission in Nasiriyah instigated to capture or kill top Baath party official Muhayfen Halwan and his number-two man, Sultan Al-Sayf. Their meeting place was in a compound near a children's school. Rather than ensure success with satellite-guided bombs, the U.S. decided to cut down on the risk of collateral damage by using helicopters with hellfire missiles. The attack did not succeed. Thus, America exhibited a willingness to fail rather than succeed with too much cost to innocent life.[30]

The U.S. did not achieve such a spotless record in its combat behavior following the initial campaign in GW2. As Nigel Biggar points out, the U.S. probably remained too long in a "war-fighting mode," and as a result more innocent civilians being unintentionally targeted than there should have been; thus the U.S. failed to meet the criterion of proportion.[31] We need to emphasize that this is a failure of proportion and not of noncombatant immunity. Allied troops were going against terrorists dressed like citizens and driving ordinary vehicles. In those kinds of circumstances, innocent civilians will be killed because the nature of the enemy's tactics makes it hard to identify proper targets. However, there is no evidence that U.S. patrols targeted innocent civilians as such. Rather, the evidence points to the initial failure of U.S. troops to switch from a war-fighting mode to a counterinsurgency mode. The British troops can be favorably compared on this point, probably due to their long experience with counterinsurgency tactics. These tactics were soon assimilated by the U.S.

One must look hard at either Gulf War to find any evidence of systematic wrongdoing at the combat level. True, the treatment of some prisoners in GW2, usually at the hands of amateurs (reservists and national guardsmen) necessary to supplement a woefully numbered professional military on the ground, was sometimes shameful and worthy of prosecution to the full letter of the law, but the combat itself was consistently just. Even the critics of the wars must admit that there exists no evidence of wide-scale, systematic misconduct in war.

IUS POST BELLUM

The idea of justice being demanded of the victors after a war is a fairly recent one, and the principles that make up the *ius post bellum* are not as broadly agreed upon as what we find in the *ius ad bellum* and the *ius in bello*.[32] Nevertheless, we can identify a broad agreement in order to apply the *ius post bellum* to the two Gulf Wars. The goal of all just wars is a just and lasting peace. When a just belligerent invades an unjust nation-state, there is a duty to see that the citizenry is given justice. At the very least, the victors owe the conquered people a return to the status quo with notable criminal behavior on both sides brought to justice. At the most, the victors owe the citizenry a better state of affairs.

There were very minimal *ius post bellum* duties for the U.S. following GW1, a war with the limited goals of removing Iraqi troops from Kuwait and inflicting enough damage on Iraq's ability to fight in order to ensure a long measure of peace. The U.S. had a duty to clear the area of armaments for the protection of everyone and, if possible, bring any captured war criminals to trial. The *ius post bellum* duties for the U.S. following GW2 are much more extensive, for the stated goal was to remove Saddam Hussein from power and to assist in forming a new government. The first basic steps toward meeting the *ius post bellum* in this case are to protect the rights of the Iraqi people and to repair the infrastructure. Unfortunately, the U.S. gave contracts only to companies politically connected to the U.S. Even if such moves were justified in the short term, Walzer is right that regulators should have seen to it that Iraqis were employed and moved into positions of authority as soon as possible.[33]

Once a strong and just protectorate is established for short-term effectiveness, the conquerors must begin to build bridges with the conquered in order to make a path toward a free and sovereign Iraq. The ultimate goal of this bridge-building process is to partner with the Iraqis to create a new political order. The U.S. achieved a political success of sorts when it disbanded the army and the national police force in a sweeping effort to end all influence of the Baath party, but the downside was so large that it more than offset any political gain, for the result was several hundred thousand resentful Iraqi soldiers without jobs, who were then easy game for terrorist recruitment. Thus, America ended up making the reconstruction of a new Iraq much more difficult that it need have been. Tellingly, the U.K. forces took a more pragmatic view and partnered with whoever would cooperate with them to establish law and order and get essential services up and running.[34] However, the worst mistake of all made by the U.S. was not fielding enough forces to achieve the nation-building goals stated in its war intention. Put simply, the U.S. plans for invasion never provided for an adequate force of occupation. Even a scholar favorable to GW2, James Turner Johnson, admits that "a particular legacy of the prewar debate was an insufficiency of resources for creating postwar peace."[35] More damning still is the official history, which records that "clearly the Coalition lacked sufficient forces on the ground in April 2003 to facilitate, much less impose, fundamental political, social, and economic changes in Iraq."[36]

DRAWING CONCLUSIONS

Human beings are not unfallen angels. Even their best acts are tainted by self-interest. There is no such thing as a perfectly just war at any phase—*ius ad bellum, ius in bello,* or *ius post bellum.* When we look at acts of force through the moral lens of the just war tradition, we do not expect to see perfection, but we do expect to see those who claim to be just making all attempts to meet the moral goals found in the tradition. When we examine the Gulf Wars in light of *ius ad bellum,* there can be little doubt that the criterion of right authority was met in both cases. There is some doubt about how well the U.S. met the rest of the criteria, especially in GW2, and much depends on how we interpret the facts. The causes for both wars seem plain enough and just on the face of it. True, we feel a gnawing awareness that oil plays a larger role in the conflicts than we would like to admit, but even when we bring that scarce resource to the forefront of the reasons for fighting, along with our concerns for regional stability, we are not deterred from declaring the Gulf Wars just. But we should remind ourselves that concerns about this scarce resource could drag us into further conflicts in the future. In other words, we need to be aware that our desire for a relatively cheap oil supply, when combined with our desire to deprive our enemies of that supply, may play a large role in where we decide to ensure stability.

Right intention, reasonable hope for success, and use of force as best means were clearly met in GW1, even though we may harbor some reservations about the ultimate political success we achieved and may suspect that more might have been done, short of regime change in Iraq, in order to have made for a more just and lasting peace. The criteria are not so clearly met in GW2, where regime change, occupation, and nation building were goals of the war but not properly planned for by our political and military leaders. The inadequate planning of the war, admitted to even by the military's own official history, can cause uneasiness about how well right intention and reasonable hope of success were met. How could we have really intended and hoped to bring a just and lasting peace to Iraq when we fielded so few troops and made such a botched job of the occupation? This basic question shows us how *ius ad bellum* concerns can spill over into the *ius post bellum*. The coalition led by the U.S. had little real chance to achieve an effective, long-term state of justice in Iraq because of the faulty planning. Evidence points to a lack of wisdom and insight rather than malicious intention, but that does not excuse our political and military leaders who planned GW2. However, it must be admitted that the intention to remove from the region a political regime as loathsome and dangerous as that led by Saddam Hussein is a good one and that there existed reasonable hope that the U.S. and its allies would succeed in creating a new government system that would, at least, be no worse than the status quo.

We may conclude on a happy note that, for the most part, America and her allies behaved in exemplary fashion in the field in both Gulf Wars. Those who did not, most notoriously those who mistreated prisoners, were tried and/or dismissed from service. We can thank the lasting influence of the just war tradition for this state of affairs.

NOTES

1. Thucydides, *The History of the Peloponnesian War*, in *The Landmark Thucydides: A Comprehensive Guide to the Peloponnesian War*, ed. Robert B. Strassler (New York: Free Press, 1998), 43.

2. Nigel Biggar, *In Defense of War* (New York: Oxford University Press, 2013), 281.

3. Craig M. White, *Iraq the Moral Reckoning: Applying Just War Theory to the 2003 War Decision* (New York: Rowman and Littlefield, 2010), 40–41.

4. An impressive number of international leaders, as well as U.S. Democrats, thought Iraq possessed WMD. See hereon Larry Elder, "Who Thought Iraq Had WMD? Almost Everybody," Townhall, May 25, 2006, https://townhall.com/columnists/larryelder/2006/05/25/who-thought-iraq-had-wmd-most-everybody-n1221067.

5. White, *Iraq the Moral Reckoning*, 43–45.

6. White, *Iraq the Moral Reckoning*, 65.

7. Human rights groups estimated that Hussein had murdered at least three hundred thousand people since 1991. See William Shawcross, *Allies: The U.S., Britain, Europe, and the War in Iraq* (New York: Public Affairs, 2004), 160.

8. Following Augustine and Aquinas, the just war tradition has held that just war causes include uses of force that attempt to defend the common good against disturbance, to avenge wrongs, to punish wrongdoing when those doing the wrong refuse to make amends, and to seek to restore what has been unjustly seized. This can put the just war position at odds with contemporary moral and legal philosophy, which tends to limit just cause and legality to self-defense and/or humanitarian intervention. This is not to say that the classic just war tradition is unconcerned about legality or self-defense, but it is to say that it recognizes categories of just use of force that may not have full contemporary legal sanction and may not be conceived as pure self-defense.

9. Intervention in another state's affairs in order to protect against terrorist acts or prevent the gain of WMD is justifiable. The rule of law cannot always be observed in such cases. Put differently, we would not wish our political leaders to be so concerned about conforming to the letter of the law on the sanctity of nation-state sovereignty that they failed to take adequate measures to protect us from imminent danger. See the very helpful discussion of this theme in Philip Bobbitt, *Terror and Consent: The Wars for the Twenty-First Century* (New York: Knopf, 2008), 529–31.

10. Thomas E. Ricks, *Fiasco: The American Military Adventure in Iraq* (New York: Penguin Press, 2006), 39.

11. Shawcross, *Allies*, 84.

12. Charles Powell, a foreign policy adviser to Margaret Thatcher, has argued that the U.N. needs to respond to these new dangers by allowing force to be used after reasonable efforts to achieve consensus within the Security Council fail and the international community as a whole is not willing to muster support (cited in Shawcross, *Allies*, 219). This argument has the advantage of recognizing that the Security Council is by no means an infallible system of maintaining justice in the world and must be compensated by the basic need of nation-state leaders to fulfill their basic function to protect their own people from unjust aggression.

13. Shawcross, *Allies*, 58.

14. Richard N. Haass, *War of Necessity, War of Choice: A Memoir of Two Iraq Wars* (New York: Simon and Schuster, 2009), 10.

15. Michael Walzer, *Arguing about War* (New Haven: Yale University Press, 2004), 153–60.

16. Andrew Bacevich, "The Real World War IV," *Wilson Quarterly* 29, no. 1 (Winter 2005): 36–61.

17. For example, Richard Haass also makes the connection between the vast consumption of oil by U.S. citizens and the Middle East as an area of strategic U.S. concern. But Haass also recognizes other U.S. concerns that led up the Gulf Wars: the spread of terrorism, the protection of Israel, WMD proliferation, and humanitarian intervention (see Haass, *War of Necessity, War of Choice*, 76).

18. Rupert Smith, *The Utility of Force: The Art of War in the Modern World* (New York: Knopf, 2005), 3, 312. Hanson argues that the very nature of ancient Greek infantry conflicts was built upon the necessity of getting the conflict over with as soon as possible. Thus, the push for the decisive battle that became so prevalent in the Western way of war through the twentieth century. See Victor Davis Hanson, *The Western Way of War: Infantry Battle in Classical Greece* (New York: Oxford University Press, 1989).

19. Smith, *Utility of Force*, 379.

20. George H. W. Bush and Brent Scowcroft, *A World Transformed* (New York: Vintage, 1999).

21. Immanuel Kant, *Perpetual Peace*, in *Kant: Political Writings*, ed. Hans Reiss (New York: Cambridge University Press, 1970; first published in 1795), 93–130.

22. George Packer, *The Assassin's Gate: America in Iraq* (New York: Farrar, Straus and Giroux, 2006), 19.

23. Ricks, *Fiasco*, 17.

24. Ricks, *Fiasco*, 3.

25. Ricks, *Fiasco*, 380.

26. Donald P. Wright and Timothy R. Reese, *On Point II: Transition to the New Campaign* (Fort Leavenworth, KS: Combat Studies Institute Press, 2008).

27. Thomas Aquinas, *Summa Theologiae* (New York: Benziger Brothers, 1947), II-II, q. 65, a. 8.

28. Packer, *Assassin's Gate*, 458.

29. Shawcross, *Allies*, 192.

30. The story is told by John Keegan, *The Iraq War* (New York: Knopf, 2004), 158–59.

31. Biggar, *In Defense of War*, 311.

32. As late as the seventeenth century, Hugo Grotius, in his groundbreaking work in international law and the just war tradition, gives victors a virtual carte blanche on how they may treat the conquered. See Grotius's *The Laws of War and Peace* (Oxford: Clarendon Press, 1925), 3.6.3. Helpful resources on the

ius post bellum include Louis V. Iasiello, "Jus Post Bellum: The Moral Responsibilities of Victors in War," *Naval College Review* 57, no. 3/4 (2004): 33–52; Davida E. Kellogg, "Jus Post Bellum: The Importance of War Crimes Trials," *Parameters*, Autumn 2002, 87–99; Michael J. Schuck, "When the Shooting Stops: Missing Elements in Just War Theory," *Christian Century*, October 26, 1994, 982–84.

33. Walzer, *Arguing about War*, 166.

34. Keegan, *Iraq War*, 209.

35. James Turner Johnson, *The War to Oust Saddam Hussein: Just War and the New Face of Conflict* (Lanham, MD: Rowman & Littlefield, 2005), 108–9.

36. Wright and Reese, *On Point II*, 573.

TWELVE

The War on Terror and Afghanistan

Rouven Steeves

INTRODUCTION: THE PURSUIT OF JUSTICE IN THE FACE OF TERROR

America's "War on Terror" arguably began on September 20, 2001, with President George W. Bush's speech to the joint session of Congress and the American people. During that address, President Bush stated, "Our war on terror begins with Al Qaeda, but it does not end there. It will not end until every terrorist group of global reach has been found, stopped and defeated."[1] Coming nine days after the infamous 9/11 attacks, the speech set in motion the subsequent wars in Afghanistan and Iraq, as well as American military involvement throughout the Middle East, the Pacific, Asia, Africa, and even Central America and the Caribbean, all of which are still ongoing in some form as of the writing of this chapter. Yet in many ways, America's war against terror is already over thirty years old, and, of course, terror and terrorism are not new phenomena.[2] What is arguably new is that today's war on terror often does not follow conventional Westphalian interstate norms of warfare, raising the question of whether traditional just war criteria are still applicable.[3] Although there are indeed certain practical difficulties, as will become evident in the following analysis, the just war tradition is sufficiently elastic to confront an often transstate enemy that is most often opposed by states rooted in precisely those Westphalian international norms and laws that embody traditional just war criteria. What is more, even if the tradition's elasticity is being stretched, possibly even to a philosophical or theological breaking point, it remains the case that there is no viable alternative to ensure a just response to what is intrinsically unjust and most often outside the historic pale of "normal" interstate warfare. Therefore, undergirding the analysis and argument herein is the awareness that the failure to adequately employ just war principles in conducting operations against terrorists, and the even more amorphous enemy, terror, will likely lead to the employment of means that are themselves terrifying. The brutality of war would only increase, and the limited gains enshrined in international law no less than mankind's aspirations for universal justice would suffer inordinately.

In the remainder of this chapter, then, I will first provide a brief history of the terms *terror*, *terrorists*, and *terrorism*, to situate an equally brief history of America's war on terror from its roots in the 1980s to the events of 9/11. The third section will examine America's contemporary (post-9/11), global war against terrorist networks, with America's war in Afghanistan against the al-Qaeda terrorist network and the Taliban regime serving as a case study to examine the prospects and problems of applying just war criteria in the modern war against terrorism. The concluding fourth section offers some closing thoughts regarding the importance of pursuing political justice in an unjust world with a particular emphasis on the duty of the statesman, who must confront the threat of terror and terrorism without losing sight of justice. Justice, after all, "is the end of government. It is the end of civil society. It ever has been, and ever will be, pursued, until it be obtained, or until liberty be lost in the pursuit."[4]

OF TERROR, TERRORISTS, AND TERRORISM

The cliché that "one man's terrorist is another man's freedom fighter" is all too true, making a unified definition nearly impossible to formulate.[5]

Jonathan Matusitz notes that there are over 200 definitions of terrorism, and a widely cited study by two social scientists examining 109 definitions derived the following statistically significant elements: 83.5% of the definitions included some conception of violence; 65% referenced political goals; 51% included conceptions of fear and terror; 41.5% mentioned psychological effects and reactions; 37.5% referenced inherent discrepancies between the targets and victims (21% referenced arbitrary and indiscriminate targeting, while 32% referenced intentionality, systemic planning, and organized action); 30.5% included references to combat strategy and tactics; and 17.5% included references to victimization of noncombatants, to include civilians and neutral parties.[6] Out of this, Matusitz attempts to devise a "most universally accepted" definition: "Terrorism is the use of violence to create fear (i.e., terror, psychic fear) for (1) political, (2) religious, or (3) ideological reasons (ideologies are systems of belief derived from worldviews that frame human social and political conditions). The terror is intentionally aimed at noncombatant targets (i.e., civilians or iconic symbols), and the objective is to achieve the greatest attainable publicity for a group, cause, or individual."[7] This definition seems comprehensive enough and more thorough than, though not in conflict with, the definition offered in the 2002 *National Security Strategy* (*NSS*), formulated in the wake of 9/11: "The United States of America is fighting a war against terrorists of global reach. The enemy is not a single political regime or person or religion or ideology. The enemy is terrorism—premeditated, politically motivated violence perpetrated against innocents."[8]

Implicit in both definitions is that terrorism's very extremism with respect to its means undermines its moral legitimacy and that it is therefore readily susceptible to the just and moral condemnation of the international community. Although key international legal documents regulating the conduct of war and the treatment of combatants as well as noncombatants—namely, The Hague (1899, 1907) and Geneva Conventions (1949) as well as the Charter of the United Nations, specifically Article 2—apply specifically to sovereign states, the moral impetus behind them arises in large part out of a broader just war tradition. Therefore, if not the laws themselves, the just war tradition and the criteria arising out of it can serve as a guide for justifying military operations against terrorist networks, specific terrorists, and even the ideology of terrorism. After all, the laws of war seek to minimize the unnecessary suffering of both combatants and noncombatants; ensure that the fundamental rights and dignity of prisoners of war, the sick and wounded, and the civilian population are not indiscriminately violated; and promote and establish a just peace. These criteria are applicable to all military engagements, including those against terrorists, and the U.S. has formulated its strategy, operations, and tactics in light of them. That is not to say that the U.S. has not sometimes fallen short or failed to live up to these standards. However, as we shall see in greater detail later in this chapter, the failures to live up to these ideals have been brought to the fore and excoriated precisely because these standards have guided American military operations. With the foregoing thoughts in mind, we turn to a brief account of America's war against terrorism up to 9/11 to situate the third section with its examination of post-9/11 U.S. military operations against terrorism, especially America's war in Afghanistan.

THE WAR ON TERROR UP TO 9/11

At the outset I suggested America's war on terror began on September 20, 2001, with President Bush's address to Congress and the American people in the wake of the September 11 terrorist attacks on American soil. All this is true enough. However, one could also argue that America's war on terror began in earnest with the April 1986 strikes on Libya in response to the Berlin Le Belle Discotheque bombing that same month. Yet even this response must be seen as the first overt military action in light of a train of terrorist attacks starting with the 1983 Beirut barracks bombings, which were followed by the June 1985 hijacking of TWA 847, the Achille Lauro cruise ship hijacking in October 1985, and finally the twin terrorist attacks at the Rome and Vienna airports on December 27, 1985. And even here the beginning is still somewhat arbitrary, for President Ronald Reagan had already announced in 1981, in the wake of the 444 days of captivity of fifty-two U.S. diplomats and citizens in Iran, "Let terrorists be aware that when the rules of international behavior are violated, our policy will be one of swift and effective retribution."[9]

Yet as the foregoing summary of terrorist attacks evinces, response was not "swift" and was often quite ineffective. From the first U.S. airline hijacking in 1961, the U.S. has struggled to formulate an effective strategy to engage terrorists and their networks. In part the geopolitical dynamics of the Cold War limited American actions, and in part the amorphous nature of terrorist networks made retaliation of any type difficult. As Laura Donohue states at the outset of her comprehensive study of U.S. counterterrorist measures from 1960 to 2000, during this period: "The United States introduced a plethora of counterterrorist measures. . . . But in its very call for immediate action, and caught up in dynamics beyond the country's control, America became further and further drawn into having to respond to each event. A complicated network marked by ad hoc adoption of counterterrorist policies ensued, and as the United States continued to attempt to defeat international terrorism, the number and range of such measures steadily expanded."[10] As Donohue notes, "Between 1994 and 2000 the U.S. doubled its annual expenditures on terrorism, bringing the total to more than $10 billion."[11]

During this time of strategic searching and ad hoc engagement, the moral questions often seemed suppressed or used as a ruse for Machiavellian realpolitik ends. In his study of modern terrorism, Matthew Carr quotes Sam Sarkesian, a U.S. low-intensity warfare theorist, who argues that "low intensity conflicts do not conform to democratic notions or tactics. Revolution and counterrevolution develop their own morality and ethics that justify any means to achieve success."[12] Carr continues, "Neither the methods nor the philosophy that supported them were unique to the United States, but few countries have so consistently disseminated the use of terror as an instrument of counterinsurgency while simultaneously engaging in a strident moralistic condemnation of 'terrorism.' And the disparity has rarely been more glaring than it was during the Reagan era."[13] Whatever the merit of this sweeping assessment (and there is some merit to it), it fails to keep in mind that though America has not always lived up to its ideals, including those that are part and parcel of the just war tradition and international norms and laws, when it fails to do so, it has been held accountable and more often than not has accepted the need to give account. This is not a universal geopolitical reality, nor has it been so at any time in human history. Moreover, the invocation of standards should not be categorically dismissed as duplicitous to justify unjust actions. Rather—and this point must be kept in mind at the forefront of any examination of justice this side of eternity—however desirable the elimination of war might be, it is a seemingly permanent and chronic ill plaguing humanity, and the purpose of statesmen of all nations at all times is to mitigate and ameliorate its horrors. It is telling in this regard that the Bush administration, which coined the terms "War on Terror" and "Global War on Terror," attempted to rebrand America's and the international community's engagement as the "Long War" in 2006.[14] The formulation of a long war better encapsulates the sense of ameliorating (not eradicating) evils and moderates public expectations, which often envision, or at least desire, wars to be short-lived.

What we then have is a long war against terrorism waged in the name of justice, which is never perfect but measured on a scale of better and worse. As Kenneth Thompson notes, "In foreign policy, the concept of elemental right and wrong is never fully realized, but it can be approximated. Even the fact that states possess an awareness of injustice indicates the possibility of justice in foreign affairs, for a sense of injustice presupposes categories of justice to which leaders have recourse."[15] In these terms, Carr's previously cited assessment requires modification and moderation. For the reality remains that America, for all its missteps and failures, remains a nation committed to the proposition "that all men are created equal, that they are endowed by their Creator with certain unalienable Rights, that among these are Life, Liberty and the pursuit of Happiness."[16] That having been said, what is no less true is that the loss of a coherent national interest—ironically the result of the triumph of the singular national interest of the Cold War, namely defeating Communism—left the U.S. adrift between visions of a globalized utopia and political realities that seemingly revealed little more than that the end of one war is the precursor to the next.

The end of the Cold War caused some political thinkers to speculate that humanity had reached the end of history and that the future would be the prosperous march of rational man building an ever more commodious, global community beholden to some form or another of globalized, democratic capitalism.[17] However, the euphoria of 1989 quickly gave way to the horrors of wars and the rumor of wars in the 1990s—especially in the Middle East, Europe, and Africa. And the first decade and a half of the twenty-first century has not slackened the pace laid in the twentieth century—a century in which over 38 million people died in wars and civil wars and over 169 million died as a result of government programs directed against their own people.[18] The Berlin Wall fell on November 9, 1989; Saddam Hussein's invasion of Kuwait began in August 1990. The relative "freeze" of regional conflicts during the Cold War thawed, and across the globe—especially in Eastern Europe with the breakup of the old Yugoslavia and the Union of Soviet Socialist Republics, and all across Africa (the Rwandan Civil War and Tutsi genocide arguably proving the most infamous)—wars raged. And terrorism, specifically a virulent Islamic strain, grew ever more powerful.

From the 1993 World Trade Center bombing to the attack on the USS *Cole* in Aden, Yemen, in 2000—a period that also included the terrorist attacks on U.S. military barracks in Dhahran, Saudi Arabia, in 1996 and the U.S. embassy bombings in Dar es Salaam, Tanzania, and Nairobi, Kenya, in 1998—a comprehensive and just U.S. response to Islamic terrorism was lacking.[19] Indeed, in response to the two embassy attacks, President Bill Clinton ordered the execution of Operation Infinite Reach, which targeted cruise missiles at al-Qaeda bases in Afghanistan and a pharmaceutical factory in Khartoum, Sudan, which supposedly contained and was developing chemicals used in VX nerve gas. The attacks were, in the words of Peter Bergen, "hardly a success."[20] Worse, they "had a major unintended consequence: they turned bin Laden from a marginal figure in the Muslim world into a global celebrity."[21] Indeed, it seems any robust strategic calculations, let alone meaningful considerations of just war criteria, were notably absent. As Bergen summarizes the operation, "It might just as well have been called Operation Infinite Overreach. Just as there had been attacks on U.S. embassies in two countries, there would be attacks against bin Laden-related targets in two countries. Tit for tat. Twice."[22] It was the first major and overt retaliation since the 1986 bombing of Libya, and it reflected a lack of strategic vision, operational clarity, and tactical precision. It reflected uncertainty about the enemy and what should be done in the face of uncertainty. President Clinton's defense secretary, William Cohen, announced in the aftermath of the attacks, "We recognize these strikes will not eliminate the problem. But our message is clear. There will be no sanctuary for terrorists and no limit to our resolve to defend American citizens and our interests—our ideals of democracy and law—against these cowardly attacks."[23] Yet without due consideration of how to wage this new war justly, the very "ideals" for which the fight was being waged were now being threatened.[24] A more coherent and cogent national security strategy was required than the one issued by the Clinton administration in 1998, which directly referenced the Kenya and Tanzania bombings and the resulting cruise missile strikes as the types of "extraordinary steps" that must be taken "to protect the safety of our citizens."[25] Extraordinary steps might well be required, but if they are intended to defeat the ideology and actions of an "adversary" that hates us "precisely because of what we stand for and what we stand against,"[26] we must be clear about our ideals and cognizant that just means must be pursued for the sake of just ends.

In sum, the period from the fall of the Berlin Wall to the September 11, 2001, terrorist attacks was a period lacking precisely this clarity. As Derek Chollet and James Goldgeier state in their preeminent study of American foreign policy in the years between "11/9/89" and "9/11/01," "In one respect, however, the 1990s were indeed a 'holiday': The end of the Cold War made many Americans and their leaders believe the world had become more benign and, therefore, of less concern. The three presidential campaigns of that era—in 1992, 1996, and 2000—spent little time on foreign policy issues."[27] That would change with 9/11.

THE WAR ON TERROR POST-9/11

Four years after 9/11, President Bush, having reflected on his first term and, looking toward his second, asserted in his inaugural address, "America defended our own freedom by standing watch on distant borders. After the shipwreck of communism came years of relative quiet, years of repose, years of sabbatical—and then there came a day of fire."[28] President Bush's first term had been transformed by the 9/11 attacks and his subsequent declaration of a "War on Terror." The end of history had proven all too short, and the invocation of the post–Cold War era revealed a truth Richard Haass understands all too well: "Such a label [post-] reveals that people know only where they have been, not where they are now, much less where they are heading."[29]

Already in 2001, President Bush, looking back on the preceding decade, saw that the expanse of time from the fall of the Berlin Wall to the rise of a virulent strain of Islamic fundamentalism that could strike American interests not only abroad but at home had been a chain of missed opportunities to formulate a coherent strategy for a world that was indeed "post–Cold War" but assuredly not at the end of history. As Chollet and Goldgeier observe in light of the above-quoted words of President Bush: "These phrases suggest that different decisions during these years could have not only prevented 9/11 but also created a new global order. 'They were not just a comment, but an argument,' says Michael Gerson, Bush's acclaimed speechwriter. They 'suggest that there was a surface calm amidst a series of emerging existential threats that had not been adequately confronted.'"[30]

President Bush would not make the same mistake as his predecessors. His 2002 *NSS* states that central to America's national security is the task of promoting and defending human dignity: "Our first imperative is to clarify what we stand for: the United States must defend liberty and justice because these principles are right and true for all people everywhere."[31] What President Bush recognized was that the battle was first and foremost one of ideas and that the battle of ideas involved winning the hearts and minds of people through words and actions that embodied and reflected these ideals. As stated in *NSS* 2002:

> The enemy is terrorism—premeditated, politically motivated violence perpetrated against innocents.
>
> The struggle against global terrorism is different from any other war in our history. It will be fought on many fronts against a particularly elusive enemy over an extended period of time.
>
> Our priority will be first to disrupt and destroy terrorist organizations.
>
> In the war against global terrorism, we will never forget that we are ultimately fighting for our democratic values and way of life.[32]

However, since President Bush first announced this "War on Terror," the debate has raged to define precisely the nature of this "war" and the appropriate terminology to describe it. The Bush administration's War on Terror (WoT) and Global War on Terrorism (GWOT) were renamed Overseas Contingency Operation (OCO) in 2009 by the Obama administration and renamed again as operations Countering Violent Extremism (CVE) in 2010.[33] The changing terminology reflected uncertainties about this new type of warfare, which itself reflected the amorphous and global nature of the threat.

Whatever the war of terms that would be waged over the course of the next decade, on September 14, 2001, Congress passed Public Law 107-40, Authorization for Use of Military Force (AUMF), allowing the president "to use all necessary and appropriate force against those nations, organizations, or persons he determines planned, authorized, committed, or aided the terrorist attacks that occurred on September 11, 2001, or harbored such organizations or persons, in order to prevent any future acts of international terrorism against the United States by such nations, organizations or persons."[34] This was the legal basis for Operation Enduring Freedom, which would be composed of several subordinate operations, the most important being Operation Enduring Freedom–Afghanistan (OEF-A), Operation Enduring Freedom–Philippines (OEF-P), Operation Enduring Freedom–Horn of Africa (OEF-HOA), and Operation Enduring Freedom–Trans Sahara (OEF-TS).[35] To these were added Operation Iraqi Freedom (2003) and Operation Inherent Resolve in Syria and Iraq (2014), as well as a range of smaller operations spanning much of the globe. Before surveying OEF-P as illustrative of these operations, I would like to first turn to Afghanistan to illuminate the prospects and problems of fighting a just war against terrorism. Operations in Afghanistan against terrorist networks are indicative of other operations with respect to moral and even political-civil considerations, whether or not the enemy is a nation-state or a trans-state actor.

THE WAR ON TERROR IN AFGHANISTAN

OEF-A officially began on October 7, 2001, with U.S-U.K. airstrikes launched against key targets in Afghanistan, including the cities of Kabul (the capital), Kandahar, and Jalalabad. The air campaign was joined by ground forces, with members of the CIA's Special Activities Division and U.S. Special Forces both having been preinserted starting on September 26. U.S. and U.K. forces supported and were supported by the United Islamic Front for the Salvation of Afghanistan, more commonly known as the Northern Alliance, a multiethnic Afghan military front united in their opposition to the Taliban. Australia, Canada, and Germany fully joined the coalition in late 2001. By November 14, the Northern Alliance had taken Kabul, and Taliban and al-Qaeda forces were retreating. Subsequent reports indicated that Osama bin Laden had taken refuge in the cave complexes known as Tora Bora in the White Mountains in eastern Afghanistan, near the Khyber Pass, which connected Afghanistan to Pakistan. In an attempt to capture or kill bin Laden and many of his fighters, coalition forces waged the Battle of Tora Bora from December 6 to 17. During this time, coalition forces consolidated their positions throughout Afghanistan and set the stage for establishing an interim Afghan government under President Hamid Karzai (who was eventually elected president in 2004 under the newly formed Islamic Republic of Afghanistan).

However, despite the Taliban having been displaced throughout much of Afghanistan and despite al-Qaeda forces being systematically hunted and targeted, long-term stability and peace still remained aloof. In December NATO established the International Security Assistance Force (ISAF) as a result of United Nations Security Council (UNSC) Resolution 1386 and as envisaged by the December 5 Bonn Agreement, which, as its official title reveals, was an "Agreement on Provisional Arrangements in Afghanistan Pending the Re-Establishment of Permanent Government Institutions," but the ISAF soon found itself confronting a determined Taliban-led insurgency. And though Osama bin Laden was finally killed in 2011, and though formal NATO and U.S.-led military operations ended on December 28, 2014 (constituting America's longest war in its history),[36] NATO and U.S. forces are still in Afghanistan supporting Afghan forces in their fight against the Taliban insurgency as part of Operation Freedom's Sentinel (OFS), which began January 1, 2015.[37] To date, the security situation in Afghanistan remains problematic at best. Per U.S. Forces Afghanistan (US-FOR-A), as of November 2016, the Taliban controls or influences 8.1% of Afghan's population (approximately 2.8 million people) and 8.7% of

Afghanistan's territory (approximately 66,000 km^2), and "28.5% of the population (~7.3 million) and 22.7% of the land (~183,000 square kilometers) is contested."[38] The long war continues,[39] and we must still consider whether it has been, and is being, waged justly—indeed if it was just to pursue the war in the first place.

THE WAR IN AFGHANISTAN: A JUST WAR?

In the following examination of just war criteria in light of America's war in Afghanistan, I will follow Jean Bethke Elshtain and remember that "a political ethic is an ethic of responsibility. The just war tradition is a way to exercise that responsibility with justice in mind."[40] And the utilization of just war criteria is not arbitrary, for as David Fisher rightly notes, though not without an awareness that "just war" is often merely a shibboleth, "Just war concepts have become part of our vocabulary in discussing war, with even politicians, at times, employing the language of just war."[41]

A fundamental criterion of *ius ad bellum* is just cause. It condemns aggression and permits legitimate defense against an unjust aggressor. Just cause does not mean one side is utterly right and the other side utterly wrong. It does mean that the injustice of one party is greater than that of the other party, which is usually reflected in the very act of aggression resulting in a just response to oppose the act of aggression and reassert a just peace. If one isolates the "evasive language"[42] of many in academia, let alone the plethora of exculpating, pseudointellectual defenses and equivocations that all, in one form or another, fail to take into account good and necessary moral distinctions,[43] it remains an undeniable fact that 9/11 was perpetrated by Islamist terrorists targeting noncombatants. It was an act of unjust aggression, and so a justifiable response was warranted.

In addition to just cause, there must also be just intention. The only legitimate intention is to secure a just peace for all involved. Neither revenge nor conquest nor economic gain nor ideological supremacy is justified. Just intention includes the right or obligation to protect innocent life and mitigate crimes against humanity (e.g., genocide and acts of such a scale as to violate or horrify the public conscience). Apart from wanting to bring the planners of 9/11 to justice, not least the leader of al-Qaeda, Osama bin Laden, the coalition sought to restore a political and civil order rooted in a substantive understanding of human rights and ordered liberty. The reality of life under Taliban rule in Afghanistan was nothing short of horrific. As Reporter Dexter Filkins noted in the wake of the Taliban's retreat in December 2001:

> The Afghanistan the Taliban left behind is a sad and broken land. To a visitor, the country seems an almost apocalyptic place, scattered with ruins and orphans and the detritus of wars.
>
> In the five years that the Taliban held the capital, their record as a government might be measured by the numbers they produced: nearly one million refugees, joining the million others who had already left and refused to come home; six million Afghans, a quarter of the country, unable to find enough food.[44]

The Taliban war on women is its own story. The Taliban's 1997 edict banning all women of any age from public education resulted in women's literacy rates falling to "some of the lowest in the world—13 percent in urban areas and three to four percent in rural districts."[45] Health care was equally abysmal, with Nicholas Kristof reporting in *The New York Times* in 2002 that "in each of the last few years, without anyone paying much attention, 225,000 children died in Afghanistan before the age of 5, along with 15,000 women who died during pregnancy or childbirth."[46] In the post-Taliban era, Afghanistan still struggles and an insurgency still rages. Yet it is equally undeniable that life has improved and that these improvements were the ostensible intent of the invasion. As PBS's *Wide Angle* reports, "In March 2002, 1.5 million children who had been barred from education returned to school. By December 2005, the number had grown to 5.2 million, of which almost two million were girls. Women's literacy levels are estimated to be up by seven percent overall."[47] Similarly, infant mortality declined by 25 percent from 2000 to 2006, and "the percentage of women in rural Afghanistan receiving prenatal care from a skilled provider increased from an estimated 4.6 in 2003 to 32.2 in 2006."[48] As Kristof notes, "Our experience there demonstrates that troops can advance humanitarian goals just as much as doctors or aid workers can."[49] The just intentions of America's military engagement bore their just fruit.

The criterion of just authority necessitates that a state of war must be officially declared by the highest, duly constituted authorities. Although Congress did not officially declare war on Afghanistan—a point causing some to question the legality of the war[50]—Congress did pass the AUMF on September 14, 2001. Similarly, the lack of an overt UNSC resolution condoning the invasion is somewhat problematic, and the U.S. justification of self-defense under Article 51 of the U.N. Charter, buttressed by invoking UNSC Resolutions 1368 and 1373—which "simply state the broad general requirement to take action to combat international terrorism"—is less than ideal. However, subsequent UNSC authorization to create ISAF, to assist the Afghan interim government, provided additional support for the criterion of just authority.[51] As the House of Commons report on the legality of the invasion of Afghanistan concludes: "Despite the problems outlined above, the U.N. and many states seemed to accept that the attacks on Afghanistan were legitimate self-defence. In a speech on 8 October 2001, the Secretary General of the U.N., Kofi Annan, stopped short of endorsing the air strikes but nor did he condemn them, acknowledging that states have a right to individual and collective self-defence."[52]

The criterion of last resort entails that war should only be pursued when alternative means to secure a just peace are not viable or have been exhausted. Such means include, but are not limited to, negotiations and compromise. One could readily argue that after all the various, albeit discordant, warnings issued during the 1990s, the final ultimatum by President Bush to the Taliban to "hand over the terrorists or . . . share in their fate" was the final straw.[53] And this ultimatum, too, was largely ignored by the Taliban, who at most sought to stall the impending invasion.[54] Elshtain is correct to point out, "The criterion of last resort does not compel a government to try everything else in actual fact, but rather to explore other options before concluding that none seems appropriate or viable in light of the nature of the threat."[55] Arguably, what is the U.S. to do when threatened with absolute destruction by a foe who views America as diabolic—even as "the devil incarnate"?[56] Bin Laden argued that his soldiers would "cure the insanity of the enemy by their 'insane' courage."⁵⁷ In such situations, war may not only be the last resort; it might well be a nation's only resort once it is attacked.⁵⁸

The last criterion of *ius ad bellum* is ensuring one fights for limited objectives. If the purpose is peace, then unconditional surrender or the destruction of a nation's economic or political institutions is an unwarranted objective. Moreover, the anticipated benefits of waging a war must outweigh the anticipated suffering and damage. This is sometimes referred to as macro-proportionality to distinguish it from the "proportionate means" criterion of *ius in bello*, which will be discussed shortly. While precision bombing and discrete kinetic targeting (both of which have more to do with "proportionate means"), as well as continued efforts to assist in the rebuilding of failed states (which have more to do with *ius post bellum*), have facilitated the implementation of the criterion of limited objectives, macroproportionality is a difficult criterion to adjudicate with respect to the anticipated benefits of success. That having been said, America's longest war has proven long precisely because America is unwilling either to utterly destroy Afghanistan or to let Afghanistan slip into a Taliban-controlled failed state, which might once again prove a seedbed for future terrorist attacks. Its limited objective is the sustainability of a sovereign and free Afghanistan, which necessitates an unlimited time commitment given the problematic nature of this long war.

Since just war criteria are not merely about initiating a war with just cause but also about fighting it justly, we must consider the criteria of *ius in bello*, specifically proportionality, discrimination, and military necessity. It is important to remember that the regulation of *ius in bello* falls into the field of international humanitarian law. In addition to the Hague Conventions of 1899 and 1907, the key international legal document related to the laws of war is the Geneva Conventions of 1949, which stipulates requirements and rights of both combatants and noncombatants and specifically delineates the rights and responsibilities of medical services like the Red Cross and Red Crescent. Here the U.S. has striven to be exemplary, which is not the same as perfect. The reality of Guantanamo Bay and Abu Ghraib and the immorality of enhanced interrogation techniques, as well as the collateral damage associated with attacking legitimate military targets, no less than the unfortunate and unintended attacks on nonmilitary targets as the result of poor military intelligence, is well documented. These facts are usually trumpeted about by those ideologically opposed to the war to make arguments that America is really no better than the terrorists. The weight of evidence, however, is that these instances, though problematic and horrific, remain exceptions and the perpetrators are held to give account.[59]

With respect to proportionality—namely, ensuring that the weaponry and the force used are limited to what is needed to repel the aggression and deter future attacks—America might be criticized for an overreliance on air power and bombings,[60] and yet targeting is almost exclusively conducted with precision weaponry when and where possible. As Elshtain reports of one Taliban claim that U.S. warplanes hit "a hospital in central Kabul, 'Lies—all lies,' said Ghulam Hussain, an emergency room nurse who said he was on duty that night, 'Not a single person in this hospital was hurt. No rockets, no bombs, no missiles. Not even a window was broken.'"[61] Such anecdotal evidence is not meant to belie the human tragedy in Afghanistan, which some estimate is around 104,000 people killed since 2001, with more than 31,000 of those being civilians.[62] These numbers are horrifying, but it is important to remember that, as Elshtain notes, "in the previous battles between Afghan warlords, over 50,000 civilians were killed, according to the International Committee of the Red Cross," and an estimated 670,000 civilians "died during the ten-year Soviet occupation."[63] This comparison is only meant to provide a bit of perspective and remind that though war is never desirable, proportionality moderates what could and would otherwise be far more horrific. This is a point even Michael Walzer understands, who for all his criticism of the Bush administration's handling of the war, still notes that good was accomplished and that it cannot simply be allowed to dissipate:

> In Afghanistan, I think, we went in rightly, but we didn't go in in the right way.... And now Obama has inherited a frightening situation which he may or may not be able to turn around. But there are two million girls going to school in Afghanistan because of our presence there. That wasn't why we went in, but they are—and we can't just walk away knowing that those girls are going to be, many of them, punished for going to school, and certainly the schools will all close. So you take on responsibilities whether you act justly or

unjustly. And there is a certain kind of hard-headed realism which says, "Okay, it's not in our interests to defend those girls. This is a mess, and we should get out of it," but that kind of realism, I think, it simply immoral.⁶⁴

The discussion of civilian casualties leads us to the criterion of discrimination, which entails making good and necessary distinctions between combatants and noncombatants such that individuals not actively contributing to the conflict (including prisoners of war, those injured and withdrawn from battle, and civilian nonparticipants) are immune from attack and not subject to maltreatment. Discrimination dovetails with the last criterion of *ius in bello*, military necessity, which demands that all military force must be directed toward legitimate military objectives and must take into account potential collateral damage while seeking to limit it. The expected military gain must be weighed in light of potential collateral damage and should not be pursued if such damage outweighs the potential military gain. As already discussed under proportionality, the weapons used by U.S. forces are meant to mitigate collateral damage and target precisely the type of legitimate military objectives permitted under international law. Moreover, these laws are part and parcel of the war fighter's training, referred to as the Law of Armed Conflict (LOAC).⁶⁵ Here again Elshtain captures very well the ground truths: If America were not concerned with considerations of *ius in bello*,

> the infrastructure of civilian life in that country would have been devastated completely, and it is not. Instead, schools are opening, women are returning to work, movie theaters are filled to capacity, and people can once again listen to music and dance at weddings. This observation is not intended to minimize the suffering and grief that has occurred in too many places, some of it the result of American mistakes in the war effort. But the restoration of a basic structure of civilian rule and a functioning state is a great benefit. We must stay engaged to this peaceful end.⁶⁶

It is to a consideration of a "peaceful end" (*ius post bellum*)⁶⁷ that we now turn, and here the prospects are glum. Although our focus in the foregoing analysis of just war criteria has been on Afghanistan, and although Afghanistan presents a more traditional political target in that it is a state and not merely a stateless transnational actor, America's global engagement against terrorist networks has not forsaken *ius ad bellum* and *ius in bello* criteria in the planning and execution of its operations, precisely because the American military upholds the Laws of Armed Conflict (LOAC). Afghanistan is also emblematic of the relative good that can come about and has come about as a result of America's post-9/11 engagements. Unfortunately, Afghanistan is no less emblematic of the limited prospects for a long-term, stable peace, a fact that has plagued almost all of the varied operations encompassing America's global war on terror.

THE WAR ON TERROR AND THE PROSPECTS OF PEACE

When OEF ended and OFS began, it was time to take the measure of the successes and failures of thirteen years of warfare and operations against terrorist networks. Apart from considerations of cost,[68] the question that still demands to be answered in light of just war criteria is whether individual states, not least America, and regions, indeed the global community, have been able to secure a just peace, or to at least bring about a more just state of affairs than there was prior to pursuing war? To address this question, I will briefly examine OEF-P as emblematic of U.S. operations in the post-9/11 era, where the stories all share some derivation of the following theme: measurable and substantive progress is marred by the limited prospects for a stable and lasting peace. What seems to be the case with respect to all of America's military engagements against terrorism to date is reflected in the understated words of Ben Farmer, defense correspondent for the *Telegraph*, and his assessment of the future of Afghanistan: "How lasting the fragile progress will be is not clear."[69]

OEF-P has reduced the capabilities of the Abu Sayyaf Group (ASG) in the Philippines, Jemaah Islamiyah (JI) in much of Southeast Asia, and al-Qaeda cells throughout the region. The result of these operations has been the degradation of ASG's fighting strength—down from 1,200 in 2002 to about 500 as of 2013—and JI has been significantly debilitated by Indonesian counterterror efforts, with "little direct US involvement."[70] However, as Mark Munson concludes in his assessment of OEF-P in the *Small Wars Journal*: "Ultimately, Operation Enduring Freedom-Philippines can be judged as a mixed success at best.... Despite success at degrading Philippine terrorist networks..., much of the resulting security gains have been transitory, and the social and economic problems causing decades of violence in Mindanao and the Sulu Archipelago are still in place."[71] And yet Operation Smiles, a humanitarian outreach of OEF-P, opened the door for a number of humanitarian relief groups to provide aid and support even as the U.S. presence spurred schooling, the digging of fresh-water wells, and much needed medical assistance.[72]

A similar assessment can be made of every other operation against terrorist cells and networks. Networks have been destabilized across the globe, and humanitarian assistance has been provided, but long-term security concerns and the prospects of peace remain aloof. Shenaz Bunglawala, Rosemary Durward, and Paul Shulte provide a compelling case, in "Just Wars, Just Outcomes—Reconciling Just Outcomes in Military Intervention," that considerations of "peace, stability and human welfare" have expanded "the already challenging Just War criteria of success following consideration of the balance of consequences. For long-term peace and stability are conditional on justice both being done and being seen to be done. Yet satisfying the contradictory concepts of justice held by all the protagonists may well be an impossibility."[73] Nevertheless,

> on moral grounds, there is a responsibility to 'make good' the job that was begun, since the consequences may otherwise be a still worse security situation with unreconciled animosities and continued human tragedy, so long as there is some expectation that it can be made good. On prudent strategic grounds, there is a case for continuing comprehensive engagement in support of modernisers because failure to do so means that whatever military outcomes might be achieved, are temporary. And such failures would betray local allies and encourage the spread of expressions of Islam, which are avowedly antithetical to the West's interests and inimical to the interests of large swathes of the indigenous populations.[74]

THE PURSUIT OF JUSTICE IN AN UNJUST WORLD

What can then be stated by way of conclusion is that however one might argue about a particular tactic exercised at a particular time or even about this or that operational requirement or strategic vision (or lack thereof), it is undeniable that American operations against terrorism in Afghanistan and elsewhere have been waged in terms of international norms and laws infused with just war criteria arising out of the just war tradition.[75] Though specific actions and events might be questioned as undermining America's high moral ideals or the criteria of just war, it is compelling that America can be held to such standards such that American soldiers and statesmen feel compelled to address criticism. The same cannot be said of America's enemies in this war. With Elshtain, I set before the reader the following words of President Bush, who in his speech to the nation on September 20, 2001, spoke the following words directed to all Muslims:

> We respect your faith. It's practiced freely by many millions of Americans and by millions more in countries that America counts as friends. Its teachings are good and peaceful, and those who commit evil in the name of Allah blaspheme the name of Allah. The terrorists are traitors to their own faith, trying, in effect, to hijack Islam itself. The enemy of America is not our many Muslim friends. It is not our many Arab friends. Our enemy is a radical network of terrorists and every government that supports them.[76]

Compare this to the al-Qaeda–sponsored Islamic Front's 1998 fatwa, which states, "The ruling to kill the Americans and their allies—civilians and military—is an individual duty for every Muslim who can do it in any country in which it is possible to do it."[77] The lack of just intention, limited objectives, proportionate means, and noncombatant immunity—to mention but the most salient just war criteria—is startling. The response by the academic no less than the politician or activist should not be equivocation but a moderated, though not uncritical, praise of American antiterrorist operations and a just, but not utterly dismissive, indictment of the Islamic Front's policy. As Berman observes, "Al Qaeda and its allied groups were a nebulous constellation, spread across many countries, and the nebulous constellation rested on solid institutions with genuine power here and there, and the institutions rested on a bedrock of conspiracy theories, organized hatred, and apocalyptic fantasies: the culture of totalitarianism."[78]

The U.S. and its allies in NATO and the international community that are embodied in the U.N. need the moral clarity to recognize that the war against terrorism is fundamentally a war against various forms of totalitarianism. The threat posed by modern terrorism is total in its objective to utterly annihilate the "other." Given its ideological roots and pernicious virility, it is not a threat that will easily, if ever, dissipate. This might give rise to the adage that extreme times (once again) call for extreme measures. Nothing could be closer and at the same time further from the truth. What is required is the extreme measure of engaging in civilizational introspection to consider what are the hallmarks of a tradition that has sought to embody, promote, and defend justice in a world that is mired in injustice. What is not required is an extreme disregard for this tradition to justify unjust acts that clearly violate the just war tradition.

THE STATESMAN AND THE PURSUIT OF JUSTICE

The global threat of would-be secular messiahs employing radical terrorism to bring about their vision of heaven on earth is not per se new, but its modern incarnation is particularly malignant, and the potential devastation even a rogue agent can wreak is magnified by the destructive capability of weapons of mass destruction, whether biological, chemical, or nuclear. It is incumbent on the statesman of the twenty-first century to be carefully attuned to the dynamic global geopolitical landscape and have in his arsenal a robust conception of justice, both with respect to war and peace. It may be all too true that there will never be a war waged with perfect justice giving way to a perfect peace. Nevertheless, to restate a point made at the outset and one that must always be kept in mind: the failure to adequately employ the laws of war and the just war tradition—

and this might prove to be all the more the case in operations conducted against terrorists and the even more amorphous enemy, terror—will likely lead to the employment of means that are themselves terrifying. The consequence of this would prove to be a general devolution of the prospects of universal justice and a corresponding increase in war's brutality and barbarism. Just war is—and it cannot be stated often or emphatically enough—not about eliminating war or giving carte blanche approval to those fighting a just war in pursuit of a just peace, but about mitigating the horrors of war, which, when left without a clear vision of justice, become all too often utterly barbaric, cruel, and violent—in a word: unjust. As statesmen, we should always keep in mind the words of the British historian, diplomat, and political theorist E. H. Carr, who makes the following important observation:

> Any sound political thought must be based on elements of both utopia and reality. Where utopianism has become a hollow and intolerable sham, which serves as a disguise for the interests of the privileged, the realist performs an indispensable service in unmasking it. But pure realism can offer nothing but a naked struggle for power which makes any kind of international society impossible. Having demolished the current utopia with the weapons of realism, we still need to build a new utopia of our own, which will one day fall to the same weapons. The human will continue to seek an escape from the logical consequences of realism in the vision of an international order which, as soon as it crystallizes itself into concrete political form, becomes tainted with self-interest and hypocrisy, and must once more be attacked with the instruments of realism.[79]

As statesmen, we must be moral realists of the Carrian variety. We must have just enough vision of utopia to believe in a better tomorrow, but pessimistic enough to recognize it may never come about, and yet realist enough to labor diligently on its behalf. In so doing, we retain the awareness that if we act otherwise, we are no longer part of a potential solution but only part of an all too real problem that has made the history of man one all too often told in terms of spilt blood and not in terms of blood ties nurturing our common humanity and our common future on this little planet.

NOTES

1. George W. Bush, "Text: President Bush Addresses the Nation," Washington Post, September 20, 2001, http://www.washingtonpost.com/wp-srv/nation/specials/attacked/transcripts/bushaddress_092001.html.

2. See Gerard Chaliand and Arnaud Blin, *The History of Terrorism: From Antiquity to al Qaeda* (Berkeley: University of California Press, 2007), 138–40. Jonathan Matusitz provides a succinct overview of the history of terrorism in "What Is Terrorism?," chapter 1 of *Terrorism and Communication: A Critical Introduction* (Thousand Oaks, CA: SAGE, 2012). See also Michael Burleigh, *Blood and Rage: A Cultural History of Terrorism* (New York: Harper Collins, 2009); Walter Reich, ed., *Origins of Terrorism: Psychologies, Ideologies, Theologies, States of Mind* (Washington, DC: Woodrow Wilson Center Press, 1998). With respect to Europe and the recent past, see Petter Nesser, *Islamist Terrorism in Europe: A History* (New York: Oxford University Press, 2016). With a particular eye on ISIS: William McCants, *The ISIS Apocalypse: The History, Strategy, and Doomsday Vision of the Islamic State* (New York: St. Martin's Press, 2015). Also Ian Buruma and Avishai Margalit, *Occidentalism: The West in the Eyes of Its Enemies* (New York: Penguin, 2004); Paul Berman, *Terror and Liberalism* (New York: W. W. Norton, 2003). With respect to the question of religious violence and terror in general and largely from a sociological vantage point, see Mark Juergensmeyer, *Terror in the Mind of God: The Global Rise of Religious Violence*, updated ed. (Berkeley: University of California Press, 2001).

3. See, for example, the critical engagements with various arguments against just war in David Fisher, *Morality and War: Can War Be Just in the Twenty-First Century?* (New York: Oxford University Press, 2011); Jean Bethke Elshtain, *Just War against Terror: The Burden of American Power in a Violent World* (New York: Basic Books, 2003). The Peace Treaties of Westphalia, signed in 1648, ended Europe's Thirty Years' War and established the principle of the territorial sovereignty of nation-states. To this day, this principle remains a cornerstone of international law and assumes the nation-state is the only legitimate actor with respect to pursuing war (*jus ad bellum* and *jus in bello*) and establishing peace treaties (*jus post bellum*). This principle and the international laws and norms which arise from it are collectively referred to as Westphalian interstate norms.

4. *The Federalist*, ed. George Carey and James McClellan (Indianapolis: Liberty Fund, 2001), no. 51, p. 271.

5. The statement, now cliché, is from Gerald Seymour, *Harry's Game* (New York: Random House, 1975), 62.

6. The data are culled from Alex Schmid and Albert Jongman, *Political Terrorism: A New Guide to Actors, Authors, Concepts, Data Bases, Theories, and Literature*, revised and updated ed. (Piscataway, NJ: Transaction Publishers, 2005). Their data are cited by, among others, Matusitz, *Terrorism and Communication*, 2. See also Boaz Ganor, "Defining Terrorism—Is One Man's Terrorist Another Man's Freedom Fighter?," International Institute for Counter-Terrorism, January 1, 2010, http://www.ict.org.il/Article.aspx?ID=1123. A substantive compilation of research on terrorism can be found in Alex Schmid, ed., *The Routledge Handbook of Terrorism Research* (New York: Routledge, 2013).

7. Matusitz, *Terrorism and Communication*, 4.

8. *The National Security Strategy of the United States of America* (Washington, DC: The White House, September 2002), 5.

9. See Ronald Reagan, "Remarks at the Welcoming Ceremony for the Freed American Hostages, January 27, 1981," *Public Papers of the Presidents of the United States: Ronald Reagan, 1981*, accessed on January 3, 2017, http://www.presidency.ucsb.edu/ws/index.php?pid=43879. The quote is also the epigraph of "The First War on Terror," chapter 9 in Matthew Carr, *Unknown Soldiers: How Terrorism Transformed the Modern World* (London: Profile Books, 2006), 223.

10. Laura K. Donohue, "In the Name of National Security: U.S. Counterterrorist Measures, 1960–2000" (BCSIA Discussion Paper 2001-6, ESDP Discussion Paper ESDP-2001-04, John F. Kennedy School of Government, Harvard University, August 2001), 3.

11. Donohue, "In the Name of National Security," 4.

12. Carr, *Unknown Soldiers*, 234.

13. Carr, *Unknown Soldiers*, 234.

14. Bradley Graham and Josh White, "Abizaid Credited with Popularizing the Term 'Long War,'" *Washington Post*, February 3, 2006, http://www.washingtonpost.com/wp-dyn/content/article/2006/02/02/AR2006020202242.html.

15. Kenneth Thompson, *The Moral Issue in Statecraft* (Baton Rouge: Louisiana State University Press, 1966), 51.

16. See the Declaration of Independence in Carey and McClellan, *The Federalist*.

17. See, for instance, Francis Fukuyama, *The End of History and the Last Man* (New York: Free Press, 1992).

18. R. J. Rummel, *Death by Government* (Piscataway, NJ: Transaction Publishers, 1997), 3–4.

19. For details regarding these events, see Bruce Hoffman, *Inside Terrorism*, revised and expanded ed. (New York: Columbia University Press, 2006).

Also Peter Bergen, *Holy War, Inc.: Inside the Secret World of Osama bin Laden* (New York: Free Press, 2001). A brief summary of what transpired can be found in "Terrorist Actions 1980–2000," The Evolution of Terrorism, http://evolutionofterrorism.weebly.com/1980s-2000.html.

20. Bergen, *Holy War, Inc.*, 125.

21. Ibid. See also Steven Emerson, *American Jihad: The Terrorists Living among Us* (New York: The Free Press, 2002), 151.

22. Bergen, *Holy War, Inc.*, 118.

23. Jamie McIntyre, "U.S. Missiles Pound Targets in Afghanistan, Sudan," August 20, 1998, http://www.cnn.com/US/9808/20/us.strikes.01/.

24. Peter Bergen cites a Western diplomat "based in Pakistan," who indicated that the strikes had "served a useful purpose because they showed 'we have reach. They served as a marker—"fuck with us and you have a major problem"'" (Bergen, *Holy War, Inc.*, 125). Such bombast and bravado may have its place to rally the troops at a moment's notice, but it has little merit with respect to a meaningful strategy informed by conceptions of justice both with respect to the war and peace.

25. *National Security Strategy*, 15–16.

26. *National Security Strategy*, 16.

27. Derek Chollet and James Goldgeier, *America between the Wars: From 11/9 to 9/11; The Misunderstood Years between the Fall of the Berlin Wall and the Start of the War on Terror* (New York: Public Affairs, 2009), 316.

28. George W. Bush, "President Bush's Second Inaugural Address," January 20, 2005, http://www.npr.org/templates/story/story.php?storyId=4460172.

29. Chollet and Goldgeier, *America between the Wars*, xiv.

30. Chollet and Goldgeier, *America between the Wars*, xi.

31. *National Security Strategy*, 3.

32. *National Security Strategy*, 5, 7.

33. Marc Ambinder, "The New Term for the War on Terror," *Atlantic*, May 20, 2010, http://www.theatlantic.com/politics/archive/2010/05/the-new-term-for-the-war-on-terror/56969/.

34. Authorization for Use of Military Force, Pub. L. No. 107-40, 115 Stat. 224 (2001), https://www.gpo.gov/fdsys/pkg/PLAW-107publ40/pdf/PLAW-107publ40.pdf.

35. There is also OEF–Pankisi Gorge, OEF–Caribbean and Central America (OEF-CCA), and OEF-Kyrgyzstan.

36. Andrew Tilghman, "Afghanistan War Officially Ends," *Military Times*, December 29, 2014, http://www.militarytimes.com/story/military/pentagon/2014/12/29/afghanistan-war-officially-ends/21004589/.

37. Dan Lamothe, "Meet Operation Freedom's Sentinel, the Pentagon's New Mission in Afghanistan," *Washington Post*, December 29, 2014, https://www.washingtonpost.com/news/checkpoint/wp/2014/12/29/meet-operation-freedoms-sentinel-the-pentagons-new-mission-in-afghanistan/. It is interesting to note that though GWOT is no longer current vocabulary, soldiers participating in OFS qualify for the GWOT Medal. Jon Harper, "Freedom's Sentinel Now Qualifying Operation for GWOT Medals," *Stars and Stripes*, March 15, 2015, http://www.stripes.com/news/freedom-s-sentinel-now-qualifying-operation-for-gwot-medals-1.334206.

38. These numbers are included in the following report, which estimates that these numbers are in truth low. Bill Roggio, "Analysis: US Military Assessment of Taliban Control in Afghan Districts Is Flawed," *FDD's* [Foundation for Defense of Democracies] *Long War Journal*, November 2, 2016, http://www.longwarjournal.org/archives/2016/11/analysis-us-military-assessment-of-taliban-control-of-afghan-districts-is-flawed.php. See also Sarah Almukhtar and Karen Yourish, "More than 14 Years after U.S. Invasion, the Taliban Control Large Parts of Afghanistan," *New York Times*, April 19, 2016, https://www.nytimes.com/interactive/2015/09/29/world/asia/afghanistan-taliban-maps.html?_r=0.

39. Andrew deGrandpre and Shawn Snow, "The U.S. Marines Are Sending a Task Force Back to Afghanistan's Helmand Province," *Marine Corps Times*, January 6, 2017, https://www.marinecorpstimes.com/articles/marines-afghanistan-taliban-task-force.

40. Elshtain, *Just War against Terror*, 59.

41. Fisher, *Morality and War*, 1.

42. Elshtain, *Just War against Terror*, 82. See also her preliminary discussion of this point on pp. 16–17.

43. Elshtain, *Just War against Terror*, 82–84. See Paul Berman's discussion of the often surreal arguments proffered by Noam Chomsky that "if 9/11 was bad, America itself was ultimately responsible." Berman, *Terror and Liberalism*, 151; cf. 44–53.

44. Dexter Filkins, "A Nation Challenged: Rise and Fall; The Legacy of the Taliban Is a Sad and Broken Land," *New York Times*, December 31, 2001, http://www.nytimes.com/2001/12/31/world/nation-challenged-rise-fall-legacy-taliban-sad-broken-land.html.

45. "A Woman among Warlords: Women's Rights in the Taliban and Post-Taliban Eras," *Wide Angle*, September 11, 2007, PBS, http://www.pbs.org/wnet/wideangle/episodes/a-woman-among-warlords/womens-rights-in-the-taliban-and-post-taliban-eras/?p=66. See also Physicians for Human

Rights, *The Taliban's War on Women: A Health and Human Rights Crisis in Afghanistan* (Boston: Physicians for Human Rights, August 1998).

46. Nicholas Kristof, "A Merciful War," *New York Times*, February 1, 2002, http://www.nytimes.com/2002/02/01/opinion/a-merciful-war.html.

47. "Woman among Warlords."

48. "Woman among Warlords."

49. Kristof, "Merciful War."

50. Bruce Ackerman and Oona Hathaway, "Did Congress Approve America's Longest War?," *Guardian*, January 27, 2011, https://www.theguardian.com/commentisfree/cifamerica/2011/jan/27/afghanistan-congress. The topic of Congress declaring war is part of the larger debate regarding the War Powers Resolution. See George Friedman, "What Happened to the American Declaration of War?," *Geopolitical Weekly*, March 29, 2011, Stratfor, https://www.stratfor.com/weekly/20110328-what-happened-american-declaration-war.

51. Ben Smith and Arabella Thorp, *The Legal Basis for the Invasion of Afghanistan*, International Affairs and Defence Section of the [U.K.] House of Commons, February 26, 2010, 3.

52. Smith and Thorp, *Legal Basis for the Invasion of Afghanistan*, 6.

53. "Text: Bush Announces Strikes against Taliban," *Washington Post*, October 7, 2001, http://www.washingtonpost.com/wp-srv/nation/specials/attacked/transcripts/bushaddress_100801.htm.

54. "Bush Delivers Ultimatum," CNN, September 21, 2001, http://www.cnn.com/2001/WORLD/asiapcf/central/09/20/ret.afghan.bush/index.html?_s=PM:asiapcf.

55. Elshtain, *Just War against Terror*, 61.

56. As Buruma and Margalit note, "The loathing of everything people associate with the Western world, exemplified by America . . . attracts radical Muslims to a politicized Islamic ideology in which the United States features as the devil incarnate." Buruma and Margalit, *Occidentalism*, 4.

57. Osama bin Laden quoted in Buruma and Margalit, *Occidentalism*, 68.

58. As Elshtain argues, "Terrorism is extremism. And Islamist fundamentalism is an extreme repudiation of modernity itself—another reason why it is impossible to negotiate and split the differences between its adherents and those immersed in the Western politics of negotiation and compromise." Elshtain, *Just War against Terror*, 22.

59. See, for example, the varied punishments meted out to those involved in the Abu Ghraib scandal: "Prosecutions and Convictions," *Salon*, March 14, 2006, https://www.salon.com/2006/03/14/prosecutions_convictions/. Also

"Iraq Prison Abuse Scandal Fast Facts," CNN, last updated March 18, 2018, http://www.cnn.com/2013/10/30/world/meast/iraq-prison-abuse-scandal-fast-facts/index.html.

60. One such salient criticism comes from Michael Walzer, who maintains a strident criticism of the Bush administration: "When it turned out that the war wasn't won, it [the Bush administration] tried to fight the Taliban resurgence from the air, still without enough soldiers on the ground, and the result was that we killed large numbers of Afghan civilians." Robert Mackey, "'Just War' Theory and Afghanistan," *New York Times*, December 10, 2009, https://thelede.blogs.nytimes.com/2009/12/10/just-war-theory-and-afghanistan/?_r=0.

61. Elshtain, *Just War against Terror*, 68.

62. "Afghan Civilians," Costs of War, *Watson Institute*, last updated August 2016, http://watson.brown.edu/costsofwar/costs/human/civilians/afghan. In addition to these deaths, an "additional 41,000 civilians have been injured since 2001."

63. Elshtain, *Just War against Terror*, 68.

64. Quoted in Mackey, "'Just War' Theory and Afghanistan."

65. Charles Stimson, "Law of Armed Conflict and the Use of Military Force: Testimony before the Armed Services Committee, United States Senate, on May 16, 2013," The Heritage Foundation, May 16, 2013, http://www.heritage.org/research/testimony/2013/05/the-law-of-armed-conflict.

66. Elshtain, *Just War against Terror*, 70. See also the relative comparison of certain statistics, which puts in context many of the numbers bantered about: Ben Farmer, "Afghanistan War in Numbers," *Telegraph*, October 7, 2014, http://www.telegraph.co.uk/news/worldnews/asia/afghanistan/11144612/Afghanistan-war-in-numbers.html.

67. With respect to post bellum considerations, see Eric Patterson, *Ending Wars Well: Just War Theory in Post-Conflict* (New Haven: Yale University Press, 2012). Also Larry May and Andrew T. Forcehimes, eds., *Morality, Jus Post Bellum, and International Law* (Cambridge: Cambridge University Press, 2012).

68. Per the Congressional Research Service, the thirteen years of war have resulted in "$1.6 trillion for military operations, base support, weapons maintenance, training of Afghan and Iraq security forces, reconstruction, foreign aid, embassy costs, and veterans' health care for the war operations initiated since the 9/11 attacks." OEF for "Afghanistan and other counterterror operations" totaled "$686 billion," or 43 percent of the total. See "Summary" in "The Cost of Iraq, Afghanistan, and Other Global War on Terror Opera-

tions since 9/11" (Washington, DC: Congressional Research Service, December 8, 2014).

69. Ben Farmer, "Afghanistan: The Uncertain Legacy of a Flawed Campaign," *Telegraph*, October 26, 2014, http://www.telegraph.co.uk/news/world news/asia/afghanistan/11189170/Afghanistan-The-uncertain-legacy-of-a-flawed-campaign.html.

70. Mark Munson, "Has Operation Enduring Freedom–Philippines Been a Success?," *Small Wars Journal*, April 5, 2013, http://smallwarsjournal.com/jrnl/art/has-operation-enduring-freedom-philippines-been-a-success.

71. Munson, "Operation Enduring Freedom–Philippines."

72. Mark Alexander, "Operation Smiles: A Legacy of Freedom," *Asia-Pacific Defense Forum*, Winter 2002–3, 24.

73. The chapter is included in David Fisher and Brian Wicker, eds., *Just War on Terror? A Christian and Muslim Response* (Burlington, VT: Ashgate, 2010), 117.

74. Fisher and Wicker, *Just War on Terror?*, 125.

75. See Oliver O'Donovan, *The Just War Revisited*, Current Issues in Theology (Cambridge: Cambridge University Press, 2003); it is also worth consulting the discussions of international norms and law in Brian Orend, *The Morality of War* (Orchard Park, NY: Broadview Press, 2006). Also James Turner Johnson, *Just War Tradition and the Restraint of War: A Moral and Historical Inquiry* (Princeton: Princeton University Press, 1981).

76. President Bush quoted in Elshtain, *Just War against Terror*, 63.

77. "Jihad against Jews and Crusaders," Federation of American Scientists, August 23, 1998, https://fas.org/irp/world/para/docs/980223-fatwa.htm.

78. Berman, *Terror and Liberalism*, 181.

79. E. H. Carr, *The Twenty Years' Crisis, 1919–1939* (New York: Harper Torchbooks, 1964), 93.

CONTRIBUTORS

J. DARYL CHARLES is the 2018/19 Acton Institute Affiliate Scholar in Theology and Ethics, serves as a contributing editor of the journal *Providence: A Journal of Christianity and American Foreign Policy*, and is an affiliated scholar of the John Jay Institute. Charles is author, coauthor, or editor of eighteen books, including *Natural Law and Religious Freedom* (Routledge, 2017), *The Just War Tradition: An Introduction* (ISI Books, 2012), *War, Peace, and Christianity: Questions and Answers from a Just-War Perspective* (Crossway, 2010), *A Return to Moral First Things: Retrieving the Natural Law* (Eerdmans, 2008), *Between Pacifism and Jihad: Just War and Christian Tradition* (InterVarsity Press, 2005), and *Virtue amidst Vice* (Sheffield Academic Press, 1997). He has taught at Taylor University, Union University, and Berry College. Charles served as a 2007/8 William B. Simon visiting fellow in religion and public life at the James Madison Program, Princeton University, and as the 2003/4 visiting fellow of the Institute for Faith & Learning, Baylor University.

DARRELL COLE is professor of ethics at Drew University. He writes regularly on the ethics of war and is the author of *Just War and the Ethics of Espionage* (Routledge, 2015) and co-author of *The Virtue of War: Reclaiming the Classic Christian Traditions East and West* (Regina Orthodox Press, 2007).

TIMOTHY J. DEMY (PhD Salve Regina University, ThD Dallas Theological Seminary) is professor of military ethics at the U.S. Naval War College, Newport, Rhode Island. He is the author and editor of numerous books on ethics, theology, and current issues and has also contributed to many books, journals, and encyclopedias. He is coauthor of *War, Peace, and Christianity: Questions and Answers from a Just-War Perspective* (Crossway, 2010) and coeditor of the three-volume *War and Religion: An Encyclopedia of Faith and Conflict* (ABC-CLIO, 2017). He serves on the advisory board of the international *Journal of Military Ethics* and is book review editor of the *Naval War College Review*.

JONATHAN DEN HARTOG is professor of history at the University of Northwestern–St. Paul, Minnesota. He spent the 2012–13 academic year as the Garwood Visiting Fellow at the James Madison Program in American Ideals and Institutions at Princeton University. He received his PhD in American history from the University of Notre Dame in 2006. Den Hartog's first book, *Patriotism and Piety: Federalist Politics and Religious Struggle in the New American Nation*, was published by the University of Virginia Press in 2015. He has published articles in *Early American Studies*, the *Journal of Church and State*, and the *Faulkner Law Review*, as well as essays in three other edited volumes. Den Hartog's research has been supported by grants from the National Endowment for the Humanities, the George Washington Library at Mt. Vernon, the American Antiquarian Society, the Clements Library of the University of Michigan, and the Gilder-Lehrman Institute of American History.

JONATHAN EBEL is a professor in the Department of Religion at the University of Illinois, Urbana-Champaign. He specializes in the religious history of the U.S. and has written on the role religion plays in shaping American soldiers' war experiences and the nation's war memories. Ebel received his BA from Harvard in 1993 and his PhD from the University of Chicago in 2004. He served as a naval intelligence officer from 1993 to 1997 and continued in that capacity in the naval reserves until 2005. Ebel is the author of *G.I. Messiahs: Soldiering, War, and American Civil Religion* (Yale University Press, 2015) and *Faith in the Fight: Religion and the American Solider in the Great War* (Princeton University Press, 2010). He coedited *From Jeremiad to Jihad: Religion, Violence, and America* (University of California Press, 2012). He received a Guggenheim Fellowship for 2017–18 to support work on his third book, a study of religion and the Dust Bowl migration in agricultural California.

LAURA JANE GIFFORD is a historian and author based in Portland, Oregon. Her publications include *The Center Cannot Hold: The 1960 Presidential Election and the Rise of Modern Conservatism* (Northern Illinois University Press, 2009) and the coedited *The Right Side of the Sixties: Reexamining Conservatism's Decade of Transformation* (Palgrave Macmillan, 2012). She holds a PhD in American history from the University of California, Los Angeles.

MARK DAVID HALL is Herbert Hoover Distinguished Professor of Politics and Faculty Fellow in the William Penn Honors Program at George Fox University. He is also associated faculty at the Center for the Study of Law and Religion at Emory University and a senior fellow at Baylor University's Institute for Studies of Religion. Hall has written, edited, or coedited a dozen books, including *Did America Have a Christian Founding?: Separating Modern Myth from Historical Truth* (Thomas Nelson, 2019), *Great Christian Jurists in American History* (Cambridge University Press, forthcoming), *Faith and the Founders of the American Republic* (Oxford University Press, 2014), *Roger Sherman and the Creation of the American Republic* (Oxford University Press, 2013), *America's Forgotten Founders* (ISI Books, 2011), *The Forgotten Founders on Religion and Public Life* (University of Notre Dame Press, 2009), *The Sacred Rights of Conscience: Selected Readings on Religious Liberty and Church-State Relations in the American Founding* (Liberty Fund Press, 2009), *The Founders on God and Government* (Rowman & Littlefield, 2004), and *The Political and Legal Philosophy of James Wilson, 1742–1798* (University of Missouri Press, 1997).

DANIEL WALKER HOWE is Rhodes Professor of American History Emeritus at Oxford University in England, and professor of history emeritus at the University of California, Los Angeles. His best-known book, *What Hath God Wrought: The Transformation of America, 1815–1848*, a volume in the Oxford History of the United States, won the Pulitzer Prize in 2006. It is available in hardback, paperback, audio, and Kindle. Howe grew up in Denver and attended Harvard University (BA, magna cum laude), Oxford University (MA), and the University of California, Berkeley (PhD). His other books include *The Unitarian Conscience* (Wesleyan University Press, 1988), *The Political Culture of the American Whigs* (University of Chicago Press, 1998), and *Making the American Self: Jonathan Edwards to Abraham Lincoln* (Oxford University Press, 2009). He is also the author of some fifty articles in scholarly journals and about a hundred book reviews. In 2014, he was awarded an Honorary Doctorate of Humanities by Weber State University in Utah.

KERRY IRISH is professor of American history at George Fox University. He has written extensively on Dwight D. Eisenhower. The U.S. Army Historical Foundation recognized his *Journal of Military History* article "Dwight Eisenhower and Douglas MacArthur in the Philippines: There Must Be a Day of Reckoning" as the best article on military history in 2010.

GREGORY R. JONES is an online instructor at the University of Northwestern–St. Paul, Grace College, and Tiffin University. He is author of "Violence on the Home Front: Democracy and Disunity in Southeast Ohio during the American Civil War," which was published in Marsha Robinson, ed., *Lesser Civil Wars: Civilians Defining War and the Memory of War* (Cambridge Scholars Publishing, 2012). He has written book reviews for the *Journal of Sport History*, *Fides et Historia*, and *North Carolina Historical Review*.

MACKUBIN (MAC) OWENS is dean of academics for the Institute of World Politics in Washington, DC, a senior fellow of the Foreign Policy Research Institute (FPRI) in Philadelphia, and editor of *Orbis*, FPRI's quarterly journal. From 1987 to 2014 he was professor of national security affairs at the U.S. Naval War College in Newport, Rhode Island. Among his publications are the FPRI monograph *Abraham Lincoln: Leadership and Democratic Statesmanship in Wartime* (2009), *US Civil-Military Relations after 9/11: Renegotiating the Civil-Military Bargain* (Continuum, 2011), and *US Foreign Policy and Defense Strategy: The Evolution of an Incidental Superpower* (Georgetown University Press, 2014) (coedited with Derek S. Reveron and Nikolas K. Gvosdev). Dr. Owens earned his PhD in politics from the University of Dallas, an MA in economics from Oklahoma University, and his BA from the University of California at Santa Barbara. He is a Marine Corps infantry veteran of the Vietnam War.

JOHN D. ROCHE is an assistant professor of history and senior military faculty member at the U.S. Air Force Academy. He earned his PhD from the University of North Carolina, Chapel Hill, in 2015 by examining the evolution of British occupation policy during the American Revolutionary War. His research interests include civil-military relations, colonization, and Atlantic history.

ROUVEN STEEVES is a lieutenant colonel in the United States Air Force and a member of the Senior Military Faculty at the United States Air Force Academy in Colorado, where he is an associate professor of humanities and political science. He earned his Master of National Security Affairs from the Naval Postgraduate School and his PhD in political philosophy from Georgetown University. A 2001 Presidential Fellow and 2007 recipient of the Bronze Star, he has served as a political-military adviser and negotiator in Iraq and worked on NATO just war doctrine during the Kosovo intervention. His most recent publications include "Dionysus versus the Crucified: Nietzsche and Voegelin and the Search for a Truthful Order," in *Eric Voegelin and the Continental Tradition* (University of Missouri Press, 2011), and "Commonwealth," in *The Encyclopedia of Political Thought* (Wiley-Blackwell, 2014). He is the 2015 recipient of the USAF Academy's Robert F. McDermott Award for Research Excellence in the Humanities.

INDEX

Abraham Lincoln (Guelzo), 117
Abrams, Creighton, 243, 244
Abu Sayyaf Group (ASG), 288–89
Acheson, Dean, 206, 207, 208, 209, 214, 215, 219, 223n6
Adams, John, 53, 81
Adams, John Quincy, 89, 104
Ad Beatissimi Apostolorum (papal encyclical), 159, 160, 163, 168, 172
Address of the Minority to Their Constituents, on the Subject of War with Great-Britain, An (Quincy and Bayard), 83
aerial warfare
    civilian casualties, 241, 242
    damage caused by, 241
    evaluation of, 240
    principle of "double effect," 242
    restriction of, 240, 242
Afghanistan
    child mortality, 283
    interim government, 281
    Northern Alliance, 281
    prospects for peace, 288
    restoration of infrastructure, 287
    status of women in, 283, 286–87
    Taliban rule, 283, 285
    war on terror in, 280–82
Afghan war
    Battle of Tora Bora, 281
    civilian casualties, 286, 287
    collateral damage, 285
    criterion of just authority, 284
    criterion of proportionality, 286
    ius ad bellum criterion, 285
    ius in bello criterion, 285–86, 287
    ius post bellum criterion, 287–88
    as just war, perception of, 282–88
    last resort criterion, 284–85
    outcome of, 286–87
    question of legality of, 284
    Taliban insurgency, 281–82
    U.S. objectives in, 285
Aguinaldo y Famy, Emilio, 147
Ahlstrom, Sydney, 51
Alaska, U.S. acquisition of, 98
al-Qaeda, 281, 288, 291
American Civil War
    "Anaconda Plan," 126
    assessment of, 125–26
    background, 117–19
    causes of, 118, 120, 122, 127
    conduct of armies in, 122–23
    cost of, 132
    Fort Pillow incident, 123, 124, 127
    historiography of, 115–16, 125–26
    Jackson's retreat to Richmond, 124
    justification of, 32, 114–15, 116, 119–22, 125, 132
    life in the South after, 128
    outcome of, 127–28, 131–32

American Civil War (*cont.*)
   role of Christian religion in, 116, 121, 122, 124
   Sherman's March to the Sea, 123, 124–25, 126, 127
   slavery and, 116–17
   split between North and South, 120
   as total war, 126
   treatment of civilians during, 124, 125–26
   violence, 123–24, 127
American colonies
   dispute over taxation of, 53–57, 59, 71n35
   sermons on opposition to tyranny in, 52–53
American Duties Act (1764), 54
American Revolutionary War
   atrocities of, 66–67
   Battle of Bemis Heights, 64–65
   battles at Lexington, 57, 60–61
   casualties, 59
   causes of, 50–51
   Continental Army, 61, 63, 65, 68
   foreign support, 63
   invasion of Canada, 61, 68
   ius ad bellum criterion, 63, 68
   ius in bello criterion, 65–67
   ius post bello criterion, 67–68
   justification of, 31, 58–59, 60, 61–62
   militia forces, 72n46
   Paoli Massacre, 64
   peace treaty, 67, 68
   protection of property during, 65
   siege of Boston, 61
   treatment of prisoners, 63–64
America's wars
   Christian perspective on, 38n5
   components of, 138
   historiography, 1–3
   just war tradition and, 3, 30
   moral scrutiny of, 2, 3
   with Native American tribes, 30
   overview, 29–36
   reflection on meaning of, 27–29
   small interventions, 30
Anabaptism, 39n11
Annan, Kofi, 255, 284
Aristotle, on virtue of prudence, 91
Arnold, Benedict, 67
Aroostook War, 35
Asgill, Charles, 65
Atlantic Charter, 193, 197
Augustine, Saint, Bishop of Hippo
   on expression of *caritas*, 8
   on just war, x, 9, 42n29
   on retribution, 15
   on serving in military, 16
   on tranquility of order, 8
   "two cities" metaphor, 40n16
Authorization for Use of Military Force (AUMF), 280, 284

Bacevich, Andrew, 256, 257
Ba Maw, 179
Bancroft, George, 102, 105
Banner, James, 87
barbarism, 28
Bayard, James, 83
Beebe, Ralph, 94n12
Beecher, Henry Ward, 119
Bell, Daniel M., 132
Bemis Heights, Battle of, 64–65
Benedict XV, Pope
   Ad Beatissimi Apostolorum encyclical, 159, 160, 163, 168, 172
   condemnation of war by, 158–59, 160–62
   meeting with Woodrow Wilson, 170–71
   on sin of the Christian West, 161–62
   on social divisions, 162
   views of the Great War, 171, 172, 173
Benton, Thomas Hart, 105

Bergen, Peter, 277, 295n24
Berlin Wall, fall of, 277, 278
Berman, Paul, 291
Bernard, Francis, 56
best means vs. last resort, 262
Better War, A (Sorley), 243
Biggar, Nigel, 264
Bill of Rights (1689), 52
bin Laden, Osama, 277, 281, 283, 284–85
Blomberg, Werner von, 185
Blum, John, 193
Bonestreet, Charles, 205
Booth, John Wilkes, 128
Boston Tea Party, 57
British Constitution, 51–52
British East India Company, 57
Brock, David, 260
Brown, Harold, 239
Brown, John, 115, 117, 118–19, 121
Brubaker, Harry, 203
Buchannan, George, 51
Bunglawala, Shenaz, 289
Bunker, Ellsworth, 243, 244
Burleigh, Michael, 185
Burnidge, Cara, 164
Buruma, Ian, 297n56
Bush, George H. W., and foreign policy, 252
Bush, George W.
  address to Muslims, 290
  on causes of the Second Gulf War, 253, 259
  declaration of "War on Terror," 278
  foreign policy, 252, 255, 259
  inaugural address, 271, 278
  national security strategy of, 279
  on 9/11 attacks, 274
  political views of, 259
  ultimatum to Taliban, 284
Butch Cassidy and the Sundance Kid (film), 138

Calhoun, John C., 79, 98, 104–5
Calhoun, William, 142–43
California
  Bancroft's naval campaign in, 102
  foreign interests in, 100
  U.S. invasion of, 101
Calvin, John, 51
Canada, U.S. invasion of, 78–79
Carp, Benjamin, 65
Carr, E. H., 292
Carr, Matthew, 275, 276
Carter, Jimmy, and Persian Gulf policy, 257
Chamberlain, Neville, 185
charity, 14, 42n29, 46n93, 47n102, 48n111, 48n116
Chiang Kai-shek, 180
China
  American Open Door policy in, 178
  Boxer Rebellion, 177
  division of, 177
  foreign relations, 177–78
  Japan's invasion of, 178–79
Chollet, Derek, 278
Chomsky, Noam, 228
Churchill, Winston, 188, 197
civil society, 28, 29
Clark, Christopher, 99
Clark, Mark W., 216
Clausewitz, Carl von, on the "fog of war," 137
Clay, Henry, 79, 89, 99
Cleveland, Grover, 140
Clinton, Bill, 254, 255, 277
Clinton, James, 66
Coates, Anthony, 14
Cohen, William, 277
Colby, William, 243, 244
Cold War, 197, 211–12
Cole, Darrell, 34, 211, 213
Collier, George, 64

combatants
  vs. civilian population, 45–46n87
  vs. noncombatants, 20
Committee of Concerned Asian Scholars, 228
common good, notion of, 28
Common Sense (Paine), 62–63
Communist Party of North Vietnam, 228
Conciliatory Resolution of the British Parliament, 62
Considerations on the Propriety of Imposing Taxes in the British Colonies (Dulany), 54
containment, doctrine of, 254, 259
Countering Violent Extremism (CVE), 280
Cuba
  American hegemony over, 149, 178
  American Red Cross in, 143
  economy, 140–41
  humanitarian crisis, 143, 148, 149, 150
  political unrest in, 140, 141–42
  population of, 142
  repatriation of Spanish troops from, 149
  U.S. trade with, 141
Cuban Revolutionary Party, 144
Cuban War of Independence
  casualties, 142
  depopulation of countryside, 142–43
  duration of, 136
  General Weyler's "reconcentration" orders, 142
  impact on U.S. economy, 141
  press coverage of, 142, 144, 145
  treatment of civilians, 142
  violence, 141–43
Cumings, Bruce, 216, 223n12

Dabney, Robert Lewis, 120
Daladier, Edouard, 185
Dearlove, Richard, 254

death, causes of, 46n93
Declaration by the Representatives of the United Colonies of North-America, A, 57–58, 59, 60
Declaration of Independence, 57–58, 59, 61
Declaration of Rights and Grievances, 55
Democratic People's Republic of Korea (DPRK)
  foreign military aid to, 208, 210
  formation of, 206
  invasion of South Korea, 207, 209
Demy, Timothy, 32
Den Hartog, Jonathan, 31
Dewey, George, 138, 147
Dickinson, Anna Elizabeth, 119
Dickinson, John, 55, 56
Dilbeck, D. H., 122
Dix, John, 105
Donne, John, 187
Donohue, Laura, 275
"double effect," principle of, 46n93, 212, 217, 242, 261
Douglass, Frederick, 117, 119
Dower, John W., 192
Dulany, Daniel, 54
Dulles, John Foster, 208
Dunn, James, 204
Durward, Rosemary, 289
Dwight, Timothy, 84

Ebel, Jonathan, 32
Eisenhower, Dwight, 219
El Caney, Battle of, 148
Elkins, Stanley, 52
Ellsberg, Daniel, 237
Elshtain, Jean Bethke, 5, 145, 157, 173, 282, 284, 286, 290
ends and means, relations between, 19

Falk, Richard A., 231, 238
Farmer, Ben, 288
Fellers, Bonner, 190

Ferguson, Niall, 187
Filkins, Dexter, 283
First Gulf War (GW1)
  air campaign in, 263
  best means in, 262
  causes of, 251, 252–53
  international coalition, 252, 267
  ius post bellum criterion, 265
  as just war, 266
  outcome of, 258–59
  overview, 34
  principle of overwhelming superiority, 259
  proportion and discrimination criteria, 263
  reasonable hope for success, 261–62
  right intention in, 258–61
  U.S. goals in, 261, 265
  U.S. troops in, 259
  as war for oil, 256–58
First World War. *See* Great War
Fisher, David, 282
force
  as instrument of justice, 12
  regulation of, 22
  vs. violence, 7, 22
Franklin, Benjamin, 55, 67
Franks, Tommy, 263
French imperialism, 197
Fromkin, David, 180, 193

Gallatin, Albert, 89
García, Calixto, 148
Garrison, William Lloyd, 118
Geneva Convention of 1949, 217–18, 219, 232, 233, 235, 273, 285
Geneva Protocol of 1925, 235
Genovese, Eugene D., 115
Germany
  aggression in Central Europe, 185–86
  amalgamation of Austria, 185
  conduct of war, 186–87
  militarization of, 184–85
  post–World War II reconstruction, 25–26
  rise of Nazi party in, 184
  Treaty of Versailles and, 184, 185
Gerson, Michael, 279
Ghent, Treaty of, 87, 89–90
Giáp, Võ Nguyên, 232
Gifford, Laura Jane, 33
Gilje, Paul, 90
Global War on Terrorism (GWOT), 280, 296n37
Goebbels, Joseph, 186
Goldgeier, James, 278
Goodman, Christopher, 51
Gottwald, Klement, 223n11
Grant, Ulysses S., 103, 124, 127
Grassey, Thomas, 151
Great Britain
  colonial policy, 52, 54, 56, 57, 59
  Declaratory Act, 56
  definition of citizenship, 77
  foreign policy, 77–78, 80–81, 100
  in Napoleonic Wars, 90
  national debt, 53
  naval violence, 77
  Whig political ideology, 51–52
Greater East Asia Co-Prosperity Sphere (GEACPS), 179
Great War
  aim of, 171
  beginning of, 158
  Benedict XV on, 158–59, 160–62
  casualties, 156, 166
  causes of, 165, 166
  cost of, 166
  cruelty of, 167
  financial interests and, 168
  historiography of, 156
  just war tradition and, 155, 156, 157–59, 172–73
  Lusitania sinking, 165
  outcome of, 171

Great War (cont.)
　overview of, 155–56
　Senator Norris's statement on, 168–69
　U.S. participation in, 156–57, 158, 159, 168, 170
　Western Front, 155, 158
Greenberg, Amy, 109
Grenville, George, 54, 55
Grey, Charles, 64
Grotius, Hugo
　on defensive war, 60
　on Dutch rebellion against Spanish rule, xiv
　on fear, 50
　on justifiable war, 10
　legacy of, 269n32
　on life of men, 59
　on means, 14
　on restraint of militarism and pacifism, 41n21
　on retributive response in warfare, 23
　on war within the bounds of law, 19
Gruening, Ernest, 228
Grundy, Felix, 79
Guadalupe Hidalgo, Treaty of, 107, 109
Guelzo, Allen C., 117, 128–29, 131
Gulf of Tonkin Resolution, 228, 248n6
Gulf Wars. *See* First Gulf War; Second Gulf War

Haass, Richard, 256, 269n17, 278
Hague Convention IV (1907), 232, 234, 235, 285
Hague Convention of 1899, 285
Halwan, Muhayfen, 263
Hamilton, Alexander, 81
Hanson, Victor Davis, 28, 258, 269n18
Harries, Richard, 18
Harrison, William Henry, 78
Hartford Convention, 83, 86–87, 92
Hauerwas, Stanley, 5
Hay, John, 136

Hayes, Rutherford B., 130
Haynes, Sam W., 109
Hearst, William Randolph, 140
Hemingway, Ernest, 187
Henry, Patrick
　Virginia Resolves, 55
Herrera, José Joaquin, 102, 103
Hickey, Donald, 87
Hickey, Doyle, 216
Higginson, Thomas Wentworth, 118
Hillsborough, Wills Hill, Viscount, 56
Hirohito, Emperor of Japan, 183, 186, 192
Hitchcock, Ethan, 101
Hitler, Adolf
　declaration of war on the U.S., 33
　on destruction of Poland, 186–87
　foreign policy, 185–86, 188
　rise to power, 184–85
Hoover, Herbert, 180
Hostages case in Nuremberg Tribunal, 234, 235
Hotta, Eri, 182
Howe, Daniel Walker, 31
Howe, Richard, 62
Howe, Samuel Gridley, 118
Howe, William, 62
Huddy, Joshua, 65
humanitarian intervention, 145–46
human sacrifice, phenomenon of, 28–29
Hunt, Michael H., 223n12
Hussain, Ghulam, 286
Hussein, Saddam
　aggression against Kuwait, 252–53
　connection to terrorism, 254–55
　elimination of, 261
　political regime of, 252, 253, 254, 268n7
　weapons of mass destruction and, 263

Idaho, U.S. acquisition of, 97
Ienaga, Saburo, 179
Indochina

Commission of Inquiry into U.S. Crimes in, 235
French re-claim of, 197
Japan's invasion of, 181
Indonesia, "War on Terror" in, 289
"Instructions for the Government of Armies of the United States in the Field" (Lieber), 122
International Committee of the Red Cross (ICRC), 240
International Law—The Conduct of Armed Conflict and Air Operations, 240
International Security Assistance Force (ISAF), 281, 284
intervention, justification of, 10, 11, 12, 268n9
Iraq
 attack on the U.N. headquarters in, 254
 Baath party, 260, 261, 263, 265
 policy of containment in, 254, 255
 regime change in, 259–60, 263
 search for weapons of mass destruction, 253
 U.S. strategic objectives in, 260, 261
Irish, Kerry E., 33
Iriye, Akira, 181
Islamic Front's policy, 290–91
Islamic ideology, 297n56
ius ad bellum
 definition, 8
 just cause criterion of, 9–12, 282
 moral efficacy of, 12
 prevention of injustice and, 9–10
 proper authority criterion of, 12–14
 right intention criterion of, 13–19
ius in bello
 definition, 8, 9
 discrimination criterion of, 19–22, 24
 proportionality criterion of, 22–24, 285

ius post bellum
 bare minimum conditions of, 25
 definition, 24, 43n34
 justice in, 26–27
 role of education in, 26

Jackson, Andrew, 87, 90, 92, 99, 100
Jackson, Thomas J. "Stonewall," 124
Japan
 alliance with Nazi Germany and Italy, 180, 181
 Allied invasion of, 191
 conduct of war, 183
 fear of "ABCD" encirclement, 181–82
 imperialism of, 177, 178, 180, 182–83, 194–95
 international treaties, 178
 invasion of China, 178–79, 182, 183
 invasion of Indochina, 181
 invasion of Korea, 178, 179, 195
 Nanjing (Nanking) Massacre, 179
 occupation of Manchuria, 178
 Pearl Harbor attack, 175
 plan of naval blockade of, 191–92
 Soviet Union's declaration of war against, 192
 treatment of prisoners of war, 183–84, 193
 U.S. nuclear bombing of, 189, 190, 191, 198
 U.S. occupation of, 193
Japanese army, Field Service Code, 183
Japanese racism, 192
Jay, John, 80
Jay Treaty, 80
Jefferson, Thomas, 76, 77–78, 94n12, 98
Jemaah Islamiyah (JI), 288–89
Jim Crow era, 130
John of Salisbury, 51
Johnson, Andrew, 128
Johnson, James Turner, 5, 18, 25, 35, 125, 146, 157, 265

Johnson, Lyndon Baines, 228
Jones, Gregory, 32
Joy, C. Turner, 218, 219
Just and Unjust Wars (Walzer), 24, 127, 145
just cause, 9–12, 19
justice
  absolutist view of, 10
  charity and, 27, 29, 48n111
  without force, 6
  legitimacy of public acts of, 12
  miscarriage of, 22–23
  notion of "unjust," 22–23
  principle of proportionality and, 22–23
  prospects of universal, 292
  relative vs. absolute, 8, 43n43
  statesman and pursuit of, 291–92
just peace, 36
just war
  on both sides, 10–11
  causes of, 268n8
  consequences of, 289
  criteria of success of, 289
  debate on justification of, xiv, 9
  early modern thinkers on, xi
  goal and rationale of, 21–22, 24, 45n76
  interpretations of, ix–x
  vs. justified war, 4
  as "last resort," 17–18
  limitation of, 24
  medieval thinkers on, xi
  vs. militarism, 22
  moral reasoning and, xii, xiii–xiv, 21, 190
  natural law and, 39n11
  operations against terrorists and, 273–74
  overview of, xiii
  passions and, 91
  prudential conditions of, 17

  representations of, xi
  scholarly studies of, ix–x
  theory of, 173
just war reasoning, xii, 5, 10, 13, 20
just war tradition
  ambiguity of, 36
  American awareness of, 4, 39n9
  distortion of classic, 6, 268n8
  elements of, xi–xii, 115
  ethic of responsibility and, 282
  humanitarian intervention and, 145–46
  immutable rules of, 8
  moral principles of, 4–5, 7, 9
  objectives of righting a wrong in, 43n42
  overview, 3–9
  vs. pacifism, 6
  representatives of, 5
Just War Tradition and the Restraint of War (Johnson), 125

Kagan, Robert, 259
Kansas violence, 118
Kant, Immanuel, 259
Karzai, Hamid, 281
Kaufman, Burton I., 223n12
Kay, David, 263
Kellogg-Briand Treaty, 178, 187
Kennan, George, 206, 209, 210, 214
Kerry, John, 236
Keteltas, Abraham, 53
Kettle Hill, Battle of, 148
Kim Chae-kyu, 220
Kim Il Sung, 206, 208, 209
Kipling, Rudyard
  "The White Man's Burden," 151
Koje Do prison camp, 217
Konoe, Fumimaro, 179
Korean peninsula
  division of, 205, 214–15
  Japanese rule on, 179, 195

Soviet presence on, 206
U.S. presence on, 205–7
after World War II, 204–5
Korean People's Army (KPA), 206, 212–13
Korean War
  armistice negotiations, 218, 219, 220
  beginning of, 207
  casualties, 212, 218
  China's role in, 208, 210, 215–16
  as civil war, 216, 223–24n12
  in Cold War context, 207–8, 211–12, 216–17, 222
  conduct of American forces in, 212, 213
  consequences of, 214, 220–21
  destruction of infrastructure, 213
  discrimination in target selection, 217, 221–22
  fictional chronicle of, 203–4
  as global conflict, 216–17, 222
  guerrilla tactics, 212–13
  historiography, 223n12
  ius ad bellum criterion, 205, 208
  ius in bello criterion, 212, 221–22
  justification of, 207, 221
  MacArthur's strategy, 214–15, 216
  as nationalist conflict, 208–9
  origin of, 204–5
  overview, 33
  principle of proportionality in, 212
  prisoners of war, 217–19
  racial component in, 212–13
  Soviet Union's role in, 208
  treatment of noncombatants, 217
  treatment of refugees, 213
  U.N. Security Council resolutions on, 209–11, 213–14
  U.N. troops in, 212, 213, 214
  U.S. intervention into, 207, 208–10, 211–12, 219, 221
Kristof, Nicholas, 283

Ku Klux Klan, 125, 129
Kuwait, Saddam Hussein's invasion of, 277

last resort, principle of, 17–19, 262
Law of Armed Conflict (LOAC), 287, 288
League of Nations, 157, 171
Lee, Steven Hugh, 217
Lee, Wayne, 67
LeMay, Curtis, 190
Lend-Lease ("An Act to Promote the Defense of the United States"), 188
Leonard, Thomas M., 109
Levine, Steven I., 223n12
Lewis, Anthony, 239
Lewis, C. S., 16
Lewy, Guenter, 228
Lexington, battles of, 57, 60–61
lex talionis, concept of, 45n73
liability, deliberate vs. unintended, 20
Lieber, Francis, 122
Lieber Code, the, 122–23
Lincoln, Abraham
  assassination of, 128
  Lieber Code signed by, 122
  opposition to, 106–7
  perspective on Civil War, 115, 131
  political career, 117, 120, 121, 122
  position on slavery, 116, 117, 120–21, 131–32
  on preservation of the Union, 131
  on Reconstruction of the South, 128, 129–30
  Second Inaugural Address, 32
Lincoln, George, 204, 205
Lincoln's Emancipation Proclamation (Guelzo), 128
Little War, the (1879–80), 136
Locke, John, xiv
  Second Treatise on Civil Government, 51

Louisiana Territory, American acquisition of, 76, 98
Lowe, Peter, 209, 212, 223n12
Lowitt, Richard, 223n5
Luther, Martin, 51

MacArthur, Douglas, 196, 212, 213–15, 216
Madison, James
  address to the Congress, 74–75
  criticism of, 86, 91
  foreign policy, 76, 79, 91–92
  plans for invasion of Canada, 78–79, 81
  trade policy, 78
  War of 1812 and, 31, 75, 90
Magna Carta (1215), 52
Maine-New Brunswick border negotiation, 35
Manifest Destiny, 31, 98, 99, 102
Mao Zedong, 208, 219
Marcy, William, 109
Margalit, Avishai, 297n56
Marshall, George, 215
Marshall Plan, 197
Martí, José, 144
Martin, Joseph W., 216
Martinez, J. Michael, 129
Massachusetts Circular Letter (1768), 56
Matusitz, Jonathan, 273
Mayhew, Jonathan, 52–53
McGovern, George, 239
McKinley, William, 139, 140, 143, 145, 146–47
McKitrick, Eric, 52
McNamara, Robert, 230, 244
means
  definition of, 7
  ends and, 7, 14
Meiji, Emperor of Japan, 177
Meiji Restoration, 177
Merritt, Wesley, 147
Mexican War. *See* U.S.-Mexican War

Mexico
  economic crisis, 100
  Slidell's diplomatic mission to, 103
Michener, James A., 203, 204
Middle East
  effect of use of military force in, 258
  U.S. policy in, 257
Molotov-Ribbentrop agreement, 186
Montojo, Patricio, 147
moral intentions, nature of, 46n94
More Civil War, A (Dilbeck), 122
Morse, Wayne, 228
Munich Agreement, 185
Munson, Mark, 289
Murray, John Courtney, 7, 28
My Lai massacre, 226, 236–37

Nanjing (Nanking) Massacre, 179, 183
National Security Strategy (NSS), 273, 279
natural law tradition, 5, 19, 39n11, 40n14, 47n109
Naval Court of Inquiry, 139, 152n6
Nazism, 23–24
New Orleans, Battle of, 90
New York City, burning of, 65, 66
Niebuhr, Reinhold, 164
Nimitz, Chester, 191
Nitze, Paul, 219
Nixon, Richard, 235, 240, 245
noncombatants, 19, 20, 21
Norris, George W., 168–69
North, Frederick, Earl of Guilford, 57
North Atlantic Treaty Organization (NATO)
  bombing of Yugoslavia, 255
  formation of, 196
No T'ae-u (Roh Tae-woo), 220
nuclear weapons, justification for use of, 21

O'Brien, William, 5, 246
O'Donovan, Oliver, 15, 39n12, 43n42

Offner, John L., 138, 140
Olive Branch Petition (1775), 60
On Strategy (Summers), 230
On War (Clausewitz), 137
Operation Enduring Freedom–Afghanistan (OEF-A), 280–81, 288
Operation Enduring Freedom–Horn of Africa (OEF-HOA), 280
Operation Enduring Freedom–Philippines (OEF-P), 280, 288, 289
Operation Enduring Freedom–Trans Sahara (OEF-TS), 280
Operation Freedom's Sentinel (OFS), 281, 288
Operation Inherent Resolve, 280
Operation Iraqi Freedom, 280
Operation Smiles, 289
Oregon, Treaty of, 35
Oregon Question, 97, 102, 103
Orend, Brian, 25
O'Sullivan, John L., 99
Otis, James, 54
Overseas Contingency Operation (OCO), 280
Owens, Mackubin Thomas, 34

Pacific war
  American conduct in, 189–91, 192–94, 198
  civilian population during, 192
  end of, 192, 196
  Guadalcanal campaign, 192–93
  Japanese conduct in, 183–84
  justification of, 176–77, 196, 198
  origin of, 180–83
  plan of naval blockade of Japan, 191–92
  racism and, 192–93
  strategic bombing of Japan, 190–91
  treatment of civilians, 183

pacifism, 4, 6, 7, 27, 45n84. *See also* religious pacifism
Packer, George, 262
Paine, Thomas, 62–63
Pakenham, Edward, 90
Panikkar, K. M., 215
Paoli Massacre, 64
Paredes, Manuel, 103
Paris, Treaty of (1783), 67, 68
Paris, Treaty of (1898), 149
Parish, Elijah, 84, 85
Paris Peace Conference (1919), 170
Park Chung Hee, 220
Parker, John, 61
Parker, Theodore, 118
Parks, W. Hays, 240
Parrott, William S., 102
peace, concept of, 6
Pearl Harbor attack, 33, 175, 176, 192
Peoples' Army of Vietnam (PAVN), 232
Perry, Matthew, 177
Petition of Right (1628), 52
Philippine-American War (1898–1902), 32, 137, 149–50
Philippines
  American annexation of, 178, 179–80
  counterterrorist operation in, 288, 289
  proclamation of independence of, 147
piracy, 13
Pitcairn, John, 61
Pitt, William, 55
Poland
  division of, 186
  German conduct in, 186–87
Polk, James Knox
  critics of, 105
  diary of, 103, 108
  diplomacy of, 101–3
  disagreements with Winfield Scott, 110

Polk, James Knox (*cont.*)
   foreign policy, 100, 103, 104, 105
   historiography of presidency of, 108–9
   invasion of Texas, 101
   legacy, 110–11
   Lincoln's opposition to, 106–7
   personality, 102
   political career, 97
   in U.S.-Mexican War, role of, 31, 104, 105–6, 107
Polk, Sarah, 102
Ponet, John, 51
Porter, David, 78
post–Cold War era, 276–77, 278
post–World War II reconstruction, 25–26
Pottawatomie Creek Massacre, 118
Powell, Charles, 268n12
prisoners of war (POWs), 63–64, 183–84, 217–18, 219
proportionality, principle of, 22–23, 24
Protestant Reformation, 51
prudence, virtue of, 91
public authority, nature of, 13
Pufendorf, Samuel von, on defensive war, 60

Quincy, Josiah, 83

Rable, George, 122
racism, 130–31, 192, 193
Raeder, Erich, 188
Ramsey, Paul, 4, 5, 48n116, 157
Randolph, John, 82
Reagan, Ronald, 274
Realpolitik, 8
Reconstruction, 127–28, 129, 130
Regan, Richard J., 211
religious pacifism, 39nn11–12
Republic of Korea (ROK)
   first democratic elections, 220
   foreign policy, 220
   formation of, 206
   North Korean invasion of, 207, 209
   "postwar" regime, 220
   withdrawal of American forces from, 206–7
"Responsibility to Protect" doctrine, 143
retribution, 15, 16
Rhee, Syngman, 206, 214, 219, 220
Ricks, Thomas, 259
Ridgway, Matthew, 218
Rietveld, Ronald D., 116, 117, 131–32
right intention, principle of, 13–14, 15
Rights of the British Colonies Asserted and Proved, The (Otis), 54
Robertson, James, 65
Roche, John, 31
Roosevelt, Franklin D.
   aid to Great Britain, 188
   anticolonial agenda, 197–98
   decision to enter World War II, 187–89
   foreign policy, 180–81, 196, 197
   on Japan's invasion of China, 178–79
   meeting with Winston Churchill, 197
   Middle Eastern policy, 257
   on Pearl Harbor attack, 175
   vision of international order, 198
Roosevelt, Theodore, 137, 149
Rusk, Dean, 205
Russell International War Crimes Tribunal, 238
Rutherford, Samuel, 51

Salisbury, Harrison, 238
Sanborn, Franklin Benjamin, 118
Sandler, Stanley, 213, 223–24n12
Santa Anna, Antonio de, 98
Sarkesian, Sam, 275
Sayf, Sultan Al-, 263
scarce resources, fighting for, 257–58
Scott, Winfield, 110, 126
Scowcroft, Brent, 259

Second Gulf War (GW2)
   American allies in, 267
   causes of, 34, 251
   cost of, 261
   critics of, 253, 256
   faulty planning of, 259–60, 261, 267
   ius post bellum criterion, 265
   as just war, evaluation of, 266–67
   outcome of, 262, 265–66
   proportionality and discrimination criteria, 263–64
   question of necessity of, 255–56
   reasonable hope for success, 261–62
   right intention, 258–61
   search for weapons of mass destruction, 253
   treatment of prisoners, 264
   U.K. forces in, 255, 264, 265
   use of force as best means in, 262–63
   U.S.'s goals in, 260–61, 265
   U.S. troops in, 259–60
   as war for oil, 256–58
Second World War. *See* World War II
Shafter, William Rufus, 148
Sherman, William Tecumseh, and "March to the Sea," 123, 124–25, 126, 127
Shigemetsu, Mamoru, 196
Shulte, Paul, 289
Sigsbee, Charles, 139
slavery
   attempts to abolish, 106, 117–18, 119
   Christian teachings and, 119–20
   after Civil War, 129
   in context of the Civil War, 116, 117
   ideological justification of, 119–21
   introduction of, 105
   Lincoln's position on, 116, 117, 120–21
   nature of, 115
   in newly acquired territories, 106
   race-based, 119
   as Southern way of life, 121

Slidell, John, 101–2, 103
Slim, William Joseph, Field Marshal Viscount, xiii, 227
Sloat, John D., 102
Smith, Gaddis, 195
Smith, Gerrit, 118
Smith, Justin H., 108
Smith, Rupert, 258
Sorley, Lewis, 244
   A Better War, 243
Soviet Union
   aid to North Korea, 206, 208
   dissolution of, 277
Spanish-American War
   American public opinion about, 144
   battle in Manila Bay, 147
   beginning of, 147
   casualties, 147, 148
   causes of, 140, 142
   conduct of combatants during, 148–49
   ground campaign in Cuba, 148
   impact on U.S. economy, 141
   in just war tradition, 137, 145
   naval campaign, 147–48
   outcomes of, 149–52
   overview of, 32, 136–38
   political decision-making process and, 138
   in popular memory, 137–38
   press coverage of, 140, 145, 150
   Spanish defeat in, 148–49
   U.S. Congress resolution on, 147
   U.S. forces in, 147
   USS *Maine* disaster and, 139–40
Spanish-Cuban War. *See* Cuban War of Independence
Stalin, Joseph, 186, 208, 219, 223n11
Stamp Act, 52, 54, 59
State-War-Navy Coordinating Committee (SWNCC), 204, 205
Stearns, George Luther, 118
Steeves, Rouven, 34

Stevens, John H., 85–86
Stimson, Henry, 191
Storm, Jane, 99
Stout, Harry S., 29, 115–16, 124, 125, 132
Stowe, Harriet Beecher, 121
strategic bombing, 190–91
Strong, Caleb, 81, 86
Stueck, William, 209, 223n12
Suffolk Resolves, 57
Sugar Act, 54
Sullivan, John, 65, 66–67
Summers, Harry
  On Strategy, 230

Taliban, 281–82, 283, 284
Tarleton, Banastre, 67
Taylor, Telford, 237, 238
Taylor, Zachary, 101, 103, 109
Tea Act, 57
Tecumseh (Shawnee chief), 78
Tenskwatawa (Shawnee chief), 78
Ten Years' War (1868–78), 136, 141
territorial sovereignty of nation-states, 293n3
terrorism
  definitions of, 272–73
  just war theory and, 34
  long war against, 276
  morality and ethics of, 13, 275
  totalitarianism and, 291
  U.S. strategy against, 275, 280
terrorist attacks
  on *Achille Lauro* ship, 274
  on Beirut barracks, 274
  9/11, 34, 251, 271, 272
  at Rome and Vienna airports, 274
  on U.N. headquarters in Baghdad, 254
  on U.S. embassy in Dar es Salaam, 277
  on U.S. military barracks in Dhahran, 277
  U.S. response to, 275, 277
  on USS *Cole*, 277
  on World Trade Center, 277
Texas
  population, 98
  southern boundary, 101
  U.S. annexation of, 98, 101
Thomas Aquinas
  on declaration of war, 12
  on foresight vs. intention, 261
  on just war, xi, 9, 10, 19
  on principle of "double effect," 46n93
  on right intention, 14, 42n24
Thompson, Kenneth, 276
Thompson, Robert, 245
Thornwell, James Henry, 120
Thucydides, 34, 51, 91, 251
Tippecanoe, Battle of, 78
Toral y Vásquez, José, 148
total war, concept of, 125
Townshend, Charles, 56
Townshend Revenue Act, 56, 57
Tripartite Pact, 180
Trist, Nicholas, 107
Truman, Harry S.
  decision on nuclear bombing of Japan, 204
  fear of spread of Communism, 211
  foreign policy, 192, 197
  Korean conflict and, 210, 211–12, 221
  relations with MacArthur, 213–14, 216
Tydings-McDuffie Act, 180
Tyler, John, 98

Uncle Tom's Cabin (Stowe), 121
United Nations, 44n56, 196, 255, 268n12
United States
  aid to postwar Western Europe, 197
  counterterrorist measures, 275
  defense agreements, 223n6
  definition of citizenship, 77

effect of the Embargo of 1807 on, 78
expansionism of, 78–79, 97–99
foreign policy, 180, 197, 198, 278
Great Britain's relations with, 74–75, 77, 78, 80
as international power, emergence of, 151–52
isolationism of, 178
Japan's war with, 175, 193
Middle East policy, 257
military conflicts of, 29–30
during Napoleonic Wars, 76
national identity, 30
Open Door policy, 178, 180
origin of, 48n118, 50
policy of containment of Iraq, 255
post–World War II, 195–96
racism in, 192
religions, 30–31
renunciation of biological warfare by, 235–36
response to Communist expansion, 223n5
strategic bombing campaign, 189–90
territorial gains, 118
trade policy, 76–77
waves of immigration, 30
in World War II, 187–89
Upon the Altar of the Nation: A Moral History of the Civil War (Stout), 116
U.S. Law of Land Warfare, 233, 234–35
U.S.-Mexican War
    casualties, 106
    conduct of American forces in, 109–10
    consequences of, 118
    dissemination of news about, 106
    end of, 107
    formal reasons for, 104
    historiography of, 108–9
    occupations of Veracruz, Puebla, and Mexico City, 110
    opposition to, 31–32, 104–5, 106–7
    peace negotiations, 107
    Polk's role in, 104, 105–6, 107, 110–11
    in popular memory, 97
    preparations for, 103
    public opinion of, 106
    in retrospect, 108–11
    Taylor's army advance to Rio Grande, 103–4
    as unjust war, 109
    volunteer units in, 109
    vote in U.S. Congress on, 104–5
USS *Chesapeake*, 77
USS *Maine*, 137, 138, 139–40, 143
USS *Missouri*, 196
USS *Reuben James*, 189
utopia vs. reality, 292

Vattel, Emmerich, 60, 63
Versailles, Treaty of, 184, 185
Viet Cong (National Liberation Front), 229, 232
Vietnam
    conflict between South and North, 228–29
    geographic importance of, 230
Vietnam War
    American operational strategy, 231–32, 233–34, 243–44
    bombing of North Vietnam, 238–40, 242
    brutality of, 230
    casualties, 240
    causes of, 229–30
    civilian casualties, 232, 238–39
    congressional support of, 228
    critics of, 227–30, 231, 238
    Easter Offensive, 244
    evaluation of, 246–47
    exercise of judgment, 234
    historiography of, 242–45
    just war tradition and, 34, 226, 228, 245–46

Vietnam War (*cont.*)
   "Linebacker II" bombing campaign, 239, 240, 245
   overview, 34
   population relocation, 232–33
   proportionality criterion in, 233–34
   Rolling Thunder operation, 238–39
   South Vietnamese army in, 244–45
   Tet offensive, 229, 243
   use of fire power during, 231–32, 235
   use of herbicides and riot control agents, 235
   U.S. goals in, 230
   war crimes, 232, 236–37, 246
violence vs. force, 7
Vitoria, Francisco de, 9, 11

Walzer, Michael
   on America's entry into World War I, 169, 170
   criticism of Bush administration, 298n60
   on humanitarian intervention, 145–46
   Just and Unjust Wars, 24, 145
   on last resort, 17–18
   legacy of, 157
   on outcome of Afghan war, 286–87
   on Second Gulf War, 256
   on Sherman's March, 124
   on surrender, 123
   on warfare and just war, 8
   on war in Iraq, 265
   on "war is hell" doctrine, 126–27
war
   as act of judgment, 1–2
   Christian thinking about, xiv
   concept of total, 125
   ethical evaluation of, 150–51
   international laws and, 273, 285
   of necessity, 255–56
   possibility to limit, 8
   proper authority and declaration of, 12
   reasons for going to, 91
   role of passion and prudence in, 91, 226
   self-defensive, 256
   Thucydides on causes of, 51, 251
war crimes, definition of, 230–31
"war is hell" doctrine, 126–27
War of 1812
   American invasion of Canada, 78–79, 81, 92
   British actions as trigger of, 80–81
   casualties, 88
   causes of, 74–75, 77, 80
   contemporary views of, 92
   declaration of, 75, 79, 81
   destruction of property during, 88–89
   Federalist opposition to, 82–84
   Fort Mims massacre, 88
   as gamble, 92
   historical and ethical evaluation of, 76
   indigenous tribes in, 78–79, 88, 89
   just war tradition and, 31, 75–76, 79–80
   level of violence, 87–88
   militia units in, 81, 88
   naval engagements, 88
   outcome of, 90–91
   peace negotiations, 89–90
   political debates over, 79, 82, 84–86
   in popular memory, 91
   position of American clergy on, 85–86
   prospect for success, 81
   public opinion about, 74, 79
   question of just conduct in, 87–89
   Raisin River Massacre, 88
   trade and, 76–78
   treatment of civilians, 88
   treatment of prisoners, 89
   U.S. Army and Navy in, 81
War of Independence. *See* American Revolutionary War

Index   321

"War on Terror"
   in Afghanistan, 280–82, 288, 295n24
   Bush's declaration of, 276, 278, 279
   cost of, 298n68
   debate on nature of, 279–80
   in Indonesia, 289
   international laws and, 274, 290
   just war tradition and, 271–72, 282–83
   in Libya, 274
   before 9/11 attack, 274–78
   Operation Infinite Reach, 277–78
   in the Philippines, 288–89
   and prospects of peace, 288–89
   renaming of, 280
   as war against totalitarianism, 291
Wars of America, The (Wells), 116
War with Mexico, The (Smith), 108
Washington, George, 61, 63, 65, 80
Washington Naval Treaty, 178, 187
Waxhaws Massacre, 67
Wayne, Anthony, 64
weapons of mass destruction (WMD), 251, 253, 255
Webster, Daniel, 110, 111
Weinberg, Gerhard, 182
Wells, Ronald, 38n5, 116
Westmoreland, William, 243
Westphalian international norms, 271–72, 293n3
Weyler, Valeriano, 141–42
Wheelan, Joseph, 109
White, Craig, 253
White League, 125
Whitman, Walt, 131
Wiley, Alexander, 210
Wilkinson, James, 88
Williams, Rowan, 18

Wilmot Proviso, 106
Wilson, Woodrow
   address to the Congress, 157, 163–64, 165–66, 168
   America's involvement in the Great War and, 158, 164, 167–68, 171–72
   critics of, 169–70
   "fourteen points" of, 184
   on Germany's warfare, 165, 167
   on just cause of war, 166–67
   League of Nations project, 171
   meeting with Pope Benedict XV, 170–71
   on preparations for war, 166
   religious views of, 163, 164
Wolfowitz, Paul, 254, 259
World War I. *See* Great War
World War II
   in the Atlantic, 188–89
   bombing of German cities, 190
   civilian population during, 190
   France in, 185–86, 188
   Germany in, 186–87, 194
   Great Britain in, 185–86, 188
   invasion of Poland, 185–86
   Japan in, 175–76
   as just war, 198
   origins of, 184–87
   outcome of, 195–96, 197
   racism and, 192–93, 194
   strategic bombing of Japan, 189–90
   U-boat attacks, 188–89
   United States in, 33, 187–88, 189–94
   as war of annihilation, 194
Wyatt-Brown, Bertram, 121

Yoder, John Howard, 5
Yugoslavia, dissolution of, 277

CPSIA information can be obtained
at www.ICGtesting.com
Printed in the USA
LVHW010544070721
692012LV00023B/1792